ACTORS' LIVES
On And Off The American Stage

ACTORS' LIVES

On And Off The American Stage

Interviews by HOLLY HILL

THEATRE COMMUNICATIONS GROUP
NEW YORK 1993

The photographs in this book are reproduced by kind permission of the following: p. 3, 241, William B. Carter; p. 11, 226, Fletcher Drake; p.22, Joe Giannetti; p. 32, Peter Krupenye; p. 42, Chris Bennion; p. 53, James Fry; p. 65, 96, 103, Joan Marcus; p. 71, 196, 235, 289, Martha Swope; p. 80, 280, Lincoln Center Theater; p. 87, Lisa Ebright; p. 112, Bruce Goldstein; p. 118, 306, Bert Andrews; p. 126, Tom Bloom; p. 132, Constance Brown; p. 139, 146, Michal Daniel; p. 154, Peter Cunningham; p. 161, Gerry Goodstein; p. 169, Suzanne Richell; p. 178, 265, 272, Martha Swope Associates/Carol Rosegg; p. 187, Merrill Holtzman; p. 206, Mark Morelli; p. 212, Teresa Snider-Stein; p. 219, Actors Theatre of Louisville; p. 249, 257, Zane Williams; p. 298, New Federal Theatre; p. 314, 323, Richard Feldman; p. 333, T. Charles Erickson; p. 340, Jim Caldwell; p. 361, Michael Jacobs; p. 369, Anita & Steve Shevett.
   All uncredited photographs courtesy of the individual actors.

Actors' lives : on and off the American stage : interviews / by Holly Hill.
   — 1st ed.
       ISBN 1-55936-062-3 (pbk.)
       1. Actors—United States—Interviews.   I. Hill, Holly.
PN 2285.A24   1993
792'.028'092273—dc20   92-41775
                                                                         CIP

Book design and composition by The Sarabande Press

First Edition, July 1993

Contents

Preface

I am a child of not-for-profit theatre. Though my parents began taking me to the Dallas Starlight Operettas and touring Broadway musicals when I was five, I really fell in love with theatre at my first play: a production of *Romeo and Juliet* at Margo Jones's Theatre '49, America's first fully professional, nonprofit resident theatre. I don't recall many specifics about the performance, but I can still "see" Juliet on the arena stage of the 198-seat auditorium where I sat enraptured. Jones's repertoire of new plays and classics set the pattern for my life: Theatre was what I most wanted to see, to be a part of, and—as I discovered eventually—to write about. The July morning in 1955 when my mother brought the front-page news of Margo Jones's death into my room is more vivid to me than the death of President Kennedy.

After receiving my degree in speech and drama from Stanford University, I began my theatre career as an acting intern at the Dallas Theater Center. Between slaving on backstage crews and taking classes in acting, speech, movement, mime, directing and playwriting, I understudied and played bit parts in a fine company (which included John Cullum, a leading man on his way to a Tony-winning Broadway career). At the end of two seasons, I had gradually won mainstage roles ranging from a five-year-old ghost in an original Mexican play to Ophelia in *Hamlet* and the Old Woman in *The Chairs*.

I came to New York dreaming of becoming a star and marrying Christopher Plummer. I had seem Plummer playing Shakespearean roles at the Stratford Festival in Canada, but—aside from my crush on him—my interest was mainly in actresses, because I wanted to be one. My earliest recollection of an actress whose name I recall is Louise Latham, an adorable, simpering Agnes with a rebellious gleam in her eye in *The School for Wives* at Margo Jones's theatre. I also remember admiring Julie Harris on tour in a forgettable play, and a graduate student in a Stanford production, Julia Curtis, who was the most moving, haunting Sonya I have ever seen in *Uncle Vanya*.

In New York in the Sixties, I feasted on exciting acting. I will never forget how Rosemary Harris made a nondescript ingenue in the APA production of *The Tavern* into an endearing character by giving her a lisp, or the mixture of elegance and playfulness in her Lady Teazle in *The School for Scandal*. I envied Elizabeth Ashley, Sandy Dennis and Barbara Harris their Broadway successes, but the actress I wanted to be like in that decade was Kathleen Widdoes, whose Miranda, Titania and other young leading ladies I stood in line to see more than once at the New York Shakespeare Festival in Central Park. Another role model appeared in 1969: Jane Alexander in *The Great White Hope*, which had come to Broadway from Washington's Arena Stage.

Experience taught me, however, that I had no special gifts as an actress. In my soul, I think I knew this all along, but I loved watching actors so much I believe I needed to be one for a while, to explore first-hand how characters are created, to feel the magical communion with live audiences, to be a part of the self-contained world of theatre before I could bear to step out and write about it. For that was where I realized my talent, if I had any, was—not on the stage, but where I had begun: in the audience; as an appreciator of the artists and craftspeople who create theatre.

The inspiration for *Actors' Lives* was a Drama Desk panel I moderated in the spring of 1989. Four outstanding supporting actors of that season—Randy Graff of *City of Angels*, Michael Jeter of *Grand Hotel*, Marcia Jean Kurtz of *When She Danced* and Stephen Lang of *A Few*

Good Men—were invited to talk about how they had created their characters and about other acting issues. They were eloquent; the event was a joy; and as I walked down the street afterwards, I realized that I wanted to write a book of interviews with actors whose careers would represent the possiblities and limitations of being a theatre actor in America during the second half of the twentieth century. Surprisingly, there was no such book which explored actors' lives since the flourishing of the resident theatre movement, the advent of television, the development of nontraditional casting and the rise of theatres dedicated to fostering and exploring the heritage of artists of specific ethnicity, gender or disability.

Actors' Lives attempts to create a mosaic of American stage experience from the Fifties to the present. While the network of resident theatres throughout the U.S. and the growth of television have created vast new possiblities for work, the diminution of commerical productions in New York, on the road and in stock companies has reduced opportunities as well. Some actors are committed to careers with resident companies, but it has become more and more difficult for even well-known actors to make a living in the theatre on a freelance basis—they must combine theatre, television and film work; they must teach, direct, write plays, create solo shows or found their own theatres if they can. When they can't, they must resort to "civilian" jobs and unemployment insurance. Actors are given too little credit for their willingness to spend all or part of their careers at theatres located away from their homes—and away from the commerical centers of film and television production, New York and Hollywood—providing the talent that enables theatre to exist, or for doing the workshops that help develop new plays and musicals that feed the nonprofit and commerical theatre.

The bi-coastal nature of the theatre, film and television capitals creates even more difficulties for American performers. British actors' lives may be precarious, but at least most theatre, film and television are based in one city, and the lucky actor can work in theatre and the media in tandem or simultaneously while maintaining a home and personal life in London. Also, the British cherish their theatre stars and will "queue" to see such actors as Judi Dench, Michael Gambon and Anthony Sher, as Americans would once have lined up for Katharine

Cornell, Lee J. Cobb and Alfred Lunt. But with such rare exceptions as Bernadette Peters and Mandy Patinkin, theatre stardom with box-office allure has not existed in America since the Helen Hayes/Ethel Merman generation. Broadway producers, and even such nonprofit leaders as the late Joseph Papp, have frequently sought Hollywood stars to boost ticket sales for theatrical ventures.

American actors must also contend with numerous misconceptions and prejudices. Among these are the fact that theatre credits outside of New York mean little or nothing to powerful agents, casting directors, directors and producers in New York and Hollywood; the belief that "real" actors have roots in the theatre, and must return to it constantly to prove themselves or else be labeled sellouts; the contradictory notions that movie and televsion stars may be good box-office but that they are to critics as Christians to lions; and the shibboleth that will not die—that British actors are better than Americans at practically everything.

Additional problems have emerged as actors of color began actively challenging casting barriers in the Sixties. What has come to be called nontraditional casting encompasses several ideas: that women, actors of color and actors with disabilities should be cast in roles they could and/or do perform in society as a whole (on tape and film this has translated into an abundance of African-American judges, many of them female); that the world of play can be transposed into a different culture (as in Pan Asian Repertory's *Three Sisters,* set in Mongolia); that actors may be cast to give a play a different resonance (Milwaukee Rep's *Our Town,* where the Webb family and some townspeople were played by deaf actors, or Yale Rep's *Pygmalion,* where Eliza was played by an African-American); or color-blind casting, in which actors are cast across or against race, ethnicity, gender or physical ability (as in the Huntington Theatre's *Iphigenia in Aulis,* where Agamemnon was played by an Asian-American, Iphigenia by a Caucasian, and Clytemnestra and Menelaus by African-American actors). Color-blind casting, in particular, is a fiercely debated issue. I once encountered an American critic who declared that British director Declan Donnellan's masterful production of *Fuente Ovejuna*—the critical favorite and a sell-out production at the National Theatre in

1989—was ruined for him the moment he saw that a black actress was playing Queen Isabella of Spain, because that was historically impossible.

Perhaps I'm just lucky that nontraditional casting has not been a problem for me. Following James Earl Jones's career through the diversity of roles he played in New York Shakespeare Festival productions—Oberon in *A Midsummer Night's Dream;* Caliban in *The Tempest;* Claudius in *Hamlet;* Othello; King Lear—and on Broadway—as Lennie in *Of Mice and Men* and Hickey in *The Iceman Cometh*—had a great influence on my attitude. Almost subconsciously, I extended my acceptance of the remarkable Jones to other actors of color (conditional, as with any actor, upon the quality of the performance); gradually, I formed the conscious attitude that the nontraditional casting of my day was a variation on a very old theatrical convention . . . for weren't the women's roles in ancient Greek and Elizabethan theatre cast against gender? Even if nontraditional casting had no such pedigree, wasn't the basic issue suspension of disbelief? If an audience at, say, *Macbeth* can "believe" that the characters are Scottish though they speak Shakespearean English with American accents; that Macbeth has encounters with witches and ghosts; that some clanging of swords is a mighty battle; that characters die but actors only play dead, why can't this acceptance be extended to a cast of mixed race, to characters played across gender, to actors with disabilities? I think nontraditional casting is *exciting*.

More important than who will be cast is what their skills are. Attendant upon the growth of nonprofit theatre has been a proliferation of new play readings and productions, as well as both inspiring and idiotic reinterpretations of the classics. (My favorite example of the latter was a *Midsummer Night's Dream* in which Lysander and Demetrius wore electric bulbs in their codpieces that lit up whenever they were supposed to be aroused by Hermia or Helena.) The resulting demand for enormous flexibility from actors contrasts strongly with the nineteenth- and early twentieth-century practice whereby actors were cast as soubrettes, character actors, leading men or ladies, or some other *type* which could confine them to playing variations on the same character for a lifetime.

University-based professional actor training programs developed to attempt to address the demands of post-war theatre. These have their admirers and detractors, both among their alumnae and among those who work with or critique the graduates. Actor training today is overwhelming—ideally, actors need to develop minds, souls, voices and bodies that respond to the canon of drama from Aeschylus, Molière and Shakespeare to David Mamet, Marsha Norman and August Wilson. Their chances of employment are increased if they can also sing and dance, and if they want to supplement the modest salaries of a career played out exclusively on the stage, they'd better learn how to act in front of a camera. It also helps if they have some show-business savvy—know how to select head shots and to write resumes, how to audition, to attract agents, to build up a network of contacts.

The professional lives of theatre actors are precarious. (A *New York Times* article on January 4, 1993 reported the Actors' Equity estimate that 41.4% of its 35,252 paid members in 1992 had worked at least *one* week.) Their personal lives pose further challenges. In what conditions do they live at home and on the road? How are their personal relationships affected by their work? What kinds of future can they hope for, much less plan?

The twenty-one outstanding artists in *Actors' Lives* were chosen, in collaboration with colleagues at Theatre Communications Group, from a list of four hundred excellent possibilities I compiled by scouring *Theatre World* from 1950 to the present, *Players Guide* and *Who's Who*, collections of theatre programs at the Lincoln Center performing arts library, and the files of the Non-Traditional Casting Project. Whittling down the list was agonizing. Interviewing the chosen few was often as exhilarating as seeing their finest work onstage.

The interviews—which took place between December of 1990 and January of 1993 in New York, Providence, Cleveland, Minneapolis, Seattle, Washington, D.C. and Spring Green, Wisconsin—averaged three to four hours. The transcripts ranged from approximately forty to one hundred forty typed pages, and from these—with the invaluable help of M. Elizabeth Osborn (editor of *Playing Joan*, my previous book on acting) and TCG Books' managing editor, Steven Samuels—I composed the actors' comments as if they were talking directly to the reader. The actors checked the final draft for accuracy and clarity.

I have assumed that readers are or can become familiar with the classics of dramatic literature; where little-known classics and new plays where discussed, I asked the actors to set their contexts. At the back of the book I have provided a chronological list of the actors' stage roles. I find these bios staggeringly impressive for the breadth of experience they record in both new plays and classics. Collectively, the actors have appeared in every Shakespeare play but the *Henry VI*s, for instance, and even those are partially represented by *The Hollow Crown.*

As New York theatre correspondent for the *Times* of London since 1983, I have been privileged to see a great deal of theatre on both sides of the Atlantic. I love British theatre and actors, but I have no sympathy for the attitude that "British is better." Considering the full gamut of performances and productions I have beheld throughout America and Great Britain, from the abysmal to the transcendent, I am probably prejudiced on the side of American productions of the classics: of twenty-three international *Hamlets* I have experienced, I most admired Garland Wright's staging at the Guthrie Theater, where Željko Ivanek was the only Hamlet who ever broke my heart; my favorite comedy of manners is the APA production of *The School for Scandal* with Rosemary Harris, Clayton Corzatte and George Grizzard; and my favorite Ibsen was Mark Lamos's *Peer Gynt* (with Richard Thomas in the title role) at Hartford Stage (though that's nearly a tie with Patrick Garland's Chichester Festival production of *An Enemy of the People*, starring Donald Sinden). The best Brecht I've seen was Andrei Serban's *The Good Woman of Setzuan* at La MaMa (with Jane Lind as the Water Seller). Even my favorite Ayckbourn was an American production: Lynne Meadow's staging of *Woman in Mind*, with Stockard Channing and an outstanding supporting cast, at the Manhattan Theatre Club.

By letting representative actors tell their stories, *Actors' Lives* pays tribute to the artists most indispensable for turning dramatic literature into theatre, and to all American performers who have brought pleasure and sometimes exaltation to audiences at home and abroad. American actors (in collaboration with fine playwrights, directors and designers) have given me more riches that I can ever repay. This book is an offering of thanks to them.

Acknowledgements

I n addition to the actors who gave so generously of themselves in the interviews, and my editors, I give special thanks to my invaluable personal assistant K.T. Baumann, and to the following: at TCG, director of publications Terence Nemeth, and Fran Kumin, Linda MacColl, Jim O'Quinn, Donna S. Moy, Michele Pearce, Stephanie Coen and Nancy Walther; from the Non-Traditional Casting Project, executive director Sharon Jensen and her assistant Beth Reif; the staff of the Billy Rose Theatre Collection at the New York Public Library of the Performing Arts at Lincoln Center; my critic colleagues Tish Dace, Sylvie Drake, Marianne Evett, William K. Gale, Edith Oliver, Sally Porterfield, Gerald Rabkin, J. Wynn Rousuck, Catherine Stadem, Dan Sullivan, Ross Wetzsteon and Robert Windeler; in New York, theatre and public relations personnel Edward Callaghan, Tisa Chang, Susan Chicoine, Terry Dwyer, Carol Fineman, John Ferraro, Kim Harding, Margot Harley, Alison Harper, Robert Knopf, Richard Kornberg, Wendy Morris, James Morrison, Ross Murphy, Doris Pettijohn, Nancy Rhodes, Ellen Rusconi, Gary Springer, Ellen Stewart and Suzanne Tighe; resident theatre personnel Neal Baron, Daniel Bauer, Dennis Behl, Sari Bodi, Michael Thomas Burgess, Flo Byron, Joan Channick, Elizabeth Clarke, Laine Dyer, Edward J. Feidner, Jan Geidt, Nicole

Hale, Elizabeth Huddle, Lynn Kelly, Kevin Kent, Dennis Krausnik, Maggi Lewis, Margaret Melozzi, Frances Oliver, Janice Paran, Michael Pauken, Dennis Powers, Mechele Pritchard, Howard Sherman, Douglas Simpson, Amy Smith, Frank Sugrue, Robert Wildmon and Anne Wittig; actor's executive assistants Caddy Granum, Bonnie Kramen and Regan McLemore; and also Helene Baker, Dresden E. Beattie, Randy Genet, Dot, George and Pal Hill, Robert J. Huven, Jerome Kilty, Lewis G. Knapp, Doris Randall and Martin Worman.

Actors' Lives is dedicated with admiration and with love to Judith Barcroft, K.T. Baumann, John Hallow, Ann Hillary, April Shawhan, Pat Starr, Kate Wilkinson and Janis Young.

ACTORS' LIVES
On And Off The American Stage

Fences *(Yale Repertory Theatre)*

JAMES EARL JONES

If I had taken all my colleagues and students at John Jay College who volunteered to play secretary when I interviewed James Earl Jones at the kitchen table of his Manhattan apartment, we would have needed the school gym. The son of actor Robert Earl Jones, James Earl Jones is of the first generation of African-American actors to attain wide success in theatre, film and television, and to break numerous casting color-barriers. His artistry and humanity have been recognized by two Tony Awards, the Commonwealth Award in 1991 and the National Medal of Arts in 1992.

I look at a great play as a great mountain to climb, and you cannot climb mountains unless you've had some experience. Shakespeare gives you the best mountains—the highest in terms of sustaining vocally through poetic phrases and long speeches, and also in terms of projecting everything out to an audience with some sort of coherence. I don't think I would have been hired for *The Great White Hope* had I not had a lot of experience playing Shakespeare, had I not played Othello a season or two before. Shakespeare in the Park is very important for actors, because there are so few places where they can grow.

An actor grows, not initially, but eventually, by being challenged by great material. It is better to be challenged by small material at first. That's why when you auditioned at the Actors Studio, at least in the old days, they didn't want you to bring in a good play, they wanted you to bring in a page from a novel, so that they could assess not how well you did a brilliant scene but how well you could act something that's not so brilliant. They wanted to see *you*. But once you get launched, what you need is good material. That keeps you encouraged, that keeps you enthralled.

It's depressing to have bad material. That's why TV can be deadly. Joe Papp gave us the best of material every summer with Shakespeare in the Park. He gave it to actors. He gave it to audiences.

My whole career, starting Off-Off Broadway in the late Fifties, has grown in small incremental steps. I can remember the summer of 1960, when I did my first work for the New York Shakespeare Festival. Alan Schneider was going to direct *Measure for Measure* in the Park, and when I went backstage after seeing another play he had directed, I approached him and said, "Mr. Schneider, I'm an actor, and in reading the plays you'll be doing this summer for Joe Papp, I noticed there's a character called Abhorson in *Measure for Measure*. It appears that he wears a mask. It shouldn't matter whether he's Caucasian, African or Asian skin color. I want to play that character." He said, "Okay, okay"—without reading me. One doesn't think of Alan Schneider being intimidated at all, but he later told me, "You were pretty large. I saw you, and you meant it."

Abhorson didn't have a whole lot to say. He was the executioner. But Joe Papp was trying to build a company, so he cast as many people in all three productions that summer as he could. The Vietnam war was looming then, and he said he wanted to have the soldier corps in *Henry V* well mixed—he didn't want them all English. So he gave me the role of Michael Williams.

After that, it often happened that I would have opportunities elsewhere, but my yearning was to get back to the Festival. Several seasons later, when my father was going to be in a very interesting movie called *One Potato, Two Potato*, I had an opportunity to audition for the character of his son, and I knew that I probably had a good chance of getting the role—a breakthrough kind of role for a black actor. But I also had the chance to do a Shakespeare Festival play with Mitchell Ryan. Mitchell was going to play Leontes, the king in *The Winter's Tale*, and I could play his major domo, Camillo. It was not a great role, but it meant working with Mitchell and playing a mature, responsible, stable, human, Shakespearean character. In the back of my mind, I was working towards a shot at playing Othello someday. So I made the decision to pass on the movie and go again to Shakespeare in the Park.

The next season, I was asked to play Othello to Mitchell Ryan's Iago. That casting, I think, is the best choice ever made, in terms of an American production of the play—to have Othello and Iago the same age, the same size, the same temperament, the same zodiac sign even. Brothers. It wasn't a bulldog and a bear. That is a different play; that is farce. The idea of a little man bringing down a big man is a joke. *Othello* is a much more psychically tuned story than that.

The third pillar of the play is Desdemona. We had a director, Gladys Vaughan, who understood that the women characters were under-written, that Shakespeare had to use young males in those roles and couldn't tax them too much. Opposite me, she cast a lady who became my first wife, Julienne Marie. Julienne had come out of musical theatre—she had just done *Foxy* with Bert Lahr; she had been in *The King and I*—so she had that kind of energy to bring to it. Julienne was finely boned and finely tuned vocally; she had the fragility, the epitome of dis-demon—the opposite of demon—Des-de-mona. Of all seven productions of *Othello* I've been in, including the big hit on Broadway with Chris Plummer, I think the one in the Park was the best realized.

Those were wonderful years Off Broadway. The spring after I played my first roles at the Shakespeare Festival, I was in the U.S. premiere of Jean Genet's *The Blacks*, which ran for several seasons. That company included many of the African-American actors you know of now— Roscoe Lee Browne, Cicely Tyson, Godfrey Cambridge, Louis Gossett. Billy Dee Williams came in later, and other younger actors as well as the original cast were recycled through—Roscoe would leave and come back, I'd leave and come back.

The Blacks connected to the awakening social consciousness of America that preceded the civil rights movement. Although I think Genet had something more absurd in mind, our production worked on that level—very effectively. Because life itself has gotten more absurd, it could not work in the same way today. In fact, two or three seasons after we opened in 1961, I noticed changes in the audience and in myself. I realized I was carrying onto the stage a racial animosity that was not very healthy. Even though we did it tongue-in-cheek, with great fun, *The Blacks* was essentially a play based on racial antagonism and satirizing racialist behavior. I found it hard to sustain. I would usually lose a lot of weight from the sweat and the grind of being onstage the whole time. I'd also lose energy. I would have to go off and recuperate, psychically as well as physically.

My father gave me a sense of the reality of the business. When I came into the theatre as a professional, he said to me, "I have not been able to make my living with this kind of work. And I want you to know that." So I came in with the realization that it was not about making bucks. Therefore I was able to sustain myself longer in both not-for-profit and for-profit theatre. I geared my standard of living to the real income. I didn't live in plush or drive plush or wear plush. In my early days, the best domicile I had was a cold-water flat in that hub between Little Italy and Chinatown. It cost nineteen dollars a month, which was ideal because it meant that I didn't have to have a certain salary just to pay my rent. I did not raise my standard of living until *The Great White Hope* in 1968. Then I decided I was able to marry and take on the responsibility of a family only because I had proved to myself that I could handle a leading role in a major theatre production.

Not-for-profit theatre is like subsistence farming. You're not there to make a killing. You're there hopefully to have a good, a fruitful, a productive season.

I was born and raised on a farm. We had some property that was our subsistence farm, and in Mississippi we even sharecropped. We moved to Michigan when I was four or five years old, and there we leased a neighbor's land to raise extra fodder.

One does not walk off a farm and say, "I want a liberal education." Not in that kind of family. Liberal education was an indulgence of the middle class. You walk off a farm and say you're going to be an engineer or a doctor or a lawyer or at least a teacher—something practical. My scholarship to the University of Michigan was for pre-med.

I found the study of science in high school a wondrous world, partly because of the teachers I had. In college, especially for the pre-med program, it was like force-feeding a goose. I did not enjoy it. And with the Korean war looming, I wanted to do something I enjoyed before I died. I then switched to the drama department, to get a degree in speech. Even then I was not determined to be an actor. It was just that my father was one.

At Michigan the faculty was fairly enlightened, so the ethnic concerns were not limiting. They tried to find roles for all the students. There were four prongs to my theatre experience there. First of all, I janitored the theatre—I was around it a lot and I got to know about theatre as architecture and as an institution. Next there was the training in drama, literature, speech, and things you could apply directly to performing. Then there were on-campus events and off-campus productions. I did several plays off-campus with an excellent company called the Arts Theatre and at the Manistee Michigan Summer Theatre.

After I graduated, I didn't die in Korea after all. They declared a truce the summer preceding my induction into the army. I was in a special unit, the Rangers, and after the Ranger course I was sent to Colorado to the Mountain Cold Weather Training Command. We worked on skis and snowshoes, with horses, mules, dogs, anything, to "negotiate" mountains. They were trying to find out things the Green Berets (Special Forces) needed in their training.

Army skiing required a great deal of endurance. A lot of it was up-hill. And for the mountain climbing, you had to have great strength, to be safe.

Coming right out of the service into the American Theatre Wing, I knew physical training. At the Wing it was called body movement and included some primitive dance taught by Sevilla Forte. I think she called it Afro-Cuban, and it was organic movement, so that you could get down to the way the human body would function at its best and its

most interesting. And we did a lot of fencing. That training continued
through all the years of Shakespeare. There was always a fencing
master at the Shakespeare Festival.

We learned at the Wing that you have to give the playwright a
chance. An actor can't right away say, "I know how the character
would say this, therefore I want you to change this dialogue." That is
not the actor's first task. The first task, even though it might feel
awkward to say a certain line, is to try it. John Berry, who directed my
early Fugard plays, would say: "Before you try to change dialogue,
experiment with it. Experiment with changes in the rhythm in a given
speech. Experiment with punctuation. Experiment with why the
pauses happen. You might find some insight into a way of saying it
that you never thought of before." I have since ended up in very serious
battles with playwrights about what's written. But I know that before I
go to battle about a line, I must have given it a chance.

There were two premier speech teachers at the Theatre Wing. One
was Fanny Bradshaw, and the other was Nora Dunfee. Nora came from
that tradition of Henry Sweet, the phonetics expert after whom
George Bernard Shaw patterned Henry Higgins. I still call on Nora,
whenever I'm doing dialogue derived from another language or another culture, or poetic drama. We always manage to get in some
sessions.

My voice is both a gift and something I worked hard for. The
genetic gift was a vocal timbre that has to do with resonating cavities,
size of body and so on, and I inherited that from my father, who is six
feet four. Then there was my farm heritage. We were never told as
children, "Hush, you'll wake the neighbors," because the neighbors
were miles or acres away. We were encouraged as farm kids to use our
voices fully, especially when it came to summoning the livestock. I had
a maybe uncanny, instinctive ability to communicate with life forms,
up through infants. When it came to human beings above infancy, I
lost it. That was part of what led me to being a stutterer . . .

I was imitating an uncle who stuttered. I was also expressing the
trauma I felt when my family moved from Mississippi to Michigan. I
had begun to solve the stuttering from the first year of high school, but
it's an ongoing process. I recently narrated an Audubon Society study
of the Great Lakes, and in the context of a long sentence, I could not

say "aquatic ecosystem." It set up a trip in my brain. That can be frustrating. I know why it happens, I just don't know how to solve it.

I often change things, change words. Occasionally I'll ask a play-wright if I can make a change for rhythm's sake. Playwrights are usually good at rhythm; documentary writers often are not. If you write something that has no kind of rhythm to it, it's not possible to speak it with any sort of coherence.

I've concluded, by the way, that speech is not natural to human beings. Sound is, music perhaps is—you find music in other forms of life. I think song is natural. But speech is an intellectual exercise that's acquired.

I had no trouble speaking *Fences* because August Wilson is a great poet. I'm from the South, and he was writing his characters from the South, so a lot of things fell right into place. Sometimes the rhythm was not familiar to me, but would be fascinating: "What you worried about what we getting into for?" You find this kind of creative distortion of English in cultures that retain what might be called a peasant class. The Irish do it, Jewish people do it when they're speaking forms of Yiddish. These flourishes of language filter up through a society. Dealing with such language is part of the fun of acting.

Most well-written material is poetically conceived. *Fences* and *The Great White Hope* are essentially poetic dramas. Jack Johnson, the fighter on whose life *Great White Hope* was based, was from Galveston, Texas. But the character was called Jack Jefferson (for legal reasons), so there was a certain poetic freedom. Howard Sackler created a sound that was not in any actual region of the country—it existed in his mind. I thought it was quite beautiful.

One of the conditions for being cast as Jack Jefferson was that I go to England to meet the trainer who had worked with Sir Laurence Olivier when he did Othello, for certain body strengthenings and a certain look. I met this trainer and he sent me back to the south of France, where I was filming *The Comedians*, with equipment—weights and so on—and I began the training. I didn't have the bulk of a fighter but I had the sinewy-ness, the flexibility. In Washington, D.C., when we were at the Arena Stage, I had a trainer named Bill

Terry who was a former fighter. He took me through the life of a boxer-in-training. Every morning you get up, you run a certain number of miles, you go to the gymnasium, you consume certain kinds of liquids and foods that are good for strength and endurance.

I had a beard I'd worn in *The Comedians*, and at some time past the halfway mark of the rehearsal period, I took the beard off and shaved my head—by then I had become pretty aware of the fighter as an ascetic. I walked into rehearsal and there was a great silence. The lady playing my mother was visibly shocked, and she walked up and said, "We want to welcome you to the company. We liked James Earl a lot, though." I thought she was kidding me at first, but she really believed I had been replaced.

At this point the physical training I had been doing came into focus and I was a different person. By then I had learned, with the director Ed Sherin's encouragement, to walk and behave physically, unconsciously, like an athlete, which I'm not. By the time I finished the run of the play and the film, I hated the training. I was not good at diets and I wanted to be free to eat what I thought my body was crying out for in terms of sustenance.

Whenever I've gone and got fancy—either with extravagant productions or where I've played sophisticated people—I've always found it important to return to what Shakespeare called the elemental man. King Lear defines him: he's got no clothes on, his ass is hanging out, and he ain't got nothin' but himself. It's always good to throw away all of our airs and play the basic human being. That's what Lennie in *Of Mice and Men* represents for me.

Ever since the American Theatre Wing, my great yearning was to do John Steinbeck's Lennie. I passed up a small role in a movie that Sidney Poitier wanted me to do with him to go out to Purdue University in Indiana to do *Of Mice and Men*. At Purdue, the psychology department was fascinated by how actors commit themselves to characters. The head of the department had done a private study of the actress who played Blanche the year before. At some performances he was convinced that the person he was watching onstage was schizophrenic. The actress was in total control, but emotionally and psychically, she crossed the line into that reality. So when I played Lennie, he

James Earl Jones (center) in The Great White Hope *(Arena Stage)*

made the same study of me—at what performances and where was I able to cross the line into being a retardate?

I used to suspend my own awareness and go with Lennie's brains. Lennie is like a child at the age when a child can talk, but takes things only literally. So when one character says, "The boss really got burned," Lennie wonders, "How did he put the fire out?" If someone tells him, "You're gonna get the can," he wonders, "Which can?"

Six years later, I played Lennie again in a production that finally came to Broadway. We started it in Dallas, at Southern Methodist University. North of Dallas, there was a community that had a center for retardates. Kevin Conway, who was playing George, and I were taken up there to spend a day. I had entered the production with the idea that I could bring to it, as part of Lennie's tragedy, that there is a hope, there is a chance. If he makes the right turn, he can become a potentially full human being, even though limited. After visiting that center, I realized there's no hope. You might be able to deal with autism, but not retardation. That's it. You don't electroshock, you don't love that person into something that he isn't. A couple of kids I met up there convinced me of that. The experience made me realize that the tragic character in *Of Mice and Men* is not Lennie but George.

George's tragedy is knowing from the time he enters that he's got to kill Lennie. George knows what I learned at the retardate center— there's no hope. When Lennie says, "I'll just go off into the hills and live in a cave like a bear," that's a wonderful dream, but George knows: no way. Lennie's too dependent on other human beings, and if he's on his own, he will kill something. And George knows he will bring about his own death someday.

George's awareness makes him similar to Hickey in *The Iceman Cometh*, which I played for Ted Mann at the Circle in the Square. I had no burning desire to do *Iceman*, but it's something I leapt willingly into, because it was another experiment.

I had seen Jason Robards do Hickey Off Broadway; in fact, my father was in that production. It's not that I couldn't get Jason's performance out of my mind. It's that I think Jason brought the kind of quixotic energy to that character that belongs there. I don't have that kind of energy. I've a much more sluggish, lethargic temperament.

I wasn't worried about the ethnic difference—the Hoosier being essentially a Caucasian from Indiana—because I'm from the Midwest. I can invoke the psyche of a midwestern human being, regardless of race.

I tried to come at Hickey from the gut. I tried to simply feel. I decided to go at him as a tragic character because he just murdered his wife.

It was an existential study for me, and an emotional study. I never wanted once to forget, "I just killed my wife." At the same time, his old friends are happy to see him. He brings in such a history with these guys. He is their savior. Whatever problems they're having, hey, Hickey's gonna solve them. So when he walks in, he's hit with that wave and he can't deny it. He wants to tell them, "I killed my wife. Can you help me?" But he has to set that aside and help *them*. That's what the whole play is about.

. . .

Before *Iceman*, I had done *Boesman and Lena* for Ted at his downtown
Circle in the Square, and I had also done *The Blood Knot* Off Broad-
way. When Athol Fugard and the director John Berry came along, I
suddenly felt I was in the presence of something very important. Later
I had the pleasure of being directed by Athol when I replaced Zakes
Mokae at the end of the Broadway run and for the tour of *"Master
Harold" . . . and the boys* and in *A Lesson from Aloes*.

I did *Lesson from Aloes* (directed by Athol himself) at the Yale
Repertory Theatre, along with Shakespeare's *Timon of Athens*, directed by Lloyd Richards. Lloyd and I have a very curious background,
by the way. I was his understudy in my first Broadway play, *The
Egghead*, written by Molly Kazan and directed by Hume Cronyn. I
never had a chance to go on because Lloyd was as diligent an actor as
he is a director. But that's how we met.

I played Timon for Lloyd, but I don't think I achieved the first act.
And without that, one in no way achieves the second. Once we had
opened that show, we started to rehearse *A Lesson from Aloes* in the
daytime. Athol would see *Timon* once in a while, and one day he said,
"You know what should have been considered for the second act?
Timon is mankind at the pinnacle. He is civilization. He is an altruist, a
philanthropist, a scholar, he embraces mankind. And when he feels
betrayed by his society, he should go on all fours: 'I'm not going to be
man anymore; I'm going to be animal.' When he encountered the
people from his former world in the second act, he should have said,
'Come down here to me or else I'm not talking to you.'" I found that
fascinating. Of course Athol wasn't directing it, and you can have
much more extravagant ideas when you don't have to test them out.
But given the frustration we were all having with the production, I
said, "Gee, we should have tried it."

Athol always said, "I'm not a director; I'm a writer who can tell the
cast very interesting stories about the characters and the events.
Beyond what I have written, I can tell them stories that they can
benefit from." And that's what he would do in the rehearsals. He
would challenge us. He was a good director. But I think I had my best
time with John Berry, because I was not dealing with the man who
wrote the play.

. . .

Later on, when I did Troy in *Fences*, I never spoke to August Wilson. I don't even know him that well. We didn't know how to talk to each other.

I did have a chance to discover August Wilson the poet when McDonald's had a scholarship program for minority groups and I was part of the ceremony. I asked August if I could read the poem he wrote to the company up at Yale on his birthday—we gave him a cake; he gave us a poem—and he gave me a half dozen more that were wonderful. Whereas I see the playwright August Wilson in racial terms, because he's a man focused on the black experience to the extent that I think he suppresses awareness of other racial entities, in his poetry it's just the opposite. He's totally universal.

I mean, his plays are universal, but in the subject matter of his poems, it's as if he could have been born centuries ago—to have that knowledge and insight about life, about the world, about mankind, he could have been born in another *country*. And of course genetically he does inherit Europe, he just doesn't deal with that right now. I think he will some day, but right now he's into his black family cycle of plays.

The year we did *Fences* at Yale, there was a consensus that it was not a viable play for any Broadway producer to take on. They all came up to see it and turned it down. We kept doing it at regional theatres hoping that somebody would give it a try. We took it to the Goodman Theatre in Chicago, where Carole Shorenstein Hays saw it. Here's a young Jewish woman, from a very wealthy San Francisco real-estate family, and she said, "This is the story of my family."

Every community is different. I think the ideal community to perform in is Minneapolis, where I did *"Master Harold"... and the boys* at the Guthrie Theater. There is no richer, healthier theatre environment than that, in terms of the way the audience is capable of receiving a play. I suspect that L.A., at this time, has a better human energy in the audience than New York does. New York has people who have seen everything: they're jaded, highly critical, highly opinionated, and fickle. They're not willing to sit and open up and listen. They're swayed by this or that political or social fad or opinion. San

Francisco, on the other hand, is where we had the weirdest experience with *Fences*.

San Francisco has that beacon on Tower Hill, like the Statue of Liberty in New York. But in San Francisco the beacon has always said, "Come unto me all ye who are fucked up. Come *here*." The audiences there didn't want to hear the play. They had concerns of their own— the AIDS problem had wracked the city; the Democratic Convention was coming there; they were having to clean up their act. They had enough problems, and they didn't want to hear about the problems of African-Americans in the 1950s. I was grateful that they left us alone. They didn't hassle us, they didn't try to infuse their own energy into the play. They just sat on their hands. Fine. That's okay. In New York we encountered audiences that contrived to disrupt the play. My father and I have had discussions about inappropriate laughter. It also happened in *The Great White Hope*. Not in the early days but after a while, when the producer was thriving on group sales.

Both plays were about black families, and you get a group of black families in the theatre—or in the case of *Fences*, a group of black church women—and it became impossible to do the play in front of them. Because they were not sophisticated enough to say, "It's just a play." They treat theatre like they do church, with the "Amen" attitude—which I resent. It's not church. And they have no right saying "Amen." I don't care how much they agree with what's going on onstage. I'm very rigid, I'm afraid, and maybe conservative in my opinions about theatre behavior. That behavior is not just cultural and ethnic. It's also from watching TV and not recognizing the difference between TV and live theatre.

I'm convinced—this is the argument I had with my father—that at a certain point, if a play becomes difficult for people to accept, they reject it through laughter. It didn't give me any solace that Hume Cronyn and Jessica Tandy came backstage one night after *Fences* and said, "Did it bother you?" Because some nights even the announce-ment of the death of Troy's mistress would evoke laughter, cruel laughter. It's me up there doing it. Once I turned to somebody laughing and said, "What's so funny?"

Jessica had similar experiences when she played Blanche in *Street-*

car, and she said that it's a phenomenon that has several causes. Playwrights like August Wilson and Tennessee Williams can draw audiences into an experience to the point that it's really now *their* experience—which is wonderful. But if you're not careful in the way you write it and perform it, when the tragedy hits the play starts walking a very dangerous thin edge.

Jessica said that when Stanley began his assault on Blanche, the audience freaked out. And she wasn't talking about groups of black church women, she wasn't talking about groups of kids raised on TV who don't have any manners in the theatre. She was talking about fully adult, sophisticated, middle-class people, who have enough support to pretty much suppress the horror of life. But Williams was asking them to confront it, and she as Blanche and Marlon as Stanley were asking them to confront it.

The audience response was a nervous laughter. They weren't *trying* to reject it, but it was happening *to them*. They were saying, "I'm not, I'm not, I'm *not* watching this. What's happening is *not* happening." Jessica said it became very difficult to play the scene because there's a part of you that's maybe ego that says, "They're not buying it." The truth is, they're buying it too much.

It's always a matter of keeping things in balance. The argument I insisted on with the playwright in the case of *Fences*, and with the director of *Great White Hope*, was that you can do certain fine-tuning to help audiences through the play. We, the theatremakers, ask them to come in and watch it. When it gets rough, we have to find ways of helping them through the experience. We *do* want them to have the experience. It's like a kid getting a shot: you gotta make it easy for them.

I discovered by accident one way to make it easy during the production of *Fences* at Yale. There you get budding talents working on plays, and the costume designer was convinced that she had to help the director with the time changes by giving little tips to the audience that certain things were day and night, and how many days have passed, by the way people dressed.

Troy comes home from the funeral of his mistress with their baby. To evoke that, he enters in black. He usually comes home with a cap on, caps which give a lot of light to the face. But after the funeral he had a hat on, the kind of wide-brimmed hat that you see on Martin Luther King. When I walked down the alley with that hat on, the audience couldn't see my face. All they saw was a dark image with a pink baby blanket in his arms, and they realized, "Oh, it's a baby." Roars of laughter. And I wondered, "Why is this happening? I haven't said anything, Rose hasn't yet given any of her delicious lines about female retribution."

One day I just arbitrarily came in with the hat off and the laughter didn't happen. I realized that all they had to keep them in focus in the play was the character—me—my face. Once I hid my face, they lost that connection. And they lost any sense of suspense about, "Now what's going to happen?" They just got an impact and took off with it. And I said to the costume designer, "I hope you can learn from this experience. The line that we offer the audience, that we throw them to hang onto, is very fragile. And however logical your reasons about how you dress a character, you don't dare interfere with that fragile line. All I have is a face. I have no dialogue. It's just my face that they know."

Another example of what I call fine-tuning, only this time it wasn't done, is when Rose has a poetic couplet that she says to Troy when she takes his baby in her arms: "A motherless child has got a hard time. From right now . . . this child got a mother. But you a womanless man."

As a couplet, it works, but sometimes people would laugh. Often the audience never registered that the baby has no mother, because they were not allowed to have any sort of connection with the baby as a human being. Lloyd Richards worked very hard as the director to make how we related to the child credible, to make the audience believe it was a real child. But the idea of a child in jeopardy never quite registered. It was just a prop. Who cares about a prop?

Carole Shorenstein Hays and her husband Jeffrey had a baby, and she wanted the baby to have an Equity card. But in order to qualify, he had to do a performance. This was just a joke, but I went for it. We put him in the swaddling cloth, I walked onstage, everything's fine. He's a bit warm because it's thick material, and he gives a kick. Now the audience knows it's a real child, and they're not laughing. When I start talking, the baby is not comfortable. He reaches up and puts his hand over my mouth, as if to say, "Will you just shut up and get me

out of here?" And it's a white hand. Some black woman in the
audience said, "I knew it! I knew she was a white! I knew he had a
white mistress!"

Everywhere we played, people who came backstage would say, "I
know a man like Troy." Then they'd ask, "Why did you treat your son
so mean?"

They didn't understand that kind of meanness—Troy not signing
the permission for Cory to get a football scholarship, and the scene
where Cory asks Troy why he's never liked him and Troy calls that a
damn fool-ass question. Maybe it's not understandable. I bought it
only because August said, "I can't write the character being totally
articulate. What he is getting at is 'If I let you go into the world
expecting kindness and friendship from anybody, I might as well shoot
you now, 'cause you're a black male child. Therefore I want to train
you how not to be liked.'" I wish Troy could've said that. August
wanted Troy to have great poetic ability, great insights, great intelligence, but not always to be able to articulate. Troy should have been
able to articulate at that moment, I think.

I had a hard time, because I had just had a son during *"Master
Harold,"* and I'm coming home to him every night. I was depressed a
lot. It seemed too painful to bear that there's such cruelty between
father and son. Their relationship had no resolution. We finally found
one that kind of worked symbolically, where Troy takes the baseball
bat and means to beat his son's brains out, and realizes he can't. This
was not written, but Lloyd, Courtney Vance as Cory, and I struggled to
find it. Once we included that symbolic resolution, I could come home
and not be depressed relating to my own son. And I learned something,
too—that when a son chooses or threatens to extract his own identity
from the relationship, it is painful. It just doesn't have to be cruel and
destructive, as it was with Troy.

Thinking of Courtney Vance . . . I think it's time to speak irrelevant
of race. I include Courtney in the battery of really vibrant young actors
that I've had a chance to work with, which includes Kevin Costner,
Alec Baldwin and Eric Roberts. I don't find many young actors as
strong as Courtney.

·   ·   ·

When I finished *Fences* in L.A., I went to Lynne Thigpen, who had taken over for Mary Alice as Rose, and to young Courtney, and said, "I didn't want to admit it until I got to this final performance, but I'm so tired I don't know how I would go on." I thought I was confessing something about me at my age: I was telling them that if we went on any further, I would probably let them down. They said the same thing to me—that they were also tired to death, deeply fatigued. I realized it was not about *my* energy, it was about the general energy.

All acting, at its best, is about entering the stage and, spiritually, going to the edge of that cliff that is the proscenium, acknowledging there is an energy there and, like a skydiver, pushing yourself off. You trust the thermal waves of energy that the audience is, and you soar.

Soaring doesn't require a lot of flapping and energy. There is a way of making it look easy. It happens in the monodrama. It did to me in *Paul Robeson.* You'd think that the one-person format would be the most fatiguing. Oddly enough, it is not.

Paul Robeson the artist—his early days—was easy. There's less known about him as a spiritual force after the Spanish Civil War. I realized at some point in Philadelphia that we were not going to get a second act with the team we had.

Lloyd Richards came in with two things: he had the ability to work with the writer, Phillip Hayes Dean; and he had a better knowledge than any other director of who Robeson really was. And he had my trust, so he pretty much salvaged that production. The first night under his direction, I was given a page-and-a-half new speech to learn. It was so well-conceived under his guidance that it gave the second act a center.

When he directed me in *Paul Robeson*, and later in *Hedda Gabler* at Yale, I thought Lloyd was one of the most daring directors I'd ever met. He belongs up there with Stanislavsky and Lee Strasberg. They have in common a broad knowledge of what the dramatic arts are all about. Lloyd has probably the broadest base of any American I know of, partly because of the way he studied, the way he trained as actor, director, teacher, administrator, all that.

What I saw happening in *Fences*, I think, was a danger signal for me, if not for him. I never told him this. I think probably the deanship at Yale, the administrative work, was beginning to erode his daring, his ability and willingness to take chances. Also he had made it his mission to give creative writers a place where they wouldn't be tampered with prematurely by the commercial world . . . but in doing so I don't think he brought to them the muscle to deal with the challenges of that world. And it took him out of the danger zone. I think, very frankly, that the need to play it safer became more important. Now that he is no longer going to be Dean of the Yale School of Drama, I think he'll get back to the danger.

Being both a producer and a director is a problem. Until Ted Mann directed our *Iceman Cometh*, he had never gotten any credit for being a good director. I don't think he *was* any good. It just happened he understood that play very well, he made it work, and he rightfully got the first good reviews I know of.

But Ted was always more proficient as a producer, just like Joe Papp's producing expertise and talent and genius far exceeded his directing. I think Joe and Ted would have been good directors if they hadn't had to do so much on the overall project. So much creative energy is spent out there, producing, it cannot be brought to directing.

I have just about decided that I won't do commercial theatre anymore. No producer can afford signing you for less than a year, and I don't want to disrupt my family. If my wife is in L.A. and our son is in school there, I would not want to spend a whole lot of time away. Short engagements of a month or two or three are always possible.

There are some plays I would like to do, some revivals, and I'd like to make theatre only the first step towards putting them on videocassette or film. I might discover exactly how to play a character onstage and it will not necessarily serve me in TV, but I'm willing to take the chance that, if I learn about the character, I can also learn how to make that knowledge work for me in the different media.

At the age of sixty, having been in the theatre for half that time, I have yet to evolve as a cinema actor. I have a lot to learn. And unfortunately, going back to the stage won't solve all those problems for me. I think TV can solve a lot of them. My series "Gabriel's Fire" had a strong potential—I just don't think we ever lived up to the pilot.

It was something to find a character like Gabriel, a man of my generation who is still hungry for life. Usually I'm asked to play retirees—underfoot and a pain in the butt.

You can get better money in films and TV, but you can't get better training or experience. So actors keep coming back to the theatre—sometimes to situations where there is no pay at all, or only the bare minimum that the union requires—because it's the experience that's valuable.

What makes an actor happy is not so much that he does a good performance, but that the whole thing works. When you get a production where the casting is right, the writing is right and the director is totally in focus, then you feel you were a part of something that was meant to be.

Hedda Gabler *(Guthrie Theater)*

I *was an MFA student in theatre history and criticism at Columbia when a professor took our class to see the newly formed Performance Group's* Dionysus in '69. *My relatively sheltered upbringing had in no way prepared me for the cultural shocks of the avant-garde groups of the sixties and seventies. One of the audience members who got as far away from the performance as I could, I gazed down at Joan MacIntosh's Agave with a mixture of horror and envy: that physically delicate young actress was giving a visceral performance more daring than I had the courage even to imagine. I never went back, and thus missed MacIntosh's Mother Courage and other portrayals that garnered her two Obies. I did not catch up with her work until she began appearing on and off Broadway in the 1980s, when her eloquence as the silent Frau Rasch in JoAnne Akalaitis's staging of* Request Concert *at Women's Interart earned MacIntosh a Drama Desk Award.*

Our interviews took place in the summer and fall of 1991, just before and shortly after she and Joseph Chaikin traveled to South Africa to conduct workshops for black theatre artists from the townships. In the fall of 1992, Joan MacIntosh was designated an Artistic Associate of the New York Shakespeare Festival.

I fell in love with theatre during my junior year in college, when I spent a semester in London. It was 1965, the year that Olivier did *Othello*, Albert Finney did *Serjeant Musgrave's Dance* and the Royal Shakespeare Company did *Henry V*, *Marat/Sade* and *The Homecoming*. I dragged my roommate to everything.

Seeing Olivier was a stunning event. This very large black man appeared on the stage and I thought, "Where's Laurence Olivier?," not realizing I was looking at him.

When I went back to Beaver College for the spring semester, I played Estelle in a production of Sartre's *No Exit*. We took our production to a college drama festival at Yale, where Robert Corrigan and Ted Hoffman were the judges. Ted later became a very close friend—I was married at his house—but at the festival he was so critical of American actors, so cutting. At a party after this event, I told him how angry I was at him. I said he had no right to criticize if he couldn't contribute to the solution. And he said, "As a matter of fact I'm starting a graduate acting program at New York University. Would you like to come to it?"

I changed my plan of going to drama school in London to going to NYU after finishing my B.A. My parents were opposed to my being an actress and coming to New York, but I was determined. Up until three days before I left, I didn't know I had gotten the scholarship that made it possible for me to be a graduate acting student instead of a suppliant, knocking at the door of La MaMa, which was my other plan.

I got a morning job at a publishing company, and later that year I also got my first job at the New York Shakespeare Festival, ushering for *Hair* when it was playing at the Public Theater. I went to NYU in the afternoons, and in the evenings I worked with the Performance Group.

Richard Schechner was a professor of mine, whom I was dating. We shared a dream of creating a great theatre, with the Berliner Ensemble as our model. That fall Jerzy Grotowski, founder and director of the Polish Laboratory Theatre and author of *Towards a Poor Theatre*, was invited by NYU to come and talk and to lead workshops in which students and faculty could participate. As a result of Richard's taking Grotowski's workshop, he started a series of workshops about a month later, using some of the techniques he had learned and transforming them.

From the infusion of Grotowski's presence, a lot of experimental theatre groups began that fall, adding to the already existing ones. Years later, we created a consortium called A Bunch of Experimental Theatres, Inc. It was a really wonderful period. We were all friends: André Gregory's Manhattan Project, Meredith Monk, Richard Foreman's Ontological-Hysteric Theatre, the Open Theater, the Ridiculous Theatrical Company, Mabou Mines, the Shaliko Company. We had parties together; we saw each other's work; we talked for hours and hours about art and transforming the world.

Richard and I and about ten other people started the Performance Group and began to find places to work. We went where we could find free space, on Saturdays and whenever we could find pockets of time. In the winter of 1968, we found the Performing Garage, an old factory in SoHo, and spent a lot of time cleaning it up. There was a period when we were on our hands and knees scraping the cement floor with toothbrushes to get the grease out of it.

The faculty at NYU was very upset that I was doing this. At my mid-semester evaluation, the panel of teachers told me that they felt I had great talent and promise and that I should not be wasting my time with the Performance Group. They called Richard Schechner a Svengali and said I needed to make a choice.

It was a major crisis in my life, and I spoke to Olympia Dukakis, my advisor, about it. She was my first acting teacher, and we have been close friends all these years. She said, "Look, just try what they want for a semester. Ask for all the best teachers, and see how you feel at the end of the year."

I did that, and I had a wonderful semester. I was taking a full day of classes. I studied acting with Olympia, Lloyd Richards and Peter Kass, circus techniques with Hovey Burgess, voice with Kristin Linklater, speech with Nora Dunfee, theatre games with Omar Shapley, and stage combat. I spent the winter and spring at NYU, and did a number of plays at school.

But I did stay in touch with the Performance Group, because by then I was living with Richard. I would go to watch rehearsals. Just before NYU told me I had to make a choice, we had started working with the text of Euripides' *The Bacchae*. What became *Dionysus in '69* was being developed very slowly.

As soon as school was finished for the year, I started working with the Performance Group again, and that summer we opened *Dionysus* and played to sold-out houses. It was a runaway hit. We could not have anticipated the impact it had on people. It was, in so many ways, a barometer of the times.

NYU's School of the Arts is near St. Mark's Place on the Lower East Side, and when I first arrived there, I felt as if I had just gotten off the bus and someone had handed me a joint. I passed through a world of marijuana smoke and bells and flowers to get to school every day. I had been very sheltered, so it was a shock, but deep inside I was also longing for that kind of impact.

The process of making and playing *Dionysus* was at times very difficult and scary, because we were in territory we had never been in before. And we were suddenly making three hundred dollars a week, which at the time was an exorbitant amount of money.

I chose not to return to NYU but to stay with the Performance Group, not because the play was a success but because we were also doing ongoing training. We were working with a t'ai chi master and continuing our vocal work, and we made a commitment to each other for ongoing physical, vocal, psychic and emotional training. Some of the exercises are described in Grotowski's book and in Richard's *Environmental Theatre*.

Our idea, also inspired by Antonin Artaud's *The Theatre and Its Double*, was that actors needed to have their bodies and voices be superbly developed and articulated instruments, and we worked every day towards that goal. We aimed at physical precision, strength, endurance and articulation, at the ability to dance and move with great specificity. We wanted to be able to swing from the rafters while singing an aria from *La Traviata*, or sing it standing on our heads or walking on our hands.

We set out to develop our inner beings through extreme states of psychological and emotional exploration. These exercises could be solitary, with partners, or in groups, and they were a torturous but joyous journey into unknown territories of the psyche. We did about

ninety minutes of exercises each day, and then Richard would take us
through an improvisation of some kind. While we were creating
Dionysus, the improvisations developed themes of the play.

The training was intense and extraordinary. It was really like going
through the flames—to use Artaud's image—to discover the deepest
inner parts of ourselves as actors, and then discover the way to manifest
this physically and vocally.

I think that an actor is a messenger, a channel for whatever there is
to be reported, from wherever the message comes, on any level—
whether it's a soap opera or a sitcom, in a film or on a stage. Theatre is
immediate and communal, and in its immediacy it has the capacity to
transform people's souls, and thereby the world.

I was with the Performance Group every day for ten years, training
and rehearsing all day and performing something at night. I learned so
much simply from having the gift of performing every night in front
of an audience. You learn what works, you learn timing, you learn how
to be honest, you learn what's truthful and what isn't. The audience
will always tell you what isn't working. And our audience was not in a
dark hole—they were lit so we could see them. I had to learn how to
concentrate on telling the story and still be open to receiving input
from the audience.

Richard coined the term "environmental theatre" for our work.
After Grotowski's model, we looked at our work as a laboratory. We
experimented with the audience's relationship to the performer. We
broke down the fourth wall. We made the whole Performing Garage
into the theatrical space so that the audience would be involved in the
environment of the play.

For *Dionysus* we thought of the audience as being in Dionysus'
camp or in Pentheus' camp. Pentheus was the ruler and represented
order, the state, conservative values, the preservation of society. Dionysus was offering an alternative of pleasure and ecstasy. A major
issue in the play is that excess of pleasure can lead to anarchy, to
violence, to death. We designed the environment so that anyone who
identified with Pentheus or felt uptight or wanted to watch from a
great distance could sit on high towers, and anyone who wanted to

participate in the Dionysian revels could sit on the floor all around and be close to the action.

There was a lot of audience participation in all the plays we did. At places in *Dionysus* the audience actually could interfere with the action and change its course. At one point, Dionysus gave Pentheus the task of asking a woman from the audience to befriend him and go home with him. If she said yes, Pentheus would escape Dionysus' wrath and the play would end there. If no woman responded to Pentheus, Dionysus would then proceed to have him torn limb from limb by his mother, Agave.

One night, a woman (who had seen the play before and planned her strategy) did say yes to the actor playing Pentheus. They left the theatre together right then and there, and the performance was over. I was playing Dionysus that night and I had a mighty disgruntled audience to explain the rules of this game to. But audiences loved to come back to *Dionysus* many times. Their participation was great fun.

In *Dionysus* we also asked the audience to join an ecstasy dance, and if they wanted to take off their clothes and dance naked, they could, and did. There had been such repression in our culture during the Fifties and the Cold War. Part of what this play was about was blasting through that repression.

In the march on Washington to protest the Kent State massacre in 1970, hundreds of people, in a moment of ecstatic union, tore off their clothes and ran naked into the Reflecting Pool. We felt this symbolized that we were free. In retrospect it seems very naive, but it was a necessary step at the time.

A play I particularly loved was called *Commune*, whose seed was the demise of the first Performance Group. There were basic disagreements in the company—the original constellation of people disintegrated—and from the pain of going through that, those who were left reexamined the nature of groups. The Charles Manson commune was in the news, as were communes in general. People were again looking for ideal societies, and theatre artists, in particular, were experimenting with communal models in our work and our lives.

We had seen Fellini's *Satyricon*, and it led us to experiment with a form of telling a story that was not linear but circular. What if the middle of the event comes first, or maybe you begin with the end and then go back to the beginning and perhaps show five aspects of the middle and then return to the end?

In *Commune* we had a scene from the My Lai massacre, a scene from the Sharon Tate murders, a scene of the pilgrims coming to America, a scene based on a Bible psalm, some text from *Alice in Wonderland*, a scene from *Lear* on the heath played by characters from the Tate story, and many other scenes. The Sharon Tate story became the apex of the event, contrasted to the transcript of Lieutenant Calley, the soldier who was tried for his role in the My Lai massacre in Vietnam. The interviewer asked, "What kind of people did you kill? Men, women and children?" and Calley answered, "Men, women and children." Then the interviewer asked, "Babies?" and Calley said, "Babies, too." Volunteers from the audience were part of the scene, and became the people who were massacred. They didn't know they were going to be. The interview happened around them, and then we acted out killing them.

We had to get fifteen volunteers for this scene, and one night we couldn't, and there was a big fight in the audience. We welcomed such controversy. We were exploring different ways of getting the audience to participate. In this case some people said, "I refuse to do that. I think it's ridiculous, it's fascistic." The whole audience broke into a debate, some people saying, "Shut up, we want to get on with the play," and others saying, "No, I agree with them!"

The play stopped for about three hours. We just said, "Okay, look, we need to have fifteen volunteers in order to continue. That's the rule we set up for ourselves. So we're prepared to stop and talk about it and we'll work it out." I threw the *I Ching*, because we used the *I Ching* in the play to see what it advised us to do; we were listening to the radio; people were breaking into groups and talking about the war and about politics; people went out and brought back food and coffee; and I think some people left.

I let the play go completely. I was reading, I was talking. We were maybe 250 to 300 people, and we all had to work together in order for the event to continue. We couldn't have disparate beliefs. We couldn't necessarily have our individual ego-needs met if we were going to get out of this mess. It's exactly what's facing us in the world.

The play finally continued when all fifteen people came to their choice to participate. I think we were all weeping by the end, the actors and the audience. It was one of the most memorable and profound evenings in the theatre I've ever had, one that brought us into the reality of what theatre is: a communal event that everyone shares; where something transpires which is unlike any other night, needing all of the energies of everyone for the event to succeed.

One of the great experiences of my life, theatrically, was playing Mother Courage with the Performance Group. We developed that production over a couple of years, in New York and on our tour of Europe with Sam Shepard's *Tooth of Crime*. To me, the whole character of Mother Courage was contingent on finding the right pair of boots to wear. Shoes are your connection to the earth, they're your foundation, they have to be right.

We were touring in many of the places that Mother Courage had followed armies with her supply wagon, and so I was getting a sense of where she had spent her time . . . and then, in Amsterdam, at a retrospective of his work, I saw Van Gogh's "Boots with Laces," and it started me on the characterization. I rejected hundreds of boots to find the right pair, and then I found *two* pairs, which didn't resemble the painting exactly, but had the right feeling . . .

I knew the whole time I was preparing the role that I was too young to play Mother Courage, but I looked at the script and saw that in the beginning the character is talking all the time, and really on top of things, and by the end she can barely speak. I knew I could take that journey from great energy to no energy. In fact, just performing the play, with its strenuous physical demands, is all you need to be spent by the end, as Mother Courage is in the story.

Because we didn't want the wagon to block the audience, we had a piece of it against the wall, and indicated it mostly with ropes that came from the walls and moved, depending on where we were in the action. We had the wagon at one end of the theatre and at the other end was the Garage door, and for the scene in which Mother Courage and the Cook stand outside the house singing for their supper, we went outside. We put on coats and we strapped the ropes to our bodies with harnesses.

It was wonderful in the winter when it snowed, and we also had the reality of the street life. Often passersby would stop and talk to us. One night Charles Ludlam and a friend came by, and we stood there and chatted in character, Charles contributing some nice little bits. The audience loved the scene for its serendipity.

At the end of the play, when Mother Courage is alone and all her children are dead, I went around the entire Garage and hooked every rope onto my back. The rest of the company were singing a chorus of the opening song—there's another army going by and Mother Courage wants to keep on going, so I'm trying to sell to the army this boot I've just taken off my daughter's body while literally pulling the entire room with me.

During intermission we served homemade soup and bread, and fruit and cheese, to everyone, like an army canteen where you would get plates and stand on line. The audience had an hour to relax and talk and eat and mingle with the actors, and we played Scott Joplin songs on the piano. We all had the same food in our bellies for the second half of the play—we had all broken the same bread—and it was wonderful.

I have never thought of myself as being old—I mean I don't *feel* old—but the director Peter Sellars said to me, "You know, when I was a little kid, you were my hero. I used to come and watch your Mother Courage all the time." Another director, Anne Bogart, said the same thing, talking about when *she* was young. But I was young then, too. I was in my twenties!

We toured that play in India, which was quite extraordinary. We did it in villages. We did it for five thousand people in a village north of Calcutta, where no one spoke a word of English, in their village square, and used an oxcart as the wagon. I still hear that I'm a great star in India because of my Mother Courage.

It's so amazing, that. A lot of us have that experience if we go away and perform. The larger issue is that I've had a profound impact on people in other countries but I sometimes feel that I barely make a dent in America. Our actors are not valued unless they become movie stars, and often the value is exaggerated out of proportion.

. . .

The Performance Group was in India in 1976, and for a year after that we went our separate ways. Richard and I went for three months on a United States Information Agency-funded tour to teach workshops and to lecture throughout Southeast Asia. We had a vacation in the Himalayas in an incredibly beautiful place called Pahlgam, where I planned my teaching for the National School of Drama, which I was to do for six weeks that fall. I went through everything I knew and really organized it. It was the beginning of my teaching career.

The last thing I did with the Performance Group was Jocasta in Ted Hughes' adaptation of Seneca's *Oedipus*, which Richard and I chose when we were in India. Once we got back from there, I had wanted to take a leave of absence to explore other possibilities for acting, and I had an agent who was willing to help me.

As it turned out, I left the Group and my marriage with Richard, taking my son with me. I had become pregnant during our year in Asia, so when I played Jocasta I had just given birth to a son and I was separating from his father. In Seneca's tragedy, the father is murdered by the son, who then marries his mother. The play was a grotesquely distorted mirror of our actual lives at the time, and the experience was very painful for all of us.

Sam was five months old when I went to live in a loft that I sublet from a friend in Brooklyn. I had no money, no job, my life was completely turned upside down. I knew it was the right thing to do, but it was terrifying, and I cried through the entire year of 1978. To keep my sanity, I started writing for the first time since college, and I started teaching acting to make some income.

I enjoy teaching, especially when I work with professionals in my own workshops. I work with one group on Monday evenings, and with people privately on a one-to-one basis. I love to talk about acting, I love connecting with people. I enjoy passing on what I know. As soon as I learn it, I want to share it.

For me, teaching is also a way of constantly refining my understanding of what acting is, and it helps me when I go back and do it. Teaching serves as a laboratory—I'm always exploring new and better ways to communicate what acting is to my students. It gives me a great

Joan MacIntosh in Request Concert *(Women's Interart Theatre)*

deal of satisfaction to hook into another actor's need, and to try to help actors get where they need to go. When I'm communicating that and the other person is receiving it and then giving it back in their work, I'm happy.

When I left the Performance Group, I basically had to start all over again as an actress. I was a star in the experimental world, but I wasn't known in the mainstream. Or if I was known, I was stigmatized. There were people who were afraid of me because I had been an avant-garde actress. But I love to do Broadway plays. I love to play comedy—I have a great sense of humor and impeccable timing. I would love to play Noel Coward. I want to do more film and TV.

When I was beginning my "mainstream" career, I was trying to get this particular agency to represent me. They sat and looked at me and talked to me and said, "Well, but you're not the Faye Dunaway type." The irony was—and I sent them a card to this effect—that a few years later I was Faye Dunaway's standby on Broadway when she did *Curse of an Aching Heart.*

I was a single parent, and I had a childcare person to whom I would literally hand over my unemployment check, which was $125 a week in 1978. I tried, with the little money I had, to get a wardrobe together for going around to meetings with agents and people in the commercial world. I'd realized that they were starting to look at me as a commodity, and the whole issue of cosmetics became paramount. I always thought it was about what's on the inside, and suddenly I was realizing it was all about what's on the outside. People were saying to me, "Well, you have a face like a happy housewife and a voice like Jeanne Moreau. We don't know what to do with you. Come back to us in ten or fifteen years, when you've grown into yourself." And I thought, "What does that mean? Here I am, at *this* moment."

Those experiences were devastating. I wanted to crawl into a hole, and just never come out again. It just seemed like such an alien world to me. I had been so sheltered in the experimental world. A lot of people said, "Ah well, you have to get knocked around and pay your dues."

I got an audition for Regan in a *King Lear* that Elia Kazan was supposed to be doing with Richard Burton. I didn't know how to audition—it was the first professional audition I had ever done—and I remember working on it in my loft, with my infant watching me. I planned every movement because I had no idea what to do. I was so rigid it must have been ludicrous. I can only imagine that they looked at me and thought, "This poor woman." But Elia Kazan was so gracious. He came and talked with me, and was wonderful.

Harold Clurman was always a great supporter. I loved him. He was a great man. He loved the theatre, and he loved everybody who loved the theatre, he was so passionate about it. Harold was very supportive of me in my early days, and his support was so meaningful because I felt incredibly inept and unprepared for life in the commercial theatre.

The second *mensch* I met in my life was Joe Papp, and I loved him dearly, too. He loved and believed in me, and to this day his spirit is with me, inspiring me and supporting me. I am so grateful to have known him. He loved Sam, too. He always told Sam that if he ever needed *anything* in his life, he should come to Papa Joe.

And Rosemarie Tichler—then the casting director at the Public—was incredibly helpful. She helped me learn how to do auditions. She is still a beloved friend.

While I was struggling to get into mainstream work, Ron Argelander of NYU, who was an old friend, offered me a job teaching there, and that saved my life. I did an Off-Off Broadway limited run of *Saint Joan of the Stockyards* because Stefan Brecht, who had loved our production of *Mother Courage* and was very particular about who he allowed to do his father's work, told the director—unbeknownst to me—"You can't do it unless you use Joan MacIntosh." I was paid a little money and got very good reviews, and that helped me survive and feel more confident.

For an audition for Liz Swados's *Alice in Concert* at the Public, I had to create characters from the book, and I did the scene where the Duchess is beating the baby and pouring salt on it. I used Sam's teddy bear for the baby, and I used him as an audience. This was the year following the Kazan audition, when Sam was old enough to appreciate what I was doing . . . and when he laughed I knew it worked, and when he didn't laugh, I knew that I couldn't use that bit.

So I began a year's work with Liz . . . and with each little thing I was getting more firmly placed. I got my monologues together, I sent my picture and resume out like everybody does, and I started getting to know people.

I met Zelda Fichandler when TCG invited me to a kind of think tank. I remember Pamela Reed was there, and Susan Kingsley, that wonderful actress who died tragically in a car crash. TCG invited people from the so-called avant-garde and the mainstream, and we all talked about the state of the theatre. I thought Zelda Fichandler was the most wonderful, articulate, full-of-heart-and-soul theatre-being. She became a role model, and when I eventually worked for her at the Arena Stage it was a wonderful experience.

She ran her theatre like a great, generous, expansive mother who is also a great, generous, expansive artist. She loves actors. There are some directors who don't, so when you find one who does, you know the difference.

· · ·

I left Richard on February 10th of 1978, and I gave myself three years
to "make it." In my moments of despair, when I thought, "I just can't
do this, I don't know how," I would think, "I'll try everything I can, I'll
go out on every audition I can go out on, I'll do everything in my power
to make it work, and at the end of three years, if my career is not where
I want it to be, I will leave the business."

My credits in the experimental world did me very little good, except
with people whom I knew from then, and one of them was JoAnne
Akalaitis. Three years to the day I had made this agreement with
myself, I thought, "I need to get out. This is just too difficult for me.
Maybe I don't have the kind of personality necessary to really fight and
to protect myself." I was walking down the street to my apartment,
thinking, "There's a nice health food store in my neighborhood. I
could work there. I'd be around healthy food and books about health,
that wouldn't be so bad." I got home and was having lunch with Sam
when the phone rang. It was JoAnne, saying, "I have this play I'd like
you to read. I don't know if it's any good or not, but I'm really drawn to
it, I think you'd be great in it, why don't you read it and let me know
what you think?" The play was *Request Concert*, for which I ended up
winning the Drama Desk Award.

It was such a risk to do—a play where the one character doesn't talk.
We thought it might be booed off the stage. And we never had a
preview, so the first public performance was when all the critics came.
I remember standing behind the front door of the set waiting to go on,
and I have never been so nervous in my entire life. My heart was
pounding against my chest and I thought, "This is a ridiculous way to
make a living. I mean, I like adrenaline, but this is a bit much!"

Request Concert is about a solitary woman spending the evening at
home. The author, Franz Xaver Kroetz, was inspired to write the play
by an obituary of a suicide, a woman no one knew anything about. In
his play, the woman comes home from work and goes through her
nightly rituals: she puts the groceries away; she cleans her apartment a
bit; she smokes some cigarettes; she watches TV; she cooks herself a
meal; she goes to the bathroom; she works on needlepoint; and she
listens to the radio—to a program called "Request Concert." The

phone, noticeably, never rings. She hums a few tunes and gets ready for bed, elaborately. She has very tactile relationships with all of her things. Those are the only relationships in her life.

We changed the setting to Queens because JoAnne felt—and I agreed with her—that setting it in Bavaria might make people say, "Oh, that's a German phenomenon, that doesn't happen here." I rode the F train to Brooklyn at the time, and I saw women just like this character every single night. The character was forty-five, the age I am now. I had some youthful fun playing somebody ten years older—fun with the fact that her eyesight was getting bad, which of course mine is now . . . all these jokes at my own expense, as I look back on them now!

Working with JoAnne was extraordinary. We both had children. (Sam was two-and-a-half then, and for years after he referred to that play as the one with the pretend toilet because he was being toilet trained at the time, so that was the most fascinating thing to him.) We rehearsed the play for a little over three weeks for very few hours a day. We worked the entire rehearsal schedule around our children, which was the only time in my life that's been able to happen. I was so relaxed because I didn't have to worry about Sam.

JoAnne and I did not talk, at first, about the psychology of the character. We started by simply doing the text, which is all description of what the woman does.

Not only are characters defined by what they do, they're defined by *how* they do it. There are at least a hundred different ways of drinking liquid, for example. So the field was open, and JoAnne would come in with ideas, and then I would have ideas, and it was just a wonderful working relationship. She suggested that I watch my own ritual as I entered my apartment every night. We looked at that, and we also listened to the radio to pick shows that were the equivalent of "Request Concert." I listened from the point of view of this solitary person.

JoAnne also asked me to think about the mask you wear when you're alone. What happens to your face when there's nobody around to look at you? Do you perform things with other people in your imagination? Is there someone you're performing for—God, a lover, a fantasy person?

When we had the actions of the script down, one day she asked me to do the entire play in slow motion. It is a seventy-minute play, and I think the improv took four hours. That was an extraordinary day, because I learned what this woman's relationship was to each of her things. Out of that came, for example, her attitude towards her clothing, which was very loving. There was one moment when I walked towards my coat to hang it up, and in that slow motion, it felt like reaching up for the arms of a lover, or a mother.

Those things began to happen because there was space for them to enter. Once I discovered that the character had an incredible tactile feeling, that led me to think she was a legal secretary who enjoyed the feel of paper in her hands, which in turn led to special care for her hands and fingernails, and wearing red nail polish.

Another director I adore is Liviu Ciulei, for whom I played Masha in *Three Sisters* at the Guthrie. He's a master, a master!

I loved working at the Guthrie. That was one of the high points of my life. I was there for six months playing Hedda in *Hedda Gabler* and Masha in *Three Sisters*, and I really felt I'd died and gone to heaven.

When I create a character, obviously I do the personalizing work and work with my imagination, but from my Brechtian training I use external things as well. I use people I know, people I see. I do a lot of reading about the time period and the history. And I look at visual aids, too. I use the public library—the picture collection—paintings, photographs.

I also find that in every play I do, I use music. In Tony Kushner's play *A Bright Room Called Day*, for example, which I did last winter at the Public Theater, my character, Gotchling, was very difficult for me to find. I shared very basic things with her, but her heart was filtered through a personality totally different from mine.

Then I began to feel that my voice, in the collection of people who were friends in the play, was like a bassoon. I wasn't asking, "What instrument am I?" I just kept feeling like a bassoon. And at the time, though I didn't make the connection on the surface, I was obsessed with a CD of the English Consort, conducted by Trevor Pinnock, playing Vivaldi's *Concerto for the Bassoon* in E-minor. I played it over and over and over again, and it helped me get inside of Gotchling.

Later it was revealed to me that in fact Tony's beloved mother, who had recently died and who was in Tony's consciousness as he wrote *Bright Room*—and particularly Gotchling—had been a bassoon player.

When I was at the Guthrie, Sam stayed with his father for the rehearsal periods and joined me once the plays opened. I tutored him in the lessons his school gave him, and while I was at the show at night, someone would take care of him.

The two times I was at the Arena in Washington, Sam came with me. I put him into a school, much like the one he was going to in New York, but he didn't like it much.

If Sam had not been the extraordinary being he is, I think my life would have been impossible. This may sound corny, but he's always been such a wise old soul—easygoing, humorous, brilliant, loving and sweet—and he was a joy to raise. All I had to do, really, was give him enough space to grow, keep the boundaries clear, and love him. The rest took care of itself.

I wouldn't advise anyone deliberately to try to be a single mother and an actress. It's grueling. I would never change having Sam for anything—he is one of the great joys of my life. It's just that the conflicts between working and caring for a child are always there, and I tried to keep a balance but, frankly, when push came to shove, I gave to Sam.

Sam is fourteen now, and at this point in my life, it's very important to me to develop my work in two general areas. One concerns my mainstream acting career: I want to move into more visible venues such as film, television and Broadway theatre. I also want to use my talents and energies to address issues in the world that need to be addressed, to try to effect some changes through theatre and film, through personal contact, and through ways I haven't even imagined yet. I don't mean to sound pretentious about that. It's just a deep conviction.

I came back from working in South Africa last summer basically a changed person, plus one who had nineteen dollars in the bank after I paid my September bills. I thought, "Okay, the old way has to go. It is no longer supporting me." To make a long story short, I'm now trying to do voice-overs, and I'm really going to go after a more commercial career. I think I expected that if you were a talented actress, somehow the universe would reward you, and I've finally realized that's not the case. The two things are separate. There is talent and good work and there is also a business sense and a way of projecting and selling yourself so that you become known.

People used to say about me, "She's the best unknown actress in New York City." When I was asked to be Vanessa Redgrave's standby for *Orpheus Descending*, I had said to myself that I would never understudy anyone again. I had done it for Faye Dunaway and in Gregory Mosher's Broadway production of *Our Town*, where I was also in the ensemble and had a very positive experience. But I said, "That's enough." Then, when this opportunity came, respecting Vanessa as I do, I thought it would be wonderful to watch her work. And it was.

People said to me then, "We need somebody who is really a great actress to understudy Vanessa." It was instructive to realize that I was considered to be very, very fine and yet not fine enough to play the leading role.

That's the last time. I've realized that one has to be very savvy.

Going to South Africa last summer was the first time I'd been out of the country in a long time. When you go away from your own culture you reckon with so many things. It shook me down to my roots and made me reexamine my entire life.

The trip that Joe Chaikin, Wendy VandenHeuvel and I took was sponsored by the USIA, largely aided and abetted by a wonderful woman, Martha Coigney, president of the International Theatre Institute. We went at the invitation of Mavis Taylor in Cape Town, who heads the New Africa Theatre Project, and Manny Manim in Johannesburg, who was with the Market Theatre and now is with the University of Witwatersrand.

We basically worked on approaches to developing original material. The students in Cape Town were in their twenties to thirties and from the townships in the area. The New Africa Theatre Project is about training people who haven't had the opportunity to go to university or acting schools, and the idea is that then they bring their knowledge and expertise back to their communities.

They were wonderful, as were the people in Johannesburg, who were individuals from various professional and what they call amateur or community-based organizations or arts alliances. We were the first people from the States to come and do something like this. I had had to write to the African National Congress to get us political clearance, because it had been a closed world for so long there, when they opened the doors they wanted to exercize control over who entered.

South Africa is the cutting edge for the future of humanity. There are people there who know that, white and black. You declare yourself, your deepest beliefs, almost with everything you do. And it's exhausting, constantly confronting and challenging. I found truly extraordinary human beings there, people who have had all of the masks, all of the defenses, all of the extraneous things that people spend their time feeling and thinking and doing, ripped away, and they're right down to the core.

Going to South Africa was perfect timing in my life. It woke me up to assuming my responsibility for the way things are in the world. I had a dream when I was there about coming back to New York and doing a workshop in the city schools dealing with racism, and two days after I got back I was talking to Kathryn Grody, and she said she wanted to do a workshop in Crown Heights. I said, "Great, let's do it." Two days after that, I met a friend who's working with the woman who sets up programs just like that in city schools!

I hope to take my artistic and teaching skills and bring them into a more social and political arena. I'm not a politician, but I want to make a more direct connection to the realities of what's happening. I saw so clearly that the most brilliant aspect of apartheid, from the white supremacist point of view, is that if you keep people separate and they never get to see each other working or living or laughing or eating or making love, they have total ignorance of each other's way of life. It's a perfect breeding ground for fear and hatred.

There is so much fear in the world. We're all afraid of the same things, and we project our fears onto each other. Maybe there's something not specifically about the craft of acting but of working with people simply to communicate with each other that I can do.

I have begun working with an organization called Earth Action, an extraordinary group of people who do volunteer service for the people of this city: the homeless, the elderly, the ill, the disadvantaged. They also work with children and the Native American population, and develop programs to preserve and protect the earth. I'm participating in a program which involves visiting the same elderly persons once a month, bringing donated food to them and spending time with them.

I am also deeply involved now with a project called Voices of Earth, which we've just incorporated. Our ongoing work addresses issues of being women and of taking care of the planet. There are five of us in the core—Olympia Dukakis, Leslie Ayvazian, Remi Barclay Bosseau, Bonnie Kramen and myself. We have a director, two producers, an executive assistant and a lighting designer. Gradually more women will come in—just in the last few days, about ten women have come up to me and said, "I have to be part of this."

We're looking for a writer, and we'll be doing workshops. We want to build and tour a piece that draws on the ancient history of women and the existence of the Goddess and of the feminine archetypal energy. People are realizing that this energy needs to be a part of our world. If we're going to survive on this planet we have to revise certain ways we've behaved—our raping and plundering of each other and of the ground we walk on. That's, in a way, what this project is trying to address.

All this is about realizing that we're *it* now. *We* have to make the world work. It's not about waiting for someone else to do it, or to *ask* us to do it. We're *it*—you and I. This is our world, and we're the ones that have to make it happen.

CLAYTON CORZATTE

Angels Fall
(*A Contemporary Theatre*)

The first New York actor I admired, Clayton Corzatte was outstanding in a stellar ensemble, Ellis Rabb's APA Company. Corzatte's comedic and dramatic talents (recognized by a 1962 Obie for his Constantin in The Seagull *and his Charles Surface in* The School for Scandal*) put paid to the view that British actors played the classics better than Americans. Corzatte has acted more than thirty roles in twenty of Shakespeare's plays—in* Hamlet *he has played Hamlet, Laertes, Osric, Reynaldo and Polonius; in* Romeo *and* Juliet *he has acted Romeo, Paris, Mercutio and Friar Laurence. He left APA for a season to be in the founding company of the Guthrie Theater, and when APA closed he relocated to become one of the first actors to build a career based in Seattle. There Clayton Corzatte and his wife Susan welcomed me to their home for two interviews in August of 1991.*

I'm sure that as a young actor I thought I was going to be a big star. And I'm not. I have had times when I thought "Oh, I could have done that," but I'm aware now that my life has turned out to be about making a life rather than a career. In the seven years I worked as an actor before going to New York, I thought I was preparing myself for Broadway; but when I got to New York, I didn't work for a while, and I had time to think about just what I wanted my life to be.

I realized what I really loved about theatre was exactly what I had had at the Cleveland Play House, which was eight or nine months a year of doing six to eight roles, rehearsing and playing all the time. For a Broadway actor, the best thing that can happen is to get into a big hit and play it for two years. Even then, that wasn't what I wanted. So I've ended up playing in companies all my life.

Looking back at my career, I am *so* aware of the people who have moved my life from one step to the next. One of the first was Marian Gallaway, who taught acting and directed plays at the University of Alabama. She was very tough, but wonderful—totally committed to the theatre, and she asked that of everybody who was in plays for her. Later I was to find that same love and commitment from Eva Le Gallienne, and those two women were like lodestars to me. Le Gallienne, who directed me in *Ghosts* and *The Cherry Orchard* for the APA company, taught me that the theatre is a noble profession if you follow it the way she did.

Marian Gallaway gave me the opportunity to play Hamlet, a chance that every serious young actor ought to have because it's the perfect part—a role that's almost impossible to fail in totally. When I was in college, the Olivier films of *Henry V* and *Hamlet* had come out and we were in love with the way he acted, the way he moved, the way he spoke. So even though I still had something of a southern accent, I spoke Hamlet well, in that kind of fluid, musical way that Olivier spoke Shakespeare, because I had him in my ear, and I had a wonderful image that relaxed me so that I was able to play with a kind of ease and truth a young man whose feelings were tremendously available to me. I had a great time, and came out of college with the feeling I could do anything.

Marian took me to the Barter Theatre—this was in 1951—to audition for Bob Porterfield. He was a New York actor who was in the original production of *The Petrified Forest* with Leslie Howard, and he had come back to his native mountains of Virginia and started the Barter in the depths of the Depression, when there were no jobs for anybody. The theatre got its name because people who couldn't pay cash would come and bring vegetables or a chicken to trade for tickets. Bob was a wonderful, folksy sort of character and also a shrewd businessman. He asked me to come as an apprentice, and arranged for me to work at the Barter Inn to pay for myself.

I played a couple of small parts and then was cast as the lead in *The Hasty Heart* for a five-week tour of schools, colleges and service installations. Midway through the summer I began to be paid for acting.

That next fall and winter, the Barter sent out a tour on which I played Bassanio in *The Merchant of Venice* and Carlton Fitzgerald in *Light Up the Sky*. On that tour, the lady who was playing Portia got ill and was replaced by an actress named Susan Willis, who became another of the people who have moved my life forward. Susan and I became very good friends and talked a lot. I kept saying, "I don't want to go to New York until I've spent more time learning how to do this job."

Susan, the ex-wife of Kirk Willis, a resident director at the Cleveland Play House, suggested I go there. At the end of the tour, she took me to Cleveland and did the audition with me, predicting that they would offer me a journeyman-level job where you were not a full member of the company. She said, "You have already worked professionally for almost a year. Tell them you want to be on the acting staff."

That's exactly what happened. I was hired at the entry-level salary. I think I made thirty-seven dollars and fifty cents a week.

During my first Cleveland season I played half-a-dozen roles. I had a huge success playing Ensign Pulver in *Mister Roberts*—I mean, whoever didn't have a success with Pulver? It's a wonderful part—and I was spotted by a marvelous German director named Benno Frank, who cast me as Haemon in Anouilh's *Antigone*.

Benno taught me to pause—for him, everything had to do with texture and relishing the moment. I met my wife Susan when she came to the Play House as an apprentice my fourth season there, and she said that when she first saw me, sometimes you could drive a Mack truck through the pauses. But I did learn, and later when I was in *Ghosts* with Le Gallienne, she took one of the longest pauses I have ever seen on the stage. Pastor Manders was going on and on about how he had saved her and them, and she walked to the window, turned back, looked at him, and stood there for an eon. The audience didn't breathe before she finally started to tell him what her life was really like.

Eben in *Desire Under the Elms* was another important role I played for Benno. People didn't think of me as an earthy person—I was the poetic or the puckish juvenile in those days. But I came out of a small town in the South, I knew what earthiness was, and I got to use that onstage.

In those days, Cleveland took shows to Chatauqua, and the first summer I did that. The second summer I had read about Group 20 in Massachusetts, a company that did classical repertory—through Fritz Weaver, with whom I'd acted at Barter, I was hired sight unseen to come play small parts. I was there three summers, and I played all the Shakespeare juveniles. I was also Brother Martin to Nancy Wickwire's St. Joan, and the Messenger to her Electra in Euripides' tragedy.

We played outdoors at Wellesley College in an amphitheatre that must have seated twelve to fifteen hundred. I had never done Greek tragedy, and I felt the Messenger called for every bit of energy, commitment and emotional bite that I could put in. Most parts only have certain moments where you let go of the whole thing—a messenger in a Greek tragedy does the most emotional speech in the play. I felt a kind of completion—as if I was totally plugged into the circuit of the play.

In those early days, just about all I had going for me as an actor was charm, sex appeal and an enormous amount of energy. I would just sock it to 'em to try to wake 'em up and make 'em come to me. I think that what I was getting from the big classical pieces, and especially from doing them outside, was a kind of economy. Outdoors it's not just a matter of playing big. It's a matter of playing with absolute clarity.

The first thing you need to learn to do with classical roles is to focus them: to stand still in the middle of them and let them play themselves through you. When you're out in a huge space, you can only be as big as you are—I'm 5'8"—but you can be so clear that the audience will want to focus on your small figure down there on the stage. If they can hear with perfect clarity what you say, and therefore understand what you're thinking, you will be able to rivet them.

I think that kind of discipline has got to be under whatever you do on the stage. Later, when I worked with Helen Hayes in *The Show-Off*, she said, "So many young actors now think that relaxing onstage means just letting yourself go. I was taught that your back ought to be a steel spring. You should look relaxed—and there is a part of you that is completely fluid and relaxed—but there is also a part that is a steel spring." And she said, "You've got those kind of legs, Clay. I love to watch you walk around on the stage because your legs are like steel springs."

I don't think I had much sense in those days of how the classical roles and the variety of modern juveniles I was doing at the Cleveland Play House were combining to make me grow as an actor. One reason I believe so totally in the value of companies where actors can be cast both to and against type is that you never know how that's going to pay off. All those years of doing juveniles was going to pay off totally when Rosemary Harris and I played Alice and Tony in Ellis Rabb's APA production of *You Can't Take It with You*.

Rosie and I were both pushing forty, but I think we were like a textbook American ingenue and juvenile because by then we knew everything there was to know about playing those parts. We were totally unafraid to be so young, and I think what killed everybody was that it was very sexy. That was because those parts are all about sublimation. You get a boy and a girl in a living room, when everybody else has gone to bed, and they want each other so badly they can hardly stand it—and they can talk about anything but that. Rosie and I knew how to play the volcano underneath. We could play all the funny, subtle, charming, lovely, touching changes on it.

What fired us was that we had played all those Shakespearean juveniles and ingenues. The same desire's driving them, and it drives them right into poetry. I see young people trying to do Alice and Tony now and I think, "You're being too cool, you're being too sophisticated." Any attempt those characters make towards sophistication is belied by the actual gaucheness underneath. You have to reach a certain age before you're willing to be that gauche and that naked.

Years later, when Ellis did the production again, Walter Kerr's review said, "It doesn't have the magic." He spent two paragraphs describing Rosemary and me playing that scene.

I've been very lucky that way. The first Off-Broadway play I did was an adaptation of *A Portrait of the Artist as a Young Man*. When a different adaptation was done, Edith Oliver said, "This is very good, but it doesn't have the kind of magic that was in the production where Clayton Corzatte played Cranley." It's good to know that people remember.

I met Ellis Rabb through William Ball, God rest his soul. Bill Ball had an absolutely incredible influence on the way my early career moved from Cleveland. We worked together as actors at Group 20, and in the spring of 1957—around the time that Susan and I were married—he called me in Cleveland and asked, "Would you be interested in coming to the Antioch Shakespeare Festival this summer? Because I'm going to direct *Twelfth Night* and I would love you to play Feste for me." I said of course I would be interested, and then Bill said, "The artistic director is Ellis Rabb, whom you haven't met. He's here in the apartment." This gorgeous, mellifluous voice came on the line, and after Ellis and I talked for a minute he offered me Oberon in *Dream*. My Titania was Chase Crosley, opposite whom I had played all those juveniles at Group 20. Ellis encouraged us to play like the Lunts of the fairy world.

The germs of my future were all there at Antioch that summer: Bill Ball, Ellis Rabb and Allen Fletcher, who directed *Henry VIII*, in which I had a small role. In the summer of 1959, Susan and I had been promised jobs playing very nice parts in a summer theatre, but that fell through. Bill and Allen were at the Old Globe in San Diego, and I called Bill and said, "I'm suddenly without a job and I really need one. Is there anything I could do out there?" He talked to Allen and told me, "I don't know where, but we can certainly use you. Will you come out just 'as-cast'?" I went to San Diego, and sent a telegram back to Susan in New York saying I've found an apartment, come as soon as you can, and I signed it "Mercutio." That's the plum I got out of going "as-cast."

After a season at the Arena Stage in Washington, Susan and I had finally settled in New York. For years we had an apartment on Elizabeth Street, below Houston, for sixty-nine dollars a month. They don't exist anymore. How the hell can young people manage to live the

kind of life we did? We could go on for years, doing what we loved to
do. We didn't have to say, "I gotta make money, I'm goin' out to
Hollywood." I guess there were periods in which we felt like we were
poor, when an evening out was to take the subway down to the Battery,
take the Staten Island ferry across and back, and take the subway
home, which cost about thirty cents. But we never felt impoverished.

Susan, at that point, was supporting us, really. The first two winters
that we spent in New York, I drew unemployment insurance as long as
I could and had a few acting jobs, while Susan worked through
temporary agencies as a typist. Then spring would come and I would
get a theatre job—sometimes both of us would. Throughout our
marriage, Susan has always wanted to go where I was. She made that
decision early on—she was never ruthless about her career. When our
son Christopher was born six years after we were married, and our
daughter Kate came four years later, Susan took time out of her acting
career to be home with them. She has always made a nest wherever
we've been, and we have not spent a lot of time apart.

While we were living in New York, I got my next big break through
Bill Ball. He was going to direct *The Tempest* at the American
Shakespeare Festival in Stratford, Connecticut, and he wanted me to
do Ariel. They wanted a star, but Bill talked them into hiring me by
telling them that I would make a perfect twin for Katherine Hepburn
in *Twelfth Night*. I was called to the Variety Arts on 45th Street to
meet Kate. She and Bill were there with Jack Landau, who was
directing *Twelfth Night.* I had been in several shows directed by Jack
at Group 20.

I was introduced to Kate, who shook hands, asked me a couple of
questions about what I'd been doing, and said "Well, they say we look
like each other. Let's see." So she took my hand and we walked over
and stood side by side facing one of the mirrors they had along the
walls. Finally she said, "I don't know that *we* look exactly alike, but boy
you sure are the spitting image of my little brother." Later I met her
brother Richard and we really did look like each other. And she and I
looked incredibly alike onstage, especially when they got us wigs and
sent us to a terribly expensive barber shop to sit in chairs beside each
other while the wigs were cut until they were exactly alike.

Sebastian isn't really much of a part, but I got wonderful reviews in it, and two of the reasons were the lessons I had learned from Benno Frank about pausing, and Kate's generosity. About the second week in rehearsal, when we got to the last scene—where Sebastian finally comes face to face with his sister—I asked Kate, "Is it okay if I kiss you here?" She said "Clay, this is your moment. You do whatever you want with it." And I did. I took a lot of time. I hugged her and kissed her, and then I turned around, looked at Olivia and thought, "Oh, this explains the whole thing!" Then I said, "So comes it, lady. You have been mistook," and the house came down.

That was a great summer for me—I was also playing Ariel, remember, to Morris Carnovsky's Prospero. I studied how to play Shakespeare as best I could, but it was only years later that I got some really fine books about Shakespearean verse, the shape and the images of it. Caroline Spurgeon's *Shakespeare's Imagery* is just wonderful. Also there are books that I have read about the shape and meter of the verse, learning how very much variety Shakespeare was able to get in the basic iambic pentameter line. If you know what the changes are and find them, they help you to release the music in the lines, and to be free with them.

I have never really liked productions that refuse to pay attention to the verse. They can't help but suffer. Shakespeare has done his work so beautifully that he makes the audience pay attention to what's being said. He's got wonderful characters and events that will carry you a certain distance, but to succeed totally you need a sense of how much mileage ought to be gotten out of what is said.

The difficulty American actors have in dealing with a role like Lear, for example, is that most have been trained to explore the visceral things that happen to a human being, and audiences are interested for a certain length of time in the visceral things that happen to Lear, but finally people are interested in what has happened in his *soul*. No amount of purely visceral, emotional power can take you to those places. You can get there only if you're willing to take that soul-journey. And the words and the images are finally what take you into those soul-places. I don't think you can take that journey unless you travel with the verse.

In the summer of 1961, I had the opportunity of working with Morris Carnovsky again, playing Gratiano when he did Shylock for

Allen Fletcher in San Diego. People often say to me something like, "Oh God, I saw you in such-and-such a play, and it was such an influence on my young life as an actor." People who saw Morris in his great roles feel that way, and I hear it especially about the APA company. Robert Farley was an assistant stage manager the last year at APA, and I worked a great deal for him when he ran the Alaska Rep and then the Alliance Theatre Company in Atlanta. All those years after, Farley said that APA was what theatre was all about to him. Well it was for me, too. Still is.

APA, which stood for the Association of Producing Artists, began when Ellis Rabb got together a bunch of us in the winter of 1960. Tyrone Guthrie had written in one of his books that people should stop griping that there's no theatre or not the kind of theatre they want, and go out and start their own. Ellis said, "So, we're going to start something." The idea was that we would work on projects in small groups and meet every month or so as a company and present what we'd worked on or discuss projects we had in mind.

The work was to be generated by the artists—actors, directors, designers. When we had a project that we wanted to see come to fruition, we would take it to somebody with money and say, "We want to do this. If you want to invest, you will make a profit, but the ideas are ours. And we won't have any tinkering with them." The power belonged to the artist, not to the people with money.

I was one of over a hundred people who were involved in this, and I was unable to be in APA's first couple of engagements because I worked at Stratford one summer, then played Puck to Bert Lahr's Bottom in a tour of *A Midsummer Night's Dream*, and then went to San Diego. During that summer in San Diego, Ellis wrote and said, "Don't take anything for the fall. I think we're going to go to the Fred Miller Theatre in Milwaukee to do a season, and I want you to be part of it."

I went to Milwaukee to play Constantin in *The Seagull* and Charles Surface in *School for Scandal*, and those productions had such an effect on my life! People talk so much about how theatrical Ellis's productions were, and they were . . . but I think what made Ellis so wonderful as a director is that underlying the theatricality were these marvelous human characters and situations that he encouraged his actors to explore.

If you think about Ellis Rabb productions that audiences just adored, they were things like *School for Scandal*. Ellis had the style but he made it be about the people. It was about Lady Teazle and Sir Peter. And about how wonderful Rosemary Harris and Will Geer or Sydney Walker were in those parts. And about me as Charles and Ellis as Joseph. I remember that from the very beginning, when I did that *Midsummer Night's Dream* with Ellis at Antioch, the mechanicals were the most wonderful I have ever seen, not because they were full of shtick but because they were six guys who wanted to do "Pyramus and Thisby" so badly and didn't know anything about putting on a play. They were so funny and touching.

To me the great quality that Ellis had is that humanity. The way he worked with actors to make them feel totally comfortable on the stage and in exploring their parts and each other is the reason that the APA was such a wonderful ensemble. We all loved being on the stage with each other.

Ellis brought in other fine directors who were important in my development as an actor. Mary Duff, who was Rosemary's acting coach at the Royal Academy in England, directed *The Seagull*, in which Rosie played Arkadina. I had never worked with anybody like Mary— none of us had—and it was terrifying. I remember Ellen Geer, who was playing Nina, was scared to death. We spent about an hour and a half on the first couple pages of the script between Sorin and Constantin, and Mary just kept stopping and picking, picking, picking at us about little things. Ellie came flying onto the stage when her entrance finally came, got out one line, and Mary said, "Just a minute." Ellie burst into tears. By then everybody was terrified.

I'm very nice on the surface, but way down I'm incredibly stubborn. I fought Mary Duff tooth and nail in small, difficult ways that finally erupted in about the second week of rehearsal, when I said something about the transition from this moment to that moment and she said, "Never mind that moment. Just give me what I want in *this* moment."

I said, "But there is some way in which I get to that from the moment which comes just before." And she said, "Never mind that. That's one moment, this is another." And I said, "Don't be ridiculous. If that moment comes then and this moment comes now, there is some kind of transition. What the hell is it?" And she walked to the back of the hall and refused to speak for an hour. I went home to Susan and said, "I got her today. If she continues to bug me I'm going to destroy this woman."

The next day we went in, and I had an hour and a half of the most brilliant rehearsal I have ever had with anyone. I can't remember any of the details, just that it was about the moments I was trying to find and Mary's helping me find them. That rehearsal brought her around to me and me around to her, and I went home and said to Susan, "I don't care what kind of pain we have to go through, this is worth it."

Mary Duff asked things of me as an actor that nobody had ever asked before. For instance, one day when I was doing something I had always done, which was to come onstage with all this energy, Mary said, "Clayton darling, you came on and were trying to tell me Constantin's whole story in the first moment. Could you just go off and come onstage and do one thing? Pick one thing and do that very simply."

Those rehearsals were my coming of age as an actor. I began to be a really serious actor, one who looked as deeply as possible into the potentialities of a role and a play and tried to define every moment that I was on the stage. Mary said, "You should be so totally involved in the moment, so in control of it, that if you want to raise a finger, you can do so and it will mean something." Well, I had never been an actor who had nearly that kind of control. I was much too hyper. Mary made me realize that acting has much more to do with focus and with understanding what you're doing. APA's vocal coach Edith Skinner was a great help in this regard—and, of course, Ellis. One of the most beautiful pieces of direction Ellis ever gave me, and he gave me this more than once, was, "Clay, I see what you're going through as the character. I don't want to see that yet." It wasn't the moment for the audience to see that. I needed to learn just to experience what I was experiencing, to wait until the proper moment to show something.

Yolanda Bavan and Clayton Corzatte in Caesar and Cleopatra *(Cleveland Play House)*

Working for Stephen Porter as Gregers in *The Wild Duck* was a wonderful experience, too. One of the things he said to me about Gregers was, "Clay, I need more stillness out of you than I've ever seen from you on the stage. Ibsen has built a huge five-act structure that has got to sit on Gregers' shoulders." Stephen helped me to focus the first scene so that audiences started out on Gregers' side, which gave them an enormous amount to deal with in the course of the play as things turned around.

APA became the resident professional company at the University of Michigan at Ann Arbor in 1962, and we started bringing the plays into New York for Off-Broadway runs. I won an Obie that year for Charles Surface and Constantin. When we did *School for Scandal* at the Lyceum on Broadway and I was nominated for a Tony, I had been playing Charles Surface on and off for five years! We had made a connection with the Phoenix Theatre and became the APA Phoenix Repertory Company. For a couple of years we thought we were going to get a large Ford Foundation grant, which would make us solvent financially. We were in Ann Arbor, doing a season whose huge success was *You Can't Take It with You*, when we found out we were not going to get the grant.

All of a sudden it seemed like we couldn't go on. T. Edward Hambleton got the idea of renting the Lyceum Theatre on Broadway to present a six-week run of *You Can't Take It with You* over the Christmas holidays. The show was an instant smash, ran the rest of the season, and turned around the history of the company. We became regular tenants at the Lyceum during the winter. We were also playing a season at the Huntington Hartford in L.A., a season in Ann Arbor, and a short season at the Royal Alexandra in Toronto. We began to bring back things that had been in the repertory, like *School for Scandal* and Stephen Porter's production of Pirandello's *Right You Are*, which had always been one of APA's successes. We did four shows a season for several years.

Unfortunately our original idea of being a company with a repertory of wonderful plays changed. The last couple of years we were putting together four new productions on Broadway, and were in a position where a couple of them had to be successful. The Broadway frame of mind—"We've got to present a big hit"—changed the focus of the work.

Maybe this is a human thing that happens to all theatre companies, but when we were working up at the 74th Street Theatre in New York, the designers and the people who built the costumes and the sets did the most incredible things for very little money. They were so imaginative and managed with so little. After we moved to the Lyceum, everything got more expensive. I do know the unions made it cost a lot more, but I also know we spent a lot of money where we could have spent a little, and where previously we would have.

I thought that was unfortunate and that if we had been an English company, for instance, standing for what we did and getting the kind of response that we did from critics and people in the business, we wouldn't have changed. If we had just stayed true to what we were and said, "We're not a theatre with a lot of money but we've got a whole lot of enthusiasm, imagination and expertise at being true to a script and to the company idea," maybe we wouldn't have gone out. I think we went under largely for financial reasons, and partly maybe because Ellis burned out. Ellis found it very difficult to give final responsibilities to other people, so a tremendous amount of weight was placed on him. He felt really responsible to the people in his company, a quality I admired hugely. When APA members became parents, for example, Ellis tried to make sure they got a salary increase. He was very concerned on a human level.

I had taken off one season from APA to be in the founding company of the Guthrie Theater. I auditioned for Tyrone Guthrie, who was so charming and put me at my ease. Auditioning or being interviewed over the years, I've found the people who are difficult and make you feel bad and tense are the ones who are not so comfortable about themselves, not the ones with huge reputations.

That opening season at the Guthrie was a terrific experience. Guthrie was directing *Hamlet*, in which I was playing Osric and Reynaldo, and I can remember coming home to Susan and saying, "He is the most brilliant director of crowd scenes I've ever known." Guthrie had a wonderful ability to put everybody at their ease so that they felt very alive about being there, and about being an individual in the crowd. He would make big moves with a group of people, have two or three people move from here to there, have little surreptitious moves where one person would take a couple of steps over and say something in another's ear—a wealth of details that were put into the crowd moments so that there was a mounting tension in the rehearsal room about what was happening.

I couldn't imagine what Guthrie was going to do with *Three Sisters*, but it turned out that he was brilliant with Chekhov, too, because his wonderful talent was seeing little bits of human behavior that tell what the whole person is like. I was playing Kulygin, Masha's schoolmaster husband, and one of the happiest moments of my life was the dress rehearsal. There was a moment in the third act in which I hid in a huge wardrobe full of clothes. I was supposed to come out sort of embarrassed, knowing that my being in the wardrobe looked very strange. In the dress rehearsal I was inside the wardrobe when I suddenly thought, "What if I come out, not even thinking, say my line, and then realize that what I have just done is really embarrassing?" I did that, and Guthrie fell on the floor laughing.

I was so proud of that. He was the perfect father figure. He could say devastatingly funny things if you were doing something silly or awkward, and you'd laugh and were never embarrassed.

I didn't have the happiest experience as Osric. When Guthrie had done a play often, he could be bored with a scene and just not interested in rehearsing it. The Osric scene with Hamlet was one of those. He gave me an idea about the way Osric should sound the very first time we went through it, and that was all the direction I or George Grizzard as Hamlet ever got in the scene.

It was a modern-dress production, and all of Osric's flourishes with a Panama hat came across as terribly effeminate. Audiences didn't find it funny; they found it off-putting. That made me self-conscious, and the scene was never as much fun as it should be. I was in a great many scenes that Osric is not ordinarily in—I was the secret service, always near the king watching—so I had been seen often before I came to play the scene with Hamlet, and in a context that was not humorous. I was not very successful in the part.

Playing Hume Cronyn's son in *The Miser*, I had a wonderful speech in which I got carried away talking about the girl that Harpagon has picked out for himself to marry, but whom I'm in love with. Tanya Moiseivitch had designed this incredible costume for me covered with ribbons. I found out in playing that when I got really excited every part of me shook, so the speech built to a point where I was ribbons flying all over the place. Hume originally followed it by giving me the finger, in order to top me. But when he saw that the speech was getting a hand, he cut the gesture because he didn't want to stop the applause. That was really generous.

The Guthrie offered me a second season, but of small supporting roles, and I wrote them rather a rude letter. Guthrie asked me why, and I said "I was very angry. You have three wonderful parts in the season coming up—Henry V, Mosca in *Volpone*, and the Dauphin in *Saint Joan*—any one of which I could play, and I think my work in the first season has earned a shot at one of those parts." They had all been offered to George Grizzard, and I told Guthrie, "George and I played together with the APA Off Broadway. He played two large parts and I played two large parts. I'm the one who won the goddam Obie. I'm furious that you would offer George all three of these plums and me nothing. If George wants to have two of them and I get one, that's great." I wasn't angry at George, I was angry at *them*. I've always had great admiration for the way George handled his career, because he was one of the first Broadway actors to take on many challenges in regional theatre. But I wasn't willing to let the Guthrie make George a star and me a journeyman actor. Guthrie said nothing, so I went back to APA.

About the last four years of APA, we lived in Oakland, New Jersey, where I was a commuting husband and Susan was a suburban house-wife. Neither of us was very happy with that, so when APA folded we cast about for a place where we could do the whole thing. We could be parents, we could be citizens of the town, and we could both work in the theatre. I wrote to Allen Fletcher, who had become the artistic director of the Seattle Repertory Theatre. There were two considera-tions: we wanted to move west, and I wanted to get into directing. I had directed a successful production of *A View from the Bridge* at a civic theatre in Ann Arbor, and had really liked doing it. The deal I made with Allen was that I would be happy to be in the company if I could also direct. That was okay with him. I directed *Summertree* the very first season I was here.

Seattle's growth as a theatre center has been absolutely incredible. When we came in the fall of 1969, there was the Seattle Rep in the winter and A Contemporary Theatre in the summertime. Supposedly the Rep was the classical theatre and ACT did contemporary plays, though that has changed somewhat over the years. The only other professional work in town was a dinner theatre where I never worked and which doesn't exist now.

The year after I got here, Burke Walker and some graduates of Duncan Ross's professional acting program at the University of Wash-ington started the Empty Space Theatre in a basement in the Pike

Place Market. Then came the Intiman Theatre, the Bathhouse Theatre and the Seattle Group Theatre. Seattle pretty quickly became a
place where actors could work—or work out of—year-round.

We bought this house on Queen Anne Hill, one of the seven hills on
which Seattle is built, eighteen years ago. We overlook Elliot Bay,
Puget Sound and the Olympic Mountains. Just about anywhere you
turn there's a view of water or mountains. The Seattle Center, which
was built for the World's Fair in 1962 and now contains the Seattle
Rep, the Seattle Opera, Intiman, Seattle Children's Theatre, Pacific
Northwest Ballet and Seattle Group Theatre is at the foot of Queen
Anne Hill.

This is a wonderful place to bring up kids, which is one of the
reasons we came, but just in general I find the western lifestyle more
salubrious. It's a slower pace. I need a lot of quiet; I need a lot of
stillness to be healthy and to do my work well. We decided to come
here while I was on the APA tour of *The Show-Off*, and when I told
Helen Hayes, her response was, "I think that's wonderful, Clay. I don't
think you are the kind of driving person who is going to have fun
staying in New York theatre. There are too many tensions involved,
too much demand to be successful every time you go out. In order to
grow, it's very important to be able to fall on your face, and it's hard to
take chances when you feel that someone's investment depends on
your success."

When I look around me now, I think, "This is where I was born to
live." These mountains and sea and greenery feed me. I couldn't be
who I am as an actor, a director or a human being without them. I
think I went through a transitional period for a few years after I came
here in which I did some work that was not totally successful because I
was changing as an actor. There were all sorts of things going on inside
of me that meant I didn't have the polish and authority that I had
when I arrived from New York. I needed to go in and tinker with what
was going on inside. I think the work that I do now is much richer.

One of my first roles here was Bri, the father of the brain-damaged
child in *Joe Egg*. People adored that performance, but Elliot Norton
came out to review the production and he got at something I was
concerned about. He made a complimentary reference to my perfor-

mance having a kind of brittleness on the surface, when you knew that underneath there were horrible things raging. I wanted to get past the brittleness. When I first came here, for instance, I couldn't have played Dr. Rank in *A Doll House* as successfully as I did in Liz Huddle's 1986 production at Intiman, because I wasn't relaxed enough. I wouldn't have bared enough of his pain, and I wouldn't have been simple enough.

We fell in love with Seattle when we came here, but as they say life is just one damn thing after another, and wouldn't you know, Allen Fletcher left Seattle Rep after one year. Duncan Ross (whom everyone called Bill) took over as artistic director, and he told me, "I don't want a company because I don't want the audience always seeing the same faces. So I'm not going to be able to use you all the time, but if you are interested in staying here I can offer you a job teaching and directing a lot of shows in the professional acting program at the university. You can direct at the Rep once a year, and you can act for me there once or twice a year." At that point, especially because I wanted to go on with directing, that seemed like a terrific offer, and actually it led to my working in regional theatres from Arizona to Alaska.

Twice I've had opportunities to play roles another actor had been cast in but couldn't do for some reason. Once Dan Sullivan called me to take over Edgar in Strindberg's *Dance of Death* during the run. Fortunately Eve Roberts, who's an old, old friend from the Cleveland Play House and New York, was playing Alice. We didn't have much of a chance to rehearse, so we found our way in front of the audience. We found that these two people stay together because they relish the way they go at each other. They wouldn't give that up for anything; they'd be bored out of their minds without it. Dan Sullivan said, "You did a wonderful job, but I still would not think of you as somebody to cast as Edgar." And I think people who know me would say, "This guy's not mean enough, not heavy enough, to play Edgar." I found something in myself and in my relationship with Eve that could make it work.

The second time was at the Intiman, when Liz Huddle had cast *The Rivals* and asked me to play a rather nice part, but I wanted like crazy to play Sir Anthony. She was very generous about it, saying "Gosh, that really is a shortcoming in me. I just thought a small man wouldn't be right in it." It turned out that the actor already cast couldn't get free from another job in time, so I got to do Sir Anthony after all.

I think that not only was my Sir Anthony a great success, but that I have a great feeling for playing eighteenth-century comedy. I had all those years at APA with Charles Surface. I feel like directors don't always think enough about what effect an actor is going to have on the company. Sometimes I believe that one of my greatest values as an actor is the effect I have on the people around me, especially in Shakespeare, eighteenth-century comedy and Shaw. It's very verbal material that actors need to be able to speak as fast as they can think it.

Actors often say to me, "Gosh, our scenes are my favorites in the show." I think that's because I bring a kind of comfort and authority to my playing of the classics and to my relating to others onstage, so they think, "Ohhhhh, this is how it goes." That may not even be on a conscious level; they may just know they're having the most fun in our scenes.

When I was in New York, I sometimes worked with young actors who had been sort of Methodized. It could be very difficult because they weren't in touch with you, they were in touch with their innards. Bill Ross, who gave me my start as a teacher, said, "If you are dealing with an emotional memory, you are dealing with the past. You are looking inside yourself, you are not relating with the other actors." The other thing about that training was that Lee Strasberg seemed to think it didn't make any difference what your body or your voice was like. You saw a lot of people trying to play a Shakespeare or a Shaw scene as if they were in their homes, behaving and speaking in the same kind of naturalistic rhythms, and it won't work. You can't make the world of the play serve you, you have to serve the world of the play. In Shakespeare and Shaw, the language makes certain demands, and you have to have the verbal facility to express yourself through those words. You have to go beyond the cerebral meaning of what you say to where the emotional drive comes from.

Take, for example, playing Jack Tanner in *Man and Superman*— you can't play Jack Tanner without nitroglycerine inside you. I went back to the Cleveland Play House in the seventies to play Caesar in *Caesar and Cleopatra* one year and Jack Tanner the next. Under Jack is this ferocious sexual drive that makes Ann Whitefield an incredible danger. He is so attracted to her, and has been ever since he reached puberty, that all he has wanted was to say, "Do whatever you want with me." In order to be his own human being, he had to separate himself from her, and he did that by pouring all his energy into being an iconoclast, a revolutionary.

He tries to make the world be honest in the way that he thinks it should be. Every time he runs into Ann, she is playing games with him and he thinks she is the most dishonest, hypocritical woman he knows, but he is fascinated by her and doesn't know why. It's a wonderful foil part. You are so smart, but there is one thing that you are just dumb about. That's why he's so charming. He's wonderful to play if you're willing to be dumb about that one thing. The audience adores it. Ann needs to be a lady, and a very sexy lady. Lizbeth Mackay in our production was just wonderful. I was hurling this explosive energy at her and she could look right at me and be laid back, knowing she was going to get me.

I started directing because as an actor I've always wanted to know how my cog fit into the machinery of the whole play and how my cog needed to operate to make the machinery work the best. I think my strong point as a director is working with the actor. I believe I do have the ability to study a play and know where it lives, and to help the actors know that life and bring it onstage.

I don't think I'm a terribly original director, or that I come up with brilliant ideas for a production—but that's not what I'm interested in. I keep telling people about Ellis on the first day of rehearsal for *You Can't Take It with You*. He said, "This set is very like the set for the original Broadway production, which was directed by one of the authors. I feel he must have known what he was doing, so we're going to start out by using the stage directions in the text." Now when we finally opened, the reviews said that our production was so different from the original one that it had its own world and tone and taste. Nobody set out to be different or original. We set out to do the play the best we could, and because of who we were and the way we worked, we arrived at something unique. That's where uniqueness ought to come from.

. . .

I directed and taught in the professional acting program at the University of Washington for four years, and then left because they were getting a little jealous of my time spent away as a professional actor and director. And as I said, "I'm a professional actor and director first, and a teacher when I can be because I love to teach." I really enjoy young people, and I'm now teaching at Cornish College of the Arts because they want teachers to be active professionals and are very flexible about teaching schedules and about faculty members working out of town.

I have seen such changes in American actors. They speak so much better, they have so much more verbal fluidity and bite than those Methodized guys had when I was working in New York. I think that professional training programs center actors. When I was at the University of Washington, I could walk down the hall in the building where we taught and tell which students were third year, because they were centered. Their whole physical demeanor was different. They were relaxed and in control of themselves. They tended to be much freer and much straighter but also much stiller.

I teach the final year of acting class at Cornish, and Susan teaches how to audition and look for work. People have said that Susan and I were the first professional actors who sometimes went away and worked in other places but who made a life in the theatre in Seattle.

In the last three or four years there has been a massive influx of actors from New York and L.A. That means it's a little trickier here now; there are a lot of jobs, but not as many jobs as there are actors.

A group of Equity actors got together and formed an organization called REACT, which brings casting directors and artistic directors from around the country here to audition the talent pool. We pay, say, five or ten dollars each to defray the expenses of bringing those people in and putting them up while they're here. And then we all go in and audition for them. Susan and I auditioned for Michael Kahn, whom I had not seen for years, and as a result we have worked at the Folger twice. We played *Other People's Money* at the Arizona Theatre Company in 1991 because David Ira Goldstein, then associate artistic director of ACT, wanted us in his production there, and it was okay

with Gary Gisselman, the artistic director in Arizona, because he had
seen us in REACT auditions here.

We've had many opportunities to work together—one of the most fun
was as Ernest and Delia in *Bedroom Farce* at the Rep—and now that
our children Christopher and Felicity Kate are grown we can go out of
town. In the past few years we've done *Painting Churches, Pack of Lies*
and *The Cocktail Hour* at the Portland Rep, and I directed Susan there
in *Driving Miss Daisy*. Susan has worked at all the major theatres in
town. We've also had an opportunity to get involved with civic
activities such as role-playing patients for doctors, nurses and office
people in the mental health field.

Soon I'll be doing *You Can't Take It with You* again, this time playing
Grandpa at the Seattle Group Theatre, with color-blind casting. That's
very important work to me. If there is theatre devoted to multiethnic
casting, then audiences will begin to just accept that the way they do at
the opera. Opera audiences don't think about whether the soprano is
black and her sister is white, and that's the way it should be.

   I think the theatre is always in a period of crisis, and I think that
crises are salutary for any art form. I know that there are great money
difficulties and that we are in an ideologically dangerous time. What's
really behind all this stuff about obscenity is that people with power
are scared of iconoclastic views, and the way that they can get at them
without admitting they're scared is to call them dirty, or dangerous, or
subversive.

   Well, of course theatre is subversive, it always has been, that's one of
its functions. Athol Fugard is this incredible man because of the
critical time and place in which he has lived. He has written out of that
dangerous place, and what he writes is pure gold because of it. The
health of the theatre comes from having to fight adversity. If there is
danger in the air, then we are going to pull ourselves together and fight
that danger. And our strengths will come out because of it.

The reason to be in the theatre is that it is the most wonderful mirror
for life in the world. Bill Ross told about being in a meeting at the

university which got kind of acrimonious because it was about budget cuts. Some history professor got up and asked, "Why are we spending all this money on theatre? Why is it important that we teach theatre at this university?" And Ross got up and said, "We teach theatre because theatre is man's oldest way of looking at himself and his place in the world. It certainly predates written history." Right on.

JOSIE de GUZMAN

Fuente Ovejuna
(Shakespeare Theatre)

Josie de Guzman is an outstanding example of a "triple threat" performer: an actor, singer and dancer. Her two Tony nomimations were for Maria in the 1980 revival of West Side Story *and for Sarah Brown in the 1992 revival of* Guys and Dolls. *In between, she spent eleven years playing Shakespeare, Lope de Vega, Molière, Marivaux, Ibsen, Chekhov and Lorca in resident theatres. Born in New York but raised in Puerto Rico, she has also starred in San Juan productions of the musicals* Peter Pan *and* Fela *in Spanish. Josie de Guzman invited me to her Broadway theatre dressing room for two interviews in the summer of 1992.*

Getting a Tony nomination was a great way to return to Broadway after twelve years. In *Guys and Dolls*, I have the best cast ever and the most supportive situation, from the crew to the staff. Playing Maria in the 1979 revival of *West Side Story* was also a magical time, but I hadn't been through the years of regional theatre and getting fired from a Broadway show then. All the hard work and all the angst paid off for me in this one show—*Guys and Dolls*.

To be ready for the performances, I like to do a physical workout early in the day and a vocal warm-up here in my dressing room before the show. Then I like to be quiet and center myself as I put on my makeup and wig.

In the warm-up I do exercises that my voice teacher, Joan Lader, gives me. Sometimes I'll work on a particular song, if there are any problem spots. Right now I've noticed I'm slipping back into talking a certain way—Joan has been helping me get my speaking voice out of my throat and more forward.

I was having vocal problems with this show. I had lost my voice because of a lot of interviews, and the pollen count was really high, and I wasn't getting to take the day just to be quiet. I need to do that or I get really tired.

Most mornings I take a floor barre exercise for alignment and strength, and may go to the health club and do some weights and the stairmaster and/or take a class. Today I came into the city to take a floor barre from the woman who invented it, Zena Rommett. She teaches at a dance studio at 74th Street called Steps. I have a tape of Zena's that I can do at home.

I find the floor barre very centering. It's almost like a yoga meditation. It stretches you out and strengthens you.

I usually keep up my dancing and singing lessons when I'm in New York. I used to drive myself crazy taking jazz and ballet classes, but I only go sometimes now. You can't do it all, but I did through *West Side Story*. I was never a dancer-dancer, but a singer-dancer.

My dream as a little girl was to be a dancer. I took Spanish dance and ballet from the age of four until I was twelve, and I was always involved in *zarzuelas*—Spanish operettas—dancing in the chorus. I sang when I was small, but my family discouraged me because they thought I could ruin my voice if I started too early. I knew I had a voice, but not how far I could go with it. In high school I played Guinevere in *Camelot*, and that's when I got hooked by theatre.

My brother had gone to Boston College and helped me get an audition for the Boston Conservatory of Music. I did a monologue from *The Member of the Wedding* and sang "Before I Gaze at You Again" from *Camelot*. I studied voice for four years at the conservatory, and we had classes in many aspects of music and theatre, but what I liked most was getting to perform a lot.

The teaching of acting technique was not outstanding, but we learned through doing and direction. I played the title role in *Gigi*, though I didn't want to—I didn't want to be the cute ingenue. The teacher who cast me said, "You might as well use what you have and enjoy it," so I did, but I wanted to play something more interesting.

My best experience was doing Kathy, the "Tick, Tock" dancer in *Company*—the role that Donna McKechnie played on Broadway. That fulfilled my dream of doing a dance solo, and it was one of the few times I forgot myself completely onstage.

I wanted to come to New York and be on Broadway. I was very lucky in having that happen pretty quickly.

I was afraid in New York. I was born here, but my family moved to San Juan when I was four. When I came back after graduation from the conservatory, I found the city gray and fast-paced and scary.

Shortly after I arrived here, I met Elizabeth Swados and she asked me to audition for her. At the time she didn't think I was right for *Nightclub Cantata*, but when it was invited to the Charles Street Playhouse in Boston and the Arena Stage in Washington, she called me because Shelley Plimpton couldn't go. She asked if I could learn the show in two weeks and I said yes.

I never slept. Liz's music is very particular to her in its rhythms and structure, and I had to learn it from a tape she sent me. I wrote down all the words as I listened. *Nightclub Cantata* was also a type of experimental work I'd never done before—Liz had set some short stories and poetry to music and the show involved ensemble and improvisational work.

In *Nightclub*, there's a song called "Once We've Started Out." It's about two people making a commitment—once we've started out there's no going back, and if you say you're with me, are you really? I remember Liz telling me just to say the words, not to embellish or "act" them. She also warned me not to get stuck in a pattern of singing a set of words, but to be open for phrases to come out differently. I had just graduated from college and I was trying to sell the song. I was stuck because I was saying the words one way, and Liz pointed out that there were other ways.

Then Liz asked me to do *Runaways* at the Public Theater. Working there was a dream come true, because I had auditioned for them when

I came to New York and they didn't even look at me. A year later, Rosemarie Tichler asked Liz, "Who's that girl?" and Liz said, "You turned her away a year ago."

Meeting Joseph Papp and working with him more than once was pretty special. He cared about actors. He was always around asking if things were okay. You don't see that very often.

From Liz I learned respect and awe for the theatre: the magnitude of the ritual onstage; the discipline of having to warm up and be prepared for the work every day. Liz taught me to learn things fast and to be consistent.

When I was in *Runaways,* learning material quickly was an incentive I liked, because the quicker you learned, the more you got to do. She might take material away eventually, but you got to go through the process of performing and working on it for a while. That made me work very hard and helped me later when I *had* to learn things fast.

Lullabye and Goodnight was another speed-learn show. Liz had originally written it for me but Papp wanted someone else, so I went off to do *West Side Story* in Paris. The other actress didn't work out and they called me. I had to learn the show in nine days. There were a lot of words and music in *Lullabye,* and the lyrics weren't easy because they were more like text put to music than songs.

Liz was a very tough critic, and she stripped me of my little tricks, of the glibness of the conservatory graduate. She taught me about the simplicity of the work, about starting from me, Josie, and not superimposing. If I concentrated on telling the story, Liz said, and not on what I was doing while saying the words, the emotional life that would come out of that would be simple and real and true.

Gerald Freedman reiterated *that* point a lot in our work together. (Liz Swados and Jerry Freedman have been *extremely* influential in my work.) If there was a very emotional scene, Jerry would say, "Do not start from the high point. Start from nothing." It's amazing, because if you start from nothing—if you're just simple—*things happen.*

I was seen in *Runaways* at the Public and cast in *Carmelina* on Broadway. I was also asked to audition for Leonard Bernstein's sixtieth-birthday concert at Wolf Trap.

There were eight thousand people in the audience for that concert, and it was televised. Rostropovitch conducted, and they did some of Bernstein's classical and show music. Steve Bogardus and I sang "Tonight," and at the post-performance party Bernstein introduced me as his "new Maria" for the Broadway revival of *West Side Story*. That was a complete surprise, and felt great. I had to audition three times during the next year . . . but it still worked out.

The dance training we had to go through before *West Side Story* was outrageous! I was taking three to four hours of dance every day for about three months—ballet mostly, and jazz. I guess the words "detailed" and "perfection" come to mind—not that I was perfect, but I learned a lot about acting, subtlety, detail and hard work.

I had a wonderful time with Jerome Robbins—I never had a problem. He yelled at me once, during the ballet, and it was my fault. I was terrified, because I was trying to do an arabesque and I thought, "This is the man who choreographed Makarova and Baryshnikov!" I was a nervous wreck, and couldn't balance on one leg. He yelled from the house, "If I didn't think you could do it, I wouldn't have cast you, so stop it!"

We took a break and he came backstage and apologized. He was very nice to me. I felt like I understood what he wanted, and I think Jerry Freedman had something to do with that. He co-directed the book and prepared us for Robbins. With Jerry we explored blocking, we started getting in gear as to what each character wanted. Robbins came in to put in the details, the colors and fine tuning that he wanted—which went on for months.

At that point in my career, I thought I had it made. *Runaways* had moved from the Public to Broadway, so I had done three Broadway shows in three years. I thought, "Okay, I'll just hang out and wait for the next one."

But I also wanted to do regional theatre and straight plays. They came to me first, and I took that path. Also, in the eighties there were a lot of big "belt" musicals, and I'm not a belter. I'm a lyric soprano with a chest voice. But now Joan Lader is teaching me how to belt.

After *West Side*, I didn't want to be categorized as a musical-theatre actress. The opportunity came to work with Liviu Ciulei in *Peer Gynt*, and I went to the Guthrie. Liviu said he knew he wanted to work with me when he saw *Runaways*. In that show we played all different sorts of characters. My one big moment was at the end of the first act when I did "No Lullabyes for Louis," a song about keeping a boy who's a junkie alive through dancing. Liviu told me he knew he wanted to work with me when he saw that.

I was thrilled about playing Solveig. I *wasn't* thrilled about being in Minnesota during the winter—I spent five months there.

It was hard to understand Liviu at first, because he's so European in his directing. He knows exactly what he wants, even physically, even line readings, and he wasn't open to any suggestions. I puzzled for a while, until Liviu showed me a gesture he wanted Solveig to make to Peer early in the play, when they are young. Peer comes to her and she says something like, "I am here," and Liviu wanted me to turn my palms towards Peer. It was a very open, vulnerable feeling towards Peer, that she was there to love him. The feeling of the arms down, my palms facing him, standing with my legs about a foot apart, felt so right for the character at that moment! Once I said to myself about Liviu's approach, "Try, and find out," the challenge was to make what he was giving me my own.

Aging Solveig was so funny. At the time, I was studying Method acting with Marilyn Fried and I was into lots of sensory exercises. When I read that I had to be blind and seventy years old at the end of the play, I asked Marilyn, "What am I going to do?" She said, "Go look at apes. Apes are good for age." So I went to the Bronx Zoo, I went to the Central Park Zoo, and I studied apes. I worked on them, and I also did sensory exercises for blindness. I got to the Guthrie and Liviu said, in his wonderful accent, "No no no no, I don't vant you to eemitate seventy years . . . she ees ageless." I had done all this work and he just wanted me to be myself! So I was myself, only a little slower. I did practice being blind, and it was helpful.

Solveig spins, and I learned how to spin thread. In one rehearsal, I was working on the spinning because I wanted to get it real, and Liviu said, "Thees you eendicate. You do not have to speen thread out of the wool. Een the theatre you eendicate." But I still got that yarn to come out, very nicely if I may add.

Solveig comes in intermittently in the play, and I worked so hard to sustain her! I did all sorts of work offstage, but during the run I realized that I had to find a balance. Gerry Bamman, who's a wonderful actor as well as translator, would be kidding around with me, telling a joke, and then he would walk on as Peer and be brilliant. I thought, "How can he do that? I can't do that! I have to *prepare*."

I would shut myself in a room and do all kinds of sensory work to get ready—what's it like not to see Peer for so many years and to be seventy when he comes again? Gerry taught me that acting is about being relaxed and open onstage and letting things happen. Of course you do the preparation, but most of it is in rehearsal, and you have to trust what you've discovered and have been directed to do in rehearsals in order to let it happen onstage every night.

Peter Gallagher and Josie de Guzman in Guys and Dolls *(Broadway)*

I couldn't let go of all that preparatory work offstage in *Peer Gynt*, but I was able to eventually.

I played Varya in *The Cherry Orchard* at Capital Rep in 1990. Varya is a highly emotional character, but she has very short scenes. I would sit in rehearsal doing needlepoint, get up and do a scene and be highly emotional. No problem. The choreographer came up to me and said, "I can't believe it. You do needlepoint, you get up and do a scene and you're hysterical!"

I'd go home and do my homework—try to figure her out—and then I wouldn't think, I'd just do it. The less you think, the better off you are—onstage. You have to prepare the character, then let the preparation work for you.

My next work was at the Great Lakes Theatre Festival. Jerry Freedman took over *West Side Story* completely when we went to Paris after the Broadway run. He became like family. He's had a profound effect on me as an actor, giving me some of the greatest opportunities to develop.

When Jerry became the artistic director at Great Lakes, I said I'd love to work for him. He had me audition and offered me Marianne in *Tartuffe* and Annette in Marivaux's *Game of Love*. I was so happy to do *Tartuffe*—it was my first classic after *Peer Gynt* and I didn't even have to sing (I had to sing a little as Solveig).

The work with Jerry grew as we went along, especially when we got to Regina in *Ghosts* the next season and to the Bride in *Blood Wedding* the third season. The great breakthrough I had with Jerry, because of the years of trust that had gone before, was in the Lorca. I'll never forget the rehearsal where he said, "In this last scene, I want you to go all the way. That means I don't want you to put up any kind of obstacle. Just go for it." I went through it and he said, "No, you don't understand. I don't want you to edit yourself." I didn't know what that meant. He showed me a little of what he wanted, and I did it, and it was devastating.

It was the scene where the bride comes to her mother-in-law after her bridegroom and the man she really loves, and has tried to run away with, have killed each other. The bride begs her mother-in-law for a place in society. Even if no one speaks to her, she needs to stay in that town. I had been emotional when I did it but I was afraid to grovel. When the breakthrough came, I was groveling and trying to get this woman to accept me—I was kissing her feet, grabbing onto her skirt, dragging myself across the floor and feeling so terrible that these two men had killed themselves over me. I forgot time and space again—it was the same feeling as in the "Tick, Tock" dance. It wasn't Josie anymore. I wasn't looking at myself doing something. I was in the moment and whatever happened, happened. One thing flowed right into the other and there was no thinking going on.

I couldn't speak for a long time after that, and that night I was emotionally drained and shook up. I had learned that if the character was out of control, it didn't necessarily mean that the *actor* had to be. I discovered the power I had, and that when you make a choice and go all the way with it, it's extremely creative and fulfilling. The choice may be wrong, but rehearsals are for actors to explore and go all the way.

Jerry is wonderful for actors. The first time you sit around and read a play with him, it's very slow and he asks you questions. You may not know the answers, but the questions make you stop and think why the character is doing this and that. He'll say things like, "What were you doing before you came in? Why were you doing that? Why did you say this to him?" He also speaks of the spine of a character, something that belongs to the character in every scene. That's a tough one. I haven't been able to figure it out as he does, but I have my own way.

When you get past the reading stage, Jerry lets you wander around and find the movement of the scene with the other actors, and then he cleans it up. I liked finding my own blocking because then it was organic.

Jerry also speaks of language, and has you work with a coach when you need it.

Language is one of the greatest joys in playing Shakespeare. Perhaps my musical training and experience makes me especially appreciate the way that the verse is like music and supports you. Viola, whom I played at Capital Rep, is my favorite of the Shakespeare roles I've done. I love the challenge of making Shakespeare make sense. Once you make sense for yourself and to the audience, it's so much fun! The characters are exactly what they say—they don't have all this subtext going on about something else. That kind of simplicity makes it very clear and the verse just sends you. It's beautiful.

Twelfth Night and *Cherry Orchard* were directed by Rene Buch. I love Rene; he is a character. He gives you free rein in rehearsals, the opposite of Liviu Ciulei. My last work in regional theatre was Rene's production of Lope de Vega's *Fuente Ovejuna* at the Folger two seasons ago.

Of Spanish theatre, I've done that Golden Age play and Lorca's modern classic. I don't know why the Spanish classics haven't been done more in the United States, except by Spanish-language theatres. It might be something as simple as Americans not being that interested in the Spanish culture until now, when there are a lot more Hispanic people in this country. It may also be a matter of translations. When you translate Ibsen you lose something, but it's still quite wonderful. If you had good translators of Spanish drama into English, you might get more productions. The translations of *Blood Wedding* and *Fuente Ovejuna* sounded British for some reason, and also kind of lyrical, not as direct and earthy as the Spanish.

I've acted and sung the title roles in two big professional productions in San Juan—*Peter Pan* and *Fela*. *Peter Pan* wasn't difficult, because I had seen it, it was easy for me to translate into Spanish because the book is simple, and it was a musical. *Fela* was all sung. That was pretty easy, but it would be hard for me to act in Spanish.

This is something I've talked about with Rene Buch, who also directs in Spanish as the artistic director of Repertorio Español. I've been acting so long in English that I think it would be hard for me to do the classics in Spanish, especially something like Lorca or Lope de Vega, in verse. The rhythms of Spanish are so different, and English is simpler in a lot of ways. I think I'm a better actress in English, but singing in Spanish is great fun, because the music supports you and I connect with it.

The only other musical work I've done outside of New York was Aldonza at the George Street Playhouse and the Denver Center,

Dracula: A Musical Nightmare at Stage West, and *Portrait of Jennie* at the Berkshire Theatre Festival.

Both productions of *Man of La Mancha* were set in Central America in the present, and unfortunately the concepts didn't work. Cervantes wrote in and about such a definite time—what could be more definite than the Inquisition?—and I think the play speaks about more than politics. To make it into this political story in Salvador, in Panama— any of the countries that have been in turmoil—is limiting. I don't think you can bring Don Quixote, who's such a recognizable character, into the present, and I can't see Spain transposed into Central America. Spain has influenced all these countries, but Central American cultures are very different.

I enjoyed working on *Portrait of Jennie* a lot. It had been a novel and then a movie starring Joseph Cotten as an artist who falls in love with Jennie, played by Jennifer Jones. Enid Futterman wrote the libretto and lyrics for the musical and Howard Marren was the composer, and the show was mostly sung. Jennie ages from six to twenty-eight, and the biggest challenge for me was that you never know whether she's real or a ghost. There is this sense of "other" you have to convey, and through the whole thing, not just at one point. (As Lucy in the *Dracula*, I died in the middle of a song and had to sing half of it alive and half of it dead.)

Jennie's director, Greg Boyd, trusted my input. I'd behave as the child, for example, and Greg said they could test the language from what I did. Maybe I'd say one tiny word didn't exist in an eight-year-old's vocabulary and he would confer with the writers and they would cut it, or find the right word, or use mine. That was true for lyrics too— sometimes I'd even sing the wrong lyric and they'd keep it! Greg said after the show that my honesty as an actor was a way to test the writing, that whatever I said that rang false was a clue to something that might be wrong.

Being given so much trust was an incredible experience. Greg directed me in both *Jennie* and *Dracula*. He's a *very* creative director—the look of his productions is beautiful and richly textured. He encourages actors to make choices that are bold and different, rather than cliched. When Jennie said goodbye forever to her painter, for example, I kept breaking into tears and Greg said, "No. No tears. This should be joyful." He didn't want her to be sentimental or maudlin anywhere, and though that was harder to play, it was an exciting choice.

When I was doing *Fuente Ovejuna* in Washington I said, "I've got to stop working in regional theatre for a while." I couldn't pay my bills! It's sad that in this country actors don't make a decent living. I was also tired of going from room to room around the country and feeling like a gypsy. I wanted to be home with my boyfriend—the relationship is important! I also wanted to be in the limelight again.

After twelve years away, I wanted to be back on Broadway and I wanted to do something big. So I auditioned for *Nick and Nora* and was cast in the role of Maria Valdez. And I got fired during previews.

I've been in two situations where I've been uncomfortable in a role, knew I wasn't getting it, and wanted to be fired but wasn't. The first time it happened I didn't understand the style the director was going for and he didn't explain it to me—I had a hard time finding it myself and felt lost; I really wanted out, but they didn't give me an out. The second time was with the same director and we were doing a piece where I thought I was miscast. I think the play called for a different person physically, and he was trying to stage it in another direction. The acting didn't go with how the character was written, and I felt lost again. There were a couple of places where it felt comfortable, and I looked forward to those and just kept it going in between. It was not a long run—that made it bearable.

So I understand what it's like to be wrong in a part, but I knew from the audience reaction to *Nick and Nora* that this wasn't so for Maria Valdez. I was terribly upset at being fired for something that wasn't my fault. I think it would have been easier if it had been, because I would have wanted out. But I also had a sense of relief, because the atmosphere surrounding the show was terrible. There was a lot of tension and pressure, and I wasn't the only person getting blamed.

I was fired on a Thursday. I cleared out my dressing room that night and never went back. The cast was very nice to me. Faith Prince, whom I'm working with now in *Guys and Dolls*, was extremely supportive. I was going to take the bus home to New Jersey, but she made me call my boyfriend Andre and wait for him to come pick me up. Kip Niven insisted on waiting with me. Joanna Gleason, Barry Bostwick and even the doorman were telling me I was better off. But I hated not having work, and also it was hard to explain to people who aren't in the theatre. My boyfriend, who's a businessman, understood because he had seen the show, but it was hard to explain being fired to his family and friends . . . and in Puerto Rico, people didn't understand. That was difficult. It's a hard thing to go through for anyone, but the fact that the show closed cleared my name, in a way. When I took over as Sarah Brown in *Guys and Dolls*, people I didn't even know sent me cards and letters saying, "There is justice after all."

If I had stayed in *Nick and Nora*, I would never have gotten into this show. I auditioned right after I got fired. I really wanted Sarah. I know that some people see her as a thankless role—the good-girl fifties ingenue. I don't. I like Sarah and I like the growth she goes through. She's one of the few characters in the show who change. It's a challenge to make the quiet role stand out.

I auditioned and lo: I got a callback, and another callback, and it was down to Carolyn Mignini and me. Jerry Zaks decided to go with Carolyn and I was heartbroken. I went on a skiing trip, and worked really hard to learn how to ski. I remember crying and saying to Andre, "I've been in the business for fifteen years and I don't know if I'm ever going to move on to another level again. It's really frustrating because I've been skiing for five days and I've already graduated to intermediate."

We came back and I was asked to understudy Sarah and be in the ensemble. I said "No, I can't march behind Sarah because I want to play her," so they gave me the standby. Accepting that position was a difficult choice, but I knew I had to do it for some reason. When I didn't get the part, I still felt like it was mine, and that hadn't happened since *West Side Story*. I *did* want to work with Jerry Zaks and be involved in the project, and thought maybe I'd get the national company. I almost turned it down, because I didn't think I'd be a good standby, emotionally. It's hard to do, because you want the best thing for the other person but you also want the best for you, and you want to do the part.

Jerry warned me three days before he let Carolyn go. We had a meeting where we went over the play and he told me how he saw Sarah and what he wanted. I had a line rehearsal with his assistant; one rehearsal onstage with the cast, costumes and props; and then I was on. You get to a point where you've done so much work and gone through so much that you are able to say, "Okay, here's your chance to enjoy yourself in a role you wanted to play. This is your night. Don't think past it."

You have to be ready, and by ready I mean knowing your character, your words, your dance steps. The dancing was amazing because I hadn't had any dance rehearsal, and in the first few days the choreographer, Chris Chadman, decided I could do more in the Havana number and he added to it. I got the new dance at four o'clock in the afternoon and had to perform it that night. It's a mambo in which Sarah is a little tipsy and lets loose for the first time. I've done mambo all my life so it was no problem—it was a lot of fun—and I have a wonderful partner in Gary Christ. I asked them if they wanted her to dance well, and they said, "Yes, we want her to really let go and do it."

The other thing about going in really fast is having the strength, and I think that comes from experience. Knowing you can do it is so important, because you can't panic.

It's funny, my ex-boyfriend spoke with me the other day and said, "That's the story of your life." When I replaced during the Off-Broadway run of *Tamara*, I had two weeks to learn the script, and my character had the longest monologue in the show!

Having been the actress fired and the actress who replaced this year, I had a mixture of feelings when I got Sarah. I felt very bad for Carolyn, and I called her. But I was very happy for me. I knew I had nothing to do with her firing, but you always feel guilty. I felt like the usurper. I saw the torment Jerry Zaks went through about it—he felt awful; he was sick to his stomach. I know how much pain it caused everybody, and I hated being a part of it.

In the ironic way things worked out, I think Sarah's a much better role for me to be seen in on Broadway than the part in *Nick and Nora*, because I've never considered myself a "Hispanic" actress and I don't like to be pigeonholed as something I'm not. Maria Valdez in *Nick and Nora* was fun, but she was a kind of Carmen Miranda stereotype. I see myself as an actress who can play a person no matter what her background is.

I am of Spanish background, but I consider myself as American as anybody else. I was born in New York and have spent most of my life here.

I don't think that ethnic pigeonholing happens in theatre as much as in television and film. I've had the opportunity to play anything and everything onstage, but in film or television, when I go in for a Hispanic role I'm not cast because I don't look like the cliché Hispanic that they're looking for, and when I go up for an Anglo role they always ask what background my name comes from.

I'm not sure what might have happened if I had changed my name. I thought when I first started working that I didn't want to change it, but for the past three or four years I've wondered, because I don't think people would think twice if my name were Josie Jackel or something like that.

My dream is that my work will speak for itself, and ultimately it won't matter. As for the position of Hispanic actors in theatre and the media, I think the more educated people of every ethnic background become about our culture, the more things will improve. The U.S. is such a huge country and so isolated that people haven't spent much time learning about cultures other than their own.

Just lately, because of this huge influx of different people and the African-Americans standing up for themselves, people are learning more about other cultures. As people become less ignorant, the Hispanic community will get roles that are not necessarily low-class and stereotypes. The more Hispanic writers and directors and producers get involved, the faster things will change, but it will take a lot of time and work.

I would like to be more involved with television and film. I had a nice part as Marisa Velez in the two *FX* movies, but I would like to be more exposed to that part of the art. A role on a good comedy or drama series or a good role in a wonderful film would be great.

I will never give up theatre, because it's where my roots are. I will do any challenging role that comes along, because I am interested in growing.

JOHN MAHONEY

The House of Blue Leaves
(Lincoln Center Theater)

Discovering new talent is one of the great thrills of going to the theatre. I was among scores of New Yorkers to feel ignited by a preview of Orphans *Off Broadway, before its official opening brought acclaim to John Mahoney and his Steppenwolf Theatre Company colleagues for their volcanic performances. Also exciting in its inspirational potential for late-starters was my subsequent discovery that Mahoney did not begin his professional acting career until his mid-thirties. Winner of a 1986 Tony Award for the Lincoln Center revival of* The House of Blue Leaves, *Mahoney has appeared in numerous feature and television films, while returning regularly to the stages of Steppenwolf. In his loyalty to Chicago and Steppenwolf, Mahoney is exemplary of the growing number of actors who may achieve success in New York and/or Hollywood, but remain devoted to their personal and artistic homes.*

I entered the acting field so late in life that a lot of the great roles are not available to me. Obviously I'm not going to play Hamlet. I'm fifty years old now, and I was forty before I started getting any decent parts.

I acted in a wonderful children's theatre in my home town of Manchester, England when I was growing up, and I had a burning ambition to be an actor, but it gradually went underground after I emigrated to America when I was eighteen. After earning my B.A. and M.A. in English, I was an English teacher and eventually an editor of medical journals and books. I had worked my way into a nice salary, nice office and nice apartment in Chicago, but by the time I was about 36 or 37, I was thinking: "What's happening to me? Is this going to be it for the rest of my life?" I remember going through a lot of problems and drinking too much and smoking too much, and I finally sat down to question myself: "What have I ever done in my life that was utterly fulfilling to me? Do we ever get to do things that we love and will satisfy us, or do we just play a little game called getting through the day?" And I thought, "The time I was most happy was when I was acting."

With this in mind—but still not committed to doing anything—I went to England to visit my family. I stopped in London and went to the National Theatre, where I saw *Jumpers*, the Tom Stoppard play with Michael Hordern, and it just inflamed my mind. Then I went home to Manchester and saw *Uncle Vanya*, with Albert Finney and Leo McKern, at the Royal Exchange Theatre, and that inspired me. My mind was in turmoil, and I was thinking, "Oh my God, if I could only do what those actors are doing. But how can I? I'm not like these people. These are great actors. Their feet don't touch the floor. These are godlike people."

Well, the morning after I saw *Vanya*, I went back to the theatre to get a ticket to go see it again. The Royal Exchange has a little coffee shop in the lobby, so I got the ticket and then had a cup of coffee. Across from me was Leo McKern. He was unshaven, with a crumpled shirt on, and he was eating a sausage roll. I looked at him and thought: "My God, that's what an actor is. Of course I can be an actor. They're people who sit around eating sausage rolls. They're people who need to shave. They're just ordinary people during the day and then they go onstage and dare to do wonderful things. But they're not godlike, they're human beings. They're exactly like I am."

Then I went back to Chicago and saw *A View from the Bridge* at the St. Nicholas Theatre. That theatre had been put together by David Mamet, Steven Schachter and W. H. Macy, and they were doing great work. In addition to plays by David, they were soliciting manuscripts from unknown playwrights. They also did the classics, but with a fresh approach.

It was a dynamic, physical, non-neurotic approach to acting. Chicago actors tend to let the words go instead of trying to act every word. If there's a pause, it's accepted as a pause as opposed to "Look at this terrible thing that I'm going through during this pause." It's a freer-wheeling type of acting than most. It's a wonderful thing—I think, anyway. Directors I've worked with in New York, including Jerry Zaks, say the same thing: let the words go. Say what you have to say. Don't be a miser: spend those words.

The St. Nicholas *View from the Bridge* was done so simply and yet so powerfully that it made me think I would have no difficulty becoming a part of that. That free, natural style is so seemingly artless that you feel you can do it. I thought, "Okay, I'm going to commit myself to this totally for at least a year," and I quit my job and enrolled in a class at the St. Nicholas school.

I had to start from scratch—right from Acting 101. We worked with the Sanford Meisner technique. The "repeating game," in particular, was a marvelous teaching tool for me, because I had never done anything like it. It lays great emphasis on giving focus to the other person and getting it off yourself, and on the importance of listening and reacting to what you hear, not to just what the lines are.

I didn't do scenes in the first class, but I graduated to a scene-study class with Steven Schachter. I lived off my savings and unemployment, and I was doing okay. Ironically, it wasn't until I began to get work that I started having financial problems, because I got less money working than I did on unemployment.

I was taking Steven's class, and when David Mamet asked Steven to recommend actors for some of the non-Equity roles in *The Water Engine*, I was among those chosen. It was so exciting. I had this little bitty part with about three or four lines . . . and no money. But I thought every moment of my life was blessed.

The play was a big hit and we extended, but some of the actors had other commitments and I was promoted to a bigger part. They said, at St. Nicholas, "You'll have to join Equity, and we'll have to pay you, because Equity demands it, but we can't afford to pay you, so you'll sign your check over to us." I said, "Okay, fine," joined Equity, and went into my big role as the grocery-store owner. When I got my first paycheck—I think it was about $75—they asked for it back. I said I'd changed my mind—I refused—and they backed right down. I had thought about it maybe a day before I did it. I hadn't decided from the *start* to pull a fast one.

In this business, you really have to learn not to be afraid. You can stand up for yourself and it's *not* going to affect your getting a job. When you're young and you're starting out, you think that if you argue about something you'll get a reputation as a troublemaker. That's nonsense. It doesn't matter. What they want is a type or a performance, and if they know an actor is capable of doing it, it doesn't matter what his or her reputation is.

Getting started as an actor was so serendipitous. Everything just fell into place. Emilia Lawrence, a Chicago agent who represented one of the other actors in *Water Engine*, came to see her client, loved me, and offered to represent me. I've never even had to make rounds at agents' offices.

Emilia was my agent until I came to New York with *Orphans*. A lot of agents don't want you doing plays, because they get no money when you're working in not-for-profit theatre and you're not available for films. I've been very fortunate. Emilia always encouraged me, and since I came to New York, my agents at ICM have done the same. In fact, when Sam Cohn visited me on the set of the film *Suspect*, he said, "Now you've done *Tin Men* and *Moonstruck* and it's about time you got back to the Steppenwolf Theatre Company." I thought that was incredible, because they're not getting a dime from me while I'm at Steppenwolf. I'm barely getting a dime myself.

John Malkovich brought me into the Steppenwolf company. We had acted together in *Ashes* at St. Nicholas, and the first play I did at Steppenwolf was *Philadelphia, Here I Come*, which was the last production they did in their first home, a church basement. Then they were invited to move into Jane Adams' Hull House, and each member of the original company was asked to recommend a new member so there would be a larger company that could do more things.

Some of the original Steppenwolf members—John Malkovich, Terry Kinney, Laurie Metcalf, Joan Allen, Gary Sinise—have since become well-known. Jeff Perry, Alan Wilder and Moira Harris are wonderful actors who have *not* become *as* well-known. Glenne Headly, Rondi Reed, Francis Guinan and Tom Irwin are actors who joined the company when I did.

At the Hull House theatre, we built walls and box offices, scraped inches of dirt and muck, all of us on our hands and knees. When we weren't cleaning and scrubbing, we were on the phone selling subscriptions. We got the theatre into great shape, and the owners rewarded us by pricing us out of it. After two or three seasons at Hull House, we took over at the old St. Nicholas Theatre, which had gone out of business.

Steppenwolf was another company that couldn't pay. But in this case, it wasn't a big, successful subscription house like St. Nicholas had been. It was obviously a group of very dedicated, very poor people. All the actors, Equity and non-Equity, worked for nothing. We signed our checks over as soon as we got them . . . which was pretty bad, because that meant I couldn't get unemployment. I was living on the remains of my savings, and I moved to Forest Park, where the rents were cheap and I didn't need a car—I could get the El into town.

Today I live in another western suburb called Oak Park, which was Ernest Hemingway's and Frank Lloyd Wright's birthplace. It's a nice little village, fifteen minutes from downtown Chicago. I'll work in other cities, sometimes for long periods of time, but I will always return to Chicago.

It breaks my heart that my parents and my sister Madeleine didn't live to see my success as an actor. Madeleine was the second and I was the seventh of eight children, and we were Irish Catholics living in Manchester. My father was a baker, my mother a housewife. There wasn't much money; I didn't do very well at school; my childhood was pretty scrungy. I guess I was close to being a street urchin—except, thank God, I had a great curiosity and was encouraged to do a lot of reading. Madeleine always gave me books—she introduced me to

Faulkner and Hemingway—and thanks to her I went from Enid Blyton to Graham Greene in one fell swoop.

I got involved in the theatre at an early age. In Manchester, there's an area called Streatford, a very nice, cultured Bloomsbury or Hampstead type of area, or it was then. I went into the Streatford Children's Theatre when I was about eleven, after playing the Fourth Tempter in Eliot's *Murder in the Cathedral* and the lead in Molière's *Le Bourgeois gentilhomme* in school. At Streatford, I was the crazy brother in *The Lady's Not for Burning*, Lord Teazle in *The School for Scandal*, Lysander in *A Midsummer Night's Dream*, Polonius in *Hamlet*. I was the youngest character actor in history.

When I was about sixteen, I dropped out of high school after being hired by the Birmingham Repertory Theatre as an assistant stage manager. My parents were just frantic. They had always encouraged me to go to the Children's Theatre, to take part in citywide acting contests and things like that, but they were afraid that being an actor was a very tough life and they thought I should get my education. They knew that I wanted to emigrate to America, so they put it to me: how did I ever think I was going to America without having a high school diploma? So I left Birmingham Rep, went home, and finished high school. I went to work in the advertising department at a department store, and saved my money. Then Madeleine gave me the fare to emigrate. She said: "Go to America. You're going to die here, otherwise. You'll end up on the dole like everybody else. Just get out."

Two of my sisters had married American farmers and lived in western Illinois, about 280 miles from Chicago. My family had visited them in 1952. Can you imagine coming from postwar England, where everything was rationed, including your clothes, food, even candy? All of a sudden to come to this country, these wide open spaces on a farm . . . and everybody had cars and looked clean and had so much to eat—it was just amazing!

It was always in my mind that I had to get back. But when I finally got here for good, I didn't know what to do with myself. I was eighteen, and I sort of wanted to be an actor, but I knew I had to make a living. I couldn't be a leech living off my sister and her husband.

At that time, if you intended to remain in the United States permanently, you had to sign a Declaration of Intent. If you did, you were eligible to be drafted. If you didn't, you couldn't stay after your visa was up. I knew I was going to stay here, so I signed the Declaration. I thought: "If I go in the army, I'll get my citizenship faster, I'll get my service out of the way, I'll be able to get a scholarship for college." I joined the army and had to serve three years instead of two, but it was the best thing I could have done because it really acclimatized me to the United States and the people here.

I was stationed at Fort Leonard Wood in Missouri, and that's where I taught myself to have an American accent. People think that an actor likes to be the center of attention. Well maybe some do, but the only time I like it is when I'm saying a line on a stage. Otherwise, I just want to blend in.

I never really had a Beatles-type accent, because my parents had always been careful about the way they spoke. They even gave me money for elocution lessons. But in this country, when people said, "Oh, I love your accent," it really bothered me. I wanted to speak like a native. I would ask friends in the army, "How do you say 'baNAHna'?" They'd say "baNANa" and I'd write it down. The funny part about that is that I was in the army with people from New York, Los Angeles, Louisiana, Nebraska—all over. I learned to say one word as if I were born and raised in Savannah and another as if I were from Newark, so I had quite a mishmash of accents when I got out. Then I went to Quincy College, a small Franciscan school in Illinois, where everybody spoke more or less the same way. That's pretty much the way I speak now.

When I'm acting, I never go very far outside the script. I've tried other people's approaches and they don't work for me. I've seen people fill their heads with so many made-up facts about a character that I don't know how divine inspiration could ever leak in.

I don't do that. In real life, I, John Mahoney, still surprise myself a great deal. The heart has reasons the reason knows not of, and although I'm a rational human being, I still do irrational things that I can't explain. All people do. So how could I presume to know a character that I'm playing inside and out? I don't try to *become* another person. I try to *portray* what is written in the script as effectively as I can.

When I work on a scene, I try to stay away from the end of the play. You read about actors who figure out what happens after the final curtain. That would be devastating for me. I think one of the most important things for me, as an actor, is to play what's happening now, without any knowledge of what's coming in thirty seconds. Obviously I know the role: there are cues I have to give, doors I have to open, phones I have to answer. But ideally, the more you can stay in the moment, the greater it is for you.

That's why I love doing Pinter probably more than any other contemporary playwright. The only way Pinter makes sense for me is to play it scene by scene. And then it's wonderful, it's marvelous. You do one scene, and then you go on to the next scene and play that for exactly what it's about *now*, without any thought about what's going to happen next. I can do this with Pinter because I can't figure out what the whole thing adds up to anyway.

Terry Kinney, John Mahoney and Kevin Anderson in Orphans *(Steppenwolf Theatre Company)*

I remember in Pinter's *No Man's Land*, I was playing Spooner, the old man who is trying to hustle his way into the house of a wealthy man. John Malkovich directed that production and stepped in for a few performances as one of the secretary-thugs who work in the house. Each of those performances was different. I recall during one performance being very afraid, thinking, "He's not acting!" I looked into those vacant and yet somehow terrorizing eyes and thought, "God Almighty, has he gone over the edge or something?" And of course he hadn't. It was just John.

John and Alan Wilder are two Steppenwolf actors who work very differently. In *Death of a Salesman*, I started out playing Charlie and then replaced our guest artist Mike Nussbaum as Willy Loman. When I took over Willy, I had this big scene with Alan as Howard, the man who fires him. I found it great to bounce off Alan, who is a very consistent actor. He really stays within what he has decided his character is, and you don't play around too much with an actor like that. You're sort of held in check.

At the same time, John was doing Biff, and he's the sort of actor who's going to do whatever moves him that moment, whatever struck that day, whatever he happened to bring with him to the theatre. He stays within the parameters of the character—if he were playing St. Francis he wouldn't make him a man who went around injuring birds—but he explores those parameters, nightly, to their extremes. That can be very exciting. It can be scary. It can inspire you. It can intimidate you.

I've encountered these contrasting types in films, too. Take Barry Levinson, who directed *Tin Men*, and Norman Jewison, who directed *Moonstruck*. You could not possibly get two more different approaches.

Barry says, "I don't want you to rehearse. I don't even want you to run lines." I'm playing Richard Dreyfuss's partner in *Tin Men*, and Richard is from a theatre background, too, and *likes* to run things. We would sneak off to run lines and Barry, catching us, would say, "Guys, I don't want you to waste all your spontaneity on this! Don't worry about the words, just play the scene!"

Then you get Norman Jewison, who rented a rehearsal hall before we shot *Moonstruck*. Everything was mapped out on the floor, just like we were doing a play: we knew where we were to walk, when to sit, how close we had to be to each other for the camera. Every last detail was planned.

I've thought many times about which approach I prefer, and the truth is that at the moment I was doing each, I loved that. I loved the aerial act of working on *Tin Men* without a net, but I also loved the safety of *Moonstruck*.

It's the same when you're onstage with somebody like Alan or John. The dependability and the knowledge of how it's going to be is comforting and gives you a lot of confidence. But at the same time, you can't deny that it's exciting to take that roller-coaster ride.

It's very difficult for me to talk about the Steppenwolf style, because everybody's approach is so different. We have twenty-three actors in our company. Some sit backstage and play cards and joke and hear their cue and run out and are brilliant. Some stand backstage staying in character and then go out and are brilliant. We've never been anything like the Group Theatre or the Moscow Art Theatre. We were never political, never had acting classes, never even discussed acting, and we certainly never tried to make one person do anything the way another person did it. I think it's from our many different approaches that the freedom comes to explode the way we explode.

And actors respond differently to different directors. I think Joan Allen, for example, does her best work with a very *strong* director. Joan went through a long period, when she started out in Chicago, of not being noticed. I think a lot of it had to do with the direction she received, which at the time was pretty easygoing. I remember after we did a play about English nurses in World War I, the reviews came out and Joan was the only actor not even mentioned. She broke down in the dressing room, and everybody was furious. John said, "She's gotta have better parts, that's what it is." I didn't agree with that. I thought she had good parts, it's just that she hadn't been properly directed.

Then Joan did *And a Nightingale Sang . . .*, directed by Terry Kinney. Now, Terry is a real ringmaster, with a whip. He's very, very specific. He wants *reality*. He wants you to dig deeper than you ever dug before. If you think you've given everything you've got, he somehow makes you find a little bit more.

Terry is very smart. He has a goal in mind and *will not* veer from the path to it. He kept Joan on that path, and I think she gave a magnificent performance in *Nightingale*. I sat on that stage for a hundred performances and watched her and she was great, she always tore me apart. Then she came to New York with the production and won the recognition she'd not been given in Chicago.

But what worked incredibly for Joan, with Terry, did not work for me. Where she blossomed, I got mad. I was raised in very similar situations to the characters in *And a Nightingale Sang . . .* and, as the father in the Chicago production, I felt I *knew* the characters, but my ideas were different from Terry's and we just never hit it off. Neither of us was ever satisfied with my performance.

It was the same with *Of Mice and Men*. I think that was one of the three best productions that we've ever done at Steppenwolf. John Malkovich was Lenny, Gary Sinise was George, Jeff Perry was Curley, Joan Allen was Curley's wife and I was the little old man with the dog. And Terry directed it to perfection. But there again, I felt that I never got into that character. I always felt that I was a marionette, that I was being manipulated and that my input was neither sought nor taken.

I don't mean that I like to direct myself. I don't. I loved working with Frank Galati, as Grandpa in *You Can't Take It with You* and as Harry Brock in *Born Yesterday*, and with Jerry Zaks in *The House of Blue Leaves*, and those directors are very, very picky. But with Frank and Jerry, you can sit down and say, "You know, I think *this*." You can come up with things about the character that interest or puzzle you, that you want to explore. With Terry, I always felt that he'd listen for a moment and then say, "Okay, I understand where you're coming from. Now this is what I want you to do . . ."

I think Terry is a brilliant actor, and I also think he's one of the warmest, most lovely human beings I've ever met. We agreed at one point that we wouldn't work together anymore as actor and director simply because our friendship meant so much to us, and it could never withstand the experience again.

.   .   .

Glenne Headly chafes even more than I do under forceful direction. Glenne, I think, does her best work when she's left to herself. She comes into a rehearsal so well-prepared, she knows what she wants to do and she pretty much does it.

When we went into *Born Yesterday*, there was no way that she was going to play Billie Dawn like Judy Holliday, which was great with Frank Galati and me. Glenne brought a wonderful sort of submerged, somnambulant quality to Billie. It was almost as if she had surrendered her life—she had *no* passion, she had no *anything*, because of the situation that she was in. As she began to get out of that situation, she gained insight into herself and gained energy along with intelligence and self-respect, which had an invigorating effect on her.

It was an amazing performance, and Glenne brought all that to it herself. I remember Frank once saying to her, "I can't tell you anything. You have a natural dignity and class about you that I simply could not improve on."

I had never played anyone like Harry Brock before. I didn't want to be *liked* by the audience. I wanted to be everything that would make Billie's standing up to me more admirable, so I went out of my way to be as vulgar and vicious as possible. When Frank suggested I might try a little softness or a little humor, I said, "It certainly is an option, but anything like that is going to take away from her eventual triumph."

To play an unrepentantly vicious person like Harry Brock is difficult. It affected me probably more than any other role has. I never thought that I retained characteristics of a character after a performance, but . . .

I remember one time, when we were doing an audience discussion after *House of Blue Leaves*, somebody asked Swoosie Kurtz, "How long does it take you to come out of playing a crazy character like Bananas?" Swoosie said, "During the curtain call, I'm thinking of what I'm going to have for dinner." I always thought I was the same way. But when I was playing Harry I found myself calling women friends "babe" and referring to "broads." The topper came when I put Laurie Metcalf in a cab one night, gave the cab driver money and said, "Take her home and keep the change." Laurie looked at me like I was out of my mind and I thought, "What is going on here?"

Maybe because Brock was so unlike me, and I had to invest so much in him, the character was difficult to drop. Thank God I was able to keep the shouting and screaming and physical violence at bay. I had female friends tell me—in fact, male friends, too—"I'll be glad when this play's over and you can get back to being yourself."

I wasn't looking to come to New York. I've done close to thirty plays at Steppenwolf—sometimes all five of the plays in a season; sometimes just one. Broadway was always more a fantasy than a goal.

My age had a great deal to do with this. When I was forty, I was still learning and trying to make up for lost time. I was never out of work, so I was ecstatic. I had discovered this passion in me that I should have been following all my life, and I couldn't get enough of it. So who cares about New York? Who cares about Hollywood? All I cared about was working.

That's what I was doing when Gary Sinise came up with *Orphans*, a play by Lyle Kessler about a very strange man named Harold who is kidnapped by two young brothers to be held for ransom and who takes over their household, puts them to work for him, and becomes a sort of father figure. Gary directed the play with me as Harold, Terry Kinney as the older and Kevin Anderson as the younger brother.

An interesting point about the Steppenwolf company is the way that actors and directors can switch jobs. As hard as Terry is on actors, he doesn't ask from an actor any more than he himself gives to a director. He'll do anything a director tells or asks him to. If he's told to do something he doesn't agree with, he'll still do it a hundred percent.

They're all like that, all the directors in our company. It's astonishing when you think of it. Terry, Gary and John have very definite ideas about what they want as directors, yet when they're acting in each other's plays, they do what they're told.

Anyway, *Orphans* was a huge success in Chicago, and the next thing I know, all these people from New York start coming. I thought, "Well, they'll just do the play in New York." Then we were told, "They want the whole cast to go," and we thought, "Oh, this'll be fun. What a great way to go to New York: to go in a play that we love and have a nice six months there and get to know the city."

Still, we were very nervous, because we were coming from Chicago and we really didn't know what to expect. When, from the first preview, they were giving us standing ovations, we *did* know that New York audiences are amazingly more demonstrative than Chicago's. They don't hold back, and they're much more sophisticated. They get things that a Chicago audience doesn't.

A perfect example is *True West*. We did two productions of *True West* in Chicago, and both of them sold out every performance. The very first line is, "So, Mom took off for Alaska, huh?" and it wasn't until the first performance in New York that the line ever got a laugh. The actors didn't know what to do. They'd played all these months in Chicago, then they come to New York, and in the first preview this line that they had never gotten so much as a smile on brings down the house.

Orphans maybe got two or three standing ovations in Chicago, but we never got them leaping to their feet like they did in New York. And then the reviews came out. . . . I don't think we could have written better reviews ourselves. It was just wonderful. We were established as national actors, and we were all offered film work and had agents coming every night after the show to wine and dine us. Kevin and I got Theatre World Awards, and I was nominated for a Drama Desk, and it opened lots of doors.

But it was still, as far as I was concerned, just a fun six months, and as soon as they were up I went back to Chicago to do Grandpa in *You Can't Take It with You* at Steppenwolf. Halfway through it, when they called me from Lincoln Center about Jerry Zaks' production of *House of Blue Leaves*, I didn't have another role in the company then and I thought, "Sure, I'll go back to New York and do a limited run," because we thought it was going to be a three-month deal in the Mitzi Newhouse. Not in a million years did we expect it to move to Broadway and win so many Tonys.

Success is a very strange thing, and I think it's more difficult to handle the older you get. You've sort of convinced yourself that you've gone as far as you deserve to go, and that's why you're not a star. Then, all of a sudden, you are twinkling in the heavens with your Tony award and you've convinced yourself that you don't belong there, so you start feeling guilty and worried. You're feeling that at any moment some-body's going to say, "Hey, you don't belong up there," and bring you back down to earth. That's a difficult situation to deal with.

If I have any great regret about having achieved success so late, it's that my sister Madeleine did not live to share it. Madeleine had lost a breast to cancer just before I started *Orphans*. I nursed her through that—she wouldn't trust any of her brothers and sisters around her but me—and then I had to come back to the States. She got cancer again, I went back over, she got better. When I came to New York with *Orphans*, and it finally looked like big things were going to happen for me, I had a ticket for her to come over, and she died of heart failure, they said. She was very sick and she wouldn't let them call me. She said, "No, wonderful things are happening for John now. Let's just let them happen for him." She was always so generous to me.

I still fantasize about Madeleine being here. I fantasize about my parents being here too, sometimes. And I know Madeleine's with me. Almost anything I am I would have to say I owe to Madeleine, for kicking me out of the country, for making sure that I got my education, for never ever laughing at my dreams but forcing me to dream even more outrageously of what should have been impossible: for some guttersnipe from Manchester like me to end up starring on Broadway.

If I feel guilty about the success that I've achieved, it's because other people equally deserving have not become successful. I come from a theatre company of twenty-three actors, many of whom have gone on to huge recognition and financial success. At the same time, we have an equal number of actors who are still at Steppenwolf and are virtually unknown outside the city of Chicago. And the sad and infuriating thing about this is that they're all as talented, if not more so in some cases, as the people who have made it. They just haven't been lucky enough to have been in the productions that brought us to New York.

It's my fervent prayer that they will be soon, because if you want career choices that include working on Broadway and in major films or television, you have to be seen in New York. Chicago is a great town to work in, and there's a tremendous amount of work there, but where would Mike Nichols and Elaine May be if they had stayed in Chicago? Or Mike Nussbaum, or Joe Mantegna, or so many others?

There's a very strange thing about Chicago. I don't know whether it is a midwestern reserve or what, but if you look in newspaper ads there, they never list the actors. I don't understand it. It's sad for me to think of actors whom I truly admire, like Alan Wilder and Rick Snyder and Rondi Reed, who do play after play at Steppenwolf and grow in stature but haven't gotten to New York or Hollywood. And I know so many actors in other Chicago companies who keep everything going, week after week and play after play and season after season, just growing and turning out this great work.

Maybe that's enough for them. I think it *would* have been enough for me. I never sought New York. I never sought Los Angeles.

No, I shouldn't say that. I don't think it *is* enough. When John Malkovich came to New York with *True West* and set the town on its ear, and all of these wonderful things started happening to him, I remember feeling, "God, I wish that could happen to me." How could you not feel that?

Sometimes I will literally sit in my dressing room and weep. That sounds stupid, but I cry with joy at what I'm doing. I still practice my religion—not as faithfully as I wish I did; but I'm a Catholic, and even if I miss Mass an occasional Sunday, I say my prayers in the morning and at night before I go to bed, and I never fail to thank God for the way my life has turned out.

There isn't one moment now that I don't love. I adore every moment of rehearsal, every moment I'm onstage, every moment of walking to the theatre and of leaving the theatre after the show, bathed in the wonderful glow of that exchange between the audience and actors. It's as exciting and marvelous and magical and mysterious and wonderful to me now as it was from the first day I did it.

Ajax *(American National Theatre)*

T he magesterial bearing of Howie Seago as an ambassador on "Star Trek: the Next Generation" was my only knowledge of the actor who had won the Helen Hayes Award in Washington, D.C. and the Drama-Logue Award in Los Angeles as the title character in Peter Sellars' 1986 production of Sophocles' Ajax. When I told my colleague J. Wynn Rousuck, theatre critic for the Baltimore Sun, that I was going to interview Seago, she remembered his performance with such enthusiasm that she looked up her review, in which she had written that the best thing about the production was " the outstanding portrayal of Ajax delivered by Howie Seago, a leading actor with the National Theare of the Deaf. He signs with gestures as strong and graphic as muscular modern dance." After a long working day in his recently adopted hometown of Seattle, Seago and his interpreter Robert J. Huven came to my hotel room to talk over dinner in August of 1991. More time was needed, and Howie Seago gave up Saturday morning with his family for a second interview.

Caliban is half man and half creature, and very often I have felt like I was a creature in a zoo. On the outside I look normal, but when I open my mouth and say some words, I get weird looks. People have all kinds of reactions because I sound different, and sometimes they make fun of me. I used that when I was working on Caliban at the La Jolla Playhouse: How did he feel? Where did he belong? Where do *I* belong?

My feelings are like everyone else's. I'm a human being, but I'm not always treated like one, just because I happen not to be able to hear and because I sound funny. This is an emotionally powerful predicament, one I have no fear of using.

Peter Sellars used it in a subtle way in *Ajax*. It's funny, because Peter never talked about my deafness. I brought it up a couple of times, and he said, "Oh, yeah, if you want to, sure, sure," but he didn't go into it. I figured it was because he had faith that I would reach down into that whole area of my deafness, my struggle as a human being to function in this world.

The last two years I haven't been working in the theatre much, except for a play called *Seeing Places* that we did in San Diego last spring. It was written by Rico Peterson, a friend with whom I did Robert Wilson's *The Forest*, and it's about our deaf experiences in school. (It's pretty well known in the deaf community that the quality of deaf education sucks.) We're going to do the play here in Seattle this fall—I will be producing and directing, in addition to working full-time and teaching an advanced course in creative uses of sign language two nights a week.

The point I'm trying to make—I'm feeling zonked-out right now because I've been working an eight-to-five job in mental health to support my family—is that my opportunities to work in the theatre have been very limited. Opportunities are limited for everyone—it's a very competitive market—but not too many people are open-minded and innovative about how to use a deaf actor in hearing, mainstream theatre. Also, I haven't taken some jobs away from home because I made a personal decision to stay closer to my family.

I have two boys who have what we call normal hearing, but they are deaf when they want to be—one is five and the other is almost two. I met my wife, Lori, in a sign-language class at California State University, Northridge. She is hearing, but she was there because she had seen students talking in sign language and was fascinated. I was the teacher's aide. Now Lori teaches English as a second language to deaf students at a community college.

We've been married fourteen years. She's been with me when I did all my theatre jobs, and I would not have gotten this far without her support. She has been unwavering in her faith in my ability to act, and she knows that my heart is in the theatre. Right now we're going through a hard time because I'm doing a working-stiff job for the first time in my life, and I don't like it. We recently moved to Seattle—I'm from Washington state, and living here had long been a dream for both of us. We're glad we came, but now we're realizing that being in the place you want to be is not enough.

We have satisfied many of our goals. We wanted to see the world before we had children, and through my theatre work we were able to go to Japan, Europe and around America. We had our children and made our dream move to Washington. But now we know that our family life must be balanced with satisfaction from our work. I want to be in the theatre again. I'm trying to figure out how to do that and— whew—it's pretty overwhelming.

I did my first play when I was in junior high school. My mother directed me in a pantomime and had someone else narrate the story, which is like a basic version of what the National Theatre of the Deaf does—matching the beauty of sign language with the beauty of powerful, well-trained voices. I enjoyed that experience, but I never really thought I could act until I was in college and my roommate asked me to be in a play.

I did not know sign language when I first went to college. I grew up with parents and two sisters who are hearing, and two brothers who are deaf or hearing-impaired. We were taught through what is called the oral method, which forbids the use of sign language. All of my life I had been forced to use speech, which is unnatural.

In college, I had the great fortune to be matched up with a deaf roommate who came from a deaf family. He couldn't speak and knew sign language. We were kind of like the Odd Couple. He is now Dr. Ted Supalla of the University of Rochester, and he travels all over the world giving lectures on American Sign Language. One of our pet jokes is that, because I am better-known than he is, people come up to him and say, "Oh, you sign a lot like Howie," and he says, "No, it's the other way around! He signs a lot like me," because he was the mentor and I the student.

While we were still in college, Ted asked me to be in a play called *The Feast*, about an angry young man. When I found out I'd have to sign I said, "No way," but he said, "Wait a minute. You can memorize the lines, and I will translate them for you and teach you what signs to use. You do the same thing every night—it's not like you have to talk spontaneously or improvise." I was a free spirit and I wanted to talk, so I thought, "Why not?" All my life I couldn't understand people or express myself to them, so it would be a real treat to take the words of somebody else and speak eloquently on a stage.

I worked on the translation with Ted, and when I performed on the stage I was a different person. I was signing fluently and the audience, which had both deaf and hearing people, ate it up. Deaf people came up to me afterwards and were signing like crazy, and I would say, "Wait, please, say that again slowly," and their mouths would drop open.

That play made me realize how hungry I was to communicate on an intimate level what I felt inside. Interacting with Ted every day, I had total immersion in the structure of American Sign Language. It's very different from how you would sign and speak at the same time, as I'm doing now. I'm speaking, and my signing is following the English pattern of the words. If I were signing in ASL, it would be different. The syntax and grammar are different, based on the subject coming first. Ted gave me the proper foundation in the language itself, and it was my introduction to meaningful communication.

I saw the National Theatre of the Deaf perform while I was in college, and attended their summer school in 1977. The NTD took me more into the world of creativity, showing me how you sign larger and make up stories to tell in sign language. That might correspond to an actor learning how to project his voice in a theatre.

I had written poetry in high school, and Ted encouraged me to change it into signs. We made a video of one of my poems, and seeing that had a great influence on my understanding the artistry of signs— the process of making things flow and using space visually and economically.

I always enjoy working with language, translating from English into any form of visual communication, whether it be ASL, mime or creative sign language. Translating poems or music is especially interesting. You have to be careful how you present song. Take a line from "Country Road" by John Denver, one of my favorite songs. When there's a lull in the music with no lyrics, I add images—I paint a picture of the mountains and the country. Repeating the sign for "country roads" over and over would be very boring for a deaf audience, so I add something each time, like a truck driving on the road and the mountain going by. For "mountain mama," I bring my hands together for the mountain and then kiss my fist and raise it. That symbolizes cherishing the mountain, which is the symbolic meaning of the words.

After graduating from Cal State and doing some work producing a TV show for deaf children, I joined the National Theatre of the Deaf because I was ready to move into professional theatre. When I did the NTD summer school, I was a typical college radical. I was not all that impressed with their translation work because I thought that it was aimed at hearing people, and that deaf people did not understand the plays very well. It's ironic, because the NTD broke a lot of ground in playing with sign language. But sometimes the signs were too fancy for deaf people to comprehend. Also, since NTD uses deaf actors who sign and hearing actors who narrate the story and say characters' lines, the signing often followed English. English is not in the natural rhythm of deaf language, so deaf people had a hard time following, and the deaf community does not identify with the NTD.

I wanted to be able to serve the deaf community more by doing more appropriate translations. We had to go through a lot of battles with that, not just me but other actors like Carol Aquiline—who became the artistic director of the Australian Deaf Theatre—Adrian Blue, Michael Lamitola and Chuck Baird. Chuck is an artist I greatly respect. Not only is his signing beautiful, but he also does set designs for NTD.

David Hays, NTD's artistic director, had his own vision—that NTD should try to reach as many people as possible all over the world. I don't know if, as a hearing person, he fully realizes the importance of the sign language being clear to deaf audiences—just as white people will never totally understand the black experience no matter what they do, and men will never completely understand what it is to be a woman. But at the same time, David has done a tremendous job of providing opportunities for deaf people to become actors. Without him, I don't know where I would be today.

I brought with me to NTD a strong understanding of the proper structure of American Sign Language and an awareness of how the deaf community perceived the NTD's way of communicating the lines. I wanted to try to make those meet. In the two NTD plays I was involved with, *Gilgamesh* and *The Iliad*, I and the others in the company insisted that our sign language not follow the English word order, and that alone made deaf people more appreciative of the work that was going on at the NTD.

I was cast as the Sumerian king Gilgamesh because they needed a tall actor, and I'm 5'11". I did it a long time ago, but I can remember two things. One is that I had almost lost my younger brother through a stupid mistake when we were mountain-climbing, and I used that when I had to work on the emotion of losing my beloved friend Enkidu. The first time in rehearsal I cried and cried, and the other people there were embarrassed. I was worried whether the scene was going to affect me that way all the time. I was able to get it under control, but it gave me a driving emotion to use the rest of the year. Whenever my energy in the play was getting low, thinking of that experience always gave me another spark to work with. That was an important discovery for me, because I had not worked in roles that called for deep emotional experiences.

The other thing I remember about *Gilgamesh* was the challenge of having to sign with one hand over my crotch. Ishtar tries to seduce Gilgamesh and steals his clothes from him. I was wearing a loincloth, but we wanted to give the feeling of my having nothing on. To keep the dialogue going I had to sign with one hand, and I would sometimes use both hands and remember that I needed one over my crotch. Sometimes I would cover myself with my leg—it became one of the funniest scenes in the play.

The NTD gave me an opportunity to develop as an actor. That was the first time I'd ever had the challenge of having to repeat a play 200 times a year and keep it fresh. The experience of a bus-and-truck tour, performing in all kinds of spaces, and in everything from great to weird and hard conditions, made me more adaptable. I remember performing in a Philadelphia cafeteria with posts obstructing people's vision. We had bamboo poles eight feet tall that we pounded on the floor, but the ceiling was so low that we couldn't pound them. The lighting was bad, but people paid to see the show, so we had to give them the best we could.

Also the experience of theatre as a family was beneficial. I come from a very close family that has always been supportive of me. It was interesting to work with all these diverse personalities in the NTD company and try to get along. There was a special feeling inside that we all belonged because we were deaf. The NTD gave us an opportunity to belong to a community, an ensemble. We might disagree on some things, but we all believed in what we were doing from an artistic point of view.

The NTD's asking me to do *Gilgamesh* was the first time that my wife said "Go" when I had the opportunity to do professional theatre. While I was with the NTD, Lori went to the University of Hawaii to get her master's degree. After two years I joined her, and in Hawaii I acted in a professional, hearing theatre for the first time. The Honolulu Theatre for Youth hired me to do four shows, which was my first repertory experience.

In *Beauty and the Beast*, I played the Beast in a full-size head mask, and I signed. That was the curse of the Beast, who was really a prince under a spell. The audience accepted the fact that the Beast could not talk for himself, and we had an actor in the shadows speaking for me. Wearing a black outfit with a long flowing cloak, he represented the evil power behind the curse. When Beauty started to fall in love with the Beast, she wanted to learn sign language. That added another dimension to the play. At the end, when Beauty loves the Beast enough for the curse to be broken, the director had me give her a rose that she had given the Beast earlier. I had changed into the costume of a young Prince, and she recognized me from the rose. If I had said anything, the audience would have known that I was deaf and that was why I had used sign language before. That director was very creative in dealing with my deafness and utilizing my talent.

The audience and the critics never knew I was deaf. I thought that was great. I got a big kick out of children coming up and talking to me after the performance. I would say, "I'm sorry, I'm deaf, can you slow down?" and they would be so amazed. Part of me wanted not to tell them that I was deaf, but there was a lot of value in their knowing that a deaf actor was able to perform like a hearing person on a stage, and that it made the play more powerful and larger than life.

At the National Theatre of the Deaf, I worked with Peter Sellars in his production of *The Ghost of Chastity Past*, a Japanese-American satire of the cowboy Western. Peter and I hit it off, and five years later he called and said, "I want you to do a play for the American National Theater in Washington, D.C."

Howie Seago in Ajax *(American National Theatre)*

I'm ashamed to say that at first I said I couldn't do it. I was teaching theatre classes and directing plays at the National Technical Institute for the Deaf in Rochester, New York. We'd just bought a house, and had a baby boy two months old. My first thought was that I would have to quit my full-time job to go and do the play for four months. Peter wouldn't take no for an answer, and thank goodness he didn't. He said it was an opportunity to show the hearing world that deaf actors can work in mainstream theatre. Richard Nichols, the chairman of my theatre department in Rochester, was a wonderful support. And my wife said, once again, "Do what you want. I will support you."

I went and played the lead in *Ajax*, and oh boy was it an incredible journey. Peter Sellars decided to do a modern adaptation of Sophocles' tragedy, using today's political issues and turmoils. We did *Ajax* at the Kennedy Center and the La Jolla Playhouse, and a year later we toured in Europe. In Washington we had mixed reactions because the play was so political. This was during the Reagan years, and we were trying to show the horror of war and what it costs people on all different levels—the generals, the soldiers, the wives, the children. La Jolla was warmer, but it's a navy town, so maybe just a little warmer.

In Europe, we received standing ovations every night. Peter was like a god; I got the red-carpet treatment; and we also blew away the deaf community there. They had never seen a deaf actor perform with a hearing theatre company on that high of a professional level, and they were just amazed. We had one special night in Belgium when a lot of deaf people came. Their sign language is different from what we use in America, so Peter had their local interpreter be the courtroom stenographer.

In Sophocles' play, Ajax is a Greek general at Troy who feels betrayed by his leader Agamemnon. The goddess Athena sends Ajax into a fit of madness in which he slays a lot of animals, thinking that he is killing Agamemnon and his other enemies. When he is sane and realizes what he has done, Ajax feels so dishonored that he kills himself. Peter Sellars set our production in a courtroom where Ajax was on trial. George Tsypin designed a huge wall like the Pentagon's front, and a metal door where water representing the ocean came out when I died. There were tables and a judge's bench, and the Chorus was the jury. I was seated onstage in a chair except for a moment when

I walked over to the soldiers and vocally spoke one line, "How can you do this to me?"

During the prologue, there was a glass box upstage, covered with a tarp. In front of the tarp, Athena tried to persuade Odysseus to work with her against me. From inside the glass box, the audience could hear water and blood sloshing around as I was killing animals—it was pieces of foam but it looked like chunks of animals. I did a piercing scream at realizing the horror of what I'd done, and then the judge ordered an MP to pull away the tarp. There I was, in full military uniform, standing in all the blood and slaughter . . . and signing—blasting out my anger.

The glass box was moved off and I was left standing there in shock. Then I walked down the raked stage with blood streaming from my costume. Peter Sellars always has something happening—soldiers were tapping their boots as I was walking, so that there was always a counterpoint and a tension. Before I killed myself, Ben Halley, Jr., a big man wearing a camouflage uniform and very large wings on his back, was singing, "Down by the riverside, I ain't gonna study war no more," while I was taking off my shirt, cleaning myself, and getting ready for the Japanese suicide ritual of seppuku. Many people told me they had to come back three or four times to take everything in because Peter packed so many details into ninety nonstop minutes.

The Chorus was composed of soldiers who spoke for me. It was very innovative and powerful, because never before had there been seven people speaking for one deaf person. That is the opposite of what the National Theatre of the Deaf does. They have seven, eight, nine deaf actors and two, sometimes three hearing people speaking for them. That can be limiting. We even had the actress who played Ajax's wife speaking an intimate scene with my son, where I told him that I was going to kill myself and gave him my last words as a father. The scene is already powerful, and having the wife speaking for Ajax and adding her own feelings wove in more emotional layers.

I work on a play from the outside in. I have to translate the language before I can do anything else. Other actors might be dealing with the sound of the word; I have to deal with how I'm going to sign it. I put in a lot of time on that. Hearing actors can work carrying scripts around and really get into it. I cannot. I have to get rid of the book and start using my tools.

As just one example of developing the signs, take Ajax's phrase about the slaughter of the animals, "the carnival of blood." I had to work a long time on how to sign that, and Peter helped a lot. There are several ways to sign "carnival": like a ferris wheel going around; or a circus tent; or making the big red nose of a clown. The image that we finally came up with was the carnival as the ferris wheel and also the animals jumping to escape being killed. The sign for animals is the first two fingers half bent over. The sign for ferris wheel is hands revolving around each other. So to communicate a carnival of terrified animals, I had the first two fingers of both hands not just half bent over but contorted as if in pain, while I moved my hands around each other in a circle.

The sign for blood is the hand moving down from the mouth with its fingers splayed out, so for "carnival of blood" one hand went up to my mouth with fingers splayed, and moved down in front of the animal/ferris wheel sign. I made my fingers flutter to intensify the feeling of blood scattering all over.

That is just one phrase—I go through any play I'm working on like that. That's what I mean by the difference between everyday signing and translating into an art form: you read the words on my body; I show you. I'm constantly revising and refining my signing in a play— I'm almost never satisfied. When we closed *Ajax* in La Jolla after doing the play for six months, I came up with a different way of signing two lines on the last night. It is a living language, a continuous process to me. Deaf people commented on the fact that I was signing in poetry.

Internally, I try to approach a play almost empty; not really empty but with no preconceived ideas or interpretations. Depending on the guidance of the director, I will try to remember things that help me. For the character of Ajax, the general who is alienated from his own soldiers and superiors, I think what Peter Sellars tapped into is that my early education—not being allowed to use sign language and having so much trouble communicating—made me feel like the alienated stranger in Camus. Peter knew I felt removed from other people just because of my deafness. I saw Ajax as a person who believed in what he was doing and was betrayed by his country. They changed the rules on him while he was fighting a war, and how do you cope with that? In my experience of growing up as a deaf person in a hearing world, *I* didn't always know what the rules were.

Ajax was my first big-time play, but I didn't feel the pressure. I knew Peter would take us where we needed to go. Playing Enkidu in Robert Wilson's production of *The Forest* (also based on the epic of Gilgamesh) was a different experience. I had never been exposed to Wilson's approach to the theatre, and I had a lot of trouble as an actor because I felt like I was being used as a pawn.

The first week of rehearsal in Berlin, Robert Wilson didn't talk about the play at all, he showed us pictures of what it would look like. At one point he said, "Okay, we're ready to start," and he showed me the picture of a big rock and a moon. There were about fifty people in this warehouse studio, and he said, "Go and lie down on the rock, wake up and do something."

"What?"

"Anything."

I had no idea what he wanted, except he told me it should be about fifteen minutes long. So I was lying on this imaginary rock, wondering what the hell I was going to do, and I woke up very slowly, took about five minutes to look around the room, reached out very slowly for the imaginary moon, held onto the moon, then walked around the room, making a figure eight and hoping fifteen minutes had passed by the time I got back onto my rock and went back to sleep. That's all I did, and Robert Wilson said, "Bravo! Bravo! That's it! Perfect!" and all the people applauded. He never changed that scene.

If I asked Robert what the rationale for something was, he said he didn't know—it just looked right. Not it *feels* right, it *looks* right. Whew, there I was, an actor, and there he was, a visual artist, using me as a prop. I was onstage nonstop, covered in green makeup, and wearing a loincloth for half the play. Very cold.

When Gilgamesh and Enkidu went on a long journey to find the great bull that was the source of immortality, Robert had us travel using three special chairs that he had designed, made out of metal, very uncomfortable to sit on. A German hearing actor played Gilgamesh, and we had to try to walk all over the stage on top of the chairs. The rule was that we could never touch the floor, because that was supposed to be a bottomless pit or something. At the very end, when I put Gilgamesh on my shoulders and had to move some chairs with my feet, the German actor said some lines and I made some sounds. I don't remember signing at all. Anytime I wanted to communicate with him it was by sounds—clucking; howling; animal noises. We had microphones on and the sound equipment made our sounds echo. All kind of weird, but the German audiences ate it up. They thought it was very profound.

I tried to create a character, and on a personal level I found some satisfaction in that I stayed with the show from the beginning to the end, which was four months. I was ready to quit three or four times. The run of the play—which we also toured in Europe and to the Brooklyn Academy of Music—was good discipline for me. Sometimes I got sidetracked and thought about other things, but for the most part I was able to stay within an internal character of Enkidu.

Being the only American in the original cast, I also became the person who stood up to Robert Wilson, because he mistreats his actors. He has fifteen-, eighteen-, twenty-hour rehearsals, all nonstop except for a meal break. Once he got a phone call and told us to stay in place while he went and took it. He expected us not to move one inch while he was gone for half an hour. I said, "To hell with this, I'm not going to stay here," and I went out and took a break. All the other actors stayed in place.

German theatre is subsidized by the government, which pays a lot of money for people to work. All the cast, crew, designers and all of Robert Wilson's very large staff were there every day. That didn't give us a whole lot of privacy to develop our roles and maybe try something that would be dangerous or vulnerable. Robert also invited his friends to watch and give him feedback, but he never introduced them to us and he never asked for our permission, which is very different from American theatre. Equity would never accept that! My role as an Equity actor was to say, "Wait a minute," and there were times when I said I would only work eight hours—that was the limit until we got into final rehearsals. The other actors always came up to me afterwards and thanked me for stopping rehearsal so they could go home and see their families, get something to eat or catch up on their rest.

The Forest was a three-and-a-half-hour play, and my wife came to see it and loved it. She found it fascinating. I have to give credit to Robert Wilson. Now I realize that there is room for all kinds of artists, and what I hope is that they will make room for me and for other artists who have special abilities.

My wife suggested that I make a proposal for "Star Trek: the Next Generation," because it is very imaginative and might be open to a deaf actor using a different kind of communication. I met with the two producers, and six months later they sent me a script. Their idea was for my character to use a headband as a communication device. I had a chorus of three people who spoke for me, but we communicated through this device, which transmitted our thoughts. The original conflict in the episode was that this headpiece got broken and their idea of a resolution was that I learned to speak verbally overnight through the use of computers.

I couldn't do that because I thought it would be psychologically damaging to deaf children, since it would give the false impression that deaf people can learn to speak overnight if only they try hard enough. I explained this to my agent, and when she called back she said, "You're a lucky bastard. They think you're right and would like to work with you on how to change the story," I was so excited, because finally somebody was willing to listen.

My idea was that my character use telepathic powers to communicate with my chorus. I played the role of a diplomat based on Henry Kissinger—pompous and egomaniacal. When I was in the middle of negotiating, the chorus got killed. I had to teach other characters sign language to communicate. We weren't able to develop that fully, but I was pretty satisfied with how far we went from where we started.

On "The Equalizer," I played an angry young man, which is nothing unusual—I find myself having to play that most of the time. I accepted the role and then learned that my fiancée in the show would be a deaf girl, played by a hearing actress. I told my New York agent I couldn't do that, but he said the casting was already set. I thought about it for several days and talked to people whose opinions I especially respect, and I decided that it was better for me to do it. If I didn't, the role might go to a hearing actor, or to a deaf actor whom I might resent for not having the guts to make the same decision I had. If I took the role, I could move one step forward in my career and maybe one day be far enough along to say, "Don't do this. We need to have deaf actors in deaf roles." It made more sense to me to go there and fight the battle *in* the system, and I'm glad I did. The producers were ready to hire hearing actors who knew sign language as deaf extras so they wouldn't have to pay for interpreters, and because they would be easier to work with. I objected, and they found deaf actors for those extras and for a small deaf role, so I had modest victories here and there.

I had several scenes with the Equalizer, Edward Woodward, including my character's wedding. A hearing actor signed and spoke the role of the priest for the wedding vows. I kissed my bride, and we turned around and the deaf extras playing wedding guests waved their hands in the air. The director blew his cool and shouted, "What are you people doing?" Someone explained to him that what we call the "deaf wave" was how deaf people showed their appreciation—we don't hear applause, we see hands waving. There was a conference and they decided to leave the waving in. Edward Woodward picked up on that, and from time to time when we finished a scene and something had gone particularly well, he would wave his hands in the air to me. I really appreciated that. Then one day, we all worked very hard on a fight between me and the bad guys. At the end of shooting, I looked up and all the guys on the crew were doing the deaf wave. I felt that I had had some impact on these people. Some of them might become directors or producers who remember working with deaf actors.

Of course I would like the money I could make in Hollywood. I don't really want the fame, because it's a hassle to deal with—though I could use fame to accomplish what I would like to do in the deaf community and for deaf children.

I would love to set up a deaf art camp, where the children would have deaf teachers as role models—but we'll get that done somehow anyway. If I could do anything I liked and money was no problem, I would start a deaf theatre company and hire all my friends—I'm often very lonely in hearing theatre, even when I have an interpreter. I would like to work in my own company, but at the same time I would like to continue to work in the hearing theatre, because there is just so much to take advantage of there. I don't want to do plays about the deaf experience only—that's limiting, boring. I *do* want to express my feelings about it, but not all the time.

I would like to do Macbeth, Othello—the whole range of human nature. Because there are so many mystical elements involved, a deaf actor could be *very* powerful as Macbeth.

There is, in deaf individuals, a deep hunger to express ourselves, to communicate with others. When this emotional power is tapped, the result is dynamic theatre.

The Tempest *(Guthrie Theater)*

Frances Conroy usually looks as if she just stepped out of a Botticelli painting, but she first bewitched New York audiences as a black-bewigged, Sophia Loren-ish Diana in All's Well that Ends Well. *She followed that 1979 New York Shakespeare Festival Central Park production the next summer with a regally delicate Desdemona to Raul Julia's Othello. A Juilliard graduate and veteran or, as she explains, survivor of two seasons of touring with* The Acting Company, *she has proven equally accomplished at playing aristocratic ladies, sensual women, the homespun Mrs. Gibbs in* Our Town, *wives driven to various stages of loopiness by inconstant husbands, and the astringent British politician in* The Secret Rapture, *for which she won a Drama Desk Award.*

I toured for two seasons, and it was hard. When I was asked to join the Acting Company after I finished Juilliard, I didn't know whether I could stand being uprooted like that. I like to travel, but travel's different from touring. On tour you don't have a home for months.

Wild things happen on tour—eccentric habits grow in a group that's become inbred from being on a bus all the time. Brooks Baldwin, a member of the company, convinced everyone to take up Transcendental Meditation and to use Erno Laslo face cleanser. He would be a millionaire if he had gotten a commission from Laslo and the TM people.

We took a crash course in TM in Evanston, Illinois, where we were playing the Ravinia Festival. Then we proceeded to do it on the bus. Everybody sat with eyes closed and palms up, zonked-out meditating, wearing whiteface cleanser. After twenty minutes, you felt you had gone into a coma, because you knew you were going to be on the bus for another six hours. It was like a traveling asylum.

Mary Lou Rosato, our Mother Courage, and David Schramm, our King Lear, had been touring with the company for six years. I don't know how they got through it. Everybody did crazy things to keep their sanity. One actress set out to shock the stage manager by opening her hotel-room door in her dishabille.

We usually stayed in motels or in university housing. The Acting Company really made an effort to make sure we were okay. The directors—John Houseman, Alan Schneider and Margot Harley—would come out to see that we were all right. We would travel four or five months, come back to New York and have three weeks to a month off, then rehearse another play and go on the road with that.

The first season I was in the company, I took over the role of Prudence Duvernoy in Tennessee Williams' *Camino Real*. She's an old woman, and I wore a beautiful, moth-like dress I think Vivian Leigh had worn in *A Streetcar Named Desire*. I also played Kattrin in Alan Schneider's production of *Mother Courage* and Cordelia in John Houseman's *King Lear*. Then, in the middle of the year, we started rehearsing George Abbott's *Broadway*. I played Pearl, one of the chorines, which was nice because it was so different from the other parts.

The second season I played Lady Capulet in *Romeo and Juliet* and—when John gave me the choice of playing Antigone or Saint Joan—the title role in Anouilh's *Antigone*. We also did Elinor Jones' *The Other Half*, about women writers, in which I played Mary Shelley, Charlotte Bronte and Virginia Woolf, among others. It was written for the Acting Company and performed Off Broadway on Theatre Row at the end of the tour.

The company really taught you to take care of your voice and not to be an idiot about keeping yourself well. There are foolish things you can do to wreck any performance, but when you're touring you really can't stay up all night partying. You've got to keep on an even keel, because you know you're in a three-hundred seat house tonight and you may play a *nine*-hundred seat house tomorrow night, and you've never seen either before.

People took turns leading the group warm-up every night, to get the kinks out of our bodies and to bring everybody together before the performance. You have to do some sort of warm-up, if only to center yourself, before going out on stage.

What I do depends on the kind of play and the size theatre I'm working in. You have to exercise your mouth—your tongue, your lips—so that you can speak and articulate. You have to get your mouth moving, particularly if you haven't talked all day long.

Lying on your back, relaxing your breathing, feeling where your breathing's coming from, feeling your ribs, your diaphragm, doing nasal warm-ups—these are all things I learned from Liz Smith, Robert Williams or Edith Skinner at Juilliard or from somebody in the Acting Company. Then there's stretching, perhaps doing some yoga to loosen up. One actor on the tour ran every day to pump himself up for performance. I don't know how you can just dash on and perform. You've got so much mishegaas from the day, you've got to get rid of it.

Doing the plays on tour was good because they were rotated. It was challenging going from Cordelia to Kattrin, for example, because Kattrin can't talk.

Touring with the company was a large, demanding experience. I hated being on a bus all the time, but doing shows over and over gave me the ability to perform in any space without fear.

I met my first husband, Jonathan Furst, during the second year of the tour. He had received an NEA director's grant and he assisted Alan and John on their productions, directed his own as well, and was director-on-the-road, keeping the shows in shape. We married two years later.

I have pleasant memories of doing school plays when I was little, although I was heartbroken in kindergarten when I came down with mumps and couldn't play the ass in the Christmas pageant. My close friend Peter Harris began a drama program in our high school, and we did some very adventurous productions, including *Our Town*, in which I played Emily. We lived on Long Island, and Peter and I would go to the Neighborhood Playhouse on Saturdays.

I loved languages and thought maybe I'd become an interpreter. I graduated from high school a year early and went to Dickinson College in Pennsylvania, a liberal arts school with an excellent language program. David and Marjorie Brubaker, who ran the theatre department, put on plays by Molière, Ostrovsky, John Arden—serious productions with some extremely gifted students. Getting involved with their productions was a wonderful further opening into drama for me.

I felt very mixed up about what I wanted to do, and left Dickinson after two years. Finding out about Juilliard from my friend Peter Harris, who was going there, I auditioned once and wasn't accepted. I worked at the Museum of Modern Art, in the gift shop and briefly as receptionist on the film department floor. I met Peter's classmates—Mandy Patinkin, William Hurt—and got to see the school a bit through their eyes. I tried out a second time and got in, auditioning with Sonia's final speech in *Uncle Vanya* and a passage from *Phaedra*.

I was at Juilliard from 1973 to 1977. There were students in my class fresh out of high school, a girl who was only fifteen years old, and a man who had been pre-med and had a master's degree. It was a mixed class that happened to have good chemistry. Our class wasn't undermined as some others were by antagonism between students or by people not liking the school. We were considered the Golden Class, after the very first one that had included Patti LuPone, Kevin Kline, David Ogden Stiers, David Schramm and Mary Lou Rosato.

Going to a school that has the extensive training of a Juilliard is a tremendous help to a young actor. Most of the people there to teach you, to critique you and to direct you, are actively involved in the theatre. At some point you will meet them again—chances are you'll work with them or you'll work with others through their recommendations. That helps, because it's a terribly difficult business.

Juilliard's a hard school. You give yourself over to it completely. If you don't, you're unhappy and you stay—or you're unhappy and you leave.

It's a full day. You take dance, voice, speech, text analysis and acting class. Classes in dramatic literature were given by professors like Maurice Valency, the translator of Anouilh and Girardoux.

In the second year, you're doing a lot of scene work and you start mounting plays on a simple scale. The third and fourth years you're having a more layered experience of doing plays, adding things like costumes to the basics of acting and speech work.

After training at a school like Juilliard, you feel comfortable working on classical and on new plays because they teach how to work on character. Over and over and over again, you work on scenes, you work on movement, you work on text, you work on roles. You're creating characters all the time.

We were exposed to Juilliard's dance, opera and music programs. We were right at Lincoln Center, so there was an opportunity to attend performances there. We had an improvisational music class, and several dance classes a week. Anna Sokolow, a great artist, taught a class and choreographed a piece with the group. In these various ways we encountered different art forms.

The costume designer Jane Greenwood came in and taught us things like how to move in a hoop skirt. She'd take us off to costume exhibits at the Metropolitan or Brooklyn Museum, and make it pleasurable by the way she talked about history and what people wore. There are certain truths of a period that are dictated by clothes.

We also took period movement—how to handle a fan in Restoration comedy, for example. That training is invaluable. You can't just schlump around in a classical play.

John Houseman, padding around Juilliard in his Wallabees, may have seemed aloof to strangers, but he loved the students. He was very shy, and he was very sweet to me. I did Nina in *The Seagull* at the end of my second year, and he said the fourth act was quite wonderful but that I was playing the end of the play at the beginning and needed to work on the first part. Whenever he gave you a comment, it was always couched in a loving, helpful tone.

Alan Schneider succeeded John Houseman as head of the drama department my last year at Juilliard, and he directed me as Antigone and Kattrin for the Acting Company. Both Alan and John meant a tremendous amount to me.

Kattrin was particularly interesting to work on. Her means of expression comes through attempting to speak, but she never gets to the point where she can be understood. I played with where the sound is located when it doesn't come out in articulated words—"uh, uh, uh" . . . it's somewhere in your throat. She had been raped, and I asked myself how that affected the way she moved. They built a padded suit for me to wear, so I was a little fat and I was aware of that as I moved. I felt like a lump on the earth. Also the clothes were so rough-hewn I felt I had had them on all my life. There were lots of senses to work with to reach who Kattrin was.

Marian Seldes is a great teacher. She taught an acting class at Juilliard and directed us in *Romeo and Juliet*, our very first production in the school. She loves young people. She was and is a tremendous inspiration to me, and I think to a lot of others. She is a brilliant woman and totally devoted to the theatre.

She has the utmost respect for the craft. She doesn't get sick. She's never missed a performance. She sees every play that's running.

Marian's father, Gilbert Seldes, was a great man of the theatre himself. Her uncle, George Seldes, was a newspaperman who knew Hitler, Mussolini, Stalin, Lenin, Trotsky—you name them, he knew them. Marian gave me a book he wrote at the age of 97 called *Witness to a Century*. There is a passion I believe runs in her family—to be involved in something one hundred percent—and she passes that on to her students.

Once I was doing a scene with another actress from a play about Mary, Queen of Scots, and Elizabeth I. We did it once, and then Marian took her fur coat and threw it around my shoulders, which had quite an effect on me as Elizabeth. That was a great, nonverbal, sensory help. She would offer the simplest suggestion in your ear—she would never embarrass anyone, never cut anyone down in class. Students are in an awfully vulnerable position, and she was only there to inspire, to nurture.

I have had the great privilege of acting with Marian on two occasions—in the original production of *Painting Churches* and in *A Bright Room Called Day* at the Public Theatre.

Frances Conroy and
Mary Lou Rosato in
Mother Courage
(The Acting Company)

Through Juilliard I met a lot of people in the business. People I wasn't even aware of saw or heard of me as I went through the school. That kind of exposure always helps.

I worked for the New York Shakespeare Festival in Central Park the summer after my third year in school, in a nonspeaking role in *Measure for Measure*, with John Cazale, Meryl Streep and Sam Waterston. In 1978, Rosemarie Tichler, then the Festival's casting director, had me audition for Wilford Leach, who was to direct *All's Well that Ends Well*, also in the Park, and he chose me to play the part of Diana, which was great fun. The scene I had with Mark Linn Baker, who played Bertram, ended up in the opening montage of Woody Allen's film *Manhattan*.

I have had some lovely experiences in the theatre. One was playing Desdemona in the Park, with Raul Julia as Othello and Richard

Dreyfuss as Iago, the summer after I had done *All's Well* and had finished touring with the Acting Company. I believe Meryl Streep was going to do the role but she became pregnant. Wilford Leach was the director.

Raul and Richard were very sweet to work with. Being in a New York Shakespeare Festival production that was so loved by everyone working on it—in that fairy-tale setting of Central Park—was an experience I shall always cherish.

One very special experience in playing the classics was going to the Guthrie in their 1981-82 season to play Miranda in *The Tempest* for Liviu Ciulei and Doña Elvira in Molière's *Don Juan* for Richard Foreman. My agents wanted me to stay in New York, but I didn't want to miss the opportunity of working on such great roles in that wonderful theatre, with two brilliant directors.

You hope that everything you do is going to bring something new out of you, and working with those two men was both exacting and rewarding. There was a total of eight weeks of simultaneous rehearsal on the two plays. We'd go from one to the other, the rehearsal processes reflecting the specific nature of each director's vision.

Liviu had done *The Tempest* in Romania and had a blueprint in his head of how he wanted the play. He wanted the actors to make very specific choices that had worked in the previous production. That was a real challenge.

Liviu's interpretation was brilliant. The set was akin to a study that a scientist like Einstein would have had. Ken Ruta, who was Prospero, was dressed à la Einstein in a cardigan sweater and glasses. Books were everywhere, and a moat of red liquid looking like blood ran around the stage, with a knight in armor, books, weapons, pieces of stairways in it. It was the debris of Western civilization and was stunning to look at. In the center, upstage, was a doorway, with about five steps going up to it. When the door opened there was a picture of a paradise that lit up, as if that's what this island looked like, this kingdom where we lived.

I came bursting out of the door in the beginning and told of the shipwreck. That first speech of Miranda's is very difficult, and Liviu from day one wanted me to run down the stairs and stop at a certain point. I was to do it that same way every time. I wasn't going to do it halfway, I wasn't going to sort of inch my way downstage—it had to be done *that way*, that committed, every time we went through it.

That's not how a lot of actors work, and some of the cast were angry. They thought they were being pushed artificially into something that they didn't necessarily believe in. They hadn't found it in their own ways.

You do somehow have to find for yourself what the director wants. In *The Tempest*, you had to go and stand in the footsteps Liviu gave you. If you had difficulty, you just had to commit to what he wanted you to do and then translate, make equivalents for yourself, like you would do with anything you'd find on your own.

Why would *I* come running out, screaming about the shipwreck? Why would *I* act with Ferdinand the way Liviu had us, looking into the water, seeing our reflections during the scene where we fall in love?

What he had us do was so beautiful. Boyd Gaines was Ferdinand. We had known each other at Juilliard, and it was sweet to be his girlfriend in the play.

Richard Foreman, on the other hand, has his own kind of blueprint, but he changes it constantly. There was an improvisatory feeling during the early stages of rehearsal, to see what worked. I had a whip, and I'd whip myself. At one point I decided that Doña Elvira seemed so childish that I gave her a regressive way of talking: "I'm wather angwy at you."

I thought Richard Foreman was so mysterious and exotic, because he's a very private person and yet impassioned about his work. He was emphatic as to what he wanted, but he was also quite fatherly when he would talk to you about it.

Rehearsing with both directors in one day just left your head spinning.

I have worked three times at Lincoln Center under Gregory Mosher's artistic direction. He worked miracles for Lincoln Center—he revitalized a dying theatre with provocative, diverse productions and made a family out of the organization for anyone fortunate enough to work there.

I was in Gregory's production of *Our Town*, and rehearsals were wonderful because he made them a time of active searching. Roberta Maxwell as Mrs. Webb and I as Mrs. Gibbs had to mime a lot of household tasks in the play, and Gregory would say, "Okay, now Roberta, go up and mime your house for a couple of minutes, and everybody's going to watch you. And now Franny, you go up and mime your house a few minutes and everybody's going to watch *you*." We had a number of sessions doing that, so we could become comfortable in the household scenes. His direction of *Our Town* was very fine indeed.

Richard Nelson's play, *Some Americans Abroad*, was lovely to work on because it was such a subtle piece. So much that was never said in the text was simmering right underneath the lines. It was a Chekhovian comedy that became quite serious at times.

The play is about a group of American academics on a theatre tour of London and Stratford. I played Frankie Lewis, a married professor having an affair with a colleague, played by John Bedford Lloyd. Colin Stinton played our department chairman. There was a scene in the Pizza Hut in Stratford where Frankie doesn't know if the chairman has found out about the affair. He and I are sitting at a table with pieces of pizza and glasses of wine, and I just can't deal with his questions, so I eat or drink to avoid answering. When my lover comes in, I realize that the chairman knows about us and the bottom of my life drops out. My lover takes the rest of my pizza and eats it in silence, and takes my glass of wine and drinks the rest. The chairman has his head in his hands because he doesn't know what to say: it was a moment of truth, and Richard put in these simple things of wine and pizza at this little table, late at night, with everyone exhausted and nerves frazzled, with things that should never be known coming out in the open. That happens in life.

You can invest your most private life-experiences into a character to bring that character to life. You're expressing intimate thoughts, clothed in the words of the play. For Frankie, I would think, "What kind of a dangerous situation have I been in that I can make the equivalent to this? What have I thought or done that I would have *died* if anybody had found out about, and how can I put that in this? Whom have I adored to the point of giving up everything and how have I

acted, how have I laughed around him?" I just keep putting those
experiences into the character and situation, and it all starts adding up
so that one becomes the other . . . and in the end it's the character and
the play.

Combining a text that is so psychologically subtle and so technically
demanding just in terms of props can be hazardous. I remember one or
two nights I choked on the pizza, and once I hit the glass of wine with
the carafe and knocked the wine—which was grape juice—all over
the table. But we kept talking.

In Richard Nelson's *Two Shakespearean Actors*, I played Catherine
Forrest, wife of Ned Forrest (played by Victor Garber), who was a
superstar of his time, the mid-1800s. In two telling scenes, the troubled
state of their marriage was revealed in all its dimensions. My time
onstage was brief, but my character was rich indeed through Richard's
eloquent writing.

It was an extraordinary experience playing three such diverse roles,
all for Lincoln Center.

Another experience working with a remarkable director was doing
Ivanov at Yale in the fall of 1990. I played Ivanov's wife Anna
Petrovna. I hadn't worked at Yale since *Tartuffe* in 1983, and I liked
the idea of going up there again. I hadn't done Chekhov since being in
Andrei Serban's *Uncle Vanya* at La MaMa, with that memorable
cast—Joseph Chaikin, F. Murray Abraham, Diane Venora, to name
only a few.

The director, Oleg Yefremov, is the head of the Moscow Art Theatre
and speaks no English. Oleg was fascinating to watch; he's so elegant
and impassioned and has great beautiful eyes. He would be talking in
Russian and you'd just be staring at him, not knowing what he was
saying. Then his translator, Victor Steinbach, would translate, and you
wouldn't know whether to nod at Victor or Oleg, and so the day would
go. Bill Hurt, who was playing Ivanov, would bring up questions
because he would be tormented trying to find the truth in a particular
moment, and he and Oleg would have these intense soul-searching
discussions in two languages, with Victor there to translate—a huge
task in itself.

It's exhausting to take a train to New Haven with commuters coming home from their day's work, and then go do a play. Then you have to get a train home at night, and since I live so far uptown I was getting off at the 125th Street station at one a.m. No one was there except the rats and maybe someone who was homeless. I'd get home and think, "Oh God, this is crazy, the way we live."

I've done a lot of dramatic roles and they have been wonderful to work on, but comedy is great fun to play. It gives you a different kind of feeling—I suppose because of what it gives the audience and what they give back to you. Comedy is certainly as exacting as drama. Indulgence is something more apt to survive in a drama than in a comedy. Precision is all in comedy.

I enjoyed playing Ann Whitefield in Shaw's *Man and Superman*, as well as Hesione Hushabye in *Heartbreak House*—two tremendous roles that are quite difficult but fantastic to play. Once within your grasp, you would soar with the music Shaw wrote for these wondrous characters.

Rehearsing intimate moments can be awkward at first, especially when others are watching. Olek Krupa and I kissed in two scenes in *A Bright Room Called Day* at the Public, and we had only just met but were lovers in the play.

In David Hare's play, *The Secret Rapture*, the kiss that Steve Vinovich and I shared at the very end fell prey to convulsions of laughter on my part until it was incorporated into the emotion of the moment and filled with all that had led up to it. In rehearsal, David Hare would say, "We've lost Miss Conroy again."

Some people assumed that Marion French, the politician I played in *The Secret Rapture*, was modeled on the then Prime Minister, but David said that he had not written Margaret Thatcher. Rehearsals were difficult, and David, who was directing, wouldn't let me work with the British accent for a couple of weeks; he thought it was getting in my way of finding Marion's character. So we blended in the accent once she became realized.

There's always a point in rehearsals where you feel you're about to crash and get sick and your throat starts going on you—your voice, or something—and I think it must have to do with the creative process of everything not quite coming together and being in this state of turmoil. I end up taking Golden Seal capsules and tons of vitamin C and nurture my body to feeling better.

I guess we got creamed by the critics. Everybody was disturbed that the show was closing. We had put our hearts and souls into it, so it hurt a lot.

I don't know what it would have been like to be in a long run of *The Secret Rapture*. Blair Brown once said, "You can't feel comfortable in one of David's plays." It's like you're walking a razor blade the whole time, because if you relax at all it won't work.

I think critics have an important function, but I don't read them. I stopped when I was damned for following the directions of a second director who came into a production in previews, whose idea of my character and of the play in general was diametrically opposite to what had been the original director's intent. In trying to accommodate his ideas to my own, I got kicked in the teeth.

Also, if you read reviews, you've got the words of the critics dancing in your head, whatever has been written. Some actors read reviews, and then there's always a fight backstage after opening night. Some people shout, "Don't anybody talk about the reviews," and others just love to talk about them. You can tell whether the notices are good or bad, anyway, from the general atmosphere backstage after opening night and the ensuing audience response.

If a play is praised, the audience walks in quite amenable to everything. Negative notices have a strangling effect on the play, to varying degrees. You do your work and see how the night ends up. But you've still got the rehearsal period within you and, unless that was a disaster, you'll be fine simply doing the work onstage.

There is heartbreak and disappointment that everyone goes through in the theatre. A role can seem impossible to figure out; bad chemistry in a cast can jeopardize rehearsals; you can be promised a role and then have it taken away, or create a role and then be replaced in a subsequent production; or you can be fired. It can happen, and you keep going.

It's difficult to support yourself in the theatre a lot of the time. If you're in a show on Broadway or pick up some film or television work, or score a commercial or voice-over, it makes things easier. Theatre is an endangered species, and more often than not the economics of being in a play are definitely not to the actor's advantage.

Aside from that, theatre leaves time for doing many other things. I go swimming, or sometimes paint, or go to museums. Living in New York City, you have the world at your feet. One summer I spent quite a bit of time at the Museum of Modern Art, seeing films and going to the garden concerts.

Los Angeles is wonderful as well. I felt like Alice in Wonderland when I first arrived there, stumbling upon the performance art and theatre scenes. My present husband, Jan Munroe, wrote and performed in many witty, concise, beautifully crafted pieces, unlike anything I had ever seen before. He and a core of other artists created a body of splendid work that I was fortunate enough to be introduced to.

I have worked on a number of plays there, in various stages of development. The Mark Taper Forum is where *Romance Language* was performed after being at Playwrights Horizons. *Mrs. California* was part of the New Play Festival there, and did so well it moved to the Coronet Theatre on La Cienega for a long run. It was about one of the homemaking contests of the 1950s, and gave a funny, revealing look at women's place in the home, and in society in general, from a feminist standpoint.

South Coast Repertory is where *Heartbreak House* was produced, and I very much enjoyed working at that theatre as well.

I've never had a picture of the career I was going to have. Some people do. But I've always seen an experience as it's come along, and gone through it, not knowing what will come next.

The future's interesting to look forward to, because it's an open slate.

Fool for Love
(Trinity Repertory Company)

Even before he began playing featured roles in films like Sea of Love *and* The Witches of Eastwick, *Richard Jenkins had earned a reputation as an extraordinary actor. On a 1980 visit to Rhode Island, Los Angeles Times critic Dan Sullivan saw a Russian play called* The Suicide *at Trinity Rep. "Twenty minutes into the piece, I got this prickly feeling: 'This is a masterpiece,'" Sullivan recalls. "Richard Jenkins played the lead, and he was superb. I wrote a rave review, and I'm told that on the basis of my review, someone decided to produce the play on Broadway. The producer hired the Trinity director but replaced Richard Jenkins with a British star. The result was terrible. I've seen several productions of* The Suicide, *and no actor has ever come near Richard Jenkins. It's a crime that an actor has to appear in New York to receive national acclaim."*

In 1990 Richard Jenkins turned his attention to nurturing other actors, taking over as artistic director of Trinity Rep. We sat in the auditorium there and talked over a February weekend in 1991.

When I started out, I was so vague about who I was as an actor that I didn't know what I was doing. I think I bought into the whole work ethic—that if I was sweating by the end of a performance,

I must have been good. I had some natural ability onstage, but I was boring myself, and naturally the audience wasn't too thrilled with me.

I was always trying to be like other people. I loved Jason Robards, and I would find myself trying to sound like him, and then realize that this wasn't the way to go. I emulated other actors because in college I had gotten the idea that if you could just be like Laurence Olivier, you would be great. "Oh, his Othello! Oh, his Hamlet!" They tell you, "Learn from the greats." Well, what you learn from the greats is that they didn't try to be like anybody but themselves. It took me forever to understand what matters: what do *I* have to offer as an actor? Am *I* interesting enough for people to watch?

I got interested in theatre my first year at Illinois Wesleyan, in Bloomington, Illinois. I was from a small farm town, and I'd never followed the theatre. I went to a play—I almost hate to say it, but it was *Hamlet*—and I thought it was incredible. So I applied for and got into the School of Drama.

I sat around for a year there because I didn't know what to do—I didn't know that you had to audition for the mainstage productions; I didn't know what the hell an audition was. So at the end of the year, the head of the School of Drama called me in and said, "Who are you? I see your name is here, but I've never seen you. You've never signed up to audition, you've never been in anything. Why don't you make room for somebody who wants to participate?"

I said, "I have no idea how to do this. You never even asked me if I had a problem. I never auditioned in my life. Aren't you supposed to teach me how?" He said, "Okay. We have a summer stock company. We'll put you in some things and see how you like it. Then we'll see about next year."

That's how I started. I appeared in the chorus of musicals and did some small parts, and had a great time. As soon as I began, I knew that's what I was going to do. There was nothing else I ever excelled at.

I don't think I've ever had that much fun. There were no stakes—"If the show's a hit, we eat tonight" didn't come into it. My one regret is that I wasn't closer to New York City. I wish I had studied where the action was, because I never felt comfortable in New York. Going to a school that is close to some theatrical mecca is a nice way to introduce yourself into the atmosphere of the professional theatre.

Theatre Communications Group started around the time I graduated from college, and I auditioned for them. I didn't make it past the first round—I didn't understand what it was that TCG was doing for us. Then I went to graduate school at Indiana University, and by the time the next auditions came around I realized how important they were. I wormed my way in and I got through that time. This led to a job in Long Wharf's journeyman program. But while I was driving a laundry truck in Wisconsin to make money over the summer, Arvin Brown said that he felt awful about it, but they'd had to drop that program. I called TCG and asked if any other theatres were auditioning. They said Trinity Rep, Stage West and a couple of others, but I'd have to be in New York to read. I said I had business there anyway, and my wife Sharon and I flew to New York. I auditioned for Adrian Hall and was hired for Trinity. I was twenty-two.

I wanted to work in regional theatre. I didn't know how else to do it. I wasn't crazy about the idea of living in New York City. I was married, and I liked the community of the theatre. I liked the feeling of being in a company; I think most young actors do. I found it exciting to start as an apprentice and carry stuff and watch and learn.

I feel fortunate that I came here to Providence, because in theatre schools, you open the book and you see how the play is blocked, and how to cross downstage left, and how to counter. You see where the furniture's supposed to go, and how in a historically accurate set they always have the chairs hanging from the wall in Quaker times or whatever. It drove me nuts. I don't think that way. Adrian Hall pushed through all of that stuff. His policy was that if you didn't need it, or if it didn't help the audience, it didn't happen.

When I was rehearsing Diomedes in *Troilus and Cressida*, Eugene Lee, Trinity's resident designer, had a truck with a cab and a flatbed onstage. We acted on the back of the truck, which looked like it had been through a war. The tires were gone, it was rusted out, it looked like it had been bombed. Everything in the play was debris. Some of the characters would get in the cab and talk; it was a terrific isolated place. I remember Adrian saying, "You know, Eugene, this cab blocks my view of some of the characters." The next day, Eugene took a blowtorch and ripped off the top of the cab. Torched it right off, and there was just a metal thing sticking up. And I thought, "What's important to Adrian and Eugene is the theatrical experience, not how the set looks. If something gets in the way, you change it or get rid of it. Theatre is about solving the problems of a production. It is an alive, breathing, living deal."

Adrian focused and clarified everything for me. Theatre made sense for the first time. The theatre is not about some kind of tradition. Traditions are killers if you let them be, and that's what I'd lived by, the tradition of trying to act like somebody else.

Adrian and Eugene would do things like hang a sign around an actor's neck that said, "Woodrow Wilson. He's five years old." They didn't go out and get a little boy and dress him up like Woodrow Wilson and have him come on and have somebody say, "Oh, Woodrow, time for dinner." Adrian's point was, if the audience knows where they are, and who they are watching, that's all they need. When we did *Ethan Frome*—it was my first leading role—the door would be the door to the house, the door to the dance hall, the door to the barn. The same door was used for forty things, but as long as the audience knew where you were going, they were with you.

We didn't always stick to our principles. When I was playing Biff in *Death of a Salesman*, we came on in a blackout, and when the lights came up there was a woman standing right between us. She turned to me and said, "I really love the show but I have to go to work," and off she went. In front of four hundred people. Had we not turned the lights off and tried to sneak on to the stage, the incident would not have happened. You set yourself up for these kinds of things by lying.

One of my best experiences was playing Stephano in *The Tempest* and finding a way to make him funny. Adrian was directing, and Peter Gerety was the other clown, Trinculo, and Richard Kavanaugh was Caliban. Richard made himself about eight feet tall by wrapping stools on his feet. He did it one day in rehearsal, and it changed everything. All of the humor evolved from this eight-foot thing standing there looking at us.

In the production, the stools weren't covered to try to make Richard

look like he was really that tall, because who are you kidding? Eugene
just bolted shoes on the stools and Richard learned to walk with them.
The first time the characters met, Richard was hiding, Peter and I
were talking, Richard stood up behind us, and when we turned around
I was looking right at Caliban's crotch.

I had an acting coach at Indiana named Harold Guskin, who told me
what I needed to hear, but I didn't hear it until years later. What he
said was, "Do it. Just do it." And I couldn't. I was doing the Gentleman
Caller in a scene class, and I did my imitation of David Wayne saying,
"Hello, Laura," and Harold Guskin said, "What?" I said "Hello,
Laura," again like David Wayne, and he said, "No, no. Tell me what
you just said," and I said "Hello, Laura," in my own voice. He said,
"Oh, okay," and the light went on for me.

You gotta begin at the beginning. You can't start somewhere else.
When I did Hickey in *The Iceman Cometh*, I would never come on the
stage intending to confess to my wife's death. I would start with
opening the door. Just open the door. It's like *King Lear*—just talk to
your kids. Start there. 'Cause if you think about where you have to end
up, you'll never get there. It's so overwhelming. So you come in and
you talk to your kids, and they aggravate you, and you go from there.

It sounds like a bizarre way to approach things, but if you really do
that, you'll get places that you wouldn't dream, because that subcon-
scious mind is a lot brighter than your conscious mind. I directed
Golden Boy here this season, and the actor who played the leading role
was having trouble with the scene where he kills the fighter. He had it
figured out that he had to feel bad about killing somebody, and he put
himself through all this emotional stuff that was always hollow and
empty.

He was a hard worker. Sometimes too hard. So in a rehearsal I said to
him, "I don't want you to cry. Don't do any of that stuff." I took all the
pressure to perform off of him. And it's a scary feeling to do a scene
where you kill somebody and say to yourself, "I don't know how I feel
about this. Let's see if it really bothers me. If it doesn't bother me, it's
fine." And it bothered him in a way he never dreamed he could get to.
He just couldn't stop crying. I mean sobbing. He didn't ask me after that
scene how it was, because if you do it, you don't have to ask. You *know*.

You're your own "Acting Police." When you're asking somebody, "How was it?" what you're really saying is, "It wasn't very good, was it?"

When I was playing Hickey, I was surprised when I started laughing at something I had never found funny before, or when I was sure I was going to be moved by something and it didn't move me. If you can get to where that's fine, that's fine. You're never going to have every moment be what you want it to be on the stage. Just let it go. And go on to the next one. And so I would, and it would be a little different. On the nights when it wasn't a little different, when it was the same as the night before, it usually wasn't as good.

I remember on stage one night in *Awake and Sing*, I started to count the knots in the tablecloth. Somebody asked me a question, I turned and I answered, and all the cobwebs went away. Moments like that are the things I remember. All my life I've been told "Pay attention," and the truth is that I was right to count those damn knots.

Those moments tell you to trust yourself, trust your instincts, because they're usually right. They are going to be as right as if you sat around and thought about it for two weeks. Try not to try. Try not to control it all the time. And don't fear going too far or not far enough. Whatever happens, happens. The best piece of advice a director ever gave me was "Breathe. Just breathe."

Playing Teach in *American Buffalo* was a breakthrough for me. We did it here, and it was well received, and then we took it to the Annenberg Theatre in Philadelphia. And I felt like my performance wasn't what it should be. It was an actor acting. Peter Gerety was playing Bobby, and he is a wonderful actor; he truly is a natural actor, and lying is not part of what he does. When we got to the Annenberg, I said to Peter, "What if this play took four hours? On opening night. What if we went out there and just talked to each other? What could they do to us?" I was talking about myself, not about anyone else. What if I just went out there and took whatever was given and responded without trying to force the play in any direction? And Peter, of course, said, "That's what I do all the time." So I said to myself "Do it. Just do it. They can't kill you." Best night I ever had. It was a lesson I never will forget . . . and we took four minutes off the play. You cannot control art. For acting to be art it must be inspired. Or it's not art. It's an ongoing process, one that I try to extract from the actors I direct.

. . .

Directing was kind of pushed on me. Peter Gerety came to me and
said, "I want to do *Billy Bishop Goes to War*. Would you direct it?" and
I thought "Gee, I can get coffee and sit around and watch Peter act,
and it will be great!" Adrian had talked to me about directing, but I
hadn't done anything yet. I said to Eugene Lee, "How shall we do this?
I've never directed." It's a one-character play. The actor has a hand
mike, there's a piano player—it's like a concert piece. You could just
stand on a stage with black curtains and talk, and do this story of Billy
Bishop's life. I said, "We could maybe put an aircraft hangar behind
him, or some kind of decoration." Eugene looked at me like I was from
the moon, and said, "Let me read it." Later he came back and said,
"Let's do it in a bar. 'Cause who's he talking to? He's talking to the
audience."

George Martin (center)
and Richard Jenkins
(foreground) in The
Suicide *(Trinity Repertory*
Company)

What a lesson. We built a bar on the stage. We served drinks. There was a bartender. There was a piano player. It looked like a Veterans of Foreign Wars bar—old, smelled like beer, had popcorn. If you wanted to buy pretzels, you went up and paid for a bag of pretzels. And while people were standing at the bar having drinks, this guy came in, took his coat off and had a beer. The piano player was playing a World War I song, and he sang along.

When they finished the first song from the show, the audience kind of applauded. The guy—Peter Gerety, of course—started talking about his life. He got up on the bar and got up on the pool table, he walked around, he opened beer, he served people and sat in people's laps and he kissed guys' bald heads, and he played seventy different parts. And I'm telling you, it was an extraordinary experience. I was swept along with it. *Billy Bishop* was changed from a concert piece to theatre.

I didn't come away thinking, "Wow, what a wonderful director I am." I didn't have a lot to do with it. I just kind of didn't get in the way. But how to do it became clear to me. From that moment on, I've always tried to find a way to bring everybody who comes to the show together with the cast. It doesn't mean we always talk to the audience, or we jump in their laps—that's not what it's about. I want audiences to feel like they can't get this experience anywhere else, that this night is for them only and it'll never be the same again.

Adrian Hall taught me that you better have a point of view about what you do. And it better be yours. He also released me from the burden of feeling that I had some kind of responsibility to be historically accurate, because that would have swamped me right out of the theatre. My style of directing has just evolved. I've taken what I loved about the way Adrian worked and I've used it, and I have my own things that I do. What really interests me is the actor, 'cause I am one.

The actor and the audience are really what I see the theatre as, and I think that sometimes the more money you have, the worse shape you're in. Because you tend to decorate, and cover up. In this theatre, we never design the set before a rehearsal. I'm not interested in historical accuracy, and I'm really not interested in anything pretty.

I'm only interested in what I would consider real beauty, which is human truth.

We're doing *The School for Wives* now, and it's the second Molière I've directed here. The trick is to take any play—a new play or one that was written three hundred years ago—and find out how it relates to today. *School for Wives* was about cuckolding in Molière's time, but what's interesting now is the way Agnes is treated, and how she deals with that. You see in this production that she deals with it in a way that truly changes her.

They always talk about the dark side of Molière—gimme a break. The only reason this guy got his plays done was he made them hysterically funny. He made the king laugh. He made the people laugh. Anybody can make it dark and mean. We're doing Molière— we're using the Richard Wilbur translation, and the costumes and set are basically of the period—but we're doing it today, for this audience.

The mural on our set is not finished, intentionally. They were painting it and I said, "Why don't we leave that? It looks like he never finished it. It looks like Arnolphe's life: it's never quite together. It's never done." You look through the door to Arnolphe's house and you see furniture stacked up. It says more to me than if I saw a pretty little picture and a little table inside. It says chaos, it says it would be interesting to go into that house. It's not decoration. What people understand as being beautiful, symmetrical and color-coordinated . . . ugh. I don't know why, it aggravates me. I love Arnolphe's costume because it's so ugly. That's a bad-looking suit. But it looks like something in which he had *tried* to look good.

Tim Crowe as Arnolphe sits on the steps next to someone in the audience and tells him his problems. The audience loves it. People have offered Tim various things. Sometimes when he is sweating they give him a handkerchief. I like him to go back to the person he went to in the first act, and the other night the guy saw Tim coming, and he gestured for him to sit down so Tim could confide in him. It was fabulous. To do *School for Wives* and have people laugh at the same things they laughed at—maybe for different reasons—hundreds of years ago, is really exciting.

·   ·   ·

You should have seen the *Christmas Carol* we did this year. That old warhorse, everyone puts it on to make money, right? Well, Adrian came back and directed it and redid the whole thing. He had Jonathan Fried as a kind of Charles Dickens narrator, taking us through the play. Adrian rethought everything. It was just wonderful, and I appreciate that so much, and the audience appreciates that. What you're saying is, "We're not just putting *Christmas Carol* up again. We want to look at it again, and we want you to look at it again."

I think that Adrian's directing style evolved partly because of a program Trinity has called Project Discovery. Adrian was doing theatre like everybody else, and then we started giving performances for high school students and they were bored shitless. Something was not connecting, so Adrian started to make the students understand that the actors knew that they were there, and that they were in this together. He tried to keep the students on their toes, and I think his style evolved more through them than through the adult audiences. The students' feelings are right on the edge, and you know exactly where you stand with them. The theatre is for everybody, and if high school audiences can't deal with it, then probably you're doing something wrong.

I love to get people who are not theatregoers here. I love when they come to the theatre and see what they've been missing. I believe if I get you here, I'll get you back. Unless it's dead on the stage, it's irresistible. We built a house this year, and I forced my contractor to come. He'd lived in this state all his life and had never seen anything here. I sat him in the front row for *Golden Boy*. After it was over he said, "What's next?" I said, "I got you, I got you!"

I like to feel at home with the people I'm acting with. Regionally, in a company, you start with no baggage. You don't have to tiptoe around. The director knows the way you work. You know the way other actors work. You can get right to it. And you feel like you're performing for friends.

It's nice for an audience to see actors do lots of things. That's the fun of it all. I love it when an audience is surprised by an actor. "I didn't know you could do that!" Or, sometimes, that you *can't* do that. You can be really bad sometimes, but they're forgiving.

As an actor, you just have to take care of your own role. If you're onstage with somebody and you're thinking, "Gee, he's not very good," then how good can *you* be? The "If he would only do that, then I could be good" syndrome shifts responsibility from yourself to someone else. I don't sit and whine when actors are different than I expect them to be and think, "No, no, don't be that way. Be the way I want you to be," and try to compensate for their not being "right" by acting twice as hard.

As a director, I constantly cast against type, because I've learned that *I* was cast against type. Adrian used to say, "Do this part, it's good for you." I didn't know what he meant. But I do now. I know we all have our limitations, but they're not as great as the commercial world would have us believe. There's always somebody taller, somebody who looks better, somebody who is thinner or fatter, so you're never gonna be the right person for a role except in regional theatre, where you make do with what you have. In a company, what becomes important is acting, not types.

A lot of the training these days seems to be technical, it seems all kind of structured and fascist. It's taken the actors' responsibility away from them and put it on the director. Actors become tools for a director, and they don't have an artistic voice. A lot of new people sing, jump, roll around on the ground, and it has nothing to do with true exploring of yourself. It has to do with being malleable and doing what a director asks you to, as opposed to finding your own way. It's boring and it's dead for me. It doesn't say anything.

The voice and the body are tools, but we all have them. And we all can do amazing things with our voice when the emotion lets us. I would rather hear somebody who talks through his sinuses and has truth in his voice than somebody who has the most wonderful voice in the world. Talking about the voice and the body excludes people because they're told that if they don't have wonderful voices with great range, and beautiful bodies, they can't be actors.

What makes an actor is inside. I've seen it proven time and time again. I mean, think of the people who have moved you—is it because their voice was wonderful? No. Think of Dustin Hoffman. Think of Charlie Chaplin. If you weigh 350 pounds and you're not graceful and you'll never be able to dance or fence, does that mean you can't be an actor? Because you cannot move or your voice squeaks? It has nothing to do with it.

It took me a long time to feel comfortable with auditions. For someone like me, regional theatre is wonderful—I'm just not a very impressive person. They don't go "Whoa!" when I walk into a room.

When I had been at Trinity a while, I decided to check out Hollywood, and I had no luck, no success. I was there for about five months in the mid-seventies, on my own, and it was the most depressing time of my life. I didn't know anybody. I talked to gas-station attendants. Nobody else would talk to me. It was horrible. And I said, "I'll never come back here without a job."

I returned to Trinity and worked for eight or nine seasons, and when I jobbed out to do Philip Barry's *Holiday* at Long Wharf, a manager named Bill Treusch saw me and asked if I was interested in doing films. I said, "I want to do movies but I don't live in New York. My kids are in school in Rhode Island." And he said "Fine. I don't care where you live as long as you're willing to come into the city." I said okay, and Bill became my manager about six, seven years ago.

My first movie with Bill was *On Valentine's Day*, and I had a small part in *Silverado*, and a very nice part in *The Witches of Eastwick*. In *Sea of Love*, I played Al Pacino's partner, who is married to his ex-wife. Maybe my favorite so far is *On Valentine's Day*. I played the town drunk, and Horton Foote is a wonderful writer—a wonderful man—and it was a great experience. It was one of those parts that I absolutely loved from the day I read it.

I really don't see a difference between acting in films and on stage. Acting is acting, but it's just tough to make a living on the stage. About seven years ago I left regional theatre to make money doing films and television. I'm not saying that I made some noble sacrifice for my family in giving up acting in the theatre—that's hooey. I love doing films, it was an ambition that had gotten pushed back because of that early failure in Hollywood.

I was at Trinity as an actor for fourteen years. (My wife Sharon is a dancer and choreographer who has done the choreography here. Adrian loves Sharon—she really will take what's given her and make something out of it that is always surprising and inventive and helpful for what's going on in the play.) You can live, working in the theatre, if you're in a company. You just can't stop working in the theatre, that's the problem. You stop for a summer, then you're broke. You can't get ahead.

We have a daughter who's now fifteen, and a son who is five. And we lived week to week. We lived hand to mouth. That's okay when you're young and there are just the two of you, but it's not okay when you have kids. My dream would be that actors could make a life here and not have to worry about making a living every week.

I see times changing and I resist it. I think that comes with getting older. That's why your grandfather is saying, "These damn kids today." What I know is from the Sixties. I'm younger than Adrian and my perspective is a little different. He revolted against tradition and even the text for many years because everything was so rigid. We did some terrific stuff, some that was really scary. The way we did the plays wasn't as important as what they were saying. But now the way that we *do* things is what interests me. I'm trying to find a way to make this experience for an audience extraordinary and different and new. So you can give me almost anything to direct and I'd be interested to see if I could do it.

The older I get, the more I like a story. I sound like an old fart, I know. When we start to put an idea on the stage, and it's not hung on anything, I find it harder and harder to go with it.

August Wilson is a wonderful storyteller. I was acting at the O'Neill Center when he was doing *Ma Rainey's Black Bottom*. I walked into a rehearsal one day, and Roc Dutton was doing his part, and I sat there and couldn't believe what I was seeing. I said to August, "Do you write any plays for white people?" He said, "You got enough."

I loved the O'Neill because it's full of actors. They're the most fun to be with. What I enjoy are actors who are willing to take a journey. That's almost what talent is—the willingness to try it. For some it's easier than for others. Some are born with that little thing in their brain that says, "That's a lie, don't do it." The rest of us have to learn.

ISABELL MONK

Agamemnon *and* Electra
(Guthrie Theater)

If Andrei Serban's Fragments of a Greek Trilogy *at La MaMa was the most exhilarating production of the Greek classics in my 1970s theatre-going, its counterpart in the 1980s was Lee Breuer's* The Gospel at Colonus *at the Brooklyn Academy of Music, in which Isabell Monk played Breuer's Antigone. She has received two Obies for appearances in productions by Breuer, a director with whom she first worked while a student at the Yale School of Drama.*

The tale of how Monk came to Yale might serve as inspiration for other aspirants to conservatory training programs: rejected in her first attempt to get into the school, Monk literally walked through a blizzard from the taxi-less New Haven railroad station for her second audition, only to arrive and find that auditions had been cancelled by the weather. Faculty members were summoned and the second audition was a success, but Monk's letter of acceptance went astray. She called the school to ask how she had fared the day before they were going to give her place to someone else because she hadn't answered their letter. "God must have meant me to go there," she says.

Having settled in Minneapolis—a city not unknown for its blizzards —Isabell Monk met me in the greenroom at the Guthrie Theater in July of 1991.

W hen I got to the Guthrie in April of 1989, to play the nurse Marina in *Uncle Vanya*, Garland Wright asked, "Where are you going to buy your house?" And I said, "Wait, wait, wait, wait, wait. What are you talking about?" He said, "I'm starting this resident company and I'd like you to be a part of it." Well, I thought about that for about two months, got up one morning and bought a car, came to the theatre and said, "I'll be here." Now I have a car, a house with a thirty-year mortgage and two dogs.

I went to graduate school because I always wanted to do repertory theatre. I wanted to be a stage actress, and for the life of me I couldn't figure out why people wanted to go to Broadway. I've been there twice and it was the biggest pain in the butt. Everything is on the line every second—it's so rigid and scary. You can't do *work* on Broadway. There's just too much pressure, and for what? It's a play, for God's sake. But it ends up being about someone's money, and you can't tamper with those bucks. In nonprofit theatre, you can take larger risks and you have a bigger playing field. It seems much more productive.

Being in a production of *Marat/Sade* at Towson State University was what got me hooked on theatre. It was the first time I'd ever merged character with self. I played the inmate who has the mad-animal speech, and the director, Paul Berman, gave me one little thing to think about as I was saying the lines: he said to think of walking across babies' bones—to really envision it. And I was a mess. After that, I thought he was God.

He *is* a deity of sorts. From about a seven-year period, when Paul was chairman of the drama department, came Roc Dutton, Dwight Schultz, Marcel Rosenblat, Ann McDonough; Sheila Keogh, who was the costume designer for "Saturday Night Live" for a long time; the director Gordon Gray; the designer Stephen Strawbridge; and Rosario Provenza, who is the artistic director of the New Mexico Rep. Roc, Marcel, Steve, Gordon and I all got into Yale Drama School.

I think Paul Berman is responsible for a lot of us loving the theatre, because he lived it. He lived for the thrill and the joy of waking people up. He is the reason why I'm an actress. Although I did maybe two plays in high school, I was going to be a teacher—which is what my mother wanted me to be—until Paul Berman got hold of me.

I'm from a tightly knit family in Maryland. From my house, you could spit in my uncle's door. There were nine kids in that house, me in my house, two other cousins at the top of the little circle, and my grandmother's house. My mom was the youngest of nine, so her house was right next door to my grandmother's. I was an only child probably because my mother was diabetic. She died at thirty-six, during my freshman year at Towson.

The next year, when I was a sophomore, I decided that life is too short to do what other people—even your dead sainted mother—want you to. So I took an acting class, and I was smitten, even though I was very shut off. You know how touchy-feely those acting classes are? I thought that was the biggest load of crap I'd ever seen. I guess I thought it was phony. I didn't talk for four years, and I couldn't stand to be touched. I think my feelings didn't have anything to do with other people. I felt unworthy or untouchable because I was always overweight.

I go from being anorexic to being huge. I weighed like three hundred pounds when I went to college . . . but the people in the drama department were all so friendly, it didn't matter to them—they respected you for what you could do, and your commitment to the work. And we did everything. I remember just living at that theatre. We did all the crews, and we rehearsed and rehearsed, even all night, and it was just great.

Paul Berman also brought in wonderful teachers. A Japanese Kabuki teacher said one thing I think I'll remember forever: "Acting is like wearing a big kimono that has lots of pockets in the sleeves. You try to live your life as fully as possible and store up all the little incidents and experiences, so that when you are on the stage you can pull from them."

The first time I applied to Yale Drama School I wasn't accepted. I then became part of a program sponsored by the State of Maryland called R.C.E.D.A.—Regional, Cultural and Educational Development Association. We toured schools in Maryland doing commedia pieces. We put up the set, did the play, took the set down, went to the next school.

The next year, they were disbanding the company and we had to come up with things like one-person shows. Gordon Gray and I got together and wrote this piece called *We Ain't What We Was*. It was basically a black history lesson in which I played a 300-year-old woman. She would go into trances, or little things that she would pull out of her bag would take her back, which led to my playing six characters. I had a couple of different versions, from one to three hours, depending on the time the school had set aside for the performance. Somebody from PBS saw it, bought an hour of it, and I won a public television award for the show.

Then I did stand-up comedy, working for Bud and Silver Friedman at the Improvisation in New York and L.A. I just didn't have the heart to do stand-up for years and years, so after about eighteen months I came back to Maryland and taught English for two years to pay off my school loans. I loved the kids, but I was a horrible teacher because I didn't want to do it. So almost six years after graduating from Towson, I applied again to Yale and was accepted.

I was twenty-eight when I went to Yale, so I was the oldest person in the acting class. The youngest was nineteen. There were five women and nine men, including Katherine Borowitz and David Alan Grier. The first day, they gave us this test that really turned me off. The summer before we started, we were all sent a list of seventy-five articles or books to read. (This was under Robert Brustein. He was the reason I wanted to go there, because I thought he was brilliant in his writing and that he did the kind of classical theatre I wanted to do.) Anyway, they gave us those bluebooks and sat us down in an examination room. We had four essay questions based on the reading list, and we were told: "Look to the left. Look to the right. One of you won't be here at the end of the year." Now that's like boot camp, and it started emotional problems for everybody in my class. One girl had a nervous breakdown six months into the program.

I already felt inadequate because my language skills weren't as developed as those of many classmates. Even though I had been teaching English, I think I had it in my head that I wasn't as good, and that's a self-fulfilling prophecy. When you don't feel good about yourself, other people don't feel good about you because you're not putting it out there.

This may be purely from my perspective, but I felt that the faculty picked favorites, and those same people were cast over and over again. I'm talking mainly about the first year, because that's when it's all set up: who is the actor and who is not. The rest of us were not really allowed to work, at least not in leading or even supporting roles. My confidence level had been completely destroyed by the time Lloyd Richards came in as Dean during my second year, and Earle Gister became head of the acting program.

Earle Gister is like rich soil. He made me feel that I was at least competent. He was always there. His door was always open, and he was human. Not that he was this big pushover. He was stern. He knew what was right and he wanted you to know that he knew, things like how far you should push yourself and how much you were really doing to get anything out of your experience. Is it our fault or is it yours? That was really, really helpful.

When you go to a professional school, you have working professionals as instructors. Wesley Fata and Carmen De Lavallade were my dancing teachers, and Carmen actually asked me if I was sure I was black because I have no rhythm. They were very patient with me, and loving. I got to do understudy work and parts in plays at the Yale Rep. In Lloyd's production of *Timon of Athens*, with James Earl Jones, I had a few lines and was a dancer. I could never remember the steps, and Wesley Fata would look at me and just roll his eyes. I understudied Novella Nelson, who I have come to love, in *Boesman and Lena*.

Andrei Belgrader directed an *As You Like It*, in which I played a tree with big green fluffy slippers and a tree costume with branches. It was so much fun! My tree had decided that it would be a fallen tree in the forest. Well, it fell hard one night. I lay down and fell asleep onstage, in a full house. Finally, I got punched by somebody: "It's time for us to go!" hissed in my ear.

The school was ultimately helpful in that it taught me I could do anything I allowed myself to do. When I graduated, my confidence level was back, especially since a degree from Yale Drama School at that time was like getting an American Express card: you didn't get the card unless you could pay on demand. It also didn't hurt to have teachers like Lee Breuer, who gave me my first job. George Roy Hill was another acting teacher at Yale, and he gave me my first film, *The World According to Garp*, with Robin Williams and Glenn Close. All four of the women in my Yale class were given roles in that film. It was like a graduation present.

I think also that the combination of all the different kinds of plays and all the different levels of directing skills was very helpful. Yale pretty much made me director-proof. I don't mean that in a negative way. You try to give a director everything he or she wants because if you don't, often *you* look bad. But you have to use your own sense and think, "Did he have time to really think about my character in the arc of the whole play?" You have to keep everything open, and be prepared to offer suggestions and not just let that poor man or woman do all the work. You do learn that.

There have been shows where I just completely missed the mark. The director can't help you because you just can't get there. I played Maria in *Twelfth Night* and I couldn't get the way the director saw the clown characters. Maria was never a real person to me, so what the audience saw was somebody flailing in the dark. Now I look back on the character and say, "What's so hard about this?" But sometimes things are going on in your life, and you don't give yourself a chance to connect. You start blaming it on other people and it's nobody's fault but your own.

Sometimes the reality of a character is evasive and you've got a director who realizes what you're going through and can help you. When I was playing Marina in *Uncle Vanya*, I didn't know who this woman was and I didn't want her to be just a servant in the house. Garland Wright said, "This woman's raised this entire family. How can she be a servant? They love her. She's their mother in a lot of respects. Just go from there." And it opened right up for me.

Also, I must say that the support system at the Guthrie almost spoils you. The research that the dramaturg staff does is incredible. For *Vanya*, Mickey Lupu brought me a book on Negroes in Russia during the time that Chekhov wrote the play. I'm not saying that everything has to be geared to me as a black actress, but I could never have thought of that. I didn't know there *were* blacks in Russia at that time. That book made me feel less like they got a shoehorn to fit me in.

It's exciting when you're struggling, struggling, struggling, and things happen to open you up. I find that when you can see the arc of the whole play and how each character functions, and you can stick yourself in there, then you get the character. That's magic for me. I've played a few roles where I've felt that the character and myself were completely merged in performance: Dorine in *Tartuffe*, Antigone in *The Gospel at Colonus*, and Linda Loman, the one I'm doing right now.

When I was told that *Death of a Salesman* with a black Loman family was going to be a part of my life this year, I thought, "Why on earth would I want to do Linda Loman?" I thought she was just the wussiest character ever. I was reminded of my aunt, who is eighty years old and was a nurse. She is meticulous and soft-spoken. She has two sons she loves and has helped to become whatever they've become, and a husband she has always loved the most. Her nails are always clean; her clothes are always crisp; her hair is always done. I used my aunt's persona for Linda.

Then I started to think about people who were married to chemically-dependent people, and that's sort of like Linda's relationship with Willy. Linda's no saint. This woman pushed this man. She wanted all the things he wanted, so she's not blameless in this tragedy.

Willy is my life. If he's not happy, I'm not happy. So what, he screams a little at me? I'm not so sure that she wasn't physically abused at some point in their relationship. But as far as I'm concerned, Linda never doubts that he loves her more than anything or anyone. She isn't hurt when he tells her to shut up. She doesn't stop talking when he tells her a zillion times. It's just part of the way they function together. He doesn't mean anything by it, and she wasn't part of a generation that knew about things like verbal abuse destroying self-esteem.

It all hits her when she gets to the requiem. She can't cry because she's so relieved that this man is gone, and guilty that she's relieved. How can she cry because she's sleeping every night again? How can she cry that she doesn't have to worry about getting a phone call in the middle of the night, that he's run off the road? I think that when she does cry at the very end of the play, it's a release: "Thank you God, I'm free. I love you Willy. I love you, but I cannot tell you what a relief it is not to have to worry about you every second of my life."

The dramaturgs gave us articles from *Ebony* magazine, in the Fifties, about black people who were in corporations in New York at that time, and also lots of articles on black people of prominence after the war. Black families could have arrived at what the Lomans aspired to—not only could have but *did*.

Mel Winkler and
Isabell Monk in
Death of a Salesman
(Guthrie Theater)

Assimilating all these ideas only happens in repetition for me. Each line and each moment now has some kind of real connection for Linda that I no longer have to think about. At the place in the second act where Biff ends up in a puddle around Willy's ankles, the thought process I went through was: "That's my baby, and he's hurt, and that's my husband who I know is gonna eat my child alive if the boy doesn't go. I've got one wounded, and I don't need one dead. I know that my baby has tried to do all he can for his father, all he can do." Now all I think about is, "My baby, my baby, my baby," and I get so full that I can just barely stand up. And still, every time we play—because we don't get to do it that often during the week—new things come to me.

Even before I started rehearsing, somebody was telling me, "Oh, you're going to do Linda Loman, that's great! I love that speech, 'Attention must be paid,'" and *did* the whole speech! On opening night, I have to admit that I knew everybody was out there going, "This is *the speech*," but as long as I get across the meaning—as long as the feeling goes from my mouth to their ears—I think I've done my job.

Not every actress approaches a speech in the same way. You can keep doing a play for hundreds of years because of the difference that individual artists find in one set group of words.

Tartuffe is the most fun play, and Lucian Pintilie's was the most fun production, I have ever done. I played the maid Dorine, and with some cast changes we did it here at the Guthrie and at the Arena Stage in Washington. It was a delight to have that beautiful verse of Molière's in Richard Wilbur's translation—to fight against those rhyming couplets to keep them from sounding sing-songy, and to bring life to this nutty, full-of-life play.

The funniest thing that ever happened to me onstage was when I was at the Arena doing Dorine. I'm sitting on the floor, leaning back on my elbows, and I have on this big seventeenth-century dress with a full skirt. Richard Bauer as Orgon is giving me a long harangue, when his false teeth fly out and land in the lap of my skirt! It's a full house—in the round—and instead of picking up the teeth with his hand, Richard puts his head in my crotch and moves his head around until he has his teeth in his mouth! Trying to keep a straight face, I thought I was going to die. The audience was howling. I think they thought it was a piece of shtick, because it was a very lusty production.

Lucian Pintilie is Rumanian and didn't speak English at the time. He spoke French to a translator. Lucian was the meanest man I've ever met in my life, and for that reason I adored him. Not mean, I guess— just brash and no bullshit. And spoiled. *Completely* spoiled. If he had been younger, you would have called him an *enfant terrible*. He was a bad boy. Whatever he wanted he wanted *then*, no waiting. He wanted to be able to see what he was asking for *immediately*. That was fun—it was a challenge. It was the first Molière I'd ever done, and to this day I don't know how I got the part, because I am the worst person to audition, ever.

I don't read cold well, and I get so defensive when I go in for auditions! I have an audition in about an hour-and-a-half for a

commercial here. . . . Oh, I hate them! It's the only time I feel that
what I'm doing is prostitution. There's no time to make anything real,
to find any connection. You are selling yourself, and to me it's so ugly!
Most people who are holding auditions try to be kind, but there is no
way to be kind. Auditioning is horrible. My stomach hurts and I can't
think and I get home and figure out exactly what I should have done,
but I don't have that next day to go back.

That's another reason I'm in regional theatre. We still have to
audition for some directors; but that's not nearly as difficult, because at
least you know you have a job in the company.

The Gospel at Colonus came to me because I had worked for Lee
Breuer before. The first time was in Central Park, when I was in the
ensemble and understudied Lola Pashalinski as Trinculo in *The
Tempest*, with Raul Julia as Prospero. I was just out of Yale, and it was
interesting to watch a great combination of professional artists working together and to see Lee's take on Shakespeare. I don't think he's
disrespectful. I think he's very playful with classical writers and tries to
breathe life into them. Louis Zorich played Stephano as W. C. Fields,
and Lola played Trinculo as Mae West. In that way, I guess Lee tried to
find contemporary icons.

The next thing I did for Lee was *The Gospel at Colonus*, which I was
a part of off and on for six years. I was here at the Guthrie doing
Requiem for a Nun, and Lee was at the Walker Art Center, which is in
the same building as the Guthrie, doing this little half-hour version of
Oedipus at Colonus, with gospel music. He asked me to come over and
read this Antigone speech. I had an hour off between the first and the
last time you saw me on the Guthrie stage, so I'd get out of my costume
and run over and do that for Lee. When Lee and his group of *Gospel*
people left, he said that they were going to go to Europe and expand
this thing and asked would I be free to go with them, and I said,
"Yeah!" I'd never been to Europe.

We did it in England and France for a few months, and it got bigger
and bigger. About a year later, Lee got Morgan Freeman to play the
Preacher and Oedipus, and the play really took off. The best performances we ever gave were at the Brooklyn Academy of Music in their

Next Wave Festival. Then we kept on touring, and finally came to Broadway, which I thought was much less wonderful. The show wasn't as spontaneous. A lot of the good stuff happened when nobody knew what they had—before they were just doing their jobs.

The hardest thing for me was to learn how to go from doing a speech, as the Evangelist, to the congregation—which was the audience—to Antigone's speech to her father on his deathbed. The idea for the production was that it took place in a Pentecostal church in which the story of Oedipus was acted out as the Preacher and others told it. I came down to my spot as the Evangelist, telling the story, and then became Antigone *doing* the story, and I had fifteen seconds to go from one to the other. Morgan Freeman was very helpful. I had the problem of holding back too much, and he said, "No, no, don't hold back. Go! This is Greek tragedy, and it's also in a gospel setting. Take it!" And so I did, and got as big as I could possibly be. Actually I didn't *do* anything. *It* did it. The music was amazingly powerful, and all I had to do was go with it.

It was great having that gospel choir, which was so alive and spontaneous, right there. They never allowed us to lie—never, until we got to Broadway, when it got to be a job. We got new costumes, glitzier sets—things that, in my opinion, took away from the innocence and purity of the piece and made it into what Lee or the producers thought people wanted to see in a Broadway play. I think that had it been as raw as it was when we did it at BAM, it would have been a welcome breath of fresh air on Broadway. Morgan said that Broadway would kill it, and he was absolutely right.

I worked with Lee Breuer on his *Lear* over four years. During that period, I became an associate member of Mabou Mines. I always want to work with Lee, and I have long been enamored of Ruth Maleczech. When Lee asked me about the *Lear*, the chance to work with Ruth was like a dream come true. I admire her guts, and how she is able to do something that a character says in *Marat/Sade*: "to turn yourself inside out and see the world with fresh eyes." That woman to me is just *alive* onstage, and fearless—not afraid of looking bad or getting a bad review or anything. She just wants to do the work, and she works hard.

I still love her work, and by now I've been with her in *Lear*, in Lee's *The Warrior Ant*, and in JoAnne Akalaitis's production of Genet's *The Screens* here at the Guthrie.

Lee had this idea for reversing the genders in *King Lear*—making Lear a queen and the daughters into sons; making Gloucester a woman and Edgar and Edmund daughters; and so on. We would meet every month or so and talk about it. We were trying to get to what the story was about in relation to how lives are lived presently. I think Lee wanted to see what it would be like if it was a matriarchal instead of a patriarchal society. When, at the end, the mother is carrying her dead son, instead of the father carrying his dead daughter, it has a different resonance. It doesn't change the play, it just changes what goes through your body and mind as a viewer.

This was a way of making it accessible in modern terms. I don't think that needs to be done all the time. I think sometimes it's good to see Shakespeare done as traditionally as possible, because we are people from a modern age and we bring that with us anyway.

Ruth Maleczech was always going to be Lear and I was always going to be Gloucester. I worked on Gloucester from my grandmother and all the older women I know. I tried to take those words and make them as much mine as possible. When Ruth and I were out on the heath, we were two old, old girlfriends and cousins who loved each other, and the pain in that scene was almost more than I could take.

Some people objected to the actors wearing body mikes, but Lee likes to use them because he feels that they allow the actor not to have to think about acting. In a lot of ways, he's right. It allowed *Lear* to be more cinematic than theatrical, and Lee really likes cinema. I think he likes to bring the essence of cinema to the stage. If we'd had a better speaker-system, people might not have been so upset by the mikes.

You know, you can't worry about what people think of your work unless the people are the actors on the stage with you. I had so much love and respect for all the people that I was working with in *Lear*, and I was doing a play with Lee Breuer . . . who cares what somebody else thinks? As long as I was doing what he wanted and what worked in the actual production we were doing—and I didn't feel like I was holding back or cheating anybody—that was enough for me. I never thought about an Obie, though I've always wanted to win one. (The *Gospel*

ensemble had won one a few years before, but four of us won individual Obies for *Lear*—Ruth, me, Karen Kandel as Edgar and Greg
Mehrten as the Fool.)

The stakes are so different when you work in experimental, regional
or commercial theatre. Like I said, when you do a Broadway play,
people are basically thinking about money. Often the last thing that's
thought about is the playwright's work, or the director's, or the actor's.
In not-for-profit theatres, the pressure lessens, but you have to keep the
subscribers coming, so it gets to be a little tug of war there, too—how
much can you grow as artists and still sell the shows? In work done by
companies like the Wooster Group and Mabou Mines, the audience is
almost the last element considered, at least in terms of how much
money it is going to bring in. To all audiences, there's always a
message that you want to get across, and no matter what the message
is, I feel that's the most important thing.

The irony of working on Broadway for me was that I made less money
there than I make here. If you're a star, I'm sure you make big bucks, but
I have earned more in regional theatre than on Broadway in *Gospel* or
Execution of Justice. I made a living in New York, and in the two years
that I spent doing films, TV and stand-up in L.A., but I make a *life* here.

I lived in New York for fifteen years, off and on, and during four of
the seven years we were together, my man-friend and I lived in a house
in New Jersey . . . but to me it was all the same. There was no way to
actually live a life in New York. It seemed like I lived from hand to
mouth.

I'm not swimming in dough here, but at least I have a garden. It's
not about what you have, I guess; it's about enjoying life. We had great
times in New York, but I lived in constant fear: fear of doing auditions;
fear of not getting jobs; fear of being unable to pay bills; fear of getting
killed on the street—afraid, afraid, afraid. I still have fears. I live in the
world. People are animals sometimes. But the quality of my life is so
much better here. I'm allowed to be not just an actress but a regular
person.

Before I decided to stay at the Guthrie, I had done one season at the
American Repertory Theatre with Bob Brustein in Cambridge. I was

so excited finally to be in a company, but I quit after nine months—the only job I ever quit. When I arrived, I was given this hellhole of a basement apartment: no welcome; no consideration for you; just, "Here's your place." It got to be a battle for just human necessities, especially if they wanted me to get to work every day and not be afraid to step out of my house or to sleep in my apartment.

I did get to work with wonderful people like Andrei Serban. I enjoy his warped mind. I played one of the gods in *The Good Woman of Setzuan* and he had us singing, going up on a swing about forty feet in the air, even though I told him I was terrified of heights. I did it because that was his vision, and if I couldn't do it, then I should have said, "Get somebody else." I stuck that out, and then I left.

I was so unhappy. Not just with ART but with Cambridge, Massachusetts. I have never in my life felt the way I did living in that town. I'm from the South. I know what it's like to be discriminated against. But I have never felt invisible in my life until I lived in Cambridge for nine months. I felt, when I walked those streets—and this is a seat of higher learning—that I did not exist. That's the only way I can explain it. I would walk into places and it was like I wasn't even in there. They didn't see you; they didn't hear you; they didn't care if you were on the planet one way or another. And Boston proper—oh!—it was the scariest feeling ever. It was worse than where I grew up. You weren't supposed to be there if you were black.

They call this the heartland. In Minneapolis people do have real big hearts and are friendly. It's cleaner here. It's less oppressive. This city has many theatres that do good work, and there's a large number of films that are being shot here because it's less expensive. Also the Guthrie is like a family. From what I see about Garland, he wants to make this troupe out of people who are from completely different theatrical backgrounds. He wants to put this hodgepodge, this goulash of acting styles, together, and make it the Guthrie style. And while he's doing that, he's giving actors a chance to be a little less gypsy-like. I think that's marvelous.

I have always wanted to play Clytemnestra, and I'm going to get to do her next season. I think the plan is to do *Iphegenia at Aulis, Agamem-*

non and *Electra*. I will get to play Clytemnestra through all three of them. She's going to be a challenge in all kinds of ways, beginning with the challenge of a diet, because I want her to look really great. I think she was very sexy. I think she was enormously passionate about her desires and her needs as a woman.

I have been very fortunate, as far as being an African-American actress. I have been allowed to play parts that not a lot of black actresses have been allowed to do. I want to do anything that is possible for me to do as an artist; I will not be limited because of my race. To be limited not because of what I have in my mind, my body and my spirit to share, but because of something as simple as the darkness of my skin, is intolerable.

My entire life has been that way. My father, bless his heart, is illiterate. I have a master's degree from Yale University. I'm the first person in my father's family to go beyond the sixth grade. I was, for a while, the only black actor here at the Guthrie. I was one of two black actors at the American Repertory Theatre. When I went to Hungary with the Actors Theatre of Louisville, I was the only black person on the tour.

It doesn't seem like race has held me back, but that is not the norm for African-American artists. I'm sure I've been discriminated against, but not to the detriment of my growing as an artist. I've played the parts that are predictable—yes, of course I've been used in that way— but then again, I've been used in other ways. People have used their imaginations and have respect and trust enough in what I have to offer as an artist to say, "You're the best person for the job. I don't care what your color is." And I'm extremely grateful.

You read in the newspaper how things seem to be changing to more like 1968—how the unrest is coming back. Fear is prevalent, fear caused by ignorance. So my daily trek out on that stage is my way of saying, "I am here. I am a part of your world. Don't you forget it!"

PAUL McCRANE

The Country Girl
(Roundabout Theatre Company)

Thirty years old when I interviewed him in the summer of 1991, Paul McCrane is the youngest performer chosen for Actors' Lives. *He began his professional career in a McCarter Theatre production at fifteen and was then chosen to create the role of Shirley Knight's disturbed young son in the original production of John Guare's* Landscape of the Body. *He has worked constantly since, interspersing stage roles with films (he created the role of Montgomery, and played and sang his own song, in the 1981 movie* Fame*) and television (he was a regular on the innovative 1990 musical series "Cop Rock"). His theatre roles have been mostly in new plays and modern classics—in the 1990-91 season he appeared in the Roundabout Theatre's revival of Odets'* The Country Girl *and the Lincoln Center production of Guare's* Six Degrees of Separation; *the following season McCrane played Andrei in Emily Mann's production of* Three Sisters *at the McCarter and created roles in several new works at the O'Neill Playwrights Conference.*

I came into this business, ironically and fortunately, through the front door. I started working at fifteen. I had some aptitude for it, and there wasn't a lot of competition for that age-range. Now that I'm thirty, I play characters from their mid-twenties to mid-thirties, and there are a hell of a lot more people auditioning for those roles.

I got interested in the theatre because my father has been involved as an actor in Philadelphia for as long as I can remember. I went to see him in a lot of plays, and I can remember going backstage after a performance and being amazed that these rickety little sets had supported a whole world that I had been completely enmeshed in. That's probably the first time I had a sense that there was something magical about that world.

When I was fifteen, I told Russ Faith, my guitar teacher in Pennsylvania, that I wanted to be an actor, and through Russ I was signed by a New York manager and started auditioning for plays. My first professional job was playing one of the three sons in Durrenmatt's *The Physicists* at the McCarter in Princeton and the Annenberg Center in Philadelphia. At sixteen, I was cast in the original company of John Guare's *Landscape of the Body*, which we did first in Chicago and then at the New York Shakespeare Festival's Public Theater.

I really had no technique at all then; I wouldn't even have known what an objective was. I was working on instinct. I remember a moment in rehearsal when this voice came out of me that frightened me. John Pasquin, the director, said, "Yeah, that's it!" and boy, that was very confusing for a while, because I had the experience of something really working and not knowing how or why.

The experience of acting can be therapeutic, but that's not its primary purpose. There are times, while working on a role, something will trigger a response which feels great in rehearsal, but then you have to apply your judgment as to whether what's coming up is helpful to the telling of the playwright's story, or if the playwright's story is now becoming a vehicle for you to address or exorcise something in your own life. That's sometimes a difficult line but a very important one to see. The *play*'s the thing. This means you must have some sense of what the hell the author's writing about, which itself is not always easy.

At sixteen I had no idea of all that. When something came out emotionally, I didn't have a sense of using it *towards* something, though I was trying to do what I thought was right. I was very tense. I

used to get tremendous headaches from trying to recreate something
that happened once in rehearsal.

Though there were a lot of great things about starting so young, there
were some very difficult adjustments, too. It was sort of like being
thrown in the pool and learning how to swim. When we went to
Chicago, it was the first time I was away from home—I was away from
my girlfriend, and I wasn't happy about that—but boy, it was a really
full experience. I must say, the people I worked with were fantastic.
Both John Guare and John Pasquin were very supportive and generous. I remember them fondly from that time.

I got an awful lot of exposure in *Landscape* when we went to New
York, but the run was difficult for me. I was going to school in
Philadelphia during the day and taking the train to and from New
York to do the show. Eventually, I had to leave the theatre before
curtain calls so that I could get an earlier train. It was a grueling
schedule, and I ended up leaving the show, mostly so that I could get
some sleep!

I finished high school, and spent the summer after I graduated
working for Lawn Doctor. I was all set to go to LaSalle College in
Philadelphia, but I went to the freshman orientation, came back home
and said, "Mom, I'm not going to school." My parents were pretty cool
about it, actually. I continued working on lawns, not quite knowing
what I wanted to do. Then I got an audition to replace someone in the
Broadway company of *Runaways.*

I got the job, and I knew I didn't want to commute again, so I moved
to New York in the fall of 1978. That first year, I lived in five different
apartments. Oh my God, do I have New York apartment horror stories!
The very first place I stayed was with another cast member who said,
"I got this big place. You wanna come? We'll share it." Great. I agreed
to it sight unseen. *Never do this.* I went with my bags to this loft, and it
was actually a great space, but he was renovating, and there was this
unbelievable gas leak. It was a construction site! I stayed there about a
week.

The next place I got was a walk-up with the water closet in the hall
and the shower in the kitchen. All the windows looked out on brick
walls about five feet away. It was very dark, and roach infested. One

time, I turned on the oven and these roaches started crawling out, so I turned on all four burners, too, and within five minutes the stove was like one living thing. The other great thing about that apartment was that it had an open steam pipe for heat. Someone had ripped off the radiator, but the valve was still there and steam came right into the room.

The next place I found was a tiny basement apartment with a couch that ran the length of the one room, literally splitting it in half. I stayed there until one night I heard a flopping around in my trash bag, turned on the light, and out ran this huge rat. I spent the next month nightly asking friends if I could sleep on their floors or couches while I looked for an apartment every day. I went back to the basement place only to change my clothes and the rat traps. That made for a pretty rugged first year in New York. Consequently, I've lived in the apartment I have now for twelve years, and I'm just moving to a new one.

After *Runaways*, I did another Liz Swados show, *Dispatches*, at the Public, and made the movie of *Fame*, where I got to play and sing my own song, "Is It Okay If I Call You Mine?" I had studied for six months with a terrific Shakespeare teacher named Robert Smith, but I needed some more basic training before I could jump into Shakespeare, and a friend suggested that I read Uta Hagen's *Respect for Acting*.

I read the book and I thought it was just great. It was not mystical in some sort of baloney way—it was very pragmatic and realistic, a down-to-earth approach to the work. I thought, "I'd like to study with this woman," so I went down and auditioned at the Herbert Bergoff Studios, made the first cut, went back to audition for Uta Hagen and was accepted into her class. I think that's probably the first time I was ever really, really thrilled to get something.

I have studied with Uta Hagen on and off for about eight or nine years. She's got an amazing eye and an ability to communicate in language that makes sense to me. I think the most important thing she does on a regular basis is ask the actors, after every scene done in class, "How did you feel?" That question encourages you to quickly reflect: "How did that go? Did it go well? *Why* did it go well? Why *didn't* it go well? Do I know?" That's the first step, because we'll never progress if we can't assess ourselves—which can be hard on the ego, especially when we want to believe we're great and don't want to see the ways that we're not very good at all.

I did a play called *Crossing Niagara* at Manhattan Theatre Club. Alvin Epstein played a tightrope walker who walked across Niagara Falls with me on his back. I was lost. I had been in class for a while, and the great thing about class is that you fail all the time—you go too far in all directions—and eventually you wind down and get a little bit closer to the truth. In *Crossing Niagara*, I finally said, "All right, face it, you don't know what you're doing. Every night, pick a moment that you know you're not sure of and just watch it. See if you can tell what's going on, what's not going on, why, and try and solve it for yourself."

I love the fact that doctors speak of *practicing* medicine and lawyers speak of *practicing* law. It took me a while to develop the perspective that every time I go out to work, it's a chance to *practice* what I do. My work extends a lot farther behind me, and in front of me I hope, than this one job or this one night. You can get locked up inside if your work is bad and you can't face that.

The best actors give bad performances. Once I decided to accept that as a fact, I developed a perspective: "Okay—every job—every time I work in class—every time I do a reading—every time I see a play—is a chance for me to try and learn more."

I may never have felt tremendously satisfied with *Crossing Niagara*, but during that play I developed the understanding that there are four possibilities in any performance: the one that we all love is when you're happy with your work and the audience likes it; the three other possibilities involve some disappointment—you like it, they don't; they like it, you don't; or they don't like it and neither do you. And that's going to happen. I guess I went into acting thinking— as I imagine a lot of young people do—that I was going to go out there and it was all going to be great. *Doesn't happen.* That attitude only interferes with real development. You have to accept disappointment and then go to work.

The most recent example of disappointment in my career is the role I'm playing right now in John Guare's *Six Degrees of Separation*. I opened with the original company at the Newhouse Theater of Lincoln Center, then went to the West Coast to shoot a television series called *Cop Rock* when the play moved upstairs to the Beaumont, and returned to the cast this summer. During the period of more than a year—from when I was rehearsing and first playing the role to when I was away from it, to now when I'm in it again—I've come to understand the difficulties I had with the character.

I play a naive young man from Utah who's come to New York with his girlfriend; we both want to be actors. My character gets involved with the con artist of the piece and ends up having a sexual experience with him in Central Park. This is more than the young man can handle. I have a speech to the audience about how my girlfriend and I have given our entire savings to this guy, and what happens on the evening I spend with him. It's a tremendous speech, but it's very difficult for me. And last year I couldn't leave it alone. I couldn't leave it at work.

You know, it's real important to separate work and your home life. No matter how serious you are about your work and how good you want to be, you've gotta have a life. A lot of people were saying they felt my work was really good in the play, but I felt something wasn't right. It just felt a bit flat somewhere, like something was rubbing the wrong way.

Sometimes when I'm having trouble with a role it's because the material triggers something in me that is too threatening, too difficult, too dangerous for me personally to look at. The problems I have in performing that material are essentially personal, as opposed to stemming from an inability to identify with it, or not being inspired by it. The challenge is to discern what's so disturbing, whether it is appropriate that it would be disturbing, and then to find some way to master the disturbance in order to perform the piece.

When you also really want to do well, and you feel the pressures of a New York opening, this kind of disturbance can make it difficult to approach the work quietly. During my first run with *Six Degrees*, I tried to set specific times of the day when I would work on my character, even if I didn't know quite *how* to work on it. I'd write about it and try to exorcise whatever demons were getting in my way. And I'd go to the rehearsal or performance, slog at it again and again, keep trying. People, for the most part, liked what I was doing, including John Guare and our director Jerry Zaks, but I was not happy.

Boy—you *gotta* trust your own instincts. Everybody says, "Oh, the audience doesn't know." First of all, I don't believe that. Second of all, it doesn't matter to me if the audience knows or not—if I know I'm bullshitting or if I know I'm having trouble, I'm unhappy. This is my *work*. And if I'm having problems performing a part, then the work is to investigate that. What makes acting interesting in the first place is trying to understand human behavior and in some way master it so that a performance is alive on its own but within parameters that you set.

I did not have a handle on *Six Degrees* during my entire first run with the part. I was really only able to do that speech in a way that felt right a handful of times. I tried to focus on the objectives as clearly as I understood them, and then to tolerate not knowing. I did the best I could, expecting that I was going to be disappointed.

I came back to the show, after a year off, with some trepidation. A friend asked me, "Why are you going back into that role when you were so miserable doing it last year?" And I said, "I don't know, but I think part of the reason is because I don't *like* not having mastered it. It beat me last time. I want to take another crack at it." All that excitement and the panic of a New York opening were out of the way, and I was much more able just to focus on the work. I was able to answer a few questions for myself that I couldn't answer a year earlier.

For example, I came to realize that some part of me had the notion that homosexuality was somehow equivalent to emasculation. Certainly it is not, but I realized that I had that equation inside, which made me feel personally humiliated, portraying on a nightly basis a character who had had a homosexual experience and described it to the audience. The character himself might have had the same equation, but if a character has a misunderstanding and the actor *also* has that misunderstanding, that does not make for playing a role well. If something is really hot emotionally for a character, and it's really hot emotionally for the actor, he's not going to be able to bring it onstage under any kind of control.

There were other personal blocks in *Six Degrees*, but I'm going to leave it at that example. When I recognized the prejudice in my ideas about homosexuality, and really examined the issue, I was able to see the character more clearly. I enjoy playing him much more now. I think the performance is more appropriate—more specific—more effective —I hope more affecting—and it's a hell of a lot more fun to do.

I believe acting, even when you're doing the most painful or most difficult moments, should have some element of joy about it. If it doesn't, there's something wrong. Art, even when it's examining the most disturbing aspects of life, has something celebratory about it.

I'd say the most difficult role I've ever tried to play was Don Parritt, the young man who has turned his mother in to the police as an anarchist, in O'Neill's *The Iceman Cometh*. I was in the Broadway production directed by José Quintero, starring Jason Robards as Hickey. I learned a really important lesson in that experience. Early in rehearsals, I was going about the work in my usual way and José, a tremendously passionate man, told me, "No, you have to dive right in! You can't hold back!" And I thought, "He's considered the master interpreter of O'Neill in our time . . . so okay."

Paul McCrane (top) and Alvin Epstein in Crossing Niagra
(Manhattan Theatre Club)

Well, I made a mistake. I abandoned my way of working. I like to take time—I like to get specific—I like to understand what it's about. I have to have a sense of what my objectives are, what it is I'm trying to accomplish.

About five or six years ago, I finally understood the term *throughline*. What it means to me is what my character wants (and is going after) in life that takes him *through* the events of the play to something usually beyond the ending. I've got someplace I'm going, and the audience gets to watch for a few minutes, while I'm on my way.

I *enjoy* diving in and just trying things in rehearsal—I do that a lot—but if I'm trying to work something up just to please the director and I don't really know what it is, I'm cutting my own head off. And that's what I did in *Iceman*, thinking José must know. Not to throw, God forbid, the whole thing on him—*I* made that choice. I didn't say, "Look, this is the way I work—if you can't live with it, I'm sorry. You can fire me."

I lived the actor's nightmare of being involved in a production of a master play with the master interpreters and getting a *Times* review that said everyone was great in it except Paul McCrane. I'd gotten bad reviews before, but I really wasn't expecting this. Jason and the company and the producers were tremendously supportive. One of the producers, Lewis Allen, sent me all these other reviews that praised me, and the experience enabled me to get some things out of the way because, in one sense, my worst fears came true. I was able to say, "Okay, I'm not going to get the *Times* to approve of me in this. Now, what's the work about?" You have to go back to work whether you get good reviews or bad, and you do the best you can. It turned out to be a freeing experience.

One of the most important things for an actor to have is a sense of humor. The times I've been most unhappy are when I haven't had it, and the times that I've been most satisfied are when I have. I used to take everything so seriously. Jason Robards was great that way, because he seemed to take the work very seriously and himself not seriously at all. When you're at work, having a sense of humor and a generous, colleague-supporting attitude is key. Because in the end, we're all trying to do something creative and productive, and life is long. It's not worth making yourself miserable.

I went back to *Iceman* and, nightly, tried to get the fears and anxieties and inhibitions out of the way, so that I could see what I needed to work on. José wanted this character to have a desperation about him. I hadn't been able to make clear for myself why Don Parritt was so desperate, and had unfortunately chosen to try to play a *general* state of desperation, which felt *awful* to do.

If someone is desperate, that implies he really wants something very badly. What is it that he wants? What's in his way? If I'm desperate to have your pen and I've got two seconds to get it, I'll get it as quickly as I can, and by the way I do it you will know, "Wow—he really needs that pen!" Understanding the circumstances and the character's drive makes actions very clean. Playing a generality makes them noisy. I felt my performance in *Iceman* was full of static.

It didn't settle and feel right until near the end of the run, after we had gone to Los Angeles. I still had plenty to work on in L.A., because having committed myself to early choices before really knowing the lay of the land, my mind sort of reflexively went to these choices. It's hard to break habits like that; but by the end of the run, I knew where I was trying to get the character to go. I wasn't completely there, but I was on the way, and that was very satisfying.

The *Iceman Cometh* experience helped me tremendously when I played Edmund in *Long Day's Journey into Night* at the Portland Stage in Maine a few years ago. First of all, it taught me a lot about how much homework I needed to do. I sat down, went through this immense play, and wrote down everything that was said about the character and everything Edmund said that referred to who he was. Uta Hagen has nine steps she talks about, and I basically did them all— on paper; *before* I went into rehearsal. And, thank God, I read the play many times.

When I first read a play, often I'll get an initial idea or picture of what the play is, who the character is—I see a face, all that stuff. I read the play a second, a third time, and it feels dead—nothing's happening; nothing's coming. *You gotta live through that time.* And do the tedious work—all of it. I think Harold Clurman, in one of his books on directing, talks about writing down whatever occurs to you as you read a play—write it down; think about it; pick the play up; read it again. You're not going to feel this great sense of inspiration or direction; but maybe over the third or fourth read, as you're writing things out, your mind starts to connect things. They start to make sense. That's when it begins to get exciting.

Preparing to play Edmund, I also read some of the O'Neill biographies, since *Long Day's Journey* is about his life, and I came to rehearsal armed with a body of understanding of what the play was about, what I believed the thrust of the play was, and what my responsibilities were as the character. Like in a football game, when the objective is to move the ball across the goal line, sometimes I carry the ball, sometimes I block other people. I found all this tremendously helpful in the collaboration of rehearsals, when sometimes I would help the director, Barbara Rosoff, see something, and sometimes she would help me.

I learned so much about how to work on plays dense with material! That had daunted me at first. I think I hadn't done some of the work in *The Iceman Cometh* because I felt, "How do I begin? It's this mountain in front of me. What do I do?" It sounds simple, but the way to start work is to start work . . . one step at a time.

Every time I've had an opportunity to do a classic, I've been given a deeper understanding of the limits of my training. Playing Orlando in Des McAnuff's production of *As You Like It* in La Jolla, and making a big mess of it, was an education in how much I don't know.

One reason I haven't done more classics is that, not having had a lot of classical training, I was probably not very good at some of my auditions for them. I think I'm better now. Another reason is that, besides work, I have struggled with the desire and the need to make money and to have a personal life.

When I did *Long Day's Journey*, we didn't cut the play, so it ran, I think, four-and-a-half hours. I was staying in a decent but slightly frayed hotel, in the dead of winter, in Maine—and having a great time doing a great play and feeling very satisfied at having tackled a writer who had given me such problems before—but I wasn't making enough money to call my friends or see the woman I was seeing at the time.

Until this past year, I have ended up out-of-town more than six months out of every twelve. I'm interested in working on more classics . . . the problem is I also want to make a living, and I want to have a family sometime. That's hard to do. I don't know how I'm going to juggle that.

When I'm in town, I'm involved with something called the 52nd Street Project, which started out about ten years ago as a collaboration between the Ensemble Studio Theatre and the Police Athletic League on 52nd Street. The project works on theatre activities with neighborhood kids from about five to fifteen years old. It's run by a playwright and actor named Willie Reale, a friend who got me involved a few years ago.

I started out just doing crew on productions, because I was afraid I was gonna screw up some little kid if I got closer. I was afraid of the kids, frankly. These are inner-city kids, some of whom come from great families, some of whom come from really bad home situations, and they go to the Police Athletic League for afterschool activities. I think the project originated when they asked for a drama teacher, and then Willie developed this whole thing.

One of the best activities of the project is called One On One: ten kids and ten adults, let's say, go away for a week to Block Island or Cape Cod or anyplace where somebody's donating a house or some space. For the week, from nine a.m. to noon, an adult and a child work together writing a five-to-seven-page play, or work on a piece that a playwright has written for them to perform. The afternoon is camp-time for the kids, when they do activities or just hang out at the beach. Toward the end of the week, all the plays are put on, and then they're brought back to the city and performed. Parents and friends come, some EST members—it's open to the public, and it's always sold out.

One of the most valuable things the project offers the kids is the discovery that they can learn. I was working with a kid a couple of years ago named Mikey Lugo, on a play already written by Leigh Curran. We were away on a One On One; it was the middle of the week; and Mikey was kind of bored and just didn't want to work anymore. I was trying to get him to learn the lines and it wasn't happening. I said, "Look, Mike, you don't have to do this. I don't want this to be a big torture for you, so why don't we just stop?" And it scared him a little. I wasn't trying to scare him, I was just trying to say, up front, "I want to respect my time and your time." He said, "No, I want to do it, I want to do it!" We started to work again, and he got through six of the seven pages off book—and he was amazed. Psychologically, it made perfect sense—he didn't want to be there so he couldn't remember a thing, and he also thought that he *couldn't* do it. So to see in his face—in his eyes—suddenly this sense of, "I can *do* this, I'm accomplishing something here," was really exciting to me. One of the biggest experiences in *my* life was learning that I could learn something, that I could develop *in* something. That these kids have that experience through the 52nd Street Project is, I think, enormously worthwhile.

Another tremendous experience has been working three summers as an actor at the National Playwrights Conference at the O'Neill. I approached the O'Neill as a sort of marathon, a proving ground of acting technique. You get three days of rehearsal to do a staged reading of a new play that may be substantially rewritten while you're working on it. I tried to take a lot of techniques I'd been working on for years and apply them under short notice and see what was not necessary and what was.

It's a great place, a great atmosphere. I really believe it is about the work. You go there and do the best you can to mount a playwright's work and expose it for what it is, both its strengths and its weaknesses, and then talk about it afterwards. When you're not in rehearsal, it becomes a matter of juggling: am I going to get enough sleep tonight or am I going to do this homework? If I don't get enough sleep, no matter how much homework I do it's not going to do me any good, but if I don't do the homework I may not be any good either.

You can learn a lot at the O'Neill about how to talk to a playwright. The all-conference critiques held after the last of each play's readings are tremendously helpful. We don't often enough sit around among colleagues and talk about techniques of acting or writing or directing. It's great to be exposed to ideas of what plays are about and what the writing is going for, and to try to understand a writer's process. I'm very grateful to have been invited there.

I used to go to everything I could see, but now I'm back and forth about going to the theatre. Unfortunately, there's a lot of bad theatre out there. If something wasn't working, I used to spend the time trying to understand why, and what would work better. But I got to a point where I was saturated. If I'm *in* a bad play, I have no qualms about friends of mine leaving.

I go to art galleries. I've had the great fortune of working in things which demanded some research into art—a play we did at the O'Neill was about Marcel Duchamp, and *Six Degrees* features a Kandinsky painting that had me going to galleries just to get a sense of John's reason for putting it in the play. These things have enriched my life.

I took a literature class and a language class at UCLA when I was out there last fall. I'm thinking about trying to get a more formal education.

For the first time, this year, I started listening to opera. I grew up listening to rock and roll and the blues, and I really like jazz now, that's what I listen to mostly. Now I'm able to appreciate opera a little more and God, it just is thrilling. I look forward to the next phase of my life, because I will have the opportunity—if I take it—to explore a lot of these other art forms.

If I take a glass and put a napkin over it, and I leave that napkin there for about an hour, or maybe even a day, you'll have a rough shape of what that glass is like. If I leave that napkin on there for a month, or two months, and let the wind and the rain get to it, you're going to have a much better, more detailed sense of what that glass is. In general, that's the way I think of the difference between film and theatre. In theatre you get to go into the detail. And also, in general, the play is a much more subtle piece than the film. It's much more satisfying to spend time with material that warrants time. I'm working on Shakespeare's sonnets now, just to play with them, just to get my mouth around the ideas and the words.

I love film—I really enjoy it. I like working in it—I love making money—and I'm very grateful for TV, too, and I've had a lot of fun with it. Film and television are different challenges for an actor than theatre, though. On film you never get a sense of building anything— it's what can you do in the shortest amount of time? That's an interesting challenge, but it's not the same kind of challenge as working in the theatre.

Thank God we still have people who write plays that warrant time spent on them. Of course we have theatre that's TV-like now, and that's okay—that's entertaining—but fortunately we also have playwrights who spend years working on what they're trying to write. They make my work interesting and fulfilling. They are the heroes.

I think it's going to be increasingly difficult to make a living in the theatre, unfortunately. I don't know what's going to happen to the commercial theatre—I'm afraid that it will all become Vegas on Broadway, to whatever degree it's not now. But I think there is an appetite for the real thing, whether it's dormant or not. The success of *Six Degrees* is encouraging. I anticipate that as long as I stay acting, I will want to be in the theatre.

A Piece of My Heart *(Philadelphia Festival Theatre for New Plays)*

FREDA FOH SHEN

Dashing between appearances on television's "One Life to Live" and preparations for an engagement at the Old Globe in San Diego, Freda Foh Shen was interviewed in Manhattan in May of 1991. Her harried schedule appeared to have no effect on one of the most effervescent personalities I have ever encountered; Freda Shen embodies her own concept of "juicy." While a student in the American Conservatory Theatre's training program, she was chosen for the original Broadway company of Pacific Overtures. *She has appeared in classics, modern plays and musicals from Alaska to Atlanta, from the Shakespeare Festival of Dallas to Manhattan's Pan Asian Rep, and has helped develop new work in such venues as the Philadelphia Festival and the O'Neill Playwrights Conference. When Freda Foh Shen was acting at the Playwrights Conference and I was teaching in the National Critics Institute at the O'Neill in July 1992, we had a second interview.*

I hadn't seen much theatre when I was growing up. My parents took us to Peking Opera, but the most I remember about it is running up and down the aisles and trying to get things to eat.

Sometimes I think it's better to know nothing. When I went to audition for the American Conservatory Theater's summer program,

I had not read any of the books or taken any classes on how to audition.
I simply went for pieces that said something to me. For my classical
monologue, I selected Emilia from *Othello*, and I chose to start with
"The Moor has kill'd my mistress! Murder! Murder!" and go all the
way through to Emilia's death . . . totally ignoring that not only was I
too young for the role, but that there were all these other characters
onstage.

For my contemporary piece—after I had fallen all over the floor
doing Emilia—I played Curley's Wife from *Of Mice and Men*, because
I've always had an affinity for the South. (When I was in high school, I
devoured William Faulkner. I think the South's strong sense of place
and of home may have appealed to me because I come from parents
who immigrated here. Or maybe I had another life there. . . .) Anyway, I was doing a southern accent, and I interpreted her as a wispy
sort of thing—a little sexual, pouty and childlike . . . completely
different from Emilia, which I guess was good. Both characters really
struck a chord in me.

After I had done these two pieces for Allen Fletcher, who was
conducting the auditions, I timorously asked, "I know this is not usual,
but do you think you could let me know within ten days whether or not
you will be able to accept me?" and he said, "I can let you know right
now. You're accepted." I collapsed on the table. That year they had
scholarships designated for Asian-American actors, and I was able to
do the whole summer program.

I had wanted to study at ACT in the first place because I had just
started studying opera in Los Angeles when I went to see Bill Ball's
production of *The Taming of the Shrew*. It was Ball with all of his flair.
He staged it in a commedia dell'arte style, and it was a transcendent
experience. It sounds silly to say that about *Taming of the Shrew*—it's
not even one of my favorite Shakespeares, now that I know a great
many—but that's what it did to me then. I left that theatre so inspired,
I thought, "Oh, I have to do this!" It was so much more exciting and
interesting to me than the opera I had seen.

I was finding that opera was not suiting me temperamentally. It
truly is all about your vocal instrument. All day long, the only thing of
concern to you is your voice: if there's a draft; whether you talk too
much on the phone; whether you're laughing too much; whether you

cry. I started to feel it was a profession that focused in on a small part of you, and as I looked down the life-tunnel for opera, it seemed to me to get narrower and narrower. After seeing the ACT play, I looked down the tunnel for theatre and it really opened up. As an actor, the whole world is your research, and every aspect of human psychology and relationships.

After the summer, I enrolled as a full-time student in ACT's conservatory training program, and I never thought anything more about my audition until I came to New York and people were talking about "how to do auditions" and advising me to read Michael Shurtleff's book on the subject. Then I went, "Oh, I did that audition all wrong!" but so what? The most important thing about actors or anyone in the creative fields, I think, is the raw material of who they are. When you're starting out and don't know how to shape the raw material, it's better to let it just hang out and not to superimpose structure and polish before you've even found out what's there.

It was the same thing when I did my first professional audition, for the Broadway company of *Pacific Overtures*. When the West Coast auditions were being held, I was a very serious-minded acting student, committed twenty-six hours a day during my first year at ACT. A wonderful acting teacher named Paul Blake, who really gave me a good grounding and a lot of love and encouragement, said I should go. So I auditioned for the show's casting director, Joanna Merlin, who loves actors and has subsequently given me a lot of support and help.

I was called back, and that audition was for Hal Prince, Stephen Sondheim and the writer of the book, John Weidman. I was thrilled. At that time there were only two people in the world I wanted to meet—Steve Sondheim and Mao Tse Tung. I was so excited about meeting Sondheim, I didn't have time to get nervous about myself. My main thought was, "How can I prolong the amount of time that I can be in Stephen Sondheim's presence?"

The callbacks were held in a small Los Angeles theatre, and I had dressed like a typical acting student, in a leotard and a black dance skirt. I sang "Villia" from *The Merry Widow*, and Hal turned to Steve and said, "Well, I don't think we need to hear anything more, do we?" and Steve said, "No, we don't need to." I was shocked. I was appalled. I thought, "What? I'm only going to spend this little time here?" and I said, "Wait, I've prepared this other 'up' song"—because they had asked for two—"and I'd be glad to do it for you." Hal said all right, and the "up" song happened to be "Gentleman Jimmy" from *Fiorello*, by Bock and Harnick, two of Steve's favorite people. For this number I had worn a teeny little dance skirt underneath. At the intro, all of a sudden I flipped off my long skirt, started doing this little tap routine, and I sang the song for them. It seems a little idiotic when I look back on it. I don't know what they thought, but they laughed.

After that, Steve was saying, "Do you have anything in high belt?" and I had nothing else, but I would just go, "Oh, yes," and I would sing a fragment of a song that I knew from memory, with no piano accompaniment. We must have gone through six or seven verses of songs like that, with Steve asking for low belt and for something in this style and something in that style—trying to find out what the limits of my voice were. Finally Hal said, "Enough of this. We've heard her sing, now we have to get to the scene."

As I was leaving, Joanna Merlin said it might be a couple of months before I heard anything, and I panicked and thought, "I'll never see him again!" So I said, "Joanna, do you mind if I just run back in there for one minute?" She said, "No, go ahead." I ran in and asked, "Would you all please autograph my music?" And in three days, Joanna called and said, "Hal wants you in the show."

But then, because I had my mind so fixed on being an acting student, I said to Paul Blake, "I don't know—I think I should stay here and finish acting school." He just looked at me and said, "Are you crazy? Do you know how rare the chance is to work with Prince and Sondheim? You go into that show! Acting school can wait! You can come back and do it afterwards!" Thank God he said that to me.

Pacific Overtures was great—I mean, what can I say? I had an incredible time. I did the Shogun's Wife in a number called "Chrysanthemum Tea," and throughout the show I was what they called a *kurogo*—a stagehand taken from Kabuki theatre, dressed all in black and supposed to be invisible. My days were incredibly full, because Steve and Hal were always changing things to make the show better, and we were constantly rehearsing so that they could see what the changes were like.

I think the thing I remember most about Prince and Sondheim was how well they worked together. There was a great deal of trust and a lot of generosity back and forth. Hal could say to Steve, as he did with the first opening number that we had while we were rehearsing in New York, "It's too beautiful, Steve. I've got to have something uglier." So we got a different opening number in Boston, and Hal said, "Steve, this is too ugly. We'll have to have something in between." And by Washington—our second month of tryouts—Steve had come up with "The planting of the rice," and Hal said, "That's it!" I never realized it at the time, but having worked Broadway shows since then, I think it's critical to have that unanimity of vision and that kind of trust, so that all the creative collaborators can do their best work.

My two years as a student at ACT—with *Pacific Overtures* in between—were very different. My first year at ACT I had a wonderful time and learned an enormous amount. The acting training was based on Uta Hagen's approach (which in turn, I suppose, is based somewhat on Stanislavsky), and there was a great deal of dedication to the work of theatre.

Also, Bill Ball had everybody study Transcendental Meditation— we had a meditation room up on the top floor. People may poo-poo that and say, "You know Bill Ball . . . he was way out in left field," but I really felt TM gave us a common ground. It emphasized to the company the importance of being centered, of taking time to allow yourself to breathe and to release daily pressures.

In fact, the whole building was oriented towards light and space. One member of the staff made it his business to put hanging plants in many of the studios that had sun. The conservatory had a feeling of openness, of expansion, of excitement. And it was thrilling, as a student, to watch the actors in the company work onstage. All of us were tremendously affected by Bill Ball's vision. I still am.

Before I went back to ACT, I had taken a summer workshop with some wonderful teachers in New York. Kristen Linklater and Peter Kass opened my eyes to so much! In terms of really digging within yourself—

getting below the surface—it was an entirely different approach, I would say, but complementary to what I had learned at ACT.

At the end of that summer, I had auditioned for the London Academy of Music and Dramatic Art, and was one of twelve students accepted for their overseas program. I had to decide between ACT and LAMDA, and I thought, "Well, I really should go back and finish what I started." I think, now, that that was a mistake. I went back to a whole new group of students and teachers, and I came in in the middle of their training.

I was in a growth period where I wanted something more than—or just different from—what ACT was giving me. ACT at that point had an acting teacher who I think was not totally grown up himself. I remember one rehearsal for a student project where he threw a hairbrush at an actor. I have to say that this man is an outstanding director in many ways and brilliant at analysis, but I saw him reduce people to tears in the acting class, and it gave me an aversion to acting schools.

I think the greatest problem in any school is how to teach without crushing the unique spirit in each student. The key word is nurture. I've seen people enter acting school with a great joy and love of acting. They throw themselves into it and get squashed, coming out much more anxious to please their instructors than to fulfill a character. So many of the unique things about them have been chopped off.

I did stick it out that second year, though. Maybe I should have left earlier. Probably where ACT excelled at that point was in text analysis, in movement, in dance, in voice, in the training of the actor's instrument. Where I needed bolstering was in exploration of how to open up emotionally.

An actor is two parts: the technical part is like the violin, and you have to train so that your technical self is a Stradivarius. Then you have the emotional part which is the violin player, who puts the content into the instrument and makes it expressive. Having worked with Peter Kass during the summer, I was much more interested in and ready to work on my emotional availability, on opening up to everything I was capable of in terms of content.

The work of Peter Kass and of Michael Howard—a teacher I studied with later—was about looking at yourself, seeing what things are there. Peter said the only difference between acting and psychotherapy is that with acting, you don't want to change anything, you just want to know where everything is and how to get to it; otherwise, you go through the same process. I think that's probably true. I mean, I think acting teachers are like therapists. You have to find the one that suits you, so the two of you can communicate.

We did our own shows in the ACT conservatory, then in the second year we did ensemble work in the mainstage shows. The show I did with Bill Ball was *Le Bourgeois gentilhomme*, with Chuck Hallihan. Chuck is a great comedic actor, and I remember his telling me that he kept a book of *lazzi*—pieces of comic business—that he would write down. And I said, "Really, you mean you would steal other people's things?" And he goes, "Oh, yes. That's the tradition. You build on everybody else's bits."

When I was playing Nerissa in *The Merchant of Venice* at Syracuse Stage, Katharine Houghton came to see the show, and she took me aside and said, "I love your Nerissa, but I want you to add something. When I played Portia, my Nerissa—Lillian Garrett—and I worked this out, and it creates a lovely moment." She showed me—I shouldn't reveal this; now every Nerissa in the world will do it—at the end of the play, when the rest of the couples are going in to talk about everything that's happened and Nerissa's husband Gratiano says, "Well, I would, but it depends on Nerissa, if she's tired and wants to go to bed," what Katharine had me do was just yawn, with a little look at Portia. It was a wonderful shared moment for the two women, and it would bring the house down. You don't have to say a thing, you just take Gratiano and pull him in with you.

When I graduated from ACT, I was thinking, "Should I go to L.A. or New York, or should I stay in San Francisco?" I went to L.A., and one morning I woke up and thought, "My God, this is like lotus land. I've been here three weeks and I don't even recall the time going by." So I asked myself for a dream, to see if it was right for me to stay. That's something I was reading about in books then, as a way of understanding what you really want or where you really should be going: before you go to sleep at night, you simplify the question as much as you can (in this case I asked, "Should I stay in L.A.?"), and you just keep asking yourself as you drift off to sleep. You try it for a couple of nights and see whether you come up with anything.

My dream wasn't very clear, but I definitely felt that it was not right for me to be in L.A. And I had also talked to Mako, whom I knew from *Pacific Overtures*, and he told me, "If you stay in Los Angeles, you'll make a lot of money; if you go to New York, you'll become an actress." I went back to San Francisco, and my acting teacher, Paul Blake, was going to be doing a musical, *Naughty Marietta*, and offered me the lead. I said, "Well, I don't know that it's right for me to stay in San Francisco," and I asked myself for another dream. That night I got a definite image of myself on the streets of New York, so I packed up and started driving across country.

I was in Colorado visiting friends when a call came from *The King and I*. They had just let their understudy for Tuptim go, and they asked if I would be interested in auditioning for Yul Brynner. I got the job, and it was like serendipity. My dreams were right.

So I understudied Tuptim on Broadway, and then later I played her at the Alliance Theatre in Atlanta. I was very lucky: both times I came to New York I came in with a Broadway show.

When I first started out, I just wanted to do theatre, period. I think the greatest outlet is regional theatre, which is much more likely to do nontraditional casting than New York. They're more willing to take risks, perhaps.

I really liked going out to regional theatres and seeing different parts of the country and meeting a lot of new people. The best thing about regional theatre is that it's a network. When you work with people and you like them and they like you, the work happens because of recommendations and mutual trust.

My first regional job was doing *Loose Ends* at Alaska Rep. I worked with Bob Farley, whom I just loved, and he recommended me to Jon Jory at Actors Theatre of Louisville. So then I went to work with Jon.

Even better is how I got cast as Lady Macbeth in *Shogun Macbeth*. An actor friend of mine from ACT, Traber Burns, traverses the country by car, going to auditions at and working in regional theatres. Traber had been working with a director named John Briggs and knew that John was going to be doing a production of *Macbeth* that he wished to set in medieval Japan. So Traber said to me, "Listen, why don't you send your picture and resume to John?"

It so happened that we all met up at Louisville's Humana Festival, attending a weekend of plays. We hung out together for a day and a half, and were sitting at a bar when suddenly John turned to me and said, "Well, do you want the role?" and I was like, "Yeah!" I mean, my mouth just dropped open. Many people would have said out of hand, "No, no, she's not right. Too young, too delicate."

That's an example of a great deal of trust between a director and an actor. Without even seeing me act or audition, John took Traber's word that I was a good actor and a good person to work with.

Shogun Macbeth was first done at the Dallas Shakespeare Festival. Tisa Chang, artistic director of Pan Asian Rep, was so taken with it that she asked John if she could produce it in New York. The only other actor who went from Dallas to Pan Asian was Ernest Abuba, the Macbeth. The Pan Asian production subsequently played at the Empire State Institute of the Performing Arts theatre in Albany.

Before I played Lady Macbeth in Dallas, I did a great deal of research and preparation, reading all sorts of analyses and reviews of different productions, and interpretations of her character. I can't remember whether I did this before the Dallas or Pan Asian production, but I also saw all of the Lady Macbeths that are on videotape. I've seen the BBC production, the Orson Welles film, and of course Roman Polanski's, and I looked at them all and thought, "That's not her. That's not her!" In other words, I had an individual take on where the character was going and what she was about. I had a very strong relationship with her, which I think is essential for an actor, because otherwise you feel, "What do I have to say about her that somebody else hasn't said already?" Luckily, I didn't agree with or care for many of the choices that the other actresses made.

Throne of Blood is the closest in essence to what I think *Macbeth* is about. Akira Kurosawa, the great Japanese filmmaker, made the Lady Macbeth in his movie into an almost nonhuman person. She's an exaggerated character, almost completely spirit. That is the only version I took things from, partly because our production was set in medieval Japan.

Ernest Abuba
and Freda Foh
Shen in Shogun
Macbeth *(Pan*
Asian Repertory
Theatre)

Kurosawa's Lady Macbeth had a wonderful stillness, and a deadly feeling about that stillness which we took and put into one of our scenes. John set the scene where Macbeth is hesitating over killing Duncan, or Shogun, in a Buddhist temple where he had gone to pray and meditate. The Buddha was behind us, and I knelt in a prayer position, but of course I wasn't praying. I was doing the exact opposite, manipulating Macbeth into an action which would take his soul to hell. I did not move at all, whereas Macbeth, in his agitation and frustration, was moving constantly.

I was aiming for great centeredness, and deliberateness. When we started rehearsals in Dallas, John had everyone learn a short version of t'ai chi. Before every rehearsal we would do the t'ai chi, and I think that drew the cast together immediately. It made everybody centered and grounded and started rehearsals off on the right foot. That fed the scene in the temple and the whole play.

Thank God for the luxury of having two full rehearsal periods for Lady Macbeth, because in Dallas it really was just thrashing around and getting a general outline, making some choices, finding out what worked and what didn't. The second time around, there was a lot more refinement and time to go into more depth. And with the same Macbeth, there was much more that we could draw on from each other. Ernie and I would talk some, but I think we both wanted more to physicalize in rehearsal. We're both very good at talking, but it really doesn't mean anything until you put it into action and feel how the other person affects you.

John would sit and watch, and Ernie and I would just go at it—I almost think of the scenes between Lady Macbeth and Big Mac as being bouts in a boxing ring. Both Ernie and I like to do completely different things all the time, and after each bout, John would say, "This is what I saw emerging from here, and this is what I saw emerging from there—why don't we try stretching this. . . ." He was wonderful at pacing the show. He would say, "This scene has to be very rough, very unfinished, but the scene in the Buddhist temple has to be smooth as glass." The rough scenes were when we'd started to fall apart after we'd done the murder. The parallel scene to the one in the Buddhist temple was when I was beginning to lose my nerve and Macbeth has sent the murderers to kill Banquo and his son.

In New York, we totally changed many of the scenes. We kept the throughlines of our characters, but in going deeper we found more effective ways to do them. For example, in Dallas, Traber was one of the witches, John's wife Judith Townsend was another, and the third witch was a man named Chika who was from Japan. Traber and Chika were in the sleepwalking scene with me. The scene was sort of a mix of Kabuki and Bunraku. As it progressed, the witches controlled me more and more.

I had opened the door to their influence with the "unsex me" speech, and they of course went right in and took advantage of this. Our decision was that this was a human's choice—a choice of free will—"Do you open that door or do you not?" and my Lady Macbeth

said, "Yes, because I want what you can give me." The witches were
onstage in the "unsex me" scene, but not prominent; they were almost
like shadows in the background. I think that John had them scurry
upstage, and that slight movement caught my eye, making me realize
that the spirits were there and that I could strike a bargain.

Just as Faust found that the devil must be paid, the witches exacted
their payment in the sleepwalking scene. Lady Macbeth's soul or spirit
is battling to get out and it cannot. They take control of me. They
would say some of my lines with me and echo others; they would be
pulling me one way and I would be resisting. At the very end, I became
completely their puppet, and I would rise, go, walk, sleep . . . whatever
they wanted.

In Dallas it was really a three-person scene. When we got to New
York, the actors we had in those two roles were wonderful at Japanese
movement but did not have as strong a sense of their manipulative
power over me. I remember one day in rehearsal, I just blew up. John
took me aside and said, "What's wrong?" I said, "John, I can't do this.
It's not the same. There's nothing going on—it's not real. I don't feel
the same things from the witches, so I, as Lady Macbeth, don't want to
react the same way. It's just not working for me."

That's the vaguest, worst thing you can say to a director, right? "It's
just not working for me." And he was so wonderful. He said, "It looks
great from the outside," and I said, "Well, maybe it looks good from
the outside, but it doesn't feel good in here." I'd really had it. He said,
"Okay, let's do another scene. I'll think about it."

A lot of directors say, "I'll think about it," and the next day they
come in and tell you, "Listen, it's all right. Don't worry about it." John
said, "I've got it. I'm going to lay down a strip of white light for you
center stage, maybe two body-widths wide. You are not allowed to get
out of that light. I want you to take everything that Traber and Chika
gave you in Dallas and have it all in your own head. Just imagine them
being there. Meantime, I'm going to backlight the sides in red, and the
two witches that we have now are going to be doing very stylized
Kabuki movements against the red light. So we'll have you center,
playing the psychological, emotional things that are happening, and
the other two doing a totally different thing."

It worked like a dream. Limiting me in that little strip of white light was so effective—trying to get out and then hearing the witches, feeling them pressing on me, was just wonderful. That is a great example of collaborative work. John made the whole scene honest and made the best use of what each actor could give.

Lady Macbeth is not a physically exhausting role, but it is emotionally exhausting because you go through that whole arc of the most intense time in a person's life, compressed into two-and-a-half hours. By the end, she's whipped and beaten; everything's gone out of her. When all the colors have just run out of me like that, I need at least a month and a half to let go and to feel fresh and ready to give life to someone else. Certain roles, I think—especially the great classical ones—suck everything out of you, and then they're still waiting for you to fill them with more. So when you've gotten through a run, you're totally drained.

After doing an exhausting role, initially I like to just putter around at home, do nothing much, maybe see movies, stand on the unemployment line, see friends, laugh, just remember what it is like to be Freda Shen. Just rest up. I know that I'm rested when I start feeling juicy. You feel that if somebody pushes you, you'll bounce back. Things are fresh again, you're a little overflowing rather than sucked out.

I think that doing the classics helps you when you're doing musicals, but that it doesn't work the other way around. Both classical and musical characters are generally larger than life, but when you look into a classic, the depth of those characters goes on to infinity. Musical characters need size to command the stage and to hold their own against elements which can easily swamp you—the music, the sets, the costumes, the lighting and the choreography. However, classical roles call for a type of acting-training that musical theatre does not necessarily give.

One of the temptations in a classic is to do what is called "singing the lines" rather than speaking them and having them make sense. The challenge when it's verse is to let the verse be beautiful in its own right, but also to make it human and specific.

One type of training that might be very useful for actors is a class, a seminar or a project in how to work on a new play—in what the

collaborative process is with the playwright and director—because I
think it's very hard. I know the first one that I went into, I didn't know
whether I should look at the play as a whole and try to help the
playwright with how my character fit into it, or whether it was more
useful to develop my character fully and simply keep pushing for her.

My first year in New York, I did a workshop of a new play directed
by Frank Chin, who's an excellent playwright in his own right—he
wrote *Year of the Dragon* and *Chicken Coop Chinaman*. It was a first
attempt at a play by a poet, and she had no preconceived ideas about
playwriting. I remember at one point she came in with rewrites: she
brought in a hat, and in the hat were little pieces of paper, sort of like
fortune cookies, which she mixed up; then she said, "Okay, these are
the rewrites. Everybody gets to choose five." It was like Dada art. We
picked out the pieces of paper, and Frank said, "Okay, guys, wherever
you wanna put that line in." It was very interesting.

I had a wonderful time working with Shirley Lauro on *A Piece of
My Heart*, which we did in a reading in New York and a production at
the Philadelphia Festival for New Plays. (Then, this past season, it was
done at the Humana Festival in Louisville, but I couldn't be in it
because I was on Broadway with *Shogun*.) The play is about American
nurses who went to Vietnam in the late Sixties, when they were
eighteen to twenty; how the country received them when they returned from the war; and how they dealt with their post-traumatic
stress disorder. My character, Leeann, was Chinese-Italian, a real New
York street girl—a little tough, a little cocky. I was able to help Shirley
with what it might mean to be Asian in an Asian country where Asians
are the enemy. She took the character and she deepened scenes with
small brushstrokes that really attacked the problems and gave Leeann
tremendous fullness.

The worst experience I had with a new play was when a director
deliberately alienated the cast from the playwright. He bad-mouthed
her, and the rehearsals began to be very edgy because the actors felt
that the playwright was unwilling to work with them. Now, I knew
the playwright from before and knew this wasn't true, but I couldn't
counteract the director's influence. It poisoned the whole atmosphere
and whipped the actors into a frenzy of saying some of the meanest
things I've ever heard people say about another collaborator. I blame

that almost totally on the director, an insecure man who wanted to be the center of authority and wanted everybody to love him at the expense of anyone else. It was really horrendous.

I went to the Old Globe in San Diego to do another new play, *Necessities* by Velina Hasu Houston, directed by Julianne Boyd, even though I've been less willing to go out for regional jobs for the past three or four years. I have my life in New York now, and I'm not so keen on disrupting it. But after doing some film and TV and a Broadway musical, I was eager to go to a regional-theatre job with an interesting and provocative play again. It was that juicy feeling. Also, the Old Globe has a great reputation, and they make it easy for actors. They were just wonderful about living arrangements and about re-arranging flights and rehearsals when I got a recurring role in a soap opera.

In terms of the living conditions and the way I've been treated generally, my regional-theatre experiences have mostly been good. I got such a deal in Alaska—someone I knew from ACT was in the show before mine, and she had her own room in a house with several other people—actually three guys, three Alaskans. They had a party at the house for the outgoing cast and the incoming cast, and my friend came up to me during the party and said, "Listen, the guys like you and they want to know if you'd like to take my room when I go," and I said, "Yeah! You bet!" It was for free! With the money I saved, I was able to rent a car, and during our days off a group of us would drive to places all over Alaska and have adventures. It was a hoot!

In Louisville I was fortunate, because the man I was living with at the time came down and we rented a large two-bedroom apartment. When I worked at the Dallas Theatre Center and the Dallas Shakespeare Festival, both of them gave me quite wonderful accommodations.

When regional-theatre housing is lacking, I know it's just a case of money, not intent. Often it's the little touches. For instance, I asked the Old Globe, "What is the cookware like?" I try to save money when I'm on the road by cooking at home, and if the theatre doesn't have good cookware, I'm forced to lug mine with me. I remember once walking into the housing and looking at the sofas, the lamps, and thinking,

"They think actors don't mind living with thrift-store pickups." It's very hard on the spirit to come home to a place that looks like a fleabag.

When you first start out, you want the regional-theatre adventure; you want that kind of education and experience. I think after you've done that for a number of years, it becomes apparent that you can't make a living that way. They just cannot afford to pay enough. At a certain point, the lifestyle of jobbing out to regional theatres is the same as film in terms of disrupting your life, but because the pay is so much greater in films, you're accorded greater hunks of your life in between. I find that you have to do film and TV and commercials in order to be able to afford regional theatre. This is what almost all actors do, after they've done regional theatre for a while. If you ever want to buy a house, buy a car, you've got to branch out.

Another reason I started to want to do film and TV is the challenge of new media and the interest of doing something completely different. I made a probably unusual decision at the beginning of my career: I didn't want to sign with an agent; I didn't want to be the Asian horse in someone's stable. So I decided to establish my identity and my reputation as an actress by myself—to go out and push for roles that I wanted to do. Trying to get agents to submit me for a whole range of roles, I freelanced with a great many, which you can do in New York but not in L.A. I only signed in the last three years, because there's no way you can do film and TV without having an agent. I find now that I appreciate the emotional factor, too—you have somebody in your corner. That's very nice to come home to.

I was up for the lead in a movie, and about the third time the director had me in to read scenes, he started calling me names, in the same way that it might happen in the script. Part of me knew that this was a directorial device to see how I would react, but he was saying things like I was "a white-bread cunt" and I "didn't know anything about Chinese people," and it started getting me very angry. He was Italian, and I said to him, "I don't see you living in Little Italy. You live uptown, you travel in your limousine," and as soon as I started attacking him he went, "Stop, stop, that's enough of that." And then he said to me, "Now do you think that's how a Chinese-American girl would react?" I found that the most insulting thing. I said, "I *am* a

Chinese-American girl, so I guess so." It seemed to me he had a certain stereotype in mind of meek and mild Chinese people, and we're not necessarily that at all.

I think that because of all the controversy over *Miss Saigon*, because of the work of the Non-Traditional Casting Project and groups like APACE (Asian Pacific Alliance for Creative Equality), people are more and more aware of their own limitations in terms of how they've been casting. Hopefully the effect will be to open up more casting to minorities. Whether it will actually have that effect, nobody can tell, because we're in a recession and as people feel more squeezed you're going get the backlash of, let's say, white actors feeling like "I can't even get a job, why should they make this particular character into a minority role?" It can get very tricky.

We have to encourage women and racial minorities, who *can* write, to *write*. We've seen more of that happening in the past five years. Then you're not taking away—you're creating new, and more. You're also telling your own story, which needs to be told. I believe that is the best thing for the future.

It's even harder for women to sustain a career in directing than men. I feel lucky to have worked with such wonderful women as Liz Huddle, Emily Mann and Julianne Boyd, and I look forward to an O'Neill project with Megs Booker.

Actually, my most recent theatre piece, *A Small Delegation*, was with Susan H. Schulman. That was one of the best all-around working situations. First of all, we had an exceptional play by Janet Neipris, set in China during the summer of 1988, about how a friendship between two women (an American professor and a Chinese translator) is affected by their different cultures. Then, the playwright and director worked well together and with the cast, being flexible, supportive and always open to suggestion and discussion.

One of the things Susan did (which I think makes a world of difference to the actor) is that up until run-throughs began, she almost always gave adjustments or notes privately, going up to the actor and talking quietly, keeping it secret from the rest of the cast. That seems to create a more intimate relationship with the director, which in turn fosters the actors' self-confidence and ability to be vulnerable and take risks. It minimizes the possibility of losing face and souring the working atmosphere. She also believes that every character should have secrets from the other characters. I think that's true, and it gives you more room to maneuver as an actor.

Another thing about Susan is that she was always prepared. She did her homework at night; she moved models around on the model set; she analyzed problems and came up with solutions; she didn't waste anyone's time and energy in rehearsal. If you were stuck or blank, she'd have an idea or a backup plan. If you were inspired or had ideas you wanted to try out, she'd always be open. She was really extraordinary.

At least fifty percent of the credit goes to Susan, and fifty percent goes to Janet (who was so good about letting go, creating new lines or scenes, and who must have been Chinese in another life). Another fifty percent of the credit must go to a cast that thrived in the inspiring atmosphere those two women created. The sum of the parts was greater than the whole.

I think sometimes actors have this secret fear: "This is the play . . . this is the one where they'll find out I really can't act at all. I'm a fake. I'm just nothing." These fantasies that go through your head are really an extension of stage fright. Sometimes I think I have no skills at all. I mean, really, you know, you start out at the beginning of rehearsal period, and you think, "Oh my God, can I do this?"

One of my teachers at ACT, Sabin Epstein, had this wonderful theory that I've thought of ever since and have experienced a lot—the popcorn theory. Sabin taught us that during rehearsal—and during your life—even when you don't think you're learning anything, you are. Knowledge is being stored in you like little kernels. All of a sudden one pops, and the illumination, the enlightenment comes.

I think it's true. All of a sudden, you go, "Oh, that's it! That's why that works!" Or, "Oh, now I understand! Why didn't I think of that before?" That's what's wonderful in doing theatre night after night. You never know when those little kernels are going to pop.

JEFF WEISS

Hot Keys (Naked Angels)

*T*he New York legend of Jeff Weiss began in a tiny theatre space on East Tenth Street called El Coyote Gallery and later the Good Medicine and Company. There Jeff Weiss acted in plays that he or his partner, Carlos Ricardo Martinez, wrote and the latter designed and directed. Dinner was included. Gerald Rabkin, theatre editor of the Soho Weekly News, wrote about a 1976 performance at El Coyote: "The night I attended Two Dykes, Part II, there was a knock on the front door during the second act and two black men entered asking if this was the place where you got free food. . . . Told they were a little late for food, the men were invited to watch the show, which they did with increasing involvement. Uninhibited by theatre etiquette, they moved their chairs right up to the area where Jeff was creating a dazzling, comic-macabre dialogue about suicide, and laughed uproariously at his virtuosity. . . . When Jeff next launched ingenuously into a black-dialect vaudeville minstrel number, I and the audience experienced a moment of apprehension. It was unwarranted. When Jeff reached the chorus of 'Who dat say "chicken" in dis crowd?' one of the black men, fully in the spirit of the proceedings, remonstrated: 'Not me! Not me!'"

Jeff Weiss also performed frequently at La MaMa, and in 1986 "went legit" with Liviu Ciulei's production of Hamlet at the Public Theater.

187

He has since appeared in many plays on and off Broadway, and he continues to do his own plays, such as his continuing late-night soap opera, Hot Keys, *which began its run at Off-Off Broadway's Naked Angels in 1992, and won Weiss his fourth Obie Award.*

Postscript: Jeff Weiss wished to add to his interview: "Carlos Ricardo Martinez now prefers the name 'Murphy,' and as for myself, call me 'Huckleberry Frankenstein.'"

Theatre was never an impulse that engaged me as a boy. I was made to be interested in theatre as a means of making me well.

I ran away from my family in Pennsylvania and arrived in New York in 1954, when I was fourteen years old. I got off the bus quite alone, and met a middle-aged man and woman who befriended me and put me to work. I didn't know that I'd be hustling, but with the first customer I understood pretty quickly what it was about. I was fairly craven and exceedingly ignorant, but animal enough to know that if you're going to survive in a hostile environment, you're going to do things you might eschew if you had an education. I lived more or less on the streets for six years, with periods of illness of a psychological nature, and took a lot of drugs.

Eventually I was scared off the street by a contretemps with another hustler and his pimp, and I ended up washing dishes at Hamburger Haven, near Saint Patrick's Cathedral. I got a one-room apartment in Brooklyn, and I was having a lot of trouble. I think probably the clinical term would have been schizophrenia. I had multiple personalities, plus several physical dysfunctions, including a speech impediment and a condition causing spasms that was similar to Tourette's syndrome.

I felt my estrangement from my family particularly at Christmases. (I found out later that they had been looking for me for many years, but I was fairly crafty in covering my tracks and using different names.) Two days before the Christmas of 1961, I went to a hardware store and bought putty, and then went to the Pioneer supermarket and bought a turkey. I spent much of Christmas Eve day puttying the windows and blocking the doors. Then I put the turkey in the oven and turned on the gas, but never lit the oven. I lay down.

That evening, the people upstairs were having a party, and one of the guests smelled gas. They followed the odor down to my door, broke it open, found me, took me upstairs and proceeded to pump me full of black coffee and walk me around the room and lean my head into the toilet until I looked like I'd be all right. The man who smelled the gas and found me was Carlos Ricardo Martinez, who got me into the theatre.

Carlos is an extraordinary man who taught me everything valuable I know about life and theatre. He was a painter with a wife and two children, from whom he had been separated for some time when we met. He moved into my apartment to take care of me.

It was very hard for people to get through to me except on the basest levels, either in some physical confrontation or through sex. I had very little to say and no knowledge of anything outside of fundamentals like getting dressed, brushing my teeth and keeping going. Carlos said, "You have to get out of this room. You've got to change something in your life!"

He had a job doing the graphics for *Odyssey*, a magazine on Greek culture, so he took me to Athens, and then to his house on Mykonos. The house was high up, and Carlos would take me out to a cliff off which the local Greeks threw their dying animals. The scavengers from the sea would pick the bones clean.

We went to this cliff early one morning, after a night when I wasn't talking or communicating with anyone. I told Carlos it was because I felt ashamed that I spoke so badly and I couldn't say what I wanted to say. I had a heavy Pennsylvania Dutch accent—flat, monotonous and difficult to penetrate. Carlos asked if I would feel better if I spoke more clearly, and I answered, "Oh God, yes," and he said, "Then let's work on that."

He said, "This is Greece, and learning should come out of the culture you're in. So I'm going to fill your mouth with pebbles and set you on the top of this cliff and give you a book of poetry. I want you to come out here every morning with rocks in your mouth and recite Gerard Manley Hopkins' 'Wreck of the Deutschland.'"

While I was imitating the Greek orator Demosthenes, I noticed these beautiful bleached white bones on the rocks. I began to collect them for Carlos, and he made extraordinary sculptures out of the bones. After six months on the cliff, I had progressed to other poems. I no longer had a Pennsylvania Dutch accent, I no longer had a speech impediment and I was never again afraid to talk.

That was my speech training (until I started doing Shakespearean roles for Liviu Ciulei. Carlos said my mouth was lazy for Shakespeare, and I would put a peach pit between my teeth and speak around the pit and still hit the consonants and pronounce the vowels. Whenever I dropped a pit, if Carlos was there he would ring a bell and keep a tally to determine if I was getting better at speaking quickly without losing control of my mouth. This exercise shows you where all the muscles are in your mouth, and it also helps you to develop different areas of the resonating box.)

Finally—one day on Mykonos—Carlos said, "We must go back to New York. But first we're going to Morocco and a leper colony in the Canary Islands, because I think you need to spend some time with lepers."

I was about twenty-one then, but I had the mind of a thirteen-year-old. I was somewhat foreshortened emotionally. Carlos wanted me to meet lepers because it would help me to stop feeling sorry for myself. He said, "I want you to see how people live and what people endure in their lives. You have no idea. You're privileged."

I found many of the lepers to have a tremendously well-developed sense of humor. They were very brave, very stalwart, and very, very funny. That had a big effect on me, and much later it affected a theme that recurs in my plays: there are the diseases we see, that are manifest, and then there are the diseases we don't see but we feel and suffer from.

All the while, I could see that Carlos was thinking, painting, making sculptures, writing and making music (because wherever he went he would get a piano and write music). I always made an appointment to see him. (I still do. We make appointments for dinner, we make appointments if I want to have a conference with him, because his time is very valuable.)

We came back to New York, he found me an apartment, and one

day he brought me to a storefront on East 10th Street, between First Avenue and Avenue A, and told me, "This is where you are going to be spending a good part of the rest of your life."

"You mean locked in here?"

"Oh don't be silly. Of course not. But you've got to find something to do. You don't want to be washing dishes for the rest of your life, and what can you do? You don't have any education, you don't have many interests. . . . I think you should be in the theatre," he said. "Theatre is theatre because it's here—it's the only present artifice. I think that's what you need: you need to convert the experience of your life into something that you can communicate to other people, and you need other people in your life. I think theatre can help you."

Carlos told me he wanted me to spend a week writing down things that had happened to me, while he made the room into a theatre. "Then," he said, "you will stand in this room and I'm going to turn a flashlight on you and I want you to tell the story." I could barely write, but I started doing it, and every night he would put these stories into an order and he would say, "Now, don't tell them as stories. I want you to tell them as though you're re-experiencing them. I want you to recall, even if you can't remember the exact words, what you said and what was said to you—and how the person who talked to you looked and sounded—and how you imagine yourself looking when you responded. Then I want you to do that." Which I did, every night.

My stories were about a pickup on the street; an assignation; a sexual encounter; a telephone conversation; trying to get a job; working at Hamburger Haven. I would play myself and the other person. Then Carlos would make me add another person, and another. He used to send me out in the afternoons to watch people and to listen to conversations and engage in conversations with other people.

I kept doing all this, and after about six months he said, "All right, next Thursday night at eight o'clock, we open. All these things that you've experienced, all these things that you've been talking about . . . I have them written down here, and I'll just call out a scene and you'll do it. If it changes, that's okay. Basically it's getting the story across." So the next Thursday night I stood there and the flashlights went on. (There was no electricity, so it was flashlights and bags of sand with candles in them as footlights.) We called our theatre El Coyote, and no one came in for months. Occasionally people would look in the window and wonder what this guy was doing in a flashlight beam, talking.

I remember the first night I performed for an audience. (I don't recall the exact date, but it was probably the spring of 1964.) These Puerto Rican kids came in, and they came back two or three times that weekend. Carlos served cheese and crackers and lemonade, so naturally the kids returned. Then they brought their parents, and Carlos said, "We'll make spaghetti, because we can't have families in here seeing this show unless there's something to eat. We can't afford to serve spaghetti unless we charge. What do you think? A dollar?" I said, "That sounds all right," so we would charge a dollar for adults, and the children were free.

Carlos moved into the apartment on the second floor, the storefront theatre was downstairs, and right behind it was my apartment. Carlos would be upstairs cooking while I was downstairs acting. I would ask him, "Am I going to do this kind of material in front of children?" and he said, "These kids are more sophisticated than you are." And of course they were. A lot of people in my first audiences didn't even understand what I was talking about. Some didn't speak much English.

I guess the first real theatre people came because somebody from the neighborhood knew them and got them down. And they kept coming back and bringing more people. We would play every weekend, and a man named Robert Sealy, who had come to see the shows, said, "I'd like you to be in a play of mine called *Waiting Boy*. It's about a waiter and the people he waits on. It's one character, and it takes place over his whole day, setting up the table, talking to people. You're the only person I know who could do it."

I said, "Really?"

He said, "Yeah, please do it. There's this woman who's just opened a little theatre. She's real interesting, and a lot of people will get a chance to see you act if this is what you want to do."

I was a strange performer. I would go into sort of a trance, but I would get so nervous midway through the performance that I had Carlos cut a hole in the back of the stage for me to run into my apartment and throw up in the toilet. I threw up before, during and after every performance. The theatre was a very small room which held comfortably no more than ten or twelve people, and the audience could hear me tossing my cookies in the back, which they found wildly amusing. *Some* people did—I guess others felt it was a slightly hairy experience.

Anyway, I did *Waiting Boy* and another of Robert Sealy's plays, *Prevarications*, at La MaMa. The interesting woman he had referred to was Ellen Stewart. *Prevarications* was the first time I worked with another actor, which I found very unsettling, even though the actress, Hortense Aldin, was wonderful. But Robert was a very good director, and one of the first things that Carlos had said to me when people started coming to our theatre was, "Always remember, Jeff, that in the theatre there are two people you must trust more than your own instincts: the writer and the director. You must assume that they know more than you do. When you get to the point where you think that no writer or director knows as much as you do, you're in trouble as an actor."

I never go into a play without putting myself entirely in the director's hands. Working with Robert and Hortense, I knew that they knew more than I did, and I was eager to learn so I wouldn't make a fool of myself. Carlos said, "What you don't want to do is disgrace yourself, if you can possibly help it. You can do a lot of tricks and you can get by, but you have to be in a space with others and you have to trust the people you're working with." That's the best advice I ever got about working with other people, and I've always acted on it.

Carlos had started me on a reading and writing program once we had opened and were running at El Coyote. During the day, he would have me going out and making notes, and he had me reading mostly poetry, and a lot of Gertrude Stein—because although he wasn't a great aficionado of Stein, he felt that her use of repetition, and of bleeding the meaning out of words and replacing them with pure emotion, was very helpful to an actor. (He made a reading list that I still have, and I still read some of the works on it. I always carry a copy of *The Psalms of Sir Philip Sidney and The Countess of Pembroke* with me—I've gone through about four.)

After the shows at La MaMa, Carlos and I went to South America,

194

ACTORS' LIVES

because he felt I needed to see more of the world. When we came back, about a year later, I ran into Ellen Stewart, who asked, "What are you doing now? People have been asking for you. They say, 'What happened to that weird actor you had working here?'" I had been trying to write down a play, for the first time, so I told her, "I'm writing a play." She said, "Great, I'll give you a date at my new theatre." She asked what the title was, and the one thing I had in my head was that I owed money on my apartment, so I told her, *That's How the Rent Gets Paid.*

When I told Carlos, he said, "Let's recreate that sick room you had in Brooklyn." So the play was me in that room where I had stuck odd pictures from magazines on every available inch of wall. Carlos created one of the most magical, theatrical sets I've ever seen. He made a room that got smaller without the audience realizing it, so that by the end of the play I was in a room the size of a telephone booth with dollhouse furniture. The changes were done in short blackouts. At the beginning, I woke up in the morning and I got out of bed naked and looked over at this table where there was an egg in the center. As I looked at the egg, it started to wobble, and very slowly it rolled off the table and broke on the floor. And for the rest of the play, the character proceeds to break, to come apart. By the end, he's in this tiny little room accepting an Academy Award, which is a can of roach spray. It was very crazy. But strangely enough, it won an Obie award for playwriting and acting.

While I was performing at La MaMa, Joe Cino came and said, "Hey, why don't you come do a play over at my theatre?" So I went to Caffe Cino and did a play that I had been working on with Carlos, a story about a young man who had been in a mental institution and was returning to his family after fifteen or twenty years. The conceit was that the audience had streamers and confetti and were members of the community welcoming this boy back from the madhouse. It's actually in front of the community that he assaults his brother sexually, has sex with his father and mother, and at the end kills the entire family. It was called *A Funny Walk Home* and I thought of it as a comedy. I won an Obie for that, too.

I didn't really think then, "Oh, now I'm in show business," although very soon an agent sent me to California to be in the movies. I hated it out there. I vowed I'd never go back, and I never have. As soon as I got back, we went right into another of our own productions on 10th

Street. I didn't want to do anything more at Ellen's for a while. I just wanted to lay off that kind of exposure.

We had changed the name of our space to the Good Medicine and Company. By this time, Carlos was making elaborate meals for our audiences. He might make a Mexican or a stir-fried dinner; a roast beef; a gingered bass—he had a contact in the Fulton Fish Market who would get him the bass. If it was a party of people, he would ask them whether there was any particular meal they would like to serve their guests. As soon as the show was over, we would move the tables in, with the candles, and we'd all sit down and drink Carlos's homemade wine, which he kept in casks in the basement, and have a hell of a good time. In those days, there was marijuana, *la buena medicina*, at every table after the show.

We were fortunate to live in a building run by a man named Albert Galante. If we were behind in the rent, Albert would say, "When you have it." We were always the supers of the building. Carlos has cooking facilities and lights because he needs them for the theatre and for his work, but I've never had electricity or a phone. I read by kerosene lamps or candles. I have no television, no radio, no phonograph. For me, they are distractions.

Our principal difficulty over the years was getting from day to day. We got so that when people would make reservations, we'd tell them to come at seven-thirty. We would collect the money and Carlos would go off and buy the food. Then Carlos said, "I want them to see what they're eating," so he took the audience shopping and that became a tradition. Ravenously, after the show was over, I would attack that dinner with everybody else and eat for the first time that day.

I don't really know how we managed to live, except that in the early years you could buy a loaf of bread, six eggs and a quart of milk for a dollar. There were times when we actually made money, like when I was a Guggenheim fellow and when I got a Rockefeller grant. To me and to Carlos that was a fortune.

We would usually do shows Wednesday through Saturday, then Wednesday through Sunday. We went into a much heavier schedule when I went legit, because Carlos felt that I was making too much money and had too much time on my hands. We did late shows six nights a week after I got back from the regular theatre. Then, when

Carlos felt that I was on an even keel, we would do Sunday and Monday nights, when the people from the shows I was in uptown would come down, have dinner with us and see the show.

Carlos encouraged me to write plays that required other people right away. He said that monologues were a dead end, that they were just jerking off. *A Funny Walk Home* had four or five characters. *The International Wrestling Match* had fifteen, twenty people in it, and it was about four-and-a-half hours long.

I've written sixteen plays so far. All my plays have been produced but not published. One publisher said, "The plays are so long. Can't you cut them?" I said, "Well, the idea is that that's what they were. If you're gonna publish the play, then publish the play. I'm not interested in publishing excerpts of my plays."

Jeff Weiss in Casanova *(New York Shakespeare Festival)*

I did a production of *That's How the Rent Gets Paid, Part Four* in Allentown, Pennsylvania, above a McDonald's, with a cast of department store clerks and waiters and workers from Bethlehem Steel. I had reunited with my family, because one Christmas—I think it was 1966—Carlos said to me, "Look, you know every Christmas I go to see my family and you always stay here. You don't want to come with me and you don't want to see your own family. It's not good. You'd better go back. You should do it now, before it's too late." So I did, I went back. It was very emotional and very shocking, because it had been so many years—it was very much like the prodigal son.

I united the Allentown cast of *That's How the Rent Gets Paid, Part Four* with the Wooster Group when we did it at the Performing Garage. Willem Dafoe played my son; Ron Vawter played my nemesis, Detective Persky; Kate Valk played my wife. I think that show finally ended up with forty people and was over eight hours long. That production was a lot of fun. Everybody was drunk, and by the end of the show some actors would be running around and others would be sleeping until somebody woke them because their scene was coming up. It was wild. And understand, unlike long evenings in the theatre with Robert Wilson, my plays are not about moving slowly. In my plays, everybody is wired. People are always in bed together or having a confrontation or getting killed.

Carlos was in one production that we did, and he used to be very much present at the others. It would drive people crazy. He'd be shining a flashlight on a scene I was doing and he'd say, right in front of an audience, "I did not believe one word of what you said! Would you like to try that one more time and see whether you could do any better?" And I'd go back and do it again.

Being part of the Off-Off Broadway movement in its early days was much less exciting than people think. Everyone was young. Virtually everyone was stoned. I would say everybody had problems with booze or drugs or boyfriends or girlfriends. There was a lot of craziness going on. What *was* exciting was people doing plays with little or no money. That was thrilling. Ellen was regularly harassed and closed. Joe Cino wasn't—he was Italian; he was white; he was male; and he was in

Greenwich Village. Ellen was black; female; and on the Lower East Side. She couldn't even get a cab to get out of the neighborhood.

When the thrill went, it went very quickly for me. Once Mayor Lindsay brought money into the movement and the grant structure kicked in, things changed rapidly. Ellen, when she started out, had this tremendous enthusiasm and energy for putting on shows, and in those days she really did leave you alone: whatever you put on, that's what you put on. And Joe was the same way. Of course that changed later, when producers—including Ellen—became auteurs of their theatres. But by that time I was no longer seeing Ellen, nor was I a part of her theatre. So I was spared the late age of La MaMa.

I've never felt that the theatre was either my calling or my obsession. I like to go to the theatre—I know so many people that I enjoy virtually everything I see, regardless of how rotten it might be.

I have a lot of fun with theatre people. I can't say that I've had a bad experience since I went legit—I've had worse experiences downtown, with monsters of one sort or another. I think when you're not being paid, a lot of very pretentious and silly people, in order to get their own out of it, set out to bust each other's balls. But if you're governed by rules and regulations pursuant to the Equity code and they are paying you a good deal of money to show up and do a piece of work, you more or less have an obligation to mind your manners. And people generally do.

I went legit five years ago, with Kevin Kline's first *Hamlet* at the Public Theater. Actually, I had played the juvenile in a Broadway hit called *Spofford* in 1967, but I wasn't ready for legit success and the trauma of that whole experience lingered for years.

Joe Papp had seen me in some of my own plays and had hired me to be in the 1972 production of *Much Ado about Nothing* with Barnard Hughes. I went to the first rehearsal and looked around at all the actors and I was terrified. I told Joe, "If I have to start—even *start* to rehearse—I'll be in a mental institution in three days." A. J. Antoon, who was the director, said, "You're kidding." Bernie Gersten was working at the Shakespeare Festival then, and he said, "Jeff, what are you talking about?" I told them, "I don't know if you can sue me, but I don't want to do this."

There have been gaps in between shows because I would disappear. I would go off by myself to New Orleans and work in construction or get into another line of work for eight months to a year, and then come back and do a play. That was something I needed to do at the time, and something that Carlos encouraged. "We're very good friends and very close," he said, "but I need to get away from you and you need to get away from me. And there is great danger to someone like yourself, in terms of the fragility of your ego." He meant that you can't get too swollen up about yourself in theatre or it starts to affect how you are with people, and neither of us wanted that.

At the time that Kevin Kline and Patti LuPone were living together, they used to come with their Juilliard class and Marian Seldes to see the shows at the Good Medicine and Company. They became friends of ours, so years later, when I was doing *Convergent Lives* at the Limbo Lounge (playing a poetry professor from Buena Vista University in Disney, California, who has an obsession with Japanese men and wants to join the Mishima Society), Kevin came and brought Phoebe Cates, whom he later married. Afterwards, he said, "Jeff, I'm doing *Hamlet* at the Public Theater and there's this director I want you to meet." And I said, "Puh-leeze!"

He left a note at the theatre and Carlos finally asked, "What is this?" And I said, "Kevin Kline is gonna do *Hamlet* and he wants me to meet this director." Carlos said, "Jeff, I have been telling you for years that you have to get out of that room down there and start earning some money. You're getting older and so am I." I told him I had absolutely no idea about Shakespeare, that I didn't like it and he wasn't crazy about it, either. "That's true," he said, "but I think you ought to consider it."

So I went to meet Liviu Ciulei, who asked me to read the Player King and Osric. He was sweet and warm and gave me a couple of very good hints about how to do them, and the next day he told me he wanted me to play those parts. I asked, "Do you think I can? Because I don't know what I'm saying. I don't know what this means." He said, "We have Liz Smith as our voice coach—she's going to help you. Don't worry about a thing. If you have any confusions, Liz will make everything clear." Which she did.

I went and auditioned again for Joe Papp, because he had to see what was going on. I had been cast for a few other roles in legit productions and not even shown up for rehearsal, and Joe said, "They're taking bets, Jeff, that you won't last past the first rehearsal."

I said, "Okay, Joe."

"You'll have to join the union, Jeff. They'll take it out of your pay."

"Okay, Joe."

So I did it, and it wasn't so bad. I'm still not crazy about Shakespeare. There are about eight zillion things I'd rather see, and that's just the way it is. I can't help myself. I don't get it. I know he's a great poet. I love the sonnets . . . but the idea of going to the theatre and seeing Shakespeare fills me with dread. When Michael Greif, a director I loved working with at the Public in Constance Congdon's *Casanova* last season, told me he was doing *Pericles* there next, I actually felt the cold hand of doom on my back. I can't even imagine sitting in a closed room watching *Pericles*. I mean, it's death on wheels.

But Liviu Ciulei was so wonderful. The man's a genius. After Carlos, nobody's ever taught me so much. I very seldom knew what he was saying, but I knew exactly what he wanted. I watched the expressions on his face, and he would communicate the exact emotional feeling of the scene simply by force of personality. He was the reason I showed up and stayed in the *Hamlet*. Then he said, "You must go with me to Pepsico to play Theseus in *A Midsummer Night's Dream*." After that, I played Menenius in *Coriolanus* at the McCarter for him.

I've done one more Shakespeare, the Broadway *Macbeth* with Glenda Jackson and Christopher Plummer. I was the First Witch, the Porter, the Murderer and Old Siward. It was grim. We had three directors— Kenneth Frankel, Robin Phillips and Zoe Caldwell—and no *Macbeth*. I don't think Christopher found Glenda as repellent as she found him. Both of them, individually, were wonderful. But if you don't have a lady and her liege who enjoy being in the same space together for two hours, you haven't got *Macbeth*.

Glenda went through plenty. She hated Christopher because he spit all over her. She used to come offstage—and I was standing there as the Porter, with a rag—and she'd say, "Give me the snot rag." She would wipe the phlegm on the side of her cheek, hanging on her eyebrows, and she'd say, "The pig, the sow, the swine!" But she's tough. She smokes three or four packs of Dunhills a day, and she goes out there and does everything. She looked like she was masturbating herself in Boston during the reading-of-the-letter scene. She was wearing this gold lamé gown, and she actually had her arm down the front of her dress. Finally, Zoe Caldwell got her to stop, but she hated Zoe after that and they wouldn't appear in the same room together. Zoe used to direct all of Glenda's scenes by intercom, because Glenda wouldn't let her in the house. But Glenda is a very wonderful woman with a great sense of humor, and she was so sweet to my mother. She wrote to my mother and they exchanged recipes.

And Christopher is terrific. He is a charmer. He's so full of himself, he just wraps himself in his own magnificence—but he's funny with it, and he is awfully brave. In Toronto, we were rehearsing the banquet scene with our new director, Robin Phillips. I was a witch dressed as a serving girl, and when the lights went out at the end of the scene, Christopher turned around and walked into my tray. It knocked the caps off his teeth, leaving these little black stubs hanging down, these little fangs. I was the Equity deputy, so he told me, "Get a dental surgeon, immediately." They called all over Toronto, but it was like two hours until curtain. They said, "What are we going to do? We're opening the O'Keefe Center tonight—it's a sold-out house!" The O'Keefe Center: six thousand seats. So he said, "Oh well, I'll just do it like this." He did the entire performance covering his teeth with his upper lip. I heard people in the house going, "What is he doing?" He had this odd lisp. As the play ended, I was standing in the wings and Christopher said, "I think they like it. I think they like it." And I said, "Yes, of course." But how would you know? Six thousand people applauding, even if they hated it, is gonna sound like a standing ovation. So he came out to take his bow, and he smiled, revealing that he had no teeth.

By the time he got back to New York, Christopher had a neck brace, braces on both knees and steel rods going down the back. He couldn't straighten up because he was wearing a double truss. He had these big duels with broadswords, and every time the swords clanged together he'd go, "Ah! Ah! Ah!" He even went on in a wheelchair. Oh, he was a darling man!

Carlos always said that whatever you do, you're in the theatre to give the best of yourself. That doesn't mean just when the lights go on. That means understanding, forgiveness, openness to different ideas, taking the direction you're given, approaching your craft with humility, realizing you're there to learn as much as to participate.

As soon as theatre made me well, it became a sanitarium in which I could easily go mad, unless I had direction and help. That's why actors have tremendous support groups. We sometimes forget that we have people making us look good, dressing us beautifully, giving us sumptuous lights and wonderful sets. We have directors who care about our performance and are leading us like babies through the shoals of the script.

Jerry Zaks is a terrific director. He taught me a hell of a lot about a different style when I was cast in the Lincoln Center production of *The Front Page*. He was very direct, very precise—he told you exactly what he wanted. It was just what I needed for a play like that. I listened to him eagerly because he knows a lot about comedy. Some people find him intolerable, because it can be closing night and he's got notes for you. But you know, you're not out there by yourself, and in a farce, if one person's timing gets off, that is detrimental to the flow of the scene. If you're the director, you have an obligation to keep the show sharp and honed. Jerry is as good at that as any director I've met.

With every director I've worked with, I've learned something different, something valuable. I played Simon Stimson in *Our Town* for Gregory Mosher, and he was very focused, calm, precise, and very sensitive to what he saw as your unique strengths and impediments. I had to conduct the choir for real in several scenes, and the musical director tried, with little success, to keep me on beat with the baton. I would break out in hives, I was so nervous. I just couldn't get it right.

Gregory must have known this, because he called me in—just the two of us—and within fifteen minutes he had me doing it right. He allowed me to find it without putting on a lot of pressure. He saw that I didn't need that—I needed something slower, less intense. He was very sweet and calming.

When we went to tape *Our Town* for television, Gregory came up to me and said, "Jeff, you've been in the theatre so long. . . . You have a wonderful face. You don't have to do anything." It was the best advice I ever had about being in a movie, and that was the only one from which I've gotten any satisfaction.

I know you can make a lot of money in a short period of time doing film, but I just don't like it. It's a medium that's removed. What I like about theatre is the presentness of it and its evanescence. I just love the idea that nobody can drag it back and enjoy it over and over again as though they were the auteurs of the experience itself. Videos and records and all those kinds of things give me a headache. When life is so dire, I think clinging to that artificiality and regurgitating it for oneself is scary. Being in the presence of a lot of people doing theatre and then walking out and having it disappear except in your mind is a beautiful idea.

I love the idea of going to the theatre and coming away charged by the experience, although I think that's overstated. I've run into a lot of people who have said to me, "Seeing your play changed my life." I say, "Thank you very much," but I'm thinking, "That's bullshit." What changes your life is when someone you love more than yourself dies. What changes your life are really big things. Other things can inform your life, can make your life more piquant or more exciting, but that's short-term. What's great about the theatre is that it's there, and then it's gone.

I would like to do more plays by Carlos. I think the first play we did of his was *Two Dykes*, about these two suburban housewives who meet at a card shop at the mall and fall in love, dump their husbands and children and run for president and vice president of the United States. It's a delightful play. It was very successful. He also writes musicals: *The Rise of Louie Bimbo, Teddy and the Social Worker, Gangster Review.* I've been in all those.

His plays are much different from mine. Mine are so intense and so volatile and so scary. I think of them as comedies, but it's an awful lot of mayhem for some people. Ricardo has this very delightful light touch and this marvelous wit and brevity. He won't write anything that's over an hour and a half. He's always thought my plays were too long, too busy and too boring.

In my years in theatre and in my relationships with people, seeing and realizing how much resentment there was against Carlos was a great enlightenment to me. If I, as a privileged white boy, had found some young, sick, Latino junkie and taught him how to act, that would be proper. But in point of fact *I* was the junkie, *I* was the Puerto Rican, *I* was the person who couldn't talk, and a Latin man was the one who went to the Sorbonne, who was a painter, who was my teacher. Oddly, that disturbs Latin and black people as much as it does whites.

Bigotry made my relationship with Carlos that much more important. It's been tested and proved over and over again: there's only one thing that can sever our relationship, and that's the death of one or both of us. I'm happiest when I'm with Carlos. I learn more about living in the world with some degree of ease and dignity from him. I could never find it myself. But it is in him and it can only do me good.

I've taken a lot of flak from people who refuse to accept that my relationship with Carlos is purely platonic and always has been. A lot of people over the years have dismissed our relationship by saying, "Oh, that's Jeff's lover." We're like brothers. Carlos's problem with me has always been to put some restraint on my carnal appetites before something would happen where I would die.

I don't think I've ever had problems in the theatre because I'm a homosexual—there are so many actors and directors who are homosexual. I think there is great prejudice against homosexual men and women in movies and television. That's a shame, but I'd say that for those who want to be in the theatre, I don't care who they are or what their appetites might be, there's a home for them if they love theatre and are willing to dedicate their time and energy and craft to it.

If I could do something else with any degree of expertise, I would. My actor's state of mind makes me sad. I think an actor, by the very nature of the task, has a tendency to become self-absorbed, and this bleeds into your personal life in ways that destroy primary relationships. The ego is a very big problem. One is encouraged by people who have a love for or a vital interest in theatre to believe that it's a much greater accomplishment than I feel in fact it is. I mean, I haven't discovered any cures for diseases.

I never felt that what I'm doing has much to do with art. If you go into the theatre thinking you're an artist rather than a member of an allied craft guild, working with a lot of other people to realize a production for an audience, I think you're playing around with something that can be dangerous. It used to be that artists were as rare as oranges in the Alps. When you said "an artist," you were talking about Degas or Matisse. You actually had to be able to transform base materials into something beautiful. I think sometimes that sense of wonderment about the theatre makes for a lot of pretentious people. I have yet to meet someone who said to me, "I'm a craftsman."

There was a time when actors were treated like prostitutes or criminals. In a way, that's a lot healthier than thinking that Katharine Hepburn is a saint.

Being an actor is a very abrasive state. The nerves are raw a lot, and many people, myself included, go through times when we think, "Do I really want to stay in something that's this hard on the heart?"

There doesn't seem to be any grace among actors as they age. There should be a time, I think, when you hang up your spurs, when it is a kindness on your part—a feeling for the audience that they don't need to see you in your palsied dotage. You simply withdraw, like Marlene Dietrich. But that insatiable, maniacal desire to be there, looking dreadful and barely able to talk . . . it's scary, it's sad.

I think how badly I would be behaving if I didn't have, and hadn't had over the years, a very assiduous brakeman to remind me of my own foolishness, self-absorption and self-delusion. I got into theatre by a stroke of providence, and I stayed in it only because of the faith of Carlos—and my mother. I love to entertain and it's meant a great deal to me . . . but I hope I'm going to get out of the theatre before I become an embarrassment to anybody. I would suggest that to any actor.

The Glass Menagerie
(*Trinity Repertory Company*)

When Olympia Dukakis won her Academy Award for Moonstruck *in 1988, the elation felt by many in and out of show business was not only for her performance but for her track record: here was a winner who had really paid her dues. She helped found two summer stock and two resident theatres, running the Whole Theatre Company in New Jersey for nineteen years. While also acting in New York and at other resident theatres, appearing in films and on television and teaching at New York University, Dukakis raised three children with her husband, actor Louis Zorich. Though the Oscar multiplied her film offers, Dukakis appears regularly on stage. Our interview was in her dressing room at Trinity Rep before a January 1992 matinee of* The Glass Menagerie. *I have also incorporated comments she made the following May in a panel discussion I moderated in Cleveland, where Dukakis was playing Mother Courage at the Great Lakes Theater Festival.*

The best experiences always have one thing in common—the courage to risk. A lot depends on the director's encouraging risk, which Richard Jenkins has in this production of *The Glass Menagerie.* When Trinity Rep asked me to play Amanda, I said I wasn't interested if the production was going to be the traditional, more or less sentimental kind. Richard said he didn't want that either. He reconceived the play in a way that has made people ask, "Why hasn't it been done this way before?"

Eugene Lee's set is a rundown hotel room where Tom, years after leaving home, is drinking and writing. He reads his first speech from a piece of paper he tears out of his typewriter. Amanda and Laura come into the action gradually—in the scene where Amanda is telling Tom how to chew his food, I'm saying the lines offstage and the audience sees Tom remembering and hearing his mother's words and reacting to her. The key to our production is his line, "The play is memory." Although Laura and I change costumes, we have only essential props like her high school yearbook, the candelabra for the Gentleman Caller scene, and the unicorn—the rest of her glass menagerie is not seen. When Amanda makes her calls, I use the phone on Tom's night table. We make entrances and exits from the bathroom and the door to the hall, and when Laura's hiding from the dinner party, she goes into the closet. At the end, when Laura blows out her candles in the hotel room and Tom is watching her in his crumpled clothes, with the whiskey bottle he has emptied during the course of the play, the audience knows that Laura will always be with him not just because he says she will, but because she's *there*, forever fixed in his memory.

With most of the stage props stripped away—like most of the genteel props Amanda had depended on—there were only memories, hopes and the warm bodies of her children to cling to. One result was to make us more fiercely loving as a family, which makes Tom's desertion a loss from which there is no recovery.

I thought Mike Nichols took a big risk casting me as an octogenarian Jewish mother in *Social Security*—for which I'm very grateful. It was what some people call a challenge and other people call an uphill fight. Norman Jewison came to the show, and that's how I got cast as Cher's mother in the movie *Moonstruck*.

One of my best experiences was Christopher Durang's *The Marriage of Bette and Boo*, which Jerry Zaks directed at the Public Theater. I played Boo's mother, a woman called Soot, who is married to an awful man who addresses everyone as "Bore" and calls Soot "the dumbest white woman alive." Jerry was urging me to think one way, and the approach wasn't getting anywhere. It wasn't wrong, but wasn't "it" somehow. I thought, "Oh, they're gonna fire me." We talked about the problem, and Jerry was wanting my character to be the person who felt responsible in trying to please everyone. What I began to realize was what she wanted was to find some measure of happiness. I think she wants to be happy, and here she is with this husband who's a horror. So she tries to rise above it.

Jerry encouraged me to follow through on that, and it worked out very nicely. I loved doing that play. We even won an ensemble Obie for it.

Jerry Zaks really likes actors. He's been one himself, so you feel you're with a colleague who understands the process.

I would like to play Winnie in Beckett's *Happy Days* five more times. I've done the play once at the Whole Theatre, and she's great. Winnie is constantly overcoming her fears, pain, bewilderment and despair, constantly trying to move forward and to affirm that every day is happy in the face of overwhelming evidence to the contrary. In the second act, when she's buried up to her neck in sand, there are periods when she's able to get away by denying her predicament and there are times when it just barrels in, the way things happen in life.

People use the word *growth*, making it seem as if you work on something and there it is. In my case, growth is drop by drop by drop. I've always felt that every time I worked I not only wanted to do the play as best I could, but to identify what I yearned to understand or get hold of or rid myself of. When I was doing *The Balcony* in Boston many years ago, I realized that I'd spent about two years doing parts in which my arms never went above my shoulders. I decided I would find ways to get my arms up during the production—sometimes growth is that simple. What I discovered was it was a deceivingly simple act which had reverberations, some pleasant, some unpleasant.

I feel that I can grow when I'm working with people who are process-oriented, who don't worry about what the results will be. What is really satisfying is to work with a director who understands the need actors have to go onstage and not to be tyrannized by themselves, by the audience, by the critics—the need to let go of any expectations.

While I'm running in a show I never read reviews. I used to, and it was very difficult because I would keep them in my head. I would keep not only the bad but the good things—"that magnificent moment when she picked up the glass"—and every time I'd go to pick up the glass that would be in my head and it made me furious!

I had a terrible time once with John Simon. He hated me in the Shakespeare in the Park production of *Peer Gynt*, and I couldn't leave the house for three days. Once it got quieter, he wrote an even worse thing about me because evidently people who liked the performance wrote him letters complaining. It's been a journey from that reaction to now, when it pleases me not to let the critics interfere with my work or my life.

You know, you're so interested in the craft, in getting noticed, in being good, in being better than somebody else. I was very competitive when I was younger, and then some things happened that changed me.

I was doing Vaclav Havel's *The Memorandum*, in a production directed by Joe Papp at the Public Theater in 1968, when I began to realize that I didn't want to act anymore. I was there with my hand on the knob feeling that I could go onstage or not go onstage. It wasn't that I was weary or cynical or bitter or whatever, I was just kind of indifferent. That was quite a shock, and it brought on a lot of soul searching. Why act if I was no longer doing it to prove to myself that I could exercise and develop a craft, or to prove to others I could do it, or to prove I was better than everyone else?

I had to figure out why I wanted to get on the stage. That's when I began to care a great deal about what a play was about and how I was a part of making it happen, so I could go beyond my own little sphere. Not only that, but I needed to stop trying to manipulate an audience.

People say things to actors like, "You had the audience in the palm of your hand," but that's an idea you have to let go of. You can't want to manipulate an audience—let them do whatever they want! You've got to do your own work, what you think and believe in, because audiences vary tremendously from night to night.

The reasons why people become actors seem to be fairly consistent, but the reasons why people *stay* actors are different. It's my experience that you can't continue to work at acting year after year, and to identify where you want to go and how you want to change and expand, if you get hung up on other issues. If you get bitter and want to score off of other people, it doesn't work. If you get too frightened and keep repeating the same thing over and over again because you want to please people, it doesn't work. Little did I know that it would take me twenty to thirty years to grapple with these problems, but it's in constantly seeking the ability to be simple and to accept myself without judgment and without shame—something Peter Kass, a really extraordinary teacher told me years ago, called "working on the work"—that has given me the reason to keep going onto the stage.

I studied with Peter Kass in graduate school at Boston University and later worked with him when he was head of the graduate acting program at New York University, where I taught acting for fifteen years. In my opinion, he is one of the best American teachers alive. In addition to the craft of acting, which he communicated so brilliantly, he taught the sense of making a total commitment to your work, of not being ashamed of who you are so that you can bring all parts of yourself to it.

The biggest lesson I had to learn was being honest and having the courage—courage is a major word for me—to trust and to commit yourself.

My parents were immigrants, and when I was growing up in Lowell, Massachusetts, my father started the Demosthenes Club, which put on plays like *Oedipus Rex* in classical Greek. During World War II my parents helped put together community shows for Greek war relief and the American Red Cross, and in one of those I played the spirit of young Greece. I took two pigeons out of a cage and released them over the audience, and being part of that was exciting, but not after the bird did what came naturally—thus began my sense of the sacred and profane on stage! Also, I have vivid memories of my brother Apollo and I forever doing backyard productions which we wrote, costumed and sold tickets for.

Looking back, it's amazing how I even got into acting. In those days—the early 1950s—physical therapy was one of the few well-paid jobs for women, which is why I chose it as a major. My junior year in college, I was appointed by the class officers to co-direct a couple of shows. To this day I don't know what they saw that made them appoint me, but I was so happy doing it I realized I wanted to be in the theatre. But I couldn't leave school and I couldn't change majors—there was no money. At that time polio epidemics were everywhere, and physical therapy was practical. After I graduated I worked four epidemics, and saved my money for graduate school. When I told my supervisor I was leaving, she said, "The world doesn't need another actress. The world needs another physical therapist." In my heart I knew she was right, but I had to go into the theatre.

I always thought I was not what would be called a commercial actress. I hoped that I would work in New York and in regional theatre doing plays and would get small roles in movies, and for a long time that's what my career was. Getting my first substantial film role in *Moonstruck* and winning an Oscar for it was an incredible turn of events, coming as it did more than twenty-five years after I started.

I think there was more opportunity for young actors to work when I began. People put on plays in any little space, so you could work on a variety of things. I got fifteen dollars a week for my first job, and then a big raise to twenty-five when I agreed to keep up the props and clean the costumes. Before I ever tried New York, I was a founding member of three theatres. Two were for summer stock—the Edgartown and Buzzard's Bay theatres in Massachusetts. The first regional theatre of which I was a founder, in 1957, was the Charles Street Playhouse in Boston.

A group of us from the Boston University graduate program took a loft on Charles Street, at the foot of Beacon Hill. There was a fish market and a German cabinetmaker below us, and we had the third floor. We did pretty well for the first couple of years, and then our lawyer and this director came in and said, "Why don't we move to a larger theatre?" We gave them our efforts and loyalties, thinking that we

John Patrick Rice, Christina Zorich, Olympia Dukakis (foreground) and Ray Virta in Mother Courage *(Williamstown Theatre Festival)*

were going to start an ensemble; meanwhile, the real plan was to get rid of most of us. And that's what happened, slowly.

I was the last to go. When I departed I was so rageful that I absconded with the period costumes. I called my cousin Michael in the middle of the night, screaming, "I've just run off with all these costumes. What am I gonna do?" I won't tell you what he told me.

I didn't get married until I was thirty, because I wanted to establish myself in a career before marriage. I didn't necessarily want to be a *successful* actress, but I wanted to feel that I was at least in control of my craft. In the years after leaving Boston I worked a lot in New York, won my first Obie, did some film and television. I'd done enough of a variety of work that I was ready.

I've been married for thirty years to an actor, and I have two words to describe what has made our marriage last: Louis Zorich. He's very, very supportive of my work. He likes to have space himself, and he gives a great deal, which is terrific. He did everything when I was working; I did everything when he was working. We made a pact that we would not take acting jobs out of town at the same time as long as any of our children still lived at home.

There were projects of his about which I thought, "Oh my God, what a waste of time," but if he wanted to do it, I would do everything I could to make it possible, and vice versa. From the beginning he cared deeply that I should realize my own dreams. Plus we really love each other. He was great with all the stuff about the Oscar. I think there was only one time he got offended, when we were both up for something that he had to read for and I didn't. But even with people calling him Mr. Dukakis, he laughed. None of that really mattered.

We're both first-generation Americans. Immigrants don't talk about husbands' and wives' roles—everybody works. Work was something I knew I was going to do early on. My mother worked in the mill, and then she ran one of her brothers' stores. During the war she ran the counter at Woolworth's.

I wanted to work when I was fifteen and my father didn't want me to. I can remember him with tears in his eyes saying, "Don't worry, you will work in this life. Right now I want you to have your youth."

My father's prediction came all too true.

In 1971, Louis, my brother Apollo, several friends and I founded the Whole Theatre Company in Montclair, New Jersey. Louis and I had chosen to settle in suburban New Jersey and to raise our daughter and two sons there because we wanted a kind of life for ourselves we knew we couldn't get in a Manhattan apartment. Living in Jersey, I was able to act in New York and to act and direct at our theatre while being at home for whatever came up. I determined that once I had children I was not going to travel. I waited until I was thirty-three to have my first child, so you can imagine how much she was wanted.

The Whole Theatre was an Equity regional theatre with a 199-seat house. We had wonderful actors come out to be in the plays, and I was able to act in and direct great plays. Running a theatre and being in a show at the same time, however, is a nightmare, because all the actors' grievances come immediately to you. I couldn't help but hear them when I was in the cast, and I was on the phone constantly with this or that problem. Then something would happen in the front of the house—there weren't enough programs, for example—and I would be on the phone about that.

We did *Mother Courage* with me playing the title role and what happened was pathetic. The director got fired, the stage manager threw the book at me and left, three actors came down with hepatitis, and my husband was in a near-fatal automobile accident. I felt like there wasn't much difference between *Mother Courage* and life at that point. I said, "I don't ever want to work in this theatre. I want to go to somebody else's theatre," but I did some of both for nearly twenty years.

Mother Courage is one of several roles I've played more than once. Among my favorite repeats is Serafina in *The Rose Tattoo*, which I did five times. When I did the role at the Whole Theatre a few years ago, her relationship with the Madonna was primary because I had become very involved with research and thinking about pre-patriarchal times and the worship of the Goddess, what Merlin Stone writes about in her book *When God Was a Woman*. It finally occurred to me that the Great Mother was on stage with me in the spirit and the image of the Virgin Mary. Ah, that was wonderful. It was great then to lose faith with her, to reject her, and finally to reclaim her again.

When I had played Serafina before I was more focused on her pride, her sexual needs, and the fact that when she lost her husband she lost her definition of herself as a person, and it was a real crisis for her to find it again. The discovery of the relationship to the Madonna was most important, which is interesting because that's also very important to another role I've played several times: Mary Tyrone in *Long Day's Journey into Night*. Mary says she's not in a state of grace and that the Holy Mother has turned her back on her and she's lost her, just as Serafina feels that she's not getting a sign as a result of her actions.

At first I didn't want to play Mary Tyrone. I thought I wasn't right for it and tried to suggest a friend of mine. Eventually, in conversation, I realized that I was probably well-equipped to play the part because I had had a problem with substance abuse. It started medically but eventually became a serious problem of dependence—so I realized that I did know what Mary Tyrone was about in a deeper sense.

. . .

My brother confronted me with a big obstacle in my work when I was doing *Long Day's Journey* the third time. Louis and I had played it together at Williamstown, the McCarter, and then at the Whole Theatre. Apollo was directing and I was having trouble with the first scene. I couldn't see Louis's eyes—whenever he looked at me he was squinting. I thought, "What is this? How can I play with him if he won't open his eyes? I can't tell what's happening." So I said to my brother something about, "Why is he doing that? When is he going to open his eyes?" And he replied, "I don't know why he does that, any more than I know why you have to control everything and manipulate the stage."

Whoa! It was like major light bulbs! He told me, "Unless somebody does what you want them to do, you won't play with them." I was furious. I was yelling and screaming and carrying on, but it was true: I was not accepting; I had an idea in my head, and I was not going to be vulnerable or forthcoming until he gave me what I thought was correct and proper.

Talk about having to work on something! My brother gave me a great gift, because then I began to try and accept unconditionally what other actors do and not ask that they change and do things my way. It doesn't mean that I don't have those feelings every once in a while, but I don't speak them and I don't honor them anymore.

The other thing I discovered from that experience was that I could now begin to trust everything in my work. My feelings of rejection, which came from Louis's not looking at me, were really part of the scene. From then on I had to try to trust what happened and know that everything was about the work, and not to misread signals.

I'm going to play Mother Courage again at the Great Lakes Theatre Festival in Cleveland this summer. The interesting thing about all these parts is that as I get older, I get more humor out of them. Also the price that Mother Courage pays is more apparent to me, more deeply felt, because of my own children. In the last production I did, at Williamstown, my daughter Christina played Kattrin and my husband played the Cook.

At Williamstown, Christina elected not to speak—to be as mute as

Kattrin is—for the rehearsal period. Jerry Freedman had suggested that she be mute for a couple of days, and she decided to do it for a couple of weeks. She learned a great deal by not talking. I really admired her commitment and discipline, especially since I know how much she loves to relish and discuss acting.

Christina is a young actress who is studying and struggling. The most difficult thing about acting, of course, is how you cope with all different kinds of people—when you're young, you're dealing with a lot of insecure people and strange people who are in it for reasons that are not necessarily healthy, and you have to survive all that. We talk about it from time to time, and Christina's father is very helpful. The only time I've ever really advised her was in *Rose Tattoo*, when she would come onstage with her hair covering her face. I'd say to her, "Why are you working so hard to walk onstage and nobody can see your face?" But she wanted that, she felt she looked "righter."

Being a working mother was very rough sometimes. I can't say my children weren't affected by it. I try to think that it's all evened out in the end. "Listen," I say to myself, "everybody has their parents, there are things they like and things they don't like," but there were times when I could have or should have or *thought* I should have been at home and wasn't.

Starting a theatre so I would be close to my family did make it easier. The Whole Theatre was in the same town; but still, I was running around *in* town. I saw them for breakfast every day, or dinner. I talked to the school counselors, I went to PTA meetings, and when my sons hurt themselves playing soccer and lacrosse for the high school, I administered the ginger-and-buckwheat poultices.

I think that growing up in the suburbs in a real house with a yard was good for my children. They're eager enough to leave home, but they say they had a wonderful time with their friends. Sometimes we'd have fifteen boys running around on the lawn, playing different sports. That was great.

The last play I did at the Whole Theatre was *Happy Days*. It was after I'd won the Oscar, and it sold out. Because I was in it, a lot of people came who never would have seen Beckett, so that was a bonus.

I was intensely and completely involved with the Whole Theatre for nineteen years, and it was one of the first regional theatres to go under when the climate in arts funding changed. We had a deficit for which there was no "quick fix," so we were forced to close.

I think that anybody who wants to start a theatre should do it. I stuck with it for nineteen years not only because I wanted a place to work or a place near my children: I wanted to make a theatre. I think one of the best things that came out of it was the contribution we made to the larger community in northern New Jersey, not just in the productions but through our outreach program, our educational programs. We—audiences, actors, directors, designers, administrators; all of us—had some terrific times in that little theatre and I think that was important.

I feel that you must not worry about what other people are going to think. If it's what you want to do, just do it. Let your life evolve out of all the things you want to do instead of what you think you should be doing to succeed and get ahead and all that other stuff which boggles the mind and poisons the heart.

Having a theatre in the town where we lived meant suffering the scorn and mockery of my New York colleagues. Ted Mann actually asked me what I was doing hiding out in New Jersey. People said all sorts of things that had me doubting and thinking, "Am I doing this because I can't cut it?" There's so much about being "successful" that has to do with making money and having a presence in the theatrical community, so people take the measure of themselves from that.

If you want to do television commercials, do them. But if you want to go off and start a small company that tours in the mountains, do that.

I've been a founder of four theatres, and it looks like the universe is trying to tell me, "Stop! Stop. Let go." But I'm not listening. The next project I want to do is called Voices of Earth. Opportunities for actresses shrink as we get older. The parts are few and far between—so many of the playwrights are men, and successful women playwrights often write in male images, which is one of the reasons that I am moved to work on Voices of Earth, a small, not-for-profit company that

Joan MacIntosh, Leslie Ayvazian, Remi Bosseau and I recently incorporated.

Among the inspirations for Voices of Earth was *The Goddess Project*, which we did at the Whole Theatre. Joan MacIntosh played The Goddess Inanna and I played her sister Ereshkigal in a play based on the Sumerian legend about the descent of Inanna into the underworld. My own interest in the Goddess began when I was playing Hecuba in *The Trojan Women* at the Whole Theatre. There's a section where she abandons the gods because she doesn't feel they are listening to her prayers and she's going to go back to the old gods.

The first thing I came across was a wonderful little book called *Perseus and the Gorgon* by an archaeologist named Cornelia Steketee Hulst. I was haunted by her phrase, ". . . and the teachings of the Great Mother were buried in oblivion and covered in silence by Perseus."

I went to another bookstore, and I know this sounds nuts, but I'm standing there and Merlin Stone's *When God Was a Woman* fell off a shelf. Those two books got me started, and last year I had the opportunity to travel to Neolithic sites in Greece with Dr. Marija Gimbutas, an archaeologist who is one of the foremost authorities on the matrilineal cultures of the Neolithic and Early Bronze Age.

The thing that drives me is my own particular search. A great modern Greek poet named Cavafy wrote, about the journey of Odysseus, that when you get to Ithaca, don't blame Ithaca if it isn't what you dreamed of—Ithaca gave you the journey.

Andronicus *(Actors Theatre of Louisville)*

*M*uch *as I have enjoyed every Joe Morton performance I've seen, my favorite is his Autolycus in the BAM Theater Company's production of* The Winter's Tale. *On both sides of the Atlantic I've found Shakespeare's rogue played with some element of vulgarity; Joe Morton gave Autolycus sensual relish devoid of crudity, and a flamboyance suggestive of a future Cyrano. Classics, new plays and musical comedies are all accomplishments of this versatile actor, who is also familiar to film audiences as the title character in* The Brother from Another Planet *and to television viewers for the series "Equal Justice." He made his New York directing debut in 1993 with the Playwrights Horizons' production of Eric Overmyer's* The Heliotrope Bouquet by Scott Joplin and Louis Chauvin.

Turning down Hamlet this summer was very hard. I've wanted to play him and have thought about the play for a long time. When I read it with the idea that I might do it in a few weeks, the thing that leapt out at me, which I'd never seen before, is that every young man in the play is either coming from or going back to university—as opposed to the older men, who are remnants of a wartime society. Other than Fortinbras and a few of the lackeys who follow Claudius around, most of the young men—especially Hamlet, Horatio and

Laertes—are involved in education. They bring the play all of its high moral ground.

Setting that contrast between the generations against the events of the plot excited me because of what was going on in America at the time. We were getting ready to go to Iraq and having the usual arguments about whether we should or should not. Hamlet thinks a lot about the idea of violence and taking somebody's life. When you go through the play, you realize that nothing has really changed. To me, it's an amazing thing that someone could write a play hundreds of years ago and we're still involved with the same problems.

Hamlet touches me in very personal ways, having to do with the fact that my father was in the military and died under suspicious circumstances. I had the opportunity to work with a director I know well— Tina Packer of Shakespeare & Company. We were going to do it in a theatre in Boston that wouldn't get a great deal of exposure, so it was perfect. Very often in this country, when you do such a role, you have to do it à la Mel Gibson, where everybody can take shots at you. I believe in England you spend a lot of time building up to parts like that.

Unfortunately, a couple of things happened to prevent me from playing Hamlet now. First, my television series, "Equal Justice," looks like it's not going to be picked up in the fall, and I felt it wouldn't be smart of me to tuck myself away and become unavailable for other projects. Second, there is a film that I may shoot in Germany in May, and I had to be available for that. I am trying to develop a film career, which is difficult enough for any actor, and even more difficult for black actors. Plus I have responsibilities—I have a wife, our three-year-old son and a daughter who's at Sarah Lawrence. So *Hamlet* won't happen this year.

It's an odd feeling, but I haven't been onstage for almost two years, since I played Hubert in *King John* for Joe Papp. That's the longest time away from the stage since I've been an actor.

I probably got my first classical roles by just talking my way into them. By saying, "There's no reason that a black actor cannot play this." What I love about Shakespeare and the Greeks is that they're greater than the characters or the plot. Their metaphors are much larger, which is why it's so difficult when you have to fight color games about who can and cannot play certain roles. The stories that are being told and the ideas about humanity and its struggles are so universal that it seems to me that anyone can do them.

I went three years to Hofstra University on Long Island, where there is a wonderful theatre facility. The emphasis was on studying the classics, and we had amazing teachers. Because I had signed up for a drama major on impulse and had no training, I didn't have any preconceptions, so I could do what my teachers told me. They were really interested in my talent and I grew very quickly, to the point that I became disillusioned with Hofstra because I wasn't getting any good roles on the main stage. When we did Shakespeare, I couldn't get anything better than Balthazar, Romeo's servant.

When I auditioned for the title role in Brendan Behan's *The Hostage* and the director said, "You could do this with your hands tied behind you, but I'm not going to give you the role because it's an Irish/English play, and if you make the hostage black it complicates everything," I left Hofstra. I thought, "If I'm going to have this much difficulty in school, I might as well have the same amount of difficulty outside, and at least get paid for anything I land."

The Hostage's director, Joe Leon, gave me an introduction to an agent at CMA named Ed Blum. It was like one of those Hollywood stories. When I walked into his office, Ed Blum had a script in front of him, *A Month of Sundays*. It was a musical update of the Noah story that was going to be Off Broadway at the Theatre de Lys. Ed set up an audition, I walked down to the theatre, and I got the job. I went from that to being a replacement on Broadway in *Hair*, to *Salvation* Off Broadway—one of the first rock musicals to deal with Christ—and eventually to playing Walter Lee in *Raisin*, the musical version of *A Raisin in the Sun*.

I started my professional career in 1968, which luckily for me turned out to be exactly the right time. Although there weren't many black actors doing Shakespeare, which was what I had come into the city to do, a lot of things were opening up for black actors who were also singers. I've never actually studied singing. I had learned guitar in elementary school during the period when everybody wanted to pick up a guitar and play, and I started singing when I got to high school. I'm not quite sure how, but I sort of developed my own style, and by the time I got to college I had a rock-and-roll band on weekends to make extra pocket money.

I guess what kept me in New York was *Hair*. Everybody wanted to get into that show, and it took me about five auditions before I was finally hired. They kept telling me to dress grungier. This may sound like an odd thing to say, but the first time I saw *Hair* I thought, "This is the best training for classical theatre." *Hair* wasn't just a story, it was an entire ritual. I thought, "Wow! To do this for six months would be great preparation for the Greeks, because you really have to get involved with giving yourself over to the gods." In that show, it was the gods of politics and drugs and rock and roll, but the names of the gods didn't much matter. You still had to strip yourself naked.

I remember the first time I did the nude scene. When you got into the show they said, "You don't have to do it if you don't want to." I was in the show for two weeks before I decided, "I just want to know what it's like. If it's horrible I'll never do it again." When I stood up I realized that I didn't feel any more naked with my clothes off than I did with them on. The stage is such a huge magnifying glass that you feel naked all the time.

Raisin was probably the most exciting of the musicals I was in. I created the role, on Broadway, and I was nominated for a Tony. That was an odd sensation—I remember going to a nomination brunch, getting a certificate and feeling like I was getting my diploma from high school.

I was in *Raisin* for two-and-a-half years. Being in a long run was one of the best experiences I ever had, because you really have to concentrate on how to keep things fresh and alive. After the first six months, that's very difficult.

I did anything and everything. There was a drunk scene at the top of the second act, and right before the act started I would wrestle with two of the guys in the chorus so I could at least be out of breath and have that as an obstacle to deal with.

When you're in a long run, you hope to have insights about the character and about the play. I would go to or call the director and then go to the other actors and say, "I wanna try something," and we would move things around a little. In a musical, you have a bit of freedom to syncopate the music, which sometimes drove our musical director crazy, but I thought, "I have to do something to keep it fresh, without going too far afield."

Actually, I left the show because of a musicians' strike. I had gotten a television series, but because I had signed a run-of-the-play contract, the only way out of the show was something like the strike, which lasted the number of days that invalidates all contracts.

I went to California, and one of the things I understood when I started doing film was why people like Brando stopped doing theatre. You can employ the same techniques and the same process in film, but you don't have to do it eight times a week. You get it right, somebody shoots it, it's cut properly, it looks wonderful, and then you can go on to the next project.

During that first part of my career, my whole effort towards not-for-profit theatre was not to get involved with it. Before leaving school, I had done what most of us did in our junior year, which was to go down to TCG and audition for regional theatres. I had been accepted as an apprentice or as a journeyman in a lot of fairly reputable theatres across the country, but my agent talked me out of it. He said, "Look, you've just spent the last three years of your life in school. Why would you want to leave New York immediately? Make a reputation inside the business first. Then if you feel there's something more creative you need to do, you can do it."

But when I had been doing musical theatre for five or six years, I felt that in order to be taken seriously in film, I had to have a *dramatic* resume. I decided it was time to do regional theatre. My agents were very supportive of my decision.

Theatre outside of New York has a wide range of possibilities. Probably the most exciting theatre I've ever worked at is the Actors Theatre of Louisville, where I've been twice. It is definitely an actors' theatre. The actors are treated like mini-gods down there. You work your tail off, but it is very rewarding. I was first there in 1977, when I went down to do two plays and ended up spending most of the season.

Jon Jory said to me, "I want to do a musical version of *Titus Andronicus*. Would you play Aaron?" I answered, "Jon, you know the last thing I want to do at this moment is a musical," but he said, "Yes, but would you like to do the arrangements of the music for it, too, and would you like to act in and direct *Sizwe Bansi Is Dead?*" So, of course, I stayed.

Jon thought that you needed a world to put *Titus Andronicus* in that would be appropriate for the amount of violence the play contains. This was in the *Star Wars* days, so he set the play way in the future: the Romans became Cronians and they were all blue; the Goths were all white; Aaron was a Calibanesque character. There were half-men, half-creature characters—the setting was supposed to be a dead, rotting planet. It was an interesting take on the play.

Unfortunately, things changed, as they do in the course of rehearsal. The first half of the play became light and like *Star Wars*, while the second half—Lavinia's rape and so forth—was very earnestly and honestly done. The audience either loved the transition into something darker or they just couldn't bear it and walked out.

I had the best time of my life during that ATL season, and I went back seven years later to be in "Shorts," their one-act play festival. I was in a wonderful play called *Advice to the Players*, which was about an incident when South African actors John Kani and Winston Ntshona had come to the U.S. to do *Waiting for Godot* and were asked by the African National Congress not to do the play, as a public protest against the government of South Africa.

Jon Jory knows my feelings about nontraditional casting, so the other play he cast me in was about an American writer who goes to Italy to write and to study and who gets wound up with various people. Doing those two plays was a terrific experience. Actors Theatre is really set up for the actor—the plays they choose, the rehearsal spaces they have—it is a very, very comfortable place to be. And because Jon has worked so hard, he has 95 percent attendance at almost every production, which is really remarkable.

When you go to a regional theatre anywhere in the country, you know that you're not going to be staying at the Ritz-Carlton. That's just given. You have to pay your own rent where you stay. The first year I was in Louisville, I had a lovely economy room with a Murphy bed in a very nice little apartment complex. In those days I was single, so when I traveled to regional theatres, which I did a lot, I pretty much brought my entire apartment with me. I would bring my electric piano, my guitar, lots of books—all the things that would make me comfortable.

In Louisville, I established a jam night on Sundays, knowing we would be off on Monday. For a while we held them in my apartment. People would bring whatever instruments they played, and if they didn't play anything they'd use wooden sticks and beat on pots and pans. I made lots of popcorn, people brought over their own beer, and we would play music and tell stories and drink and carry on till all hours of the night. Neighbors didn't particularly care for us, but you needed somewhere to blow off steam, and you didn't always want to go to a bar or a club or someplace where you had to spend money.

These Sunday-night parties got so huge, however, that we changed our location to the bar downstairs at the theatre. It's great—I don't know of any other theatre in the country where you walk out of the dressing room into a bar. Everybody knows that most actors enjoy sitting in a bar after the show and talking about the work and drinking.

I met a young apprentice down there named Ron MacIntyre, and he played saxophone. He and I wrote music together, and some of us became so friendly that after the season was over, one of the stage managers and a couple of the actors and I got together in the back of a van and drove from Louisville down to Key West for a vacation. Ron MacIntyre is still a friend, and his first son is my godson. Leo Burmester, an ATL actor, and I are still close friends. There are a lot of people who came out of Louisville who remain good friends. It was that kind of theatre.

Once you're no longer rehearsing during the day at a regional theatre, what you do is still geared to acting. Playing at night means you begin to prepare, usually just mentally, around five o'clock, so you don't have a lot of time. You've probably been up late the night before, so you don't get up till noon. Most of the day you're really just concentrating on your work. You may take time to read, go to the local library, a museum, a movie—whatever that particular town has to offer. Most regional theatres are set up so that if you're not working on another production, you may be involved in a reading of a play that

they're considering. If the theatre is run at all like Louisville, they keep
you occupied most of the time.

The second time I was in Louisville, I was traveling with my daughter,
who was then about eleven years old. Once I wasn't rehearsing, the
daytimes were spent with her. My daughter's name is Hopi, and she's
been living with me since she was ten. Her mother and I separated
many years ago, so for a while I was a single parent.

Hopi traveled with me to Louisville; to GeVa in Rochester; to do a
television film by Kenneth Cavander called "The File on Jill Hatch."
I'm an army brat, so I've traveled most of my life, and when Hopi came
to live with me, I thought, "I need to travel at this point, 'cause I need
to continue doing this work. If taking her along doesn't work out, I'll
make another plan. But if I don't at least try it, I'll feel as if she's taken
something away from me, even though it won't be her fault."

*Shezwee Powell
and Joe Morton
in* Raisin
(Arena Stage)

What I would do is hook up Hopi's school with on-site tutors I had arranged for, which worked fine. I wanted to have a day-to-day relationship with my daughter. She had really only known me from whatever she'd seen on TV or onstage, which looked kind of glamorous. When we traveled together, Hopi could see that I had to go to rehearsals every day, that there were lines to learn, that acting takes a great deal of effort—it's not just about lights and people recognizing you on the street. We became very, very close, and she's been with me ever since. I'm really proud it worked out that way.

Another regional-theatre highpoint was being in *How I Got That Story* at GeVa, brilliantly directed by Steven Katz. I played the Historical Event, which is twenty-six characters, plus I did all of the sound effects for the show. Amlin Gray, the playwright, came to see the production and to give a talk to the audience. The first thing he said to them was, "At this time the last thing I wanted to do was to see yet another production of *How I Got That Story*—especially in Rochester, New York, where you have to travel by train, and it's cold. But by far, including the production that's now rehearsing in New York, this is the best production of my play that I've ever seen." That made us feel very proud. I got to use a great deal of myself. Those kinds of opportunities made me feel like things were going to work out, because each one gave me a chance to grow.

Another opportunity for growth came in 1979 with the BAM Company, which purported to be a dream come true: a resident repertory company of thirty-odd actors doing the classics at the Brooklyn Academy of Music; an artistic director, David Jones, who had been with the Royal Shakespeare Company. Every actor would like to have a home from which to work. The problem with the BAM Company was trying to have it in New York.

In New York, everything you do is viewed as if it's a Broadway or Off-Broadway play, so the reviews keep you alive or kill you. Because David Jones was from the RSC, critics expected us to be brilliant— forgetting that it took a long time for the RSC to *become* the RSC. So we died, unfortunately, after two years. (Probably the closest New

York can get to a major repertory company is to have a group of actors and directors who fairly consistently kind of float through a theatre, which is held together by the kind of work that's done there. The Public Theater has had that reputation; so do La MaMa and Second Stage.)

At BAM, in a play called *Johnny on the Spot*, I was Lucius, keeper of the gate. He was the stereotypical black character wearing a bellman's uniform with a pillbox hat, and it just made me feel miserable. It was one of the most embarrassing things I've ever done. But the play was in the repertory, so I did it. And it worked out, because I was able to do Oedipus the following season.

One of my best experiences in the BAM Company was playing Autolycus, the rogue in *The Winter's Tale*. I have heard that actors have played Autolycus dark and vulgar, and I don't see where that is in the script. I think you break the sense of what Bohemia is about if you do that. To me, Autolycus is sensual. I think he has the greatest fun trying to win. That's what he wants. Winning a woman, winning a purse, winning whatever, it is just the idea that he can do it. It has nothing to do with being evil. That is the way he gets through life.

Some of the costume choices emphasized his flair and sense of fun. I had a large leather cape which had dozens and dozens of pockets, so I could pull whatever I wanted out of them, and one of those wonderful Elizabethan silk shirts that was covered by I don't know how many vests that all tied, so there were lots of strings, and a wonderful red hat that had a butterfly and a feather. . . .

I'm the kind of actor who comes in with my own home version of whatever the costume is going to be like. For Autolycus, I rehearsed in a very large Nigerian robe that stood in for the cape. When I did *Cheapside*, a play about Shakespeare's contemporary Robert Greene, at the Roundabout, our costumes weren't necessarily of the period because the director, Carey Perloff, wanted to open up its resonances to the present. For rehearsals, I wore my purple Elizabethan-style jacket, and underneath it a hooded sweatshirt, because my character, Cutting-ball, is the kind of guy you might see today in the streets if you were roaming in the wrong part of town. I have a knife that has a handle made from a deer's hoof, so I'd wear that. I took some lariat and strapped it around my boots because I thought he would wear those kind of shoes. As things occur to me, I add or subtract from what I bring in. For *Cheapside*, a lot of what I wore in rehearsal is what the costumer ended up putting together.

When I played Caliban at Shakespeare & Company, I stole my costume from an African book. I took some flour and water and made paste, put it in my hair, and had six feathers sticking up; rubbed artist's charcoal all over my body so that I would be pitch black; and put yellow paint on my face, with black around my eyes. I had on leather gloves that gave me claws; a loincloth; and a very long, wide tail. . . .

The Shakespeare & Company theatre is outdoors, in the Berkshires, on the former estate of Edith Wharton. It's gorgeous, and there was a magic over that production of *The Tempest*. Two things would always happen during the pageant when the goddesses appear: one, it would stop sprinkling; two, a tiny mouse came to the wall and stood there—I mean literally got up on his hind legs—to watch.

Behind the stage, there is a small dirt road that leads to some property away from the estate. One night, in the middle of the play, I'm backstage with Rocco Sisto, and suddenly we hear music. It's getting louder and louder and we can hear that it's in a truck or a car, coming down the dirt road toward the stage area. Rocco's gotta make an entrance, and I say, "Go, I'll take care of it." A truck appears and I run out and leap onto its side and I keep saying to the guys inside, "Turn it off, turn it off!" These guys start driving crazy and finally they stop, 'cause they're just looking at this vision in yellow and black and feathers. . . .

I've played Caliban twice—it was my first major classical role, at the Shakespeare Festival in Stratford, Connecticut. I've also played Oedipus twice—the first time was the BAM production that Emily Mann directed; the second time was in *The Legend of Oedipus* at the Williamstown Theatre Festival in 1988. Kenneth Cavander took all of the House of Laius plays and wove them together, starting with Oedipus as a young man coming in and destroying the Sphinx at Thebes and ending with him as an old blind man dying at Colonus.

Getting the part was an interesting process in itself. Nikos

Psacharopoulos originally called me to play one of the gods. I said, "No, I've already played Oedipus and I think I got it half right the first time, so I want to do that character again. If that's not possible, thank you, but I'm not interested." So he considered it and I had three auditions in his apartment in New York. The third was more like the two of us sitting down to talk, to make sure that we were going to be doing the same play. I'd heard all the stories about how difficult Nikos could be on actors, but I just found him a wonderful man. We had a great time together, and I think this production is one of the best things I've ever done on stage.

Talk about opportunity to stretch! There was so much to deal with—the set was like something out of an opera; there were forty people just in the chorus. I needed to make the production mine as quickly as possible, so the rest of the cast would know who Oedipus was. I asked Nikos if the very first time I rehearsed, we could do the scene when Oedipus galvanizes the community to look for the murderer. I had this idea, which I probably got from *The Gospel at Colonus*, that since I was a black man, the way to do the scene was almost like a revival preacher. The first time I did it, everybody liked it, but they didn't respond. I said, "No, no, I need you to respond to what I'm doing." Well, we tore down the rafters. It was great. And it established what kind of Oedipus I would be and what kind of relationship he had to Thebes. There was lots going on—there were two vocal coaches; the chorus had to learn music—and I felt that every time I walked in, it was important that they had to deal with me as the king. That's how I approached it and it really did work very well.

The first major thing I had to do was learn the words. We had only ten days to learn a script that was over three hundred pages long. Most people lived on or near the Williams College campus. I had them give me a house very far away. It was a converted barn, and I would get up with the sun and go out to this lovely, expansive farmland. I would work all morning long so that, depending on what scene we were doing that day, I would be basically off-book. No one could understand how I could be off-book so quickly. I was off-book completely in five days. Doing that was part of my saying, "If I work hard, they'll work hard." We were asking everyone to do a great deal in a very short period of time. And I think we were successful.

.   .   .

When I read a play, I read it the first time for the story. Then I start reading the play asking, "What's my character's journey through this piece?" The more you do that, the more you realize what the writer is trying to say. And that's when everything begins to play. There's a wonderful moment when Oedipus is looking for the murderer and one of the messengers comes back to tell him that his parents have died. It's such a relief for Oedipus—he feels so free—that when we did it I not only broke into tears but started to laugh all at the same time.

The Greeks and Shakespeare will always be my favorites. I played Orestes in Carey Perloff's production of Ezra Pound's *Elektra* at CSC. Pamela Reed was Elektra, and Pamela and I became as close as sister and brother because of that play. With classics, there is nothing that is impossible. There's this great breadth of emotion and possibility that doesn't necessarily exist in modern theatre.

The last Oedipus I did made a big difference in terms of what I thought I could do in classical theatre. I suddenly thought, "Now I'm ready to think about doing Othello"—although I don't believe I'm ready to do Othello. "Now I'm ready to do Hamlet." It filled me with a lot of hope.

When I did Hubert in *King John*, Joe Papp, who could easily infuriate me, said, "You know, Joe, you're really good in the show. Some actors get to a point and they just level off. Every time I see you, you get better and better." To me, that's the name of the game. Growth plus some good luck—which is opportunity meeting preparedness. That is why I tell actors to go to regional theatres. If you've spent enough time to learn what it is you want to do, and you've learned to do it really well, when the opportunities make themselves available, you can take advantage of them. It's terrible to feel like something is happening and you're not ready for it.

Very slowly, during the last decade, I began to pull away from regional theatres to get more involved in doing film. I started doing smaller parts, because no one knew me in that part of the industry. I'd already done a television series and hated it a lot. It was a sitcom called *Grady*, a spinoff of *Sanford and Son*, and it fulfilled every fear I ever had of doing sitcoms. It was just ridiculous.

I made a point of not doing the roles of pimps and drug dealers that were being offered to black actors. Gradually, I began to build a reputation, and I think what finally sort of flipped me over was John Sayles' film, *Brother from Another Planet*. It's a movie about a black extraterrestrial slave who escapes from his planet and accidentally winds up in Harlem. He looks like he knows what's going on, but has no idea what's happening. He has no facility for speech. It's a wonderful film, and it presented a great challenge to me because I had to go through everything without speaking.

I haven't had the opportunities in film that I have had in the theatre; I think that's left for the future. So far *Brother from Another Planet* is my favorite, and it has a lot attached to it. I met my wife, Nora Chavooshian, doing that movie. She was the production designer.

In television, I've done some wonderful films and gotten a chance to work with some great people. Probably the best to date is "The Howard Beach Story."

I feel fortunate that I was able to do a series like "Equal Justice." I think most people approach television—certainly I did, and will in the future—with a great deal of trepidation, because you don't know how something's going to wind up. With Thomas Carter and everyone on his "Equal Justice" staff, there was a sense of a greater universe, where people are trying to talk and to do something about things that need to be talked about and done.

Since I started acting professionally, some major changes have come about in dealing with stereotypes. A white director can no longer say, comfortably, "I need you to be blacker than that." People are beginning to realize that there are lots of different kinds of black people in the world, just as I think they're beginning to realize there are lots of different kinds of women, and gradually they will understand that Oriental is not the proper word—that there are different kinds of Asians in the world—and they all have their own particular points of view.

John Sayles, as a director, surrounds himself with women. He doesn't allow himself to have a completely male point of view. He also makes sure that there are black people behind him as well as white.

I've always wanted to direct. Directing *Sizwe Bansi Is Dead* at the Actors Theatre of Louisville was one of the high points in my career. It was great to put the whole thing together, and then we got the best reviews of any play that season. I felt really proud of that production.

I'm going to Sundance in Utah this summer to adapt and direct a film segment. It's from a play by Bill Gunn called *Black Picture Show*. As a director, I go to the music first. That usually helps give me a clear picture of what I'm trying to create. In *Black Picture Show*, the music that's talked about is jazz samba. It has to do with a man's hallucinations: he actually thinks he sees a band and they start playing samba. I've decided to go all the way and make it absolute samba. I was able to find a wonderful range, not only of samba songs, but also some incredible music written for an orchestra in the Andes, made up of traditional instruments like nothing you've ever heard before.

I'm only doing one very long scene. I hope that leads to an opportunity to make the entire film, because I would like to be instrumental in presenting images of black people that have never or seldom been seen. My preferences are different from Spike Lee's. I think what he's trying to do is fine, but I'm talking about images that have to do with my own personal background, that come from novels and plays. There's a book called *Cane* by Jean Toomer, a series of short stories and poems that are beautifully written—amazing stories in very poetic prose, which is what my bent is. I'd love to make films out of Zora Neale Hurston's *Their Eyes Were Watching God* and Toni Morrison's *Tar Baby*.

In the future, I'd like to make enough money so that we can buy a house outside of New York. Like most people in the world, I would like not to have to worry about bills. I am trying to get more and more involved in helping my wife, who is a sculptor. (She became a production designer so she could put enough money together to sculpt.) The television series afforded us enough money to put some away in our savings and deal with my daughter's college, and now we're using a lot of it to get Nora's pieces cast. Sometimes I am able to take my paycheck and hand it over to her and say, "This money is to be used for nothing but your sculpture." It's very hard for new visual artists to get off the ground, because people say, "That's really good," but few of them buy. We theatre people think *our* business is screwy—we have lots of friends who are artists, and I just don't understand how they do it.

As an actor, I want to continue to present images that are slightly different from what people are used to seeing. If the opportunity to play Hamlet should, God forbid, pass me by, I hope I get a chance to direct the play.

I want to go on playing or directing Shakespeare and the Greeks. I think it's important that the theatre community and audiences understand that the voices that have been behind those plays are not the only ones that can speak through them.

Largo Desolato (New York
Shakespeare Festival)

*A*mong *the remarkable qualities of the* Hamlet *starring and directed by Kevin Kline at the Public Theater in 1990 (then filmed and shown on the PBS "Great Performances" series) was the Polonius of Josef Sommer. Handsomely gray-bearded, sophisticated, wily and witty, he was believably a prime minister and patriarch whose loss might unhinge Ophelia and Laertes. Character actor extraordinaire, Josef Sommer spent most of the theatre seasons between 1962 and 1970 playing twenty-four roles in twenty-one productions at the American Shakespeare Festival in Stratford, Connecticut. Though he eventually became a country squire in upstate New York, where he and his wife Nina welcomed me to their home for our interview, Sommer has worked extensively in resident theatre and has built a film career in such parts as Harrison Ford's nemesis in* Witness, *Meryl Streep's lover in* Still of the Night, *and numerous roles in television series and other movies.*

The theatre is a profession that seems to me to have no structure. There are no ladders to climb—you don't get to one level and then automatically step up to the next one. My experience has been that you climb to a certain point and then suddenly find yourself down at the bottom, and climb up again.

The rises and falls may look more exaggerated from the inside. My wife often points out that when I finish a role, and two weeks go by and I haven't gotten another offer, I become a little hard to live with. The future can look so blank to an actor at the end of a job . . .

It is clearly harder for a woman than it is for a man in the business, particularly in those middle years. Older character women and men— those of us who have stuck it out—can have things better. But I think a woman in her thirties and forties has a terrible time.

Actually, I had a worse time as an actor when I was young, because I was never really a juvenile. One of the worst experiences I can remember is a production of *Androcles and the Lion* at Stratford, in which I was hopelessly miscast as the romantic captain. I was bad in the part and didn't know what to do, and the actress I was playing opposite and I didn't get along, so it was just terrible. I was not comfortable as an actor until I got into my late thirties.

When I came out of Carnegie Tech in 1957, regional theatre as we know it today was just an idea. I had done summer stock at the Gateway Theatre in Bellport, Long Island, between my college years, but I wasn't ready to face New York. I spent a year teaching English at a school in Switzerland, which was just a way of getting to see something of Europe. Then I got drafted into the army and was sent to Cleveland to protect the city from air attack by Russians, and I actually succeeded: the Russians didn't attack Cleveland the entire time I was there.

Next I got a Fulbright to go to Germany, where my intention was to become a bilingual actor. I was born in Germany, and we came to America when I was a small child, so I knew some German to begin with. I thought, "I will study in Germany and maybe I will be able to act in German *and* English." This was kind of a pipe dream, but I did see lots of European theatre, and that further encouraged my hope to find resident theatre work here.

When I came back in 1962, my Carnegie Tech teacher, Allen Fletcher, had become head of the company training program at the American Shakespeare Festival in Stratford, Connecticut, and invited me to join the company. Stratford had just gone through its star phase (when

Katharine Hepburn and Jessica Tandy were its leading ladies), then they decided to make it into a repertory theatre and conservatory. The Ford Foundation gave a great deal of money to hire a group of us to train during the winter and to perform during the summers, and this meant year-round employment for actors—unheard of at that time. You got a contract that covered your entire year, with not a generous but a living wage. There were some wonderful actors in the company: Sada Thompson, Hal Holbrook, Phil Bosco, Roy Scheider.

We were paid to go to school for voice training, movement, style, scene work, all that stuff. Some of the training was good, some of it was kind of bullshit. Maybe it's just me—and movement training has never been my strong point anyway—but we would have these sort-of dance classes, leaping about. I felt that was not very useful.

We had to learn a lot of fencing and fighting, which was very good for those who were adept at it. I'm not. I've always avoided fencing in plays, and my directors know to work around *that* problem.

I was with the company at Stratford for eight years. Not eight *consecutive* years (since regional theatre really got going in the mid-sixties, and I did three seasons in Seattle and a season each at ACT in San Francisco and at the Long Wharf in New Haven). I would say after each year, "This is it. I don't want to say any more of this Shakespeare crap. I want to do some 'Hi. How are ya? Stick 'em up' kind of jobs." And then, the next year, I'd be back again.

I remember with great affection one of my first productions at Stratford, the *King Lear* that Morris Carnovsky did. I thought Morris's Lear was a wonderful performance, a very open and innocent approach that was staggering. On the opening night of this *King Lear* that I was so proud of being in, I was one of about ten soldiers who were standing behind Lear as he made his pronouncements in the first scene of the play. We all had big heavy costumes on, and big boots. We were carrying enormous padded shields that looked like ironing boards, with a handle on the back so we could hold them up in front of us. There was a lot of trumpeting at the end of the scene, and everybody made big sweeping exits offstage. I was one of the last soldiers to leave, and I tripped on my costume, fell flat onto my ironing board and—as I was still gripping the handle—I couldn't get up! There was this poor, hopeless soldier, flailing about onstage. Finally the lights went away

and I could struggle off. I remember being so humiliated and apologiz-
ing endlessly to everybody . . .

It seems to me we had a *lot* of trouble with costumes. I remember a
Julius Caesar that we did on a raked stage. I was playing either Cassius
or Caesar—I played them both, at different times—and we had all
been costumed in tunic dresses, with a very narrow skirt opening at the
bottom. When you're trying to make a fast exit on a raked stage in a
narrow skirt, you keep going down and there's nothing you can do to
stop yourself. You become one of those little walking toy ducks that
just goes by momentum. And on the big Stratford stage, the wings are
about twenty miles away, so you say your last line and fifteen minutes
later you're still trying to hobble your way off the stage in this cute
dress . . .

Stratford was full of that kind of thing. Because of the size of the
stage, everything had to make a big statement, including your acting.
You always had to make a gesture so the audience could see who was
talking . . .

I had the very fortunate experience of playing Malvolio twice. The
first time was at Stratford, where you had to get a little bigger than
you wanted for it to carry; then, the following year, I played Malvolio
at the Old Globe in San Diego, which is a rather intimate theatre.
The size difference was very important, because at the Old Globe I
was able to become far more detailed and truthful and believable in a
comic role—which is the essence of comedy—instead of slamming it
across . . .

One of the important points for me in acting is to play against the
obvious. I don't mean fighting the text, but making tension out of
resistance. If you have a character whom the playwright has strongly
drawn in certain colors, those colors are there—you can't make them
go away. What you want to do is find your own colors that will contrast
and create a tension. I can't honestly remember whether that had fully
formed in my mind as Malvolio, but it's something I have worked on,
and was certainly thinking about when I played Polonius in Kevin
Kline's production of *Hamlet* at the Public Theater . . .

What Shakespeare did with Polonius is quite complex, in and of
itself. But I have often seen Polonius played not as Shakespeare's

complex character but as a buffoon—comic relief, perhaps, and a bit of a bore. Knowing those negatives about the part, I set out to find the opposites, which are that he's an interesting guy, with a strong sense of self-worth and a terrific sense of humor. Polonius's advice to Laertes, for example, is very good advice. The only way to play it, certainly from his point of view, is to give excellent advice to a young man, who may well not know these things. I think it's a mistake for Laertes to play it as if he's heard all this stuff a thousand times.

When Polonius does his "tragical-comical-historical-pastoral," or his "That he is mad, 'tis true; 'tis true 'tis pity" speeches, he is deliberately finding the amusement in saying things like that. I think he finds managing to be alliterative and talking in this convoluted way amusing and quite elegant. He's certainly not saying it because he doesn't know what he's doing.

Kevin's approach to the part as a director was very much in sympathy with mine. Before we even decided to work together, I laid out why I wanted to play the part and we had a long discussion. So our intentions were the same.

It was Kevin's idea to do an actor's production of the play. He had no big concept behind the production other than to do the play as honestly and directly as possible, to strip it of all extraneous matter, and to focus on actors speaking the play, which may not sound as revolutionary as I found it to be.

This approach is a very rewarding one from the acting point of view. As both director and leading actor, Kevin was extremely giving, making sure that every actor, to the smallest part, had his moment.

I tend to be rather distrustful of "concept" productions, having been in some pretty terrible ones. There was a *Love's Labour's Lost* we did at Stratford, soon after *Hair* was the big show. It was done in that hippie style, with motorcycles coming onstage. I thought it was pretty damn hopeless. I was playing Don Armado, who is supposed to be the flamboyant character. Well, everybody else was so flamboyant that Don Armado looked like wallpaper!

I do like things that are actor-oriented, that are collaborative. I'm attracted to directors who work this way, and perhaps they are attracted to me. I don't have a lot of experience with putting myself in the hands of concept directors, though one example of a concept production I really enjoyed was *The Merchant of Venice* at Lincoln Center. Rosemary Harris played Portia, Chris Walken was Bassanio, Sydney Walker was Shylock, I played Antonio and Ellis Rabb directed. This was a modern-dress production set in 1960s Italy.

I never can speak about these productions from the audience's point of view, but I found this one great fun and terribly interesting and I loved doing it. I was dressed so elegantly and looked so good! Ellis, Chris and I jointly made a decision to hint at a homosexual relationship between Bassanio and Antonio—we never did anything overt, but we gave the audience something to think about, and that fell right in with the Via Veneto setting. There was a style about doing this *Merchant of Venice* that was very satisfying to me.

Another fabulous experience was playing Tartuffe for Allen Fletcher, who became the artistic director of Seattle Rep. I'm an actor who works a great deal out of instinct—I'm not very good at thinking about acting; it seems to me that acting is doing and not thinking—so I just leapt into Tartuffe. Allen was like a safety net for me. I would try anything and he would catch me.

Seattle was very exciting for me because it was my first real break away from Shakespeare, and it was a good company. The big thing there—which was absolutely thrilling, and I would still love to go back to—was playing in repertory. We did a different play every night. I played Tartuffe, and a very small part in *The Visit*, and we continued that way, mixing all kinds and sizes of roles.

One of the joys of working in a company atmosphere is getting to play so many kinds of parts. Places like Long Wharf and Hartford that job in actors out of New York are perhaps a little more rigid in their typecasting than what I experienced in Seattle, when we were all stuck out there and were going to play the parts whether we looked like what the author had written or not.

I moved my wife and daughter to Seattle for three years. That was really uprooting my family, and generally a positive experience, except for the fact that I didn't care that much for Seattle as a place to live. I did get to know people outside of the theatre, and felt very much a part of the community, which I liked. I just didn't like being in

Seattle itself. I find that I'm not much of a West Coast person, and I include the entire West Coast. It's just something about me—I feel like I'm falling off the edge of the world when I'm out there.

After about two years of working in Seattle, the atmosphere at the theatre began to resemble slightly that of a factory. It's peculiar, because what we were making in this factory was really great stuff. I had major roles to do in important plays, but because you would go from one production to another without any of the time to prepare yourself to start on another role, or even to be out of work and be *grateful* for another role, it became a little routine and pat, which I think hurt the work. You sort of said, "Oh yeah, now I'm playing Serjeant Musgrave in *Serjeant Musgrave's Dance.*" It was an enormous undertaking to play that part, but it came right after having played another wonderful part, and you were sort of thrown right into it. I

Josef Sommer and Kenneth Welsh in A Walk in the Woods *(Yale Repertory Theatre)*

began to feel like I was not paying enough attention to what I was doing.

If I had stayed in Seattle for, say, twelve years, I don't know if I could have gone on acting. I don't know that I would have been any damn good at all. I hate to say it, because I hate unemployment, but maybe lack of routine is not a bad thing for actors. I'm very grateful for the fact that later on, after all these theatre experiences, I've been able to move between doing film and television and theatre. Change keeps me more alive.

On the other hand, you can spend too little time putting up a production, and that makes for a different kind of factory atmosphere. I've been to the Williamstown Theatre Festival, and the short rehearsal space in a summer theatre schedule is terrible! The first time I went there was to do *The School for Wives*. It was Molière; Richard Wilbur's translation, uncut; Arnolphe—wonderful part, wonderful comedy . . . and ten days rehearsal. Impossible! You're learning a million-and-a-half rhymed couplets, and you're lucky to get the lines right, much less do anything with the part.

As much as I liked the artistic director, Nikos Psacharopoulos, and the atmosphere of Williamstown, I decided that I was never going back except to do cameo roles. When I played the Troll King there, in *Peer Gynt*, I had a fabulous time, because the part was not demanding.

Playing the classics demands more of you than do the "hi-how-are-ya" parts. And that demand for imagination and the breadth of what you have to do to work in the classics has got to be helpful when you get down to playing some television detective. I think it often doesn't work in the reverse. My experience has been that a young actor who can get away with saying "Stick 'em up" in a television show or film is not prepared to say anything more complex in the theatre.

The first film I did was while I was at ACT. They were shooting the first *Dirty Harry* movie in San Francisco, and I played a district attorney who chews Clint Eastwood out for having violated the rights of his suspect. That was in 1971, just before I came back to the East Coast and committed to New York . . .

My life until then was very itinerant. We never really had a home—

we moved from apartment to apartment in various cities—and I don't think that was particularly good for my daughter. I regret that.

I think there's some trade-off as far as raising a family and doing regional theatre goes. In terms of the relationship in a marriage, I think that depends entirely on the individuals. There are some very happy acting couples.

I was married to someone who was not an actress, and she supported us. She did secretarial work and really crappy New York jobs. She was a wonderful singer, and did have a brief career, bringing in income that way. . . . All of that made it possible for me to stick with the theatre. I am grateful to her.

After a number of years, the marriage ended in divorce. I don't know if that was particularly because of the strains of my being an actor—but it didn't help.

After I settled in New York in the early Seventies, I got my first break on television from being seen at the Long Wharf in Lillian Hellman's *Autumn Garden*, directed by Arvin Brown. The production attracted a lot of attention, and my role in the PBS production of *Mourning Becomes Electra* came almost directly out of that. *Autumn Garden* was also the first time that Mike Nichols saw me, and I subsequently worked with him both in the theatre and in film.

My first New York play was Off Broadway—*The Trial of the Catonsville Nine*, directed by Gordon Davidson. I replaced in that, and I was lucky, because Gordon had seen my work and I did not have to audition for him—auditions are a horror. *Catonsville* moved to Broadway. My next show there was a flop murder mystery with Gwen Verdon.

I've done only a handful of Broadway shows. At first, going backstage in a Broadway theatre, belonging to a Broadway company, is thrilling—going to Charlie's and all that kind of nonsense. It's exciting for a while, but then you begin to look around and ask, "What am I doing in a Broadway theatre? I'm playing this lousy little part in this crappy murder mystery!"

My longest Broadway run was in *The Shadow Box*. I had a smaller part and then took over a major role from Larry Luckinbill and played it for six or seven months. I found once the buzz had gone that I was playing by rote. I had a soliloquy about five minutes long, and I opened my mouth one afternoon and nothing would come out. There was nothing in my head. All I could say was, "Excuse me, I'm leaving now," and walk offstage. The play had to go on without the soliloquy. Well, that scared the life out of me. I realized I was not paying attention to anything anymore, except that I had a job. It was a humiliating experience that taught me a lesson. The part was wonderful, and I had to refocus myself in it because it had become so easy and glib. I wouldn't want to be in another Broadway long run . . .

Even as I say that, however, probably my most bitter experience in the theatre was doing the original production of Lee Blessing's *A Walk in the Woods* with Kenneth Welsh at Yale Rep, and neither of us getting to do the show on Broadway. I loved working with Ken—a wonderful actor—and I thought we had done an excellent job at Yale, and the press had said so.

There was a lot of gossip about the situation, and I don't know the truth. When they wanted to do the play on Broadway in the fall, I was doing a television series and was not available; but when they actually did it in the winter, I *was* available, and they went with two actors who were bigger names. I thought that was a bit of a betrayal and felt very badly about it. But I did not get along with the director at Yale to begin with, so perhaps his point of view was that he didn't want to deal with whatever difficulties I was presenting him.

I really would like to have done the role in New York, though. Very much.

I was glad to work with Lee Blessing, the following year, on his play *Cobb*, at Yale. Working on the character of Ty Cobb, the baseball player, I found that a photo told me something about the way he was physically.

Sometimes just the way you stand influences the way you think, behave, talk. A photograph might not even look much like the character, but something in the turn of the head—the way the person's holding himself, the way he sits in a chair—speaks to you. Then everything else can fall into place.

Something similar can happen if I'm having trouble with an extensive role that has a number of scenes. One scene will be more comfortable and begin to fit. The others don't, so I find myself saying, "What the hell is wrong with *this* scene when *that* scene is right?" I often realize that a little thing—a gesture, or even a phrase—is making one scene work. Then I have to understand how I can apply that to the other scenes.

I love doing new plays. I've done a lot, and I like working with the playwright there, unless the playwright is a complete idiot. I especially enjoyed *Lydie Breeze*, a very dense play by John Guare, about the relationship of a man and his daughters on an island. I played the man, and Louis Malle directed—his first stage play.

Some of my best directors have been film directors—I wish more of them worked in the theatre. Mike Nichols is one exceptional talent who moves back and forth. For Mike I did an E. L. Doctorow play at the Public, *Drinks before Dinner*. It was very exploratory, and the critics hated it, but it was a fabulous actor experience. Mike has a wild imagination and will try anything. The script didn't have a lot of structure . . . so Mike tried to create more of a play out of it, and we got to explore all sorts of dead ends.

My character, as I ended up playing him, was the antagonist, whom the hero has tied up in a chair and provoked with a pistol. Finding out how to deal with this guy who is threatening me—to become totally superior—was fascinating. I understood that a man sitting in a chair, tied up, faced with a gun, can—with the right mental attitude—dominate the situation.

That is another example of what I mean by playing against the obvious. If you're playing a villain, you can slide down the path of grimacing and saying, "Aha, I have you now!" or you can say—here is the harder route—"I'm going to be your best friend and I'm not going to allow you to see that I'm going to do anything bad to you. I'm not going to show you or the audience or anybody that. You'll find it out. My job is to not let you see this." (This process had much to do with my part in the film *Witness*, in which I played the villain. Through the first half of the picture, it was my job not to let Harrison Ford's character know that my character was actually doing dirt . . .)

I wouldn't say there was a specific point, but film and television just began to take over my life. And once you get to depending on them, you really can't make those long-term commitments to theatre, particularly to regional theatres. When you begin to have things like alimony and mortgages, a long-term commitment at a regional theatre salary is almost beyond financial possibility. The many actors who *do* go must subsidize those theatres to a certain extent by teaching and other activities. I wouldn't know how to do that anymore.

Perhaps I brought that on myself, by insisting on having a house and a particular lifestyle. When I had to get out of my last New York City rental, I suddenly realized that for the amount of money it was going to cost to buy a one-bedroom apartment in a not very desirable part of Manhattan, I could have six acres and a house and a garden upstate. I was at a point in my career where I didn't have to be in New York because I was no longer doing much auditioning.

One of the things that made me come back to the theatre was that film taught me a lot about the use of subtlety and detail. Sydney Pollack was sort of the Allen Fletcher of film for me. I played Sally Field's newspaper editor in *Absence of Malice* for Sydney, and he taught me a lot about detail and reality in film.

A good director or a good teacher doesn't teach you how to do something; he brings out what you're doing and says, "Yes. I'm gonna film this. Let's do it again and see if more comes out," and more *does* come out. Then he says, "Okay, now we'll drop that take, let's do one more," and each time you go through it—when you've got a good actress like Sally Field opposite you—new things happen.

It's perhaps the improvisational quality in film that translated for me to the stage. I found that complexity and detail, which you may not trust so much onstage, can be projected in the theatre and can be as effective as it is in film.

When I started out as an actor, I felt uncomfortable improvising. I always wanted words and the scene set out for me, because then I knew what the limits were. In film I've learned to trust my imagination a great deal more. And I like to work that way in rehearsal for the stage, too—just to let things happen. Even with Shakespeare, there are a lot of things you can ad lib, things that you will not say later on but which will help in the rehearsal process. Now I feel comfortable doing that. I even prefer it.

The process of working with Kevin Kline on *Hamlet* (to choose one instance) was one of exploration—trying different things, going down different paths. For example, it's Hamlet who drives the "words, words, words" scene. *He* decides how that scene is going to go, and Polonius responds. Kevin, during rehearsal—and I think during performance—would take very different approaches: maybe one time he would be into himself—introverted—and I would have to try to crack through that shell; at other times he would be attacking me and I would have to try and protect myself.

It's terrific fun to follow many different paths. Shakespeare opens up so much for actors. It's not dictated that a scene has to be down one line.

I have also been able to transfer the improvisational approach I learned in film to television, where the time squeeze is much tighter, and the scene structures and words are not always that deathless, so that you can rewrite it as you're going along to a certain extent.

I've done two series. I just finished twelve episodes of one called "Undercover," and my reward for having spent five months in California doing it is that I'm about to go off to the Goodman Theatre in Chicago to play Anton Schill in *The Visit* . . .

When I was offered the role, my first inclination was "Naw, this is an old chestnut that nobody needs to revive." Rereading it, I thought, "Oh, this is a very interesting and pertinent play!" The director has good ideas about making it immediate . . .

I like the idea of casting the black actress, Rosalind Cash, as Claire Zachanassian. Non-traditional casting seems to me obviously the way to go, the way it should be in the theatre. At times the casting can be colorblind, as it was with Peter Francis James as Horatio to Kevin Kline's *Hamlet*. In the case of *The Visit*, it adds something interesting to make a specific racial comment.

Right now doing theatre can be a financial loss for me. I've got to really want to do the part. When I first came to New York as a young actor, anything that would bring in income was fine. Maybe I'm in that same position now with film and television: unless they're just terrible, I'll take most jobs that will give me a boost financially, so I can do some theatre.

There's no way I could earn a living in the theatre now. I don't see how anyone can. I like moving back and forth between the mediums anyway, and I love to work in good films and good television. But the grass is often greener. If I'm doing a film for three months, I think, "Oh boy, I can't wait to get onstage!" and if I'm doing two or three months in a play, I begin to say, "God, to have the life of doing a film!"

But there are rare times in the theatre, when you connect on an intimate artistic level with a director—I keep thinking back to Allen Fletcher, Ellis Rabb and Kevin Kline. . . . I was saying before—about the experience in Seattle, where it became kind of routine and I began to get jaded about doing one great role after another—I feel regretful about Seattle, because maybe I wasted some of those opportunities. Now, at this point of my life, the theatre experience has become very precious to me.

The Merchant of Venice
(American Players Theatre)

When I told New Yorker *critic Edith Oliver that I was going to the Midwest to interview Randall Duk Kim, she barked, "Say that I'll never forgive him for leaving New York!" Many of us who watched Randy Kim (as he called himself in his first Off-Broadway appearances in 1970) in the four seasons he spent acting in New York share a sense of loss. He ascended through a variety of roles in new plays and classics to a 1974 New York Shakespeare Festival season in which his Trinculo won the St. Clair Bayfield Shakespeare Award, and his commanding Pericles raised hopes for seeing his interpretations throughout the Shakespeare canon. But from Kim's early founding of a theatre company in his native Hawaii, he had dreams beyond his acting career. For over a decade he pursued and partially fulfilled them at the American Players Theatre in Spring Green, Wisconsin, where we talked in July of 1991. Kim and his APT co-founders Charles Bright and Anne Occhiogrosso have resettled in Hawaii, where the Honolulu Theatre for Youth received a 1993 National Theatre Artist Residency Program grant from The Pew Charitable Trust for Kim and Occhiogrosso to develop a series of productions of classics.*

I love doing research. I find it stimulating to know where we've come from, who our ancestors were, what they thought about, what they felt, how they lived. I never find history boring. It increases the possibility of characters living and breathing on their own terms, not on mine. And any opportunity I have to transcend my limitations—beginning with the fact that I'm five feet four inches tall—I'll take.

In all my Shakespearean work, I try to look at Shakespeare's sources and get to know the stories that affected his imagination, so that I can see what may be assumed in the text that isn't directly there. For example Gertrude, in *Hamlet*, is sometimes seen as almost secondary, but she becomes very important on the basis of the older "Hamlet" story in Saxo Grammaticus. He wrote in around 1200, and according to him Gertrude was Queen of Denmark in her own right. It was by marrying her that old Hamlet and Claudius became king. So she has a very strong position in that society. Also, in the older story, she was considered the most virtuous of all women.

I've played Hamlet three times. I never thought it would be my favorite role. I was frightened of it and had no original vision of the character.

When I played Hamlet for the first time, at the Honolulu Theatre for Youth, I'd already done three seasons at the Champlain Shakespeare Festival in Vermont and played Trinculo and Pericles for the New York Shakespeare Festival. I had a fight on my hands from the start: the director wanted to cut the script to ninety minutes. I'm convinced that if the play is done excitingly, an audience will sit there for the full four hours. We could not perform the full text, and my anger spilled over into the character. My first Hamlet was a pretty self-righteous and indignant young man.

When I got to the Guthrie to play Hamlet in their 1978-79 season, some of that angry interpretation carried over, but I did manage to see other elements in his character—generosity and nobility in his treatment of people—but he was still intensely passionate and active. I had a fight at the Guthrie too, again over cutting the text. The director felt that certain performers were not able to handle their tasks and began to cut lines from them. But actors must be guided. You've hired these performers, *work* with them! Don't start cutting up the text in order to save moments, because that doesn't fix it. All you're doing is mutilating an exciting story, diminishing the challenge to your actors, and showing the depth of your mistrust.

The third time I played Hamlet was here at the American Players Theatre, which Charles Bright, Anne Occhiogrosso and I founded in 1979. The three of us have been working on plays together for a very long time. We're the closest of friends and life partners. We do research and discuss the plays endlessly, exploring all the material that might make it possible to understand and perform them better. Anne is probably the most important influence in my life and work, and she demands and provokes clarity of vision. Annie directed the APT *Hamlet* in 1986, and that is the Hamlet I carry with me now.

I tried to find a man highly accomplished, extraordinarily intelligent, active, not prone to self-indulgent introspection—I think the circumstances in the play *force* him into introspection. He's a highly ethical man, noble, compassionate and just. When a man like that uncovers the kind of deceit that exists in the world of the play, it's agonizing. You watch him struggle with his conscience, with what he's been commanded to do by his dead father, knowing that there's a judgment beyond this life that he must face (which he does most beautifully—his dying thoughts are for his people). As an audience member, you should sit there and think, "God, if such a man had governed, what would it have been like?"

I think I accomplished more of the character the third time I played it. I'm too old now, but if I had it to do again, I'd attempt to find more places to show what Hamlet was like before the funeral and the marriage—as in his responses to Marcellus, Bernardo and Horatio when they come to tell him what they've seen on the battlements; in his first greeting to Rosencrantz and Guildenstern before he realizes that they were sent for; in his dealings with the Players and with the Gravedigger. What I sense now in Hamlet is a sadness that corruption in the world can be profound, and not so much a rebellious youthful rage.

Over the years, in working with the character and uncovering layers in the story, you begin to form a picture of such a wonderful man, that you throw your own life up against that vision. Hamlet teaches you. He's taught me a lot about my life and forced me to look at myself and the kind of man I would like to be. From Hamlet I have learned a great

deal about compassion and courage. I have thought of him during the
battles we have had at the American Players Theatre, fighting for its
very existence. He's helped me there. I treat Hamlet as a guide.

The genesis of the American Players Theatre goes back twenty-five
years, to when Charles Bright and I founded, and ran for two seasons,
a small nonprofit theatre company in Honolulu, the Ensemble of
Theatrical Artists. Chuck and I were fellow students at the University
of Hawaii and fellow employees of United Airlines.

I've always been interested in theatre—well, really in the art of
transformation. I was raised on a farm in Hawaii and there were not
many neighbors and kids around, so I would make believe a lot in my
playing. Then I became fascinated, through film and books, with the
possibility of physically becoming another person, taking on another
life. And I've always had a great love affair with myth, fairy tale,
legend and history.

I was at the University of Hawaii, majoring in religion and philosophy, for a long time, because I was studying, working *and* doing plays.
For the theatre that Chuck and I ran, I did one-man shows of Mark
Twain and Edgar Allan Poe. We necessarily staged plays that were
small-scale, like *No Exit*, *Rashomon*, *Endgame* and Chekhov's *The
Marriage Proposal*. With government, corporate and private funding,
we toured the islands, giving performances not only in theatres but at
senior citizen centers, prisons and the leper colony at Kalaupapa on the
island of Molokai. I was also doing roles in university and community
productions—Damis in *Tartuffe*, Sir Oliver Surface in *The School for
Scandal*.

I left school and Hawaii in 1969 to be in *Hair*, my first professional,
commercial production. The Michael Butler organization was going to
do a production in Hawaii but couldn't find a space, so they took all of
us "kids" and made us the Las Vegas company. It was an enormous
culture shock—we had to get to the stage door through the casinos!

I was in *Hair* for about four months, and then left and went to live
in Los Angeles for a year. I was trying to write a one-man show based
on Tolstoy's life and work, and was also looking to find a way to stage
the trial and death of Socrates. Those are still on the burners.

I moved to New York when friends invited me to play the lead in

Charley's Aunt with the Brooklyn Heights Players. Then I was a guest artist playing Monsewer in Brendan Behan's *The Hostage* at Hunter College, directed by my friend Allen Belknap. There I met Anne Occhiogrosso, who played Teresa in the production. Charles Bright had also moved to New York, and the three of us began discussions on the formation of a classical theatre company.

I started going to auditions, and I swore very early on that I would work at a Shakespeare Festival during the summers. Edward Feidner, the head of the Champlain Shakespeare Festival, gave me an opportunity to do that right away, casting me as Gremio in *The Taming of the Shrew* and Cassius in *Julius Caesar*.

That first season was wonderful—the freshness of the experience, the challenge of doing two such extreme roles. It was in the third season that I took myself too seriously and had regrettable arguments with the director about my interpretation of Richard III. He was right in his vision of it, but I wasn't listening. He wanted to find much more humor in it and I was after a Richard that was heavy and dramatic and thoroughly evil, and a total bore! I'm afraid I was pretty pigheaded and stupid about it.

Titus Andronicus, which I acted during my second summer at Champlain—and again here at APT—has always been a favorite character to do. The play is like an introduction to tragedy. It's almost adolescent in its action—blood and thunder and sex and violence. But unlike slasher movies, it has a moral framework. At Champlain, I tried to incorporate some of the Japanese style of acting into my performance—Titus killed his youngest son with a spear thrust, in the manner of a Samurai warrior.

After the *Titus* at Champlain, in the fall of 1972, Anne, Chuck and I tried to put together a production of the play Off Broadway, with Anne directing and Chuck producing. We received nearly 1400 pictures and resumes and auditioned almost 650 actors, but we couldn't raise the money and the production was aborted. In the spring of 1975 we tried to do the play in an Off-Off Broadway workshop, and failed miserably. We went into initial rehearsals and it got totally out of hand. Our exploring the reality of the tale led to its violence spilling over between actors. In trying to go deeper, we went too far and put an end to the proceedings.

We accomplished more when we did *Titus* here at APT. I've played many roles more than once—Hamlet, Titus, Gremio, Puck, Prospero, Stockman in *An Enemy of the People*—and it has been a wonderful adventure—one's life experience brings something brand new to each interpretation. You can run on naive decisions and choices when you first do a part, and it's all broad strokes. But to get to the under-levels, you've got to live with a role over a period of time and have a chance to do it again.

I loved my stay in New York. Playing Trinculo in Edward Berkeley's production of *The Tempest* at Lincoln Center was great fun—*hell*, but fun. The magical set by Santo Loquasto in the Newhouse Theater was a sand pit, and I'd carry sand with me everywhere—it was in my hair, my ears, between my toes, in my bed. But it was wonderful to do pratfalls in the sand, to get drunk in the sand—for the clowns in that show, the sand was a perfect surface to play on. But the best, best time was working in the Park, playing Pericles for Ed Berkeley. *Pericles* was where I got the bug to do more classical plays under the open sky.

When Pericles is told that his beloved father-in-law has died, he says, "Heavens make a star of him." And each night I said that line, a star was there, right above our heads, and word and reality were joined for a moment. Suddenly it all became very real, very sacred. A poet doesn't use nature metaphors as fancy, meaningless talk. His purpose is very specific. I think sometimes in enclosed spaces we lose touch with the realities that language attempts to point us towards. Working in the outdoors, particularly with Shakespeare, reality is very present. *Pericles* in the Park was a most significant experience for me.

In 1976, Charles Bright, Anne Occhiogrosso and I decided to put our partnership to a test. We did a full production of *Richard II* Off-Off Broadway—with me playing Richard, Anne directing and Chuck co-producing and managing. It was a reasonable success and we determined that we would work together as a producing unit. We founded the American Players Theatre as the only regional theatre in the country dedicated exclusively to doing the classics uncut, in rotating repertory.

In our time, there's an intense obsession with new plays and with finding new ways to do old plays. I think there is too much attention paid to our own time. It's almost narcissistic. The theatre should point us to where our root systems are. *Do* these old plays, do *more* of them. There are children and young people in our country who have never seen the classics of world theatre, and it is necessary for them to see these wonderful stories.

We wanted APT to do the plays in the settings of, and with visual choices appropriate to, the worlds where the playwright placed his stories. We wanted our company to be highly versatile and skilled. We wanted the audience to be nurtured and educated in such a way that they would be intensely curious. (If we did, say, *The Spanish Tragedy*, we hoped they would come to see it just because they didn't know it.)

We looked at a map and chose the Midwest, near the heart of the continent. While I was at the Guthrie doing *Hamlet* and three other plays during the 1978-79 season, we began looking here in Wisconsin. We looked at over forty sites in a nine-month period, and then found the Spring Green property near Taliesin, Frank Lloyd Wright's home and studio, about an hour from Madison. We leased seventy-one acres in the midst of a beautiful valley along a river. Our goal was to have the theatre purchase the property for a public sanctuary where the classics would be researched and produced and performed in a natural environment.

Anne, Chuck and I took everything we had saved and moved here. The property had a few buildings on it. What are now the administrative offices was a small farmhouse, where we lived at first.

When our first company got here, the theatre was a sand pit up on the hill. With a lot of local volunteer help, we all got to work on it. It took something like 6300 hours of labor to build a wooden thrust stage and amphitheatre in a natural bowl at the top of a hill in the woods. There are two trails to the theatre—a short and a longer climb, and access for the handicapped via vans. There are 800 cushioned seats on three sides of the stage, which is framed by oaks and pines. The wood of the stage is like that on an old barn—gray and worn because of wind, rain, the elements. I look at it as an old, old ship that has now sailed to many places, seen a lot of things, and survived beyond its time.

I was called the artistic director, Anne was associate director, and

Chuck was the managing director. I tried to urge a lot of people to settle here, but our inability to maintain the company year-round eroded the ensemble and undermined our quality.

For our first season in the summer of 1980, Ed Berkeley came and directed *Titus Andronicus* and *A Midsummer Night's Dream*, and we gave a total of ninety performances to skeptical and tentative audiences. By the end of the second season, we started to realize some of our dreams. To the plays done in 1980 we had added *King John*, *The Comedy of Errors* and *The Two Gentlemen of Verona*. The audiences had grown not only in size but in curiosity and enthusiasm. We hoped to do Shakespeare's comedies and tragedies in the order in which he had written them, and the history plays in their historical order. We planned to add plays written by Shakespeare's predecessors or contemporaries, to give additional insight into his world. All of this was to build our understanding of how Shakespeare and this group of men at the Globe finally arrived at the great plays towards the latter part of his career. All that experience must have fed into the richness of those pieces. We wanted ourselves and our audience to start at the beginning and slowly grow towards the masterpieces.

Shakespeare is part of a twenty-year production plan. One day, we wish to explore such subjects as the Trojan War—perhaps to do Peale's *The Arraignment of Paris*, Euripides' *Iphigenia in Aulis* and *The Trojan Women*, Shakespeare's *Troilus and Cressida* and Aeschylus' *Oresteia* to explore the epic from different points of view and different times. There are so many wonderful plays and playwrights—Lope de Vega and Calderon. . . . I would love to see Goethe's *Faust* onstage. We're doing our first Molière this summer and I would love to do more, as well as Racine and Corneille, whom we almost never see in this country.

After our first season, most of our productions were co-directed, often by Anne Occhiogrosso and one or two others. Our idea in having collaborating directors present during the run of the productions was to continue the research and to explore new ideas throughout the entire process to the last performance. Every actor and director was expected to look up the definitions of each word in the text (using, in Shakespeare's case, the First Folio of 1623) and to become intimately acquainted with the world in which each play takes place. We wanted

Randall Duk Kim and Benjamin Reigel-Ernst in The Merry Wives of Windsor *(American Players Theatre)*

to create fresh productions where audiences would understand every word that was said not just because they would be spoken clearly and with understanding, but because everyone on the stage was part of an unfolding story.

I always guide myself by asking, "What are you saying?" and "Why are you saying it?" It is out of the *sense* and the circumstance that the music comes. If it's written by a poet, the music will be there and suited to the sense. But make sense first.

Vocally, I've had coaches who have come through my life, but mostly it's been my own practice. I envision what I want to do and try to find a way to get there. I don't like amplification through mikes and speakers. That's technology getting between me and the people I'm playing for. Doing plays outdoors without amplification—now there's a real challenge! You have to find a way to almost carry your own resonance within your entire body, and to project so that you can be heard clearly two hundred feet away, say, even when you're not letting out screams that echo in the hills.

It can be totally unbearable—intolerable; awful—to work out-of-doors. APT has taught me that. For all the beauty and the things you can learn with regard to truth and the connection between poetry and reality, there are conditions that make you ask yourself, "Why do we put up with this?" It's like masochism. It's either extraordinary heat and *very* warm costumes—so it feels like you're carrying around your own personal sauna—or extreme cold, rain or wind. God! When that wind comes up over the hill and hits our stage, it makes you feel insignificant—blows your voice, your performance, right out of the theatre.

It can work for some things. I remember a few Lears when I actually got to do the storm scene in a storm—the line between theatre and reality genuinely blurred at that moment when the audience didn't know whether to sit and watch the crazy old man or flee the theatre for their own safety. Exhilerating to do *Lear* in a storm! On the other hand, the weather can make things ludicrous. Just the other night, as Stockman, I had to rip my mustache off because half of it was blowing over my mouth! Falstaff, however, was fun to do (despite some blazingly hot summer performances), not only because I would not normally be cast as such a character, but because the costume was such a wonderful design—I was huge, and my padding was filled with ice packs to keep me cool.

With the second season here, we were also able to explore another dream, the American Players Theatre Academy, with a full schedule of classes, for every company member and apprentice, in research, acting, voice, speech and movement. It was a chance to educate ourselves and to train like a team. We hired a man named Jerry Gardiner, a martial arts expert who knew t'ai chi, because we wanted our people to know t'ai chi as a way of centering, of getting in touch with the breath, and of relaxation. He taught us many things for quite a few years when the company was at its strongest. We had lessons with a great theatre man, Professor A.C. Scott, who was a leading authority on Asian theatre. From him we learned something of artistry, dedication and discipline.

Later, we had the pleasure of classes with Patrick Crean, gentleman and master fencing choreographer, as well as Phoebe Brand and Morris Carnovsky, elders in the American theatre.

One of the things we learned was that research can be limiting if not balanced with imagination. When we did *Tamburlaine, Part I*, our first—well, our only—Christopher Marlowe play, in 1983, we did a lot of historical research only to find that Marlowe took many liberties with history and created something brand-new and very theatrical. We did not follow Marlowe's lead very well. We designed costumes for the Persians, Arabians, etc., that may have been *too* accurate and not theatrical enough for that play. We did not strike the most exciting balance between history and fantasy.

With *Julius Caesar*, though, it was helpful to read Plutarch, to learn as much history as possible in order to understand who those people in the play were and to get a feel of what Roman life could have been like. That research gets onstage and is evidenced in the ease with which the actors have stepped into their characters' shoes.

For me, acting is literally doing that. I believe that reading a lot, looking at paintings and sculptures, and listening to music from the period in question can help you live and breathe the place and time. I would say, for example, that in our current production of *Tartuffe*, the pieces of music by Charpentier, Mouret and Couperin, used before the play and between scenes, certainly help create the atmosphere of Louis XIV's France. The combination of trumpet and organ suitably exemplifies the two elements of state and religion in the play. The music fills you with a spirit of the time, a sense of grandeur and elegance.

One of the greatest experiences I've had here was being directed by Morris Carnovsky in *King Lear* in 1989. I had seen him do Shylock at the Old Globe in San Diego when I was just starting out as an actor, and his performance made an enormous impression on my life and work. I vowed that I would try to do precisely that kind of acting. He had such enormous humanity, not just as an actor spouting speeches or looking or sounding pretty, but down to the depths of the heart and soul. Morris's Shylock was the vision that set my spirit on its journey. When I had a chance to do Lear here, he kind of passed on his performance to me and planted seeds that are now incubating.

Morris and his wife Phoebe Brand came in two different seasons, to co-direct productions of *Ivanov* and *Lear*. They brought all their experiences with the Group Theatre, and the years afterwards, to try to show us how to find truth in acting. Working with them was wonderful . . . eye-opening, inspiring.

Morris gave me certain sounds that Lear would make—he conceived him as an old enraged dragon in the first scene and again later, when he berates Goneril. He would do bits and pieces of it himself, and we all sat around spellbound. There were moments when what I did was pure imitation of him. I said to myself, "I will imitate and I will learn from this."

In Oriental theatre, that's how young actors are trained—when you have attained your middle age, *that's* when you can begin to innovate. I like that mode of teaching, and I loved it from Morris. I chafed at the beginning, I must say, but I learned to be quiet and to receive—as a first step in attempting that character—what Morris could teach me.

In 1988 I needed time away from APT, and I worked at the Arizona Theatre Company, at ACT in San Francisco and at the Williamstown Theatre Festival, where I was the Storyteller in Nikos Psacharopoulos' production of Kenneth Cavander's *The Legend of Oedipus*. I did the final Messenger speech from *Oedipus at Colonus*, telling about old man Oedipus' miraculous end. I wasn't onstage a lot, but I loved watching Nikos work with the chorus.

When I got back here I persuaded Annie to try our first Greek tragedy. Like doing any great play for the first time, our production of *Oedipus* was in broad strokes. The one strong thing I carried away with me was that I wasn't just doing a play, I was actually participating in a religious ritual. For the first time, a theatre performance was much more than show biz, and mattered much more. It was a hymn to the gods!

We had twelve in our Chorus, and did a lot of unison work. Whether vocally or physically, American actors find it difficult to operate as one. We're just not taught to do that kind of work, so it was a big challenge, but I think we arrived at some pretty nice moments for them. We used masks—I've always loved masks and makeup. When you're acting in Greek-tragedy masks, you have to act down to the soles of your feet.

I'd love to do more of the Greeks, who are so unflinching in their view of things, so ruthlessly honest. My great regret this season is that I wasn't given the opportunity to play Hecuba in *The Trojan Women*. Yes, I want to play a woman's role! I will not kow-tow to the kind of thinking that allows me only to play characters that I'm biologically suited for. I want to play men, I want to play women, I want to play gods, demons, young people, old people—I want to experience the full imaginary range of characters. I want to bend and shape my body and my voice and my mind and my heart to give a home to those characters.

It has always been difficult to sustain APT. We didn't expect it to be easy, but it has became impossible for us. Chuck Bright left four years ago. Anne became artistic director and I the associate director then. Annie and I are leaving for good at the end of this season and going to live and work in my home state, Hawaii.

We faced enormous skepticism when APT came to Wisconsin. Classical theatre in the country? A lot of people believe that the best craftsmen and artists go to the big cities, making it impossible to have exciting theatre in such a rural area.

The winters were the toughest for us, when there were no performances and, therefore, no income or exposure. Annie, Chuck and I had to keep afloat somehow and prepare for the summer season. We sent out a newsletter that had not only appeals for support together with information about the upcoming season, but also information about theatre history, famous actors and productions, to stimulate public interest.

I had a one-man show called *What Should Such Fellows As I Do?* that we toured locally to encourage support. It opened with Chekhov's *On the Harmfulness of Tobacco*, in which I played a henpecked husband, and then I stripped off the makeup and did the balcony scene from *Romeo and Juliet* intertwined with a story of Julia Marlowe, who was famous for her Shakespeare heroines. With the *Hamlet* section, I told a story about Edwin Booth and the news that his brother had shot President Lincoln. The two-act program was designed to celebrate the classical theatre.

Those initial years were very rough. We would go out and talk to different groups, trying to raise interest and support, not always succeeding. We expected to draw audiences from the immediate area and from Madison; eventually, we thought we would get people from Milwaukee, Minneapolis, Chicago and the outlying areas, who would come for the weekend and see three or four plays in repertory.

We knew that would take time. We did not know how difficult it would be. But after twelve seasons, audiences have increased steadily and have confirmed our belief that once people began to see how wonderful these old plays are, they would come back to see others, and bring their children.

Four years after we opened we still carried the first year's debt. Our Board panicked and began to demand artistic sacrifices. They asked us to bring only one new play into the fifth season, which we consented to, believing the assurance that things were to be more secure. Midway during that fifth season we were asked to disband the training academy for the rest of the season. That was the beginning of its end, and is one of my great disappointments. I just don't know how you can build a first-rate classical repertory company without training the ensemble.

What Chuck, Annie and I wanted and attempted but never quite succeeded in doing was to join administrative and artistic vision, so that our public image was at one with the work itself. Since Chuck's leaving, APT is two separate entities: those who work on the hill and those who market the theatre. The play is no longer the thing— packages are. There was a time when the three founders sat on the Board and had voting power, but we were advised that because we were drawing salaries there was a conflict of interest, so we separated from the Board. That was a fatal mistake. Artistic concerns could not be voiced or defended by vote, and APT was doomed to lose its unique mission.

The American Players Theatre is not what we set out for it to be. Long-term artistic vision is of no consequence to those who govern it. Ignorance and manipulation are acceptable. After all, the bottom line is money, isn't it? Classical summer stock! Get these plays up fast! There's no time or money for study and training and collaborating productions into existence.

We wanted this theatre to be a special place—a sanctuary, a beacon, an entity that had an ethical and spiritual center. I wanted it to be a place where people could leave the city, get out of the concrete, come to a place with other living creatures around them, and watch the enactment of a great poet's vision.

I would say that most people think that's a nutty idea. And I would say that most people in the theatre wouldn't care to give themselves or their lives to such a project, because of the demands it makes. There is certainly no mass media fame or money in it. But I think all the time about Shakespeare and the men of the Globe. I think about Molière's company spending those early years together touring the provinces and then coming back to Paris. And I think about the Japanese Kabuki theatre I love—those men spend all of their life practicing their craft and they are given enormous respect.

I've had the honor of working with many dedicated actors and of being enriched by their experience and their long devotion to the theatre—people like Sydney Walker and Ruth Kobart at ACT. I'm ecstatic working with the older ones. I also love working with and watching young performers, especially those just beginning. I guess the troublesome ones are those near my own age—we seem to be so turbulent in our motives.

I know right now that America is bedazzled by technology and mass media. I hope we get through this stage and begin to realize that there is something very special in going to a live performance and seeing a real person, who's here for only a brief period of time, embody such astonishing characters as Antigone or Prometheus. I hope we can regain the appreciation of our life—of our mortality—that the theatre offers.

As Americans, as people who claim to hold a philosophy of democracy, we have to ask how the arts function in our society. It appears that we understand more about sports in the making of character—we seem to have no idea that the *arts* may have an ever greater function in making and serving the character of the citizenry. Once you have heard a great piece of music like Beethoven's Ninth, or seen Michelangelo's David, or watched *Hamlet*, you are forever altered.

. . .

Right now Annie and I are in the process of saying goodbye and packing up to rejoin Chuck in the first home and garden we've ever owned. I'm going back to Hawaii and looking forward to the chance to study. I had my first lesson in ancient Greek this week—I want to *know* ancient Greek theatre. I am ready to take on a regular job if I have to, but I also want to get in touch with some of the Hula schools, where the kids are very good at unison performance. I was thinking— well, just dreaming right now—that perhaps a production of *Antigone* or *The Trojan Women* could use those skills.

I'd be ready for whatever opportunities are possible for doing classical theatre in Hawaii. Perhaps the timing may be right for such a venture. Hawaii is in a unique place, with its own ancient culture and its own blend of East and West.

I think I would like to have an interracial troupe of young people in Hawaii doing classical plays. A smart, intelligent, sensitive, vividly imaginative group of kids, highly disciplined and dedicated, trained with a great deal of intensity. My hope now lies with the young ones. They must be educated and nurtured correctly—must be exposed to the world's great plays early enough, so that by the time they're teenagers they're not afraid of poetic language, and the stories themselves are familiar friends to be respected and loved.

After all the turbulent years with APT, I saw the light this past Sunday. I saw the first glorious fruits of our long twelve-year labor.

The children who have literally grown up with this theatre took it upon themselves to do an uncut version of *A Midsummer Night's Dream*. They were astonishing. After years of watching, of lessons learned silently, these children conducted themselves as performers of a classical play with a joyous craftsmanship and a maturity of judgment far beyond their years.

These children are the gold we have toiled for. Each of them is at the beginning of what could be a most miraculous journey, and I am sure we will meet them again. Annie and I are bent upon finding some way to keep working with youngsters like these and watching young imaginations catch fire with tales of our ancestors. Pray for us.

JANE LIND

The Summer Face Woman
(*La MaMa*)

*A*mong the most unforgettable productions I have ever seen were
Andrei Serban's The Trojan Women *and* The Good Woman of Setzuan
*at La MaMa in the mid-seventies. In researching the actors for this book,
I was amazed to realize that the ravaged Hecuba and the cunning Water
Seller I had relished were both played by a young actress who had barely
begun her career, having left New York University's acting program to
help found the first Native American Theatre Ensemble at La MaMa in
1972. A few years later, Jane Lind had toured with NATE and Serban's
company throughout America and abroad, playing at the Edinburgh
Festival and festivals in Paris, Rotterdam, Berlin, Vienna, Athens and
Shiraz, Iran. She has continued to travel not only as a stage and film
actress but also as a director, choreographer, producer and author in the
vanguard of the multicultural movement in the theatre.*

W hen we opened *Fragments of a Trilogy* in Athens in 1975, we
thought we were going to be blown to bits. The production had
made Andrei Serban an important director in New York, where we
had played at La MaMa. On tour in Europe, we were getting top
billing at Edinburgh and other festivals; but in Athens, there had been
articles in the papers about this American company that dared to do

Greek tragedies with a company of mixed races, and to do them in Ancient Greek. We expected the worst, because this was *their* stuff.

We were playing in a theatre at the top of Athens, on Lycabettus Hill. During the Greek civil war, the woman who owned the property had said something against the government and her theatre had mysteriously burned down. For *The Trojan Women*, we needed just such a place of ruins. But we went thinking, "Boy, they're going to really shred us."

Andrei was nervous just as the actors were. At the opening, police surrounded the thousand-seat amphitheatre, where two thousand people were waiting for us. Ellen Stewart was out in the crowd somewhere, and we were up . . . way up in the ruins. As Hecuba, I had to lead the procession of captive women in chains. There was a lot of noise, and all I could make out was Ellen screaming to us, "Babies, babies, run, run!" The crowd had broken the police barricades and was rushing in.

Hecuba's chant started at the top of the hill, and we came down into the theatre. Astyanax, Hecuba's grandson, was brought in, and this child made such a pitiful sight that it quieted the crowd. Then we knew we had them. We were outdoors, and it was magical. Our voices, the feeling of being on that piece of earth that was so old—everything worked for us. We did *Trojan Women*, *Medea* and *Electra*. At the end there was a little applause, a stop, and all of a sudden this roar, and bravos.

An interpreter told us that the reviews were wonderful, and quoted one as saying, "Some of the ancient sounds reawakened our myths that we should nurture. A young American company had to come to give them back to us."

During rehearsals for *Fragments* we had had a person teaching us Ancient Greek, but we also used Latin and a mixture of languages. There was some Aleut in it, too. I contributed that.

I grew up on the Aleutian Peninsula in Alaska, in a culture that always had theatre, though I didn't know it was theatre then. I think I saw my first bright lights in the rocks and ash spilling up from Mount Veniaminof, the volcano near my village of Perryville. I remember the volcano always threatening to move us, and the clothes my grandmother had washed and hung out to dry getting covered with soot. It was so dramatic—we had volcanos, windstorms, the sea. I think something was stirred in me very early.

Also, being raised as a Russian Orthodox was important, because that church has such pageantry, and I was always taken by it. I sang in Russian in the church choir.

I have something between a sixteenth and a fourth of Russian in me. You can see it more in some of my brothers and sisters. I think I've taken more of the Aleut side, but my grandmother always said, "You identify with everything in you, or you're going to have trouble as you grow up."

Every January, the 14th to 17th, during the Russian Orthodox Christmas holiday season, the Aleuts do something called *Masqualante*, which is our word for masking. When night comes, we dress in costumes and masks and dance from house to house, where people try to guess our identities. You can't talk—you have whistles you can talk with—and I loved doing that. I was pretty good, and I was one of the youngest ever to take a role.

I had a lot of dolls I'd create drama with. We held huge doll funerals, and when animals died, kids would say, "Go get Jane," and we'd walk the animals around the church. I held many funerals in Perryville. I made all the kids dress up. The girls had to wear veils like Orthodox women do when they're married, and dustpans were the holy pictures—this was a whole production.

I worried my father, but he did not stop me. He was afraid I was too hyper. I wanted to know why I couldn't fly like the birds. When they handed out vitamins at school and told us to take them because they would make us healthy, I took about half a bottle. I was very much a tomboy—I played hard, climbed trees, jumped off high places—I mean, my mom didn't have *four* sons, it was *five*.

Then all of a sudden, at age fourteen, I began to say, "I don't want to be a man really. I think I like being me."

I was orphaned at that age. My mother died when I was eight, and my father about six years later. Then I was raised by my incredible grandmother, my mother's mother. She took in all seven of us, and my brothers and sisters are tight to this day. My grandmother told us things like, "If you are afraid, just make a loud sound and scare the spirits away." Or if you were going to go through the forest, she'd say, "Make these sounds to tell all the other beings to get away so that you do not step on them or surprise them where they may hurt you."

There was a great deal of mystery surrounding my childhood—like you don't play at night because that's the time for the night people to come out. I remember throwing a rock at the ground once and my grandmother screamed, "Jane, aya, don't! It's your mother you're hurting, it's alive!" Way back then, she taught us to treat the earth with the highest respect, because if you do not, it's going to hurt you. A lot of the Aleut ways were there, and my life was very rich.

I didn't want to go away to school, but until the 1970s we were required by law to go to boarding schools. All Native or Indian kids, or Native Americans or American Indians—whatever they call us now—were forced by the United States government to go as far away as possible from our home grounds. My sister Virginia and I went to the Chemawa Indian School in Salem, Oregon.

The first thing required was not to speak your own language. It was sad. They herded us into these dormitories, and we had to get up at six o'clock to start our details before we went to school, and you had demerits if your detail wasn't done. We had to line up to go to breakfast, lunch and dinner, and we couldn't hold boys' hands. A lot of damage was done. The self-esteem of students suffered because they were told they were not worth anything. In those schools, you were basically taught to be a maid, a gardener, or a mechanic. And I had great aspirations. I thought you could be anything. That's what my dad said—it's in your mind, you can do anything you want.

When I went to Chemawa, my sister Virginia got me up on stage. She was a natural singer, and we'd perform at school functions. I'd sing the main line and she'd do harmony. I was always flat, and she'd hit me to make my voice come up. The audience loved that, so we left it in our act. We were a success at performing, but they tried to pull me back academically because I was ahead for my age. Some of the Navajo students in my class were in their mid-twenties and had been working instead of going to school, and Chemawa said that it would make them feel bad to see me in there.

I was saved by Lee Udall, wife of Stuart Udall, who was Secretary of the Interior. She came to visit the school, saw that I was very artistic, and asked, "Jane, why don't you go to the Institute of American Indian Arts in Santa Fe? It's a wonderful school for all aspects of the arts, from traditional to contemporary. You could focus more on theatre, and you'd have a regular high school curriculum." I asked my family, and they said I should go.

At the Institute I was introduced to Rolland Meinholtze, an incredible drama teacher. He pushed me right into the Greeks, into Shakespeare, into contemporary work, and demanded of us standards just as high as those of a college. In *Oedipus Rex*, I asked Mr. Meinholtze, "Why can't we do it Native American?" and he said, "That's a very good idea." I said, "Why can't we take some of the sounds and make them Indian sounds?" and that's when I began to think, "Hey, this wildness in me, there's a place for it!" Mr. Meinholtze directed me as Jo in *A Taste of Honey*, and from that I was asked to play Rosa in Gene Frankel's production of *The Rose Tattoo* at the Greer Garson Theatre.

I lived in the arena of the stage. It was like home, it was like my blood, but I never thought that I would make a living at it—I just knew I loved it. I knew I loved the applause, and that the exchange between the audience and myself was holy. I got deeper and deeper into it and I graduated with the highest honors. My Tonys were Hopi Kachina dolls. I won best all-around theatre person two years in a row.

I went home, and was working in the cannery and not liking it, when Lee Udall contacted me again, and said, "Come, let's go to New York."

I asked my grandma, who said, "Go go go go go. Go see." From looking at movies and magazines when I was growing up, my mind had always stretched to other places. My father was a part of that, too. He used to let us sit Sunday mornings and listen to all the different languages on the broad-band radio, and he'd say, "See how many kinds of people there are?"

I came to New York during a garbage strike, and I hated the first few weeks, but strangely. . . . You know, I really believe there's a "click," and when you find that click, it's yours. I found mine in New York.

All of a sudden, New York's energy felt rejuvenating, and I saw different things, and my eyes were being filled—my ears, and my heart. It was the diversity of people—all different kinds—and doing what they wanted to do. For the first time in my life, I didn't feel out of place. I didn't feel that my emotions were too big and I had to cap them.

Lee brought me and Keith Conway, a Blackfoot dancer who had been at the Institute, to meet Michael Miller, who is now associate dean but was then director of the theatre program at New York University's School of the Arts. I couldn't conceive yet that I was auditioning to attend the school. I thought I was going to go home and get married, because that's what women did, but then they sent me a letter offering me a scholarship to New York University, to be a full-fledged theatre person. I could not believe it.

The school was a nurturing haven. Michael Miller was always stopping and talking to us, and if we were going astray there would be a gentle hand and, "You've got to pick up, Jane." He was like the image of an elder, a caretaker for us.

I took acting classes with Lloyd Richards, but Olympia Dukakis was my major acting teacher. Oh, she was unbelievable. Her classes were very emotional. She wouldn't start small. The emotions were always big, and then she'd let us trim it down.

That's a rehearsal process I have treasured to this day. Most of the teachers there had that quality about them: larger than life, because that's what you were dealing with.

I attended NYU for only three years, and then I got an offer from the Native American Theatre Ensemble. Hanay Geiogamaha, a Kiowa playwright, wanted to start the company to do plays by Native Americans. I had a meeting with Lloyd Richards and Michael Miller, and they said, "Well, this is what we're trying to train our students to have, a livelihood."

Hanay founded the first Native American theatre with Ellen Stewart at La MaMa in the early seventies, and we toured the U.S. and Europe, doing both realistic and traditional plays. *Body Indian*, one of Hanay's contemporary plays, was about alcoholism. I played one of the aunts, all of whom were drunkards who didn't want to talk about it. Alcoholism in the native peoples is very much alive—it rules a lot of our lives, and some of us did not want to do the play because we didn't want to be stereotyped as drunken Indians. Then Hanay had us read the script, and to this day I'm glad I did it, because the story was about Hanay's real family, and so true and so ugly—some of the characters rip off a man's wooden leg to sell it for money to buy alcohol.

People who came didn't see it as just about Indians. It was so honestly done, it was universal. We had many people who quit drinking after they saw it—they wrote and told us. Or we'd be in a residency and someone would say, "Well, I've been dry for about two weeks, and you're the cause." We'd go back to a place six months to a year later and hear, "You know, I quit drinking because of the ugliness I saw in that play." The contemporary plays were the hardest to deal with, because they were so close to us.

One of the traditional plays was *NA HAAZ ZAN*, which is Navajo for the beginning of the creation, when the people believe that they came from the underworld to the earth. I played the wolf, and I had a great affinity with the character. A lot of my work was becoming one with the animal. My father was a hunter and trapper, and he told me that when you hunt, you ask the animal's permission. If it's meant to be yours, it will give itself. So when I do my character work, I ask for permission, and then begin to do the research.

With the wolf, I started to work with sounds, because I have a great range in my voice. I worked towards sounding like a wolf—the baying or bathing of the moon we called it at home, when wolves would wash the moon with sound. We live around water back home, and bathing the moon is great magic.

For the performance I had a wolf's mask worn like a hat on top of my head. I'd put the mask on, and I'd "see" my sound going to the top of the wolf's mouth, and try to become this thing making the sound. There was some chanting, and when the chanting went into my upper register and became howling, that was the release into bathing the moon.

The Aleuts believe that a mask or disguise contains a spirit which might enter the body if the wearer does not wash it off. After twelve o'clock, when we did the *Masqualante* in my village, we had to wash our faces to make sure we didn't take our characters with us. It was very easy to carry that tradition to the world in which I lived afterwards, to respectfully put my character away when I leave the theatre. I always wash my face to say to the character, "Okay, it's time for me to go and you to stay."

I was with the Native American Theatre Ensemble for about three years, and then I needed to move on. Being in the company had given me the certainty that I could make a living from acting, and had also made me very proud of who I was. Eventually, it also gave me the desire to go back to my people and say, "Hey, we have legends that are worth remembering and recording, let's look at them. It's grand to set up businesses for Native Americans, but what about the soul?"

To me, that's what theatre is. It's the soul. NATE gave me the sense of what I had, and Andrei Serban's company gave me permission to experiment with what I had.

Jane Lind (foreground) in Fragments of a Greek Trilogy *(La MaMa)*

. . .

Andrei had seen me in *NA HAAZ ZAN*, and asked me to join his Great Jones Repertory Company at La MaMa. He created an ensemble that cared immensely for each other. We worked so hard on *Fragments of A Trilogy* that sometimes we felt like our bodies and minds didn't belong to us anymore. Andrei would have us do improvs, Elizabeth Swados would come in with new songs, and we were working so intensely with the linguistic person that it was like our tongues weren't ours.

Andrei would ask, "How would you come down from Troy in chains, after your city is burnt? Where are the soldiers? Which ones are going to take you off to be their slaves in Greece?" We'd all talk about a scene and then do it, because talking about it is quite different from the action itself. We would do it as a dance, a movement, an improv. We were so tired.

Andrei was looking for a ritual, because he came from ritual in his native Romania, from the Orthodox faith there. A lot of the stage pictures in *Fragments* had the quality of icons. I especially remember the washing of the child—preparing Astyanax for burial—that was like a holy picture.

I thought Andrei's images were gorgeous. In *The Trojan Women*, we had almost violent physical action in which the audience was treated like nonspeaking actors, like survivors of Troy being herded around by the Greek soldiers and watching as the Trojan noblewomen grieved, heard their fates and revenged themselves on Helen. Then all but the principals were seated for *Electra*, in which I was one of the Chorus. We went from being very active to very still, sitting on stools for fifty minutes, with just the upper torso moving. That was a lesson in how to keep the lower body alive, because the blood begins to stop. Some of the Chorus didn't do so well because they didn't practice, starting with five minutes sitting in one position and increasing gradually until they got up to the full amount of time. That created for me an enormous discipline.

Andrei had the ability to make a group of actors follow him in taking great risks. Priscilla Smith jumped off a fourteen-foot platform and wore a live boa constrictor around her neck as Electra. Joanna Peled had her head shaved for Helen of Troy, and in performance she was stripped naked, covered with mud, hung by her arms on a pole and carried around by two soldiers to be spat upon by the Trojans. That was extremely difficult for everyone.

Joanna had beautiful red hair. They called her "Gingy" at rehearsals. The company had a big talk just before she shaved her hair, and it was very sensitive. Joanna was feeling already bare, and she was scared of being stripped. We were all saying how supportive we were of her, and there were people crying. Andrei was trying to give us a reason why he wanted that picture of her, and he said that he was trying to show the rape of a people. So many people on both sides died in the Trojan War, and Helen started it. He wanted the audience to feel that rape . . . but it was another thing to us to have to do it to Joanna. As friends, we identified with her, and felt like we were *all* getting raped.

There was always this one actress who started putting the mud on Joanna, and if it hadn't been for her, I don't think the rest of us could have done it. *I* couldn't. When they brought Joanna up for me to spit at her and curse her, it was difficult. We were very close friends. I had to see Joanna as a woman who had robbed my people, and play Hecuba as my grandmother, as a woman of a people that had been robbed.

I went to my grandmother's spirit and asked her, "Please can I use you as Hecuba?" Both Hecuba and Grandma brought so many children into the world, and all nine of my grandmother's children died before she did—and her two husbands, and most of her friends.

I felt Grandmother's heartbeat, and the lines in her skin. At times it was very hard for me to rehearse. I'd feel like I was being choked with emotion. Being chained as Hecuba was actually a help, because while I was restricted bodily I felt that the emotion and the sounds were my freedom and I could go anywhere with them.

After *Fragments*, we did Brecht's *The Good Woman of Setzuan*, in which I played the Water Seller. He was a trickster, the one the gods first contacted, who mediated between them and Shen Te, just like the Kachina dolls do between humans and the gods. Andrei wanted the character to be androgynous. He said, "If they see you as a woman, it's fine; if they see you as a man, it's fine." He had me in silk pants for the first preview, and I said, "Andrei, this is a person who lives in the ghetto. I wouldn't be walking around like this. Let me make a statement, please." He said, "Okay, go find something . . . go find, go find." I came back with old worn clothes like people would throw away, and he said, "Ah, this is very good." You could converse with Andrei.

Good Woman was a challenge in that we were so wild with *Trojan Women*, whereas in the Brecht it was, "We walk here, we go up there, we do this." Everything was very disciplined. My buckets had to hit a place at a certain time—it was very much like Carl Weber, a director at NYU who was precise in everything he did. I was lucky to have worked within different kinds of restrictions and to be challenged to find freedom within them.

For the Water Seller, I found how to make my emotion fit within the blocked area. At times I'd lose my pitch, because when I got too emotional I couldn't hear the note in Elizabeth Swados's score for me to come in on. I'd be in rehearsal, and Andrei would say, "Put down the emotion, put down the emotion!" But sometimes he would get very supportive when I'd get the emotion and say, "See, it's alive, what she's doing."

As with Andrei, I did not ask to work with Peter Brook. They asked me. I did not know who they were. I had been amazed by the film of *Marat/Sade*, never dreaming that I would work with this man.

I first met Peter when he came to do a residency with NATE while he was working on *The Ik*. He wanted to study our dance and our rituals. I took workshops with him in Paris at his International Centre of Theatre Research while on tour with *Fragments*, and was in a workshop production of *The Birds* at the Brooklyn Academy of Music. There, again, I was working from my animal backgrounds, and ritual.

I actually worked with Peter Brook for only a short period of time, compared with the three years I spent with NATE and with Andrei's company; yet within that time, there was so much given, because I had learned to make use of the time, and I watched intensely. Now that I am a director myself, I find that when I get a little boisterous, I remember Peter, who moves people with his gentleness. Seeing people of all colors within his company, and watching him observe other people's ways with such respect, taught me to respect myself more.

I got into directing, and into helping to record and dramatize the legends of my own people and other Native Americans, when I went to play Kate in *The Taming of the Shrew* for Robert Farley at the Alaska Repertory Theatre in 1982. I worked with a wonderful actor named Dana Hart as Petruchio, and I loved our production. It was not that hard for me to identify with Kate, coming from a culture where ladies are ladies and the oldest daughter is supposed to marry first. My father had a certain standing in the tribe, and there was a way you were supposed to behave. Jane didn't follow that.

During the run, Dana and I were asked to go into the schools and teach drama as a way to help children with their educational skills and self-esteem. We did theatre residencies in eight rural communities around the state, performing a program combining drama, comedy, storytelling, dance and music, and conducting creative dramatics workshops.

The students had tremendous personal problems. Many had attempted suicide. In a matter of weeks, I had them speaking, I had them organizing, I had them doing everything.

I must say here that a lot of the teachers, however good and caring they might be, were white, whereas I was a native person whom the students could identify with. The role model became very important for them, and began to cut barriers like crazy.

When I understood whom I was working with, I felt I had to give them more time. The time that I spent out of New York took me away from what I wanted as an actress, but I felt I must start giving something back.

I have worked with a lot of native peoples and their elders to record their legends. The first were the Inuit people in Bethel, Alaska. Renee Patten and I co-founded the Spirit Theatre, did research on Inuit legends, and commissioned Dave Hunsaker to write up the legends in script form for us. I directed Dave's play *The Spirits in All Things*, which we toured to villages in southwestern Alaska, the Arctic slope, Fairbanks and Anchorage.

Based on the legends of the Athabascan people, Renee and I co-wrote and I directed *The Potlatch*, which is a tourist piece, a half-hour play showing the heart, strength and beauty of the people. There are many villages up north that want to work so that what they present to the tourists will be of dignity.

I just came back from the town of Glenn and Allen, about two hundred miles from Anchorage, where we did a tourist piece based on local history. *The Glenn and Allen Show* project was a bit touchy, because I had to work with natives and whites, with people ranging in age from a baby to a sixty-six-year-old man . . . and to make them work together was a challenge. Anne Hanley wrote the script and we developed some dialogue between the Athabascan natives in rehearsal. But the Atnas felt there were not enough lines for them, and also that they were being moved all around the stage. Finally, I asked the most outspoken Atna, a boisterous man named Clarence, to sit in the audience and watch while I had someone stand in for him. I explained that I was moving the native people around because it showed them always present but their land shrinking, and after Clarence watched he said, "Oh, man, Jane, I didn't know this was happening. The picture's quite different from being up there."

It is difficult to get the trust of the peoples and their elders because they have been ripped off so often. Theatre or dance people have come and studied their cultures, and then done their own interpretations that haven't passed through the elders and do nothing for the peoples. I try to make sure that the last step in the projects I work on is getting the sanction of the elders, so the respect is there.

The hardest battle I have to fight is that, while I am a Native American, I am a woman. They do not expect a woman to do what I do. A woman is still supposed to be home with the babies. And wearing a wedding ring doesn't help. Too many guys try to make passes at you, and say about your man, "What's wrong with him, can't he control you, or are you a loose woman?" Especially when they find out I'm in theatre—they associate theatre with looseness.

They find that I'm very disciplined and I've done my research, and I have the highest respect. Still, sometimes they say, "Why should we trust you?" I say, "Why should you not? Don't let your stories die because *I'm* trying to do them. If you die tomorrow, you're guilty for taking your heritage to the grave instead of sharing it with the next generation."

They sometimes get very upset about how I'm doing it, because I cut one part off to make the storyline flow, but I'm trying to go for the heart. I try to bring in the traditional dances, for instance, but I'll say,

"I've got to cut here. I cannot let you sing for ten minutes. I want only three minutes, for the essence." Your own people begin to doubt you in the process of your getting to what is really theirs. After they see it they say, "Oh, yes." The audience still gets the gist of the whole thing. I did not cheat that much. I just didn't do twenty repetitions.

I was also asked to work with Native Americans in Oklahoma— Pawnee, Sioux, Cheyenne and Kiowas. Christopher Sergel, who wrote *Black Elk Speaks*, made a play called *Footprints in Blood* from their history. I played the female lead in the first production and then directed it in Tulsa with two Equity actors of Seminole/Potawatomi and Sac/Fox heritage in the leading roles.

I've been alternating or combining acting, directing and teaching for nearly ten years. For the past five I've directed operas for a multicultural ensemble, the Magic Circle Opera Repertory Company in Manhattan. Thank God I have a cheap rent. My husband Michael Trammell and I still live downtown, just as we did when NATE first developed. That's how we met. Michael's a lighting designer and a computer graphics designer who was with the company. He's Sac/Fox, Delaware, and Irish—quite a combination. We live simply, and I am able to sustain myself—knock on wood—through my work.

The Magic Circle wants me to commit more of my time, and in Alaska they want me to do a professorship for a year, but the actress in me gets very jealous if I do too much other work.

My last acting was in a leading role as Chuck Connors' Inupiaq Eskimo wife in Percy Adlon's film *Salmonberries*, which won first place in Canada's 1991 film festival. In the planning stage now is a production of *Black Elk Speaks*, Christopher Sergel's new version of his play that we first did at the Folger. I will choreograph it and recreate my role of Yellow Woman, a Cheyenne married to a white man. The play covers such events as Wounded Knee and the death of Crazy Horse, and Yellow Woman loves her husband but leaves him. Before she goes she describes witnessing a massacre where an Indian child is sent out holding a white peace flag and is gunned down by the cavalry. It's a magnificent and very taxing role.

· · ·

I'm trained enough to do all aspects of the theatre, film and television, and I would wish to be treated as such, but no agent will sign me because they believe I'm not sellable. I got *Salmonberries* because I saw a casting notice in *Backstage* and faxed my photo and resume to Percy Adlon. He had read many actresses but not found what he wanted, and he flew me to Seattle to audition for him.

There's always been a casting problem, even when I was young. If Indian things come up, I'm overqualified, I speak too well, I'm not dumb enough. More recently it's been, "You're too sophisticated." When I wanted to be considered for the Mazola Oil commercials, casting directors said I would outshine the product. I said, "But the person in the commercial now is very beautiful and you still know it's Mazola Oil. Please be honest with me. Is it my appearance, my acting, am I too heavy?" They said, "It's the way you come across. You're too sophisticated. We don't expect native people to be that sophisticated."

I auditioned and was called back twice for the Scottish play at a major New York institutional theatre. They wanted some women with wild, mad sounds to do the witches. That's easy for me, and also I've studied with Kristin Linklater, one of the finest teachers of speech and diction, so I know how to play Shakespeare. At the second callback they kept asking me to do different lines and screams and wild things. They were taking notes like crazy, and I knew I did an exceptional audition because they did not speak for about thirty seconds after I finished. Then they said, "Well, you come highly recommended and we'll be calling you," but they did not call. I had heard many other actresses at the auditions and none did anything like me. I went to see the production, and they had taken some of the ideas from my audition and given them to the witches.

I so wanted to work at that theatre, and thought I was good enough. So I try to make my own work. And one day, like Grandma said, "When your time comes, you will know it."

To have hopes and dreams is very important. I hope there will be more work for all native peoples. We've been around for hundreds of years, so use us!

Anything Goes *(Lincoln Center
Theater)*

*T*he quintessential chameleon-like actor, Anthony Heald created the
role of Charlie, the title character in The Foreigner, *Off Broadway. I
found him so endearing that I wrote in my review that if the producers
needed money, they could raffle him off. Two seasons later, at intermission of* Principia Scriptoriae *at the Manhattan Theatre Club, I wondered, "Who's that gorgeous blond hunk playing the American
reporter?" Looking at my program, I gasped, "It can't be the same actor
who played the shrimpy guy in* The Foreigner!*" Skip to another intermission, at a press performance of* Anything Goes *at Lincoln Center,
when I check my program to see who the British actor is playing Lord
Evelyn, and it's Anthony Heald again. So I get an assignment to find out
how he works his wonders, and at interview time I pass right by Heald
standing outside his Lincoln Center dressing room because I don't recognize him!*

*Tony Heald was the first actor interviewed for this book, in December
of 1990. After an interval—while he rehearsed and opened as Henry
Higgins in the Roundabout Theatre production of* Pygmalion—*we
talked again the following spring.*

*Postscript: in 1992, Anthony Heald, his wife Robin Herskowitz and
their son Dylan welcomed an adopted baby girl into their family.*

I wasn't Tony Heald until I came to New York twelve years ago. My full name is Philip Anthony Heald, and I was Phil Heald until my first season of Equity stock, at the Houghton Lake Playhouse in Michigan in 1963. The character man was named Phil Smith, so I said, "I'll use my middle name," but I was Phil Heald in the children's shows because those programs were already printed. One night a woman said to me, "I have seen everything this summer, and you're just wonderful. I saw your brother Phil this afternoon and he's not as good as you are." So I became Anthony Heald professionally from then on. My family and old friends still call me Phil, but when I came to New York it had gotten too complicated to be two people, and I started introducing myself as Tony.

I grew up in Massapequa, Long Island, where my parents were amateur actors. They started a playreading group at our house, and were instrumental in forming a community theatre. The first time I was ever onstage was as Santa Claus in the fifth grade, but it wasn't until a tenth-grade play, in which I had five lines and got applause on my exit, that I got hooked. The following year I played Higgins in *Pygmalion*; my senior year I directed a play; and then I went to Michigan State University as a communication arts major. That summer I did my first stock job. I was making fifteen dollars a week and living in a bat-infested cottage, but I was working, and it was nonstop after that.

I had very helpful teachers at Michigan State, like Mariam Duckwall and Sidney Berger, but I've learned mostly by doing. I was in a few mainstage shows a year, three or four arena productions, and many acting and directing scenes and directing projects. I was in rehearsals constantly, playing a wide range of characters.

I went to college full-time only in '62-'63 and '66-'67. In the intervening years I was taking one course at a time and working. I had jobs as a camera-store salesman and as a simulated patient in the medical school, but mostly I was working in the scene shop as a stage carpenter.

I've worked as a designer, tech director, stage manager and producer, and I've taught. I think it's good to have an understanding of all those things relating to people you're working with.

.   .   .

I left school in '67 two terms shy of graduation because I got a job at the Asolo Theatre in Florida. Eberle Thomas, one of Asolo's founders and co-artistic directors, was at Michigan State in the Performing Arts Company, which was composed of graduate assistants who were being paid to act in the company and teach some classes. In Eb's second year at Michigan he translated and directed *The Lovers*, a Goldoni play that had never been performed in English before. I thought, "If I can do a really good audition and get the part and do a real good job, maybe he'll ask me to come down and join his company," which is what happened.

I got my Equity card at Asolo in the summer of '67. It was a great company that included Charlotte Moore, Polly Holliday, Albert Stratton, David Colson and Paul Weidner.

My first classical role there was Balthasar in *Romeo and Juliet*. David Colson played Romeo and Bob Strane, who was Asolo's co-artistic director, was directing. Bob said, "David, you and Phil go over there and work on the Balthasar-Romeo scene."

David had an approach that was totally improvisational, and it seemed like anything was possible. I had the idea that the proper way to do the classics was somewhat staid and restricted. David's whole bent was to make it real, to surprise people. He's one of those actors who's sort of dangerous. I watched and I liked that.

I did Bardolph in *Henry IV*, with David as Prince Hal and Al Stratton as Henry, and watched them carefully. I've always been a good mimic, and I picked up things. Also for Bardolph, I got very involved with makeup, because in a rep season you try to disguise yourself.

I was at the Asolo for two summers and one winter season, and did about twelve to fourteen productions. I played Lysander in *A Midsummer Night's Dream*, Haemon in *Antigone*, Mick in *The Caretaker*, Cliff in *Look Back in Anger*. Mostly I was the juvenile who did character work.

I realized I was a character actor. I've always been conscious of the fact that actors who are a little bit taller than I am—I'm 5'8"—were perceived as more leading-man types. It may have been rationalization, but I saw leading men as people who had to play basically the same kind of role all the time, while I was having a delightful time doing the spectrum.

At the Asolo I learned the crucial importance of discipline. We would rehearse the first play from ten in the morning until one, the second play from two to five, and the third play from seven to ten in the evening. Once we had opened the first play we would be rehearsing the fourth play. We were working constantly and you had to be flexible. You had to key in to what was crucial about each play and character.

It was wonderful training for understanding the importance of doing your homework and coming to the theatre early enough to clear your mind of extraneous matter and lock into whatever you were rehearsing or performing. The dressing rooms were crowded and noisy, so you had to be able to construct a bubble and get your concentration going. That experience was very, very valuable.

The Asolo was a large company under a lot of strain, so learning how to maintain good working relationships with people was also very important. I tended to be friendly with the technicians in the apprentice corps. In a situation where the set has to be totally changed twice a day, you learn that theatre isn't stars and underlings: everybody has a crucial function to perform.

The most memorable acting experience at Asolo, and an important turning point in my career, was *Look Back in Anger*, directed by Paul Weidner. I think Paul is one of the greatest unsung directors, and performing Cliff was the furthest, the deepest into a part I had ever gotten. Since it was the last show of the season, they constructed the set and put it up in the rehearsal hall. We had the set and all the props right from the beginning, and were encouraged to bring in things from home—photographs or pots and pans. The stove actually worked. I would go in hours before rehearsal began and have my breakfast on the set. We did improvisations, and for the first time I got a glimpse of what naturalistic theatre could be, the sense of what living a part is like. I had such a crush on Charlotte Moore at the time, as Cliff does on Alison, and that fed into it.

I loved that production, and later Arnold Wesker's *The Kitchen* at Milwaukee Rep, because it was strongly naturalistic. In naturalism small aspects of behavior are significant. The way you handle something is *always* important, but in naturalism you can handle more things and the kind of physical texturing you can do is greater.

I've always been a "proppy" actor. If you're doing a classical piece without a lot of props, you have to do it vocally. And though I've always felt confident with accents, I've never seen myself as a vocal actor.

I like to get involved with the physical life of the character. Naturalistic productions reward that.

The week we opened *Look Back in Anger*, Paul Weidner learned he had been chosen as the new artistic director at Hartford Stage, and he asked Charlotte Moore and me to be members of his company. In the fall of 1968 I came up to Hartford and began with Constantin in *The Seagull*, my first and only Chekhov.

My best experience that season was playing Joey, the boxer in *The Homecoming*, because it was the most extreme physical transformation I'd ever tried. When you play a part you feel physically too small and too light for, you find ways to fill more space. I made pectorals out of foam rubber and taped myself into them every night. I put lifts in my shoes and threw my back out doing this kind of lumbering walk. I used nose putty to flatten my nose a bit, to show that Joey's had been broken a few times.

I worked with an adenoidal sound, and his accent wasn't hard for me . . .

I had developed an ear for accents by imitating my father, who was from England, and Cockney, Welsh and Irish characters in British movies I saw on television. But I've had both brilliant and bad coaches for accents. The good speech coach understands that character comes first. The way a character speaks is made up of a great many things *including* the accent, which is only a tool.

Tim Monick worked with me in 1982 doing the Yorkshire accent for *Quartermaine's Terms*, and he is brilliant. He was able to sit listening to the whole cast and take accent notes for everybody. He'd have seven sheets of paper, jotting down just the word, the inflection, the timbre you needed to make it better. His notes were incredibly specific but they never trespassed into the interpretive area. The less successful speech coach indulges in extraneous talk about what the character is like and why he talks a certain way, which is my job and the director's.

I had one of my very best experiences at Milwaukee Rep (where I went with my first wife, an actress at Hartford Stage, after we got married), in *The Kitchen*, playing Peter, the German short-order cook who goes crazy. Doing a German accent in Milwaukee, with its large German population, was terrifying. I audiotaped all of Oskar Werner's scenes in *The Spy Who Came in from the Cold*, and worked on imitating him. I would do his dialogue and then I'd read my lines over and over and over. It seemed to work. I got some positive comments and no negative ones.

A few years later, at the BoarsHead Theatre in Michigan, I was playing a character with a Brazilian/Portuguese accent in Christopher Hampton's *Savages*, and somebody who spoke Portuguese came up to me after a performance and said I had all the sounds wrong. I had tried to do it from a book. When I try an accent I live in terror of somebody saying, "That's not the way it sounds," and that ruining the experience for them.

I use accents from the moment I audition for a play. For Lord Evelyn in *Anything Goes* I read P.G. Wodehouse books out loud for hours when we were in the beginning stages of rehearsals, just to get that rhythm, that sense of how it sounds. For *The Foreigner*, Charlie's English accent had to be London middle class but not too cultured. Then I had to find the accent for when he is pretending to be foreign, and that was interesting to work on because it had to be a Londoner's image of what a middle-European accent would be, colored by the fact that he was learning American slang from Southerners.

Accents are always freeing, because they make me forget myself and think that anything is possible. I love playing with sounds and rhythms. I think that finding the voice and finding the walk are the critical bookends to character.

I did my second Lysander, in *A Midsummer Night's Dream*, at Milwaukee. Playing parts twice can be interesting; it depends on how the first experience went. My first Lysander was grim because we were in pumpkin pants—that horrible Elizabethan shape. In Milwaukee the costumes were Cavalier—long flowing things, and the set was an impossible number of steps with weird angles. In tech, this wonderfully fluid production, directed by Boris Tumarin, became about making sure you didn't fall, and the whole production fell apart. I realized the value of simplicity and of not letting the technical elements get in the way of the acting.

It's hard to make the transition from rehearsal room to stage, because in the rehearsal room, where everything is pretend, you make what you have work for you and it connects with your imagination. You find yourself sitting a certain way on the chairs that are put together to make a sofa, and that feeds into the physicality of the character. You pitch your voice in a certain way to fit the acoustics of the room. Then all of a sudden you're in another room where you're asked to perform, and you're wearing different clothes and surrounded by different objects.

To go from the womb of the rehearsal hall through tech is an agonizing process, and I learned fairly early how to use tech rehearsals constructively. Actors do a lot of sitting around while lights get refocused or set problems get worked out. I try to use every moment to work with the chairs, to practice with a door, to see where the step is and how it affects the turn on an entrance.

But doing *Look Back in Anger* on the actual set was wonderful, because the transition from hall to stage was minor. And at the first rehearsal of *Anything Goes*, for Lincoln Center, Tony Walton presented a model of the set on which every part that was going to move *actually moved*. You could see exactly how it was going to be, so the transition from rehearsal hall to *that* set was also a relatively easy process.

In part that was because there's never been anybody who does his homework more carefully or completely than the show's director, Jerry Zaks—it's one reason he's the preeminent theatre director in New York today. And he has the perfect collaborator in Tony Walton. Together, Jerry and Tony even solved the great bugaboo of the Vivian Beaumont Theater at Lincoln Center by discovering and making use of a sweet spot on that stage, of maybe eight-to-ten square feet, where you can be seen and heard by everybody. The set and Jerry focused everybody into that area—as he basically did in *The Front Page* and *House of Blue Leaves*. There are a lot of things around the area that add to the picture, but he got you into that sweet spot for the scenes. The staging was very simple that way.

. . .

Working with costume designers goes both ways—you each contribute something to the character. For Lord Evelyn in *Anything Goes*, Tony Walton suggested the monocle; I suggested the mustache. He had the idea that, before the tango Patti LuPone and I did, Lord Evelyn should take off his jacket and fold it very carefully. He said, "It's white. If you just throw it on the ground it will get dirty, so could you turn it inside out and fold it?" This turned out to be a very nice bit.

I find now that I need to know very early in rehearsal what kind of clothes I'm going to be wearing. When I did Jules Feiffer's *Elliot Loves* last year, I knew the character wore a jacket and tie, so I dressed that way for every rehearsal. I prevailed upon the designer—and have for as long as I've had the opportunity—to get me the shoes as early as possible so I'd know how I would be walking.

I may be very impatient with physical things, but the *Midsummer Night's Dream* in Milwaukee was a frustrating experience followed by an even worse one—an original play, ludicrously overproduced. I had to make an entrance on a twenty-foot platform, blindfolded, with my hands behind my back, trip down six steps onto another platform, and fall face forward onto a sixteen-foot slide that arched down to the stage. Seeing the money poured into that lavish production made me feel that this was not what I wanted to devote my life to doing!

This was during the Vietnam War, and I had become radicalized. I thought, "I'm just a tool of the ruling class. I have no say over what plays get done or how they get done. I've got to run my own theatre! I've got to direct! . . . But if I want to direct, I've got to go to Yale or Carnegie Mellon." I applied to those places, and they said, "Not without your B.A.," so I went back to Michigan State to get my degree.

During my last two terms, I got involved in a political street theatre, which answered all my needs. I ended up staying with that and abandoning the idea of going to grad school.

I wanted to do a play about how girls are conditioned to accept certain things in their lives, and I thought a street theatre group called the Streetcorner Society would be a wonderful company to do it with. They were students or former students from Michigan State in a large, loose, pacifist commune. We worked on a piece called *The Woman Play*. I would have ideas for improvs which we would do and then discuss. I took notes on the improvs and discussions like crazy. I'd go home and smoke dope and take amphetamines and stay up all night typing. In the morning I'd go into the department office and mimeograph the script, and that night we'd stage it. We worked out a forty-five minute play that way.

I was taking great heat from my political party—the Young Socialist Alliance—that I shouldn't be directing this play about women's liberation because I was a man. The society was getting a lot of heat from women's groups around the state, but we were bringing local people from the women's movement to watch rehearsals and give us feedback about what we were missing.

Finally, we did the play in the lobby of the Student Union at Michigan State during a weekend congregation of women's groups. It was the acid test, the most critical and informed audience, and we got an enormous response. We took the piece on tour, performing for women's groups in churches and basements and dormitories. It was hugely successful.

We went back into rehearsals that summer and did a drug play that was underwritten by the governor's office on drug abuse, and it was videotaped to be shown in schools. We were being asked to perform at conferences, and we shared the stage with Gloria Steinem and Candice Bergen at an abortion-rights rally. But during all that time some of the women's groups were clearly not happy that men were involved in the plays. And I, as a believer in discipline, was battling the freewheeling-communal-hippie approach of some of the people involved in the group. That was a real frustration to me, and finally it bubbled over into the splintering of the group and my being forced to resign.

I left the Streetcorner Society and started a radio-theatre group. I was working as a waiter, I had been divorced and had gotten married again, I had my degree, and I had directed shows in the community theatre. Then I was asked by the BoarsHead Theatre to audition. It was a very poor theatre in terms of its financial resources, so nothing was overproduced. The accent was on the acting and direction, there were some very good productions, and I ended up staying for four winter and three summer seasons.

Madeleine Potter and Anthony Heald in Pygmalion *(Roundabout Theatre Company)*

In the winter season we did a play every three weeks, and in the summer every two weeks—mostly good solid plays like *The School for Wives, Misalliance, Savages, The Hot l Baltimore.* I was acting in virtually every show, directing every fourth or fifth show, designing every show that I directed *and* some others. I was company manager/associate producer, and I was teaching at the community college. The most I made with everything was $170 a week my last season.

One of my jobs as associate producer was to make up the budget, and mine was a little grandiose. Halfway through the season we had to lower everybody's salaries and lose some people. That brought home the negative side of producing. The concerns were distracting me from doing my best work as an actor, and realizing that led me to leave this poorly paying but very rewarding, secure birth in Lansing and come to

New York just to act, and see if that was where I wanted to be. It
turned out that it was.

One of the first things I did in New York was an NYU directing project
of *A Doll House.* I was Dr. Randy Rank. The director had decided to set
it in 1966, and in my first scene with Nora we rolled a joint and got
stoned together. It got worse and worse.

It's criminal how few good directors there are. When you have a
terrible director and look at those weeks of rehearsals stretching ahead
of you, knowing you have to stick with it because of some other goal,
it's like serving time.

I think the reason why there are so few good directors is similar to
why there are so few good Presidents. It's the hardest job. A director
has to be everything, and he has to be different for each production and
each cast. He has to have a clear idea of what he wants the play to say,
and he has to be open to ways of saying that. He has to have a clearly
defined production scheme, but he's got to be collaborative in arriving
at how to realize that scheme. He has to time the development of every
actor in every role so they don't peak too soon and get tired, or don't
hold others up. He has to deal with producers and designers.

It's a horrendously hard job. I have enormous respect for directors
who are good at it.

I was doing dreadful workshops in New York and I was totally
poverty-stricken. My money ran out, unemployment was gone, and
the Actor's Fund turned me down. My second marriage and a subsequent relationship had broken up, and I was all alone. I was working
doing telephone surveys, living in Hoboken, and it was the absolute
low point of my life. Then I became a contestant on "The $20,000
Pyramid" and won $20,000.

At virtually the same time, I was offered a part in Paul Weidner's
production of *Galileo* at Hartford Stage, and he asked me to stay and do
The Matchmaker with Sada Thompson, and then the lead in Michel
Tremblay's *Bonjour, La, Bonjour,* so it was a wonderful season creatively. I had $20,000 in the bank, and I came back to New York
determined not to take any more out-of-town jobs.

The artistic rewards of working in regional theatre were wonderful, but it was terribly frustrating trying to get in to see agents and casting people who would look at my resume and say, "What have you done in New York? What would I have seen you in?" It became clear to me that you can work anywhere and work well, but you can only have a *career* in *theatre* in New York. People who will be exciting and important for you to work with will work with you if they've seen your work. Very rarely will they take an unknown out of an audition, and certainly not somebody with my unprepossessing physical and vocal attributes.

Nearly a year after I left Hartford, I got a workshop production at Playwrights Horizons. The $20,000 had about run out, I was living in a cheap place in Brooklyn and working as a waiter on 72nd and Broadway.

I spent the summer after the workshop going to every open call, as I had for a year, beating my head against the wall, trying to get a theatre job in New York, still determined not to go out of town. Finally, that fall, I got cast as Tom in *The Glass Menagerie*. Julie Haydon was Amanda, and we played on Theatre Row. Tennessee Williams came to see it with the agent Audrey Wood, and Miss Wood told her acting agency, ICM, to sign me. I got some high-powered agents and started getting good auditions.

Then I did four shows at the Roundabout, and the second was my big breakthrough. I played Gunner in *Misalliance*. Frank Rich wrote a very nice review, I got a Theatre World Award, and the show ran for a while, so a lot of people saw it. That made me feel like I had made the right decision about staying in New York.

Misalliance was the second big artistic turning point in my career. I had done two other productions of this Shavian comedy, playing Joey Percival in Milwaukee and Johnny Tarleton at the BoarsHead. I'd always wanted to play Gunner, and at the Roundabout I was working with Philip Bosco, who's an extraordinary actor, so there was a chance of going to a real extreme with my character. I felt a great sense of confidence about my right to make bold decisions and follow through on them.

The Roundabout *Misalliance* was my eighty-fifth professional production. I had had lots of opportunities to take those kinds of chances and, I guess, to varying degrees I had. There's something special, however, about taking risks on a New York stage with an actor of Phil Bosco's caliber, when you know that in the audience there could be anybody, and you're going to be reviewed by the New York critics. I think having the confidence to make those decisions and play them fully is an outgrowth partly of where you are and who you're doing it with, and partly of what kind of experience you have behind you. By then I was nearing my late thirties and had worked sixteen years in theatres outside of New York.

Another turning point was the New York Shakespeare Festival's Central Park production of *Henry V*, starring Kevin Kline. I wanted the role of Fluellen, though I felt right from the start that I was too small. I thought that Fluellen should be played by someone 6'5", weighing 240 pounds, so I concentrated on trying to act and look *big*. I did a lot of pounding around to sound heavy. I remember wanting the earth to shake when I stamped on it.

Through a variety of factors, I had a great success and won an Obie. One factor was that the low comedy scenes in that production did not work particularly well, so the audience was hungry for humor. Another was that Kevin had decided, as we got through rehearsals and into performance, that he wanted to pare down the humor he had brought to Henry and play the regal, majestic side of the character. The field was pretty clear for me to make an impression comically.

Fluellen, no matter who plays him, is a great role, but it became a role that got more attention and focus, I think, than anything that I'd done in New York, and after that I was seen for major roles.

Then came Charlie in *The Foreigner* Off Broadway, two parts at the Manhattan Theatre Club—the title role in *Digby* and Bill, the American reporter covering a South American revolution, in *Principia Scriptoriae*—Figaro in *The Marriage of Figaro* at Circle in the Square, and Lord Evelyn.

Sometimes I have a specific image for a character. My image for Fluellen, for instance, was one of those fish that blow themselves up to intimidate other fish. For Lord Evelyn, I thought, "Ramrod straight, high energy, very positive." For Charlie, I felt that he starts pulled in and ends opened up. In *Principia*, what struck me about Bill was how full of himself he was. Both verbally and physically, I tried to take up more space. He kind of strutted. I also tried to make him initially as expansive as possible, so that as the first act progressed and he grew more insecure he could kind of contract—the opposite of what happened to Charlie.

Sometimes a specific physical characteristic will occur to me. In *Anything Goes*, Jerry Zaks said that in the middle of a break in the music of "Blow, Gabriel, Blow," he wanted Lord Evelyn to have a fit. He suggested it be a religious fit. I tried, but couldn't find anything that felt right. Then it occurred to me that Evelyn says to Reno Sweeney in the first act, "I had a smashing time in your club. Your singing drove me into a frenzy, pulled me out of my seat, got me dancing around like Bojangles," and I thought, "That's what I should do for my fit! I should dance around like Bojangles!" So I started doing this crazy tap dance, which evolved into a "fit" that felt right for the character.

Every character has a signature; that signature may express itself in both vocal and physical ways. Also, I try to find an adjective that describes the character for me. With Evelyn, "passionate" was the word. He falls madly in love with Reno Sweeney—the oddest person for him to love. He talks about the gypsy in him, this passionate side that escaped only when he was with Plum Blossom years before. His passion can't have disappeared in the meantime; I wondered how he had sublimated it, and decided the answer lay in his enthusiasm for American slang and in the way he approaches life. He's a true English eccentric, very passionate about the oddest things. I decided to play Evelyn with enormous energy and great joy, just loving everything that was happening, so that when it comes time for him to be sexually passionate with Reno, the audience buys it because they've seen the seeds.

I get off the book as soon as I can. I try to memorize each scene before it is blocked, and then I try to stay as open as possible to whatever happens to me by inspiration. When I stop performing one role and go on to another, I try to lose the old role. It's much better to start with a blank slate.

The three things I hear people talk about the most are *Anything Goes*—because more people saw that than anything I've done—

Henry V and *The Foreigner*. I had a very frustrating time playing the part in *The Foreigner*, however, because it was so exhausting. Larry Shue, who wrote *The Foreigner* and played Froggy, was an old friend from Milwaukee days, and working with him was a joy, but I went on and never stopped, and at the end of the play I could literally ring out my shirt. It got terribly draining, especially on the Off-Broadway schedule of seven- and ten-o'clock shows on Saturdays.

Paul Gallo, a wonderful lighting designer, had designed *The Foreigner* so that if you moved three feet during a scene, there was a light cue bringing this area up and that area down. It was that carefully calibrated, and it meant that you were rigidly locked into the staging that Jerry Zaks had given. Because of an authoritarian stage manager, you were also locked into the line readings and interpretation. And because of the nature of farce, there was only so far you could go in exploring the characters before you hit bedrock. The process became one of perfecting the moves that you had, which was like engraving on the head of a pin.

Although *The Foreigner* was a lot of people's favorite show and is a big hit everywhere it's done, it turned me off to farce. There's so much yelling you have to do in farce, so much running around! The humor comes out of situations, not out of character. It's tied up in "bits."

I probably did three hundred-and-some performances of *The Foreigner* and of *Quartermaine's Terms*. *Misalliance* was somewhere between a hundred fifty and two hundred performances. *The Lisbon Traviata* was a reasonably long run, *Anything Goes* was an *extremely* long run—I think I did over six hundred performances.

I love getting up to seventy-five to a hundred performances; that's when it really starts to crackle. By a hundred and fifty, you're starting to go "Oh no," and then it starts to revive again. A frustrating thing about not-for-profit theatre is that most runs are forty-some performances. You don't have a chance to play it enough to really get inside it.

You make choices in rehearsals, and performing is about demonstrating those choices. After forty to fifty performances, I begin to take some choices that are the cornerstone of my performance and question them. In a long run I'll have, say, ten moments, and I'll make my choice for how to play each. Then as I get to the fiftieth performance, I say,

"Well, I can do that choice, but I can also do this choice; and here I could do that choice or I could do this choice." In a really long run, you have seven different variations on the first moment and five on the second—twelve different things that you've tried. A performance almost becomes like being in a supermarket and deciding what you're going to have for dinner, and you're making those decisions as you're performing. You say, "How would this choice work with this audience?" And you hear how it works and think, "Oh, they'll love this next choice—I'll do this!" And putting those two choices together suddenly leads you to the discovery of a fourteenth way of doing the next moment.

The one other enormous turning point in my career thus far was *Elliot Loves*. We were in Chicago rehearsing and playing at the Goodman for around eight weeks. I was away from my family and making very little money, but it seemed a good investment because I thought we'd work on the play, bring it to New York and be a huge hit. I said, "I will do this play for a year because this is a part I can live in and people I can work with that long."

We had a collection of geniuses: Mike Nichols, Jules Feiffer, Tony Walton, Ann Roth, Paul Gallo, a wonderful cast—and it did not work. I don't think you can blame the critics for killing it, because they didn't like it in Chicago *or* New York.

I learned it really is a crapshoot to do a play in New York, because you just can't count on anything. It also taught me not to take even geniuses on faith. No rewriting was done! When we were rehearsing, I thought, "How does this scene tie in with what's going on? Seems like this doesn't work here," but nobody else said anything and I didn't pursue it. I accepted it as an unusual and quirky aspect of the play, and said to myself, "Don't deal with that, because clearly it's not bothering Mike Nichols and it's something Jules Feiffer has created."

I think the next new play I do, I'm going to be very vocal if I'm not satisfied or I don't understand it. I owe it to myself to raise the issue and see if anybody else feels the same way, or at least to put my doubts to rest.

My decision to take roles in not-for-profit or commercial theatre, in television or film, is mostly based on my wanting to do something different. My goal has always been to get the audience to wonder who I am from performance to performance, to make them say, halfway into a show, "Oh, *that's* the guy who was *so-and-so!*" I think that goes back to the period when I was performing at the BoarsHead for the same audience for four years and felt, "You daren't keep doing the same kind of roles because they'll know it's you. You gotta do something different, otherwise they won't want to watch you." I want to be as totally the character as possible, and from my standpoint that makes the work much more interesting.

For example: after *Anything Goes*, I was offered the uptight gay character in *Lisbon Traviata*. I said, "This is diametrically different. This is what I should do next." *Then* there was a possibility that I might be doing the Bill Hurt role in the musical *Kiss of the Spider Woman*, but my wife and I thought, "Is another Terrence McNally gay character the next thing to do?" The chance to work with Mike Nichols on *Elliot Loves* was much more appealing. After that, I had said I wasn't going to do *any* plays until Terrence's *Lips Together, Teeth Apart* at Manhattan Theatre Club this spring, but the film roles weren't coming, and the opportunity to play Henry Higgins for the Roundabout turned up. It's a great role, the kind of role I've tried to prepare my career to have the opportunity to do.

There are classical characters I would love to play, but it's become such a package. I can't think of a worse experience than doing a role you've always wanted with a mediocre supporting cast, or a director who doesn't understand what he or she is doing, or in a theatre that doesn't get enough technical support. It can be tremendously fulfilling to play a minor or a supporting role in a brilliant production . . . much more fulfilling than playing Hamlet in a mediocre one. So I'd love to do Hamlet, or Bottom, or Iago, with the right director and cast and theatre, but not in other circumstances.

I'll be forty-seven this summer. The time to go to the hinterlands to do great roles was before. I'm in New York because I think this is the place where I can work with the best. That coincides with the fact that I really can't afford personally or financially to work out of town.

I've used the quote a lot: "They say there's no subsidized theatre. It's not true; it's subsidized by the actors." Actors subsidize it by working for peanuts and then making better money somewhere else to live on. But theatre is labor-intensive, and as people need more and more money to live in this society, theatre becomes more and more anachronistic. How can a producer pay everyone associated with a show a real living wage without charging audiences an astronomical amount of money? And if they charge that much, who will come? What will they come to see? They'll come to see people they know from movies or television, or to see spectacle.

It would be great if the government could support theatre, but the government doesn't have the money to support *schools* . . . or is not *willing* to pay the money to support the schools. I'm pessimistic about where we're going with theatre because I don't see anybody being able to support a good, comfortable lifestyle working there. I don't think it's theatre's fault; I don't think it's producers' fault; I don't even necessarily think it's the government's fault.

In 1982, when I was just getting cooking in New York, I turned down a Broadway revival at Circle in the Square to go up to New Haven and do *Quartermaine's Terms* at the Long Wharf because I thought, "This is a great role in a great play and this play has a future." I was right there, because not only did we come in for a good run Off Broadway and win some Obies, but that's where I met my wife Robin Herskowitz, who was our stage manager.

Robin and I became parents during tech week of *Anything Goes*, and during the run we bought a home in New Jersey. With Robin teaching creative dramatics at the elementary school in Montclair, a son who's now three-and-a-half and, hopefully, another child, logistics get very complicated. Before I met Robin, my career was who I was. After I met her, my career and marriage were the dual centers of my life.

Now that we have Dylan, my family is my life and my career is what I do to support my family. The whole focus has gone through a subtle but enormous shift.

I think the less single-focused you are, the less obsessed with career, the better and freer your work is. Having a family has changed my whole perspective.

FRANCES FOSTER

Do Lord Remember Me
(New Federal Theatre)

Frances Foster's 1985 Obie for Sustained Excellence of Performance illustrates the esteem in which she is held by the theatre community. As a member of the original Broadway and national touring companies of A Raisin in the Sun *and a founding member of the Negro Ensemble Company, she has not only lived the career dreams of countless aspiring actors but has helped advance opportinities for African-American actors, writers and directors. Among her best-remembered NEC portrayals are Alberta Warren in* The Sty of the Blind Pig *(which she also played at Houston's Alley Theatre), Wilhemina Brown in* The River Niger *(which the NEC took to Broadway) and Ash in* Zooman and the Sign. *She has also appeared in the works of Brecht at Lincoln Center, Arthur Miller at Arena Stage, Fugard at the Manhattan Theatre Club and August Wilson at Seattle Rep. Frances Foster gave me two interviews between Broadway performances of the Langston Hughes-Zora Neale Hurston play* Mule Bone *in 1991.*

The kids in the cast tease me. They say, "Tell us about *Raisin*. Tell us about Lorraine Hansberry running down the aisle."

A Raisin in the Sun was so important in my life—as a matter of fact, this was Sidney Poitier's dressing room. When I heard we would

be doing the Lincoln Center production of *Mule Bone* at the Ethel
Barrymore Theatre, I wondered whose room this would be. In *Raisin*,
my dressing room was up on the sixth floor. It was a thrill when the
Mule Bone company walked in for the first time and I saw my name
among several on this door.

When I was a young actress, I knew there was less work, fewer
opportunities for black actors. You'd have to be a jerk not to know that.
But a group of us had gotten together and were organizing to put on
our own plays. We would have meetings and decide what we were
going to do and how we were going to raise money. They were casting
Raisin in the Sun, which we all knew about. Diana Sands came in, and
she was going to play Sidney's sister Beneatha. Lou Gossett was cast as
George Murchison, then Lonne Elder was going to be Bobo, and
Douglas Turner Ward—he was just Douglas Turner then—was un-
derstudying Sidney and playing one of the Moving Men.

It seemed like everybody in the group but me was going to be in
Raisin, and I was feeling very unhappy. One day the phone rang, and it
was the *Raisin* office saying that Lloyd Richards would like me to
audition to understudy Diana and Ruby Dee, who was playing
Sidney's wife, Ruth. So I went in and read for Lloyd, whom I had
known first as a wonderful young actor before he became a director. I
got the job, and that was the beginning of an unbelievable experience.

No theatre in New York wanted us. We weren't booked for Broadway when we started the tryout tour in New Haven—it was Lloyd's
first Broadway show, Lorraine's first, all the principals were black. We
knew *Raisin* was special, but we had no idea if it was going to be a
success.

We got wonderful reviews in New Haven and in Philadelphia,
where they held us over. Then the Shuberts decided that maybe we
had something, and booked us into the Blackstone in Chicago . . . until
the Ethel Barrymore Theatre was free.

We opened on Broadway March 11, 1959, and I almost went on that
night. That morning, our stage manager called and said, "Diana Sands
has laryngitis. You have to come in and rehearse." I worked all day
with Sidney, Ruby and Claudia McNeil—who was Mama Younger—
and the rest of the cast. Then they found a doctor who sprayed Diana's

throat every time she came off, so she was able to play that night, and she was brilliant.

One of my favorite memories is seeing Lorraine run down the middle aisle on opening night. You see movie scenes where a Broadway audience is crying "Author! Author! Author!" but it really happened after our final curtain. Sidney, Lou Gossett, Douglas Turner Ward, Ivan Dixon, Lonne Elder and Glynn Turman all reached over and lifted Lorraine up on the stage. When that happened, we realized it was a history-making evening.

Several years later, I'm at a reception for Paul Robeson and a gentleman sitting next to me introduced himself as Dr. So-and-So. I said, "I'm Frances Foster, and I'm an actress." He asked, "Oh, do you know Diana Sands? I'm the doctor who sprayed her throat the opening night of *A Raisin in the Sun*," and I said, "Well, I'm the actress you kept from going on!"

The understudies hung out in Sidney's sitting room, and he used to tease us. He used to tease me particularly. One night an African leader came to see him, and he called me to "Come in here girl, and let me introduce you before you faint!"

Beah Richards, who understudied Claudia, and I used to watch the parade of celebrities who came backstage to see Sidney, and we'd whisper at each other, "Is that Laurence Olivier?" "Yes, it's Olivier!" You can imagine how it was to be a young actress and suddenly look up into Laurence Olivier's face. When Paul Muni came, Sidney took the cast out on stage and introduced us to him, and we each shook his hand.

Sidney was a very gentle guy who felt a great sense of responsibility, because he had become a big movie star. He was doing the play to further this black woman playwright, and to create employment for the rest of us. That eventually included a national tour and a London company. We all admired Sidney and appreciated what he was doing. In 1959 this theatre was next door to a movie theatre, and there was another movie theatre on Broadway between 46th and 47th. It made us very proud to stand on the corner at Broadway and see Sidney's name on three marquees at once—*Raisin in the Sun*, *Porgy and Bess*, and *The Defiant Ones*.

I went on for a week or two when Ruby got sick, and then she left to do the film and I played Ruth for the rest of the Broadway run.

Before *Raisin*, I had replaced Vinnette Carroll as Tituba in an Off-Broadway production of *The Crucible*, and experience had taught me that the important thing when you understudy or replace is to give the same performance as the person you're replacing so as not to disturb the other actors or the balance of the play. Gradually you make the character your own. That process is mainly internal, though someone once told me that, at some point after I'd taken over for Ruby, there was an argument in understudy rehearsal about how Ruth was "doing something." The stage manager said, "That's the way Ruth has always been played," but he was talking about a change I'd made so gradually it hadn't been noticed and had become part of the production.

I think I wound up playing Ruth longer than Ruby because I also did the national tour. I wouldn't want to do it now, but then I had never been anywhere except maybe New Jersey, and it was a great experience. I loved to travel, and we went by train all over the country and to Toronto. We were on the regular Theatre Guild tour, and the reception was just fantastic.

I played Ruth with three different actors—with Ossie Davis, who replaced Sidney; then briefly on the national tour with an actor who was fired because he had an alcohol problem; and then with Douglas Turner Ward.

Ruth would have had different reasons for marrying the Walter Lee as played by each of those three actors. Ossie is one of the kindest, most gentle men in this business, so it wasn't difficult to figure out why Ruth would marry *him.*

In the national company, there was a moment when Doug as Walter Lee said, "That is just what is wrong with the colored woman in this world. . . . Don't understand about building their men up and making 'em feel like they somebody." I remember that really hurt me. Doug's reading of the line was more wounding than either of the other Walter Lee's, and I had to adjust my reaction.

Those differences are nice to work with. When you listen for the first time every time and *hear* those differences, they keep the performances fresh.

·   ·   ·

At that time, the only life I had was the theatre. Maybe it sounds strange, but my work was all I thought about, and what was important to me was doing the best I could every performance. I was my own worst critic. I'd think, "That scene didn't go well last night," then I'd sit there and analyze it. Or I would discover new things and say "Mmm, see what happens if I do so and so." I was constantly trying to improve, and I didn't realize it then, but I was trying to put into practice an expression that we used at the Negro Ensemble Company years later: I was deepening the role instead of making it bigger.

I always wanted my work to be honest. In the back of my head I never wanted people, black people particularly, to be ashamed of what I was doing. I wanted them to recognize the character I was acting.

I liked playing Ruth—though she was harder to play than Beneatha, because Ruth seems to be an average, uncomplicated woman. I've not played Mama yet, and I would like to.

I had always wanted to be an actress. My parents wanted me to go to Howard University and become a lawyer. I had a godmother named Frances Atkins who was a dancer, and when I got into plays at the Harlem YMCA as a kid, my godmother told my parents, "She's not going to get into any trouble at the Y," so they let me go there.

One of the plays we did was Oscar Wilde's *Salome*, and I was Salome and did the dance of the seven veils—very modestly. The people loved the performances, but someone told the YMCA board we were doing a dirty play, and I had to go before them and speak about it. I said I didn't see any reason why we couldn't tell a Bible story, and they let us continue.

That was in the early days of the American Negro Theatre, a group that was founded in 1940 and produced *Anna Lucasta* and other plays. Alice Childress, Ruby Dee and Ossie Davis, Fred O'Neal—who became president of Actors' Equity—Sidney Poitier and Harry Belafonte were all a part of the ANT. The first theatre they worked in was at the Schomburg Library at 135th Street, which was right across the street from the Harlem YMCA. Word got to these professionals that there was a little girl over at the Y who was pretty good. So Fred O'Neal and a few others came over and saw me in *Salome*. Fred took me out for coffee afterwards, or maybe it was an ice-cream soda, and told me about scholarships that were available at the American Theatre Wing. He asked was I interested, and I told him, "Yes, sir." I was graduating from high school, and without telling my parents I auditioned and was awarded a scholarship for three years.

The training I received at the Wing was wonderful. It was my foundation, which still serves me today. The school was on 44th Street between Eighth and Ninth Avenues, and the people with whom I studied were the working actors and directors of the day. They could share with us, as I do now with my students, things that had worked for them. You can't really teach anybody how to act—you can only share your knowledge and experience as a working actor. I had such teachers as Margaret Webster for Shakespeare, Dorothy Sands for Restoration comedy, Arthur Hanna for radio, and Ezra Stone for TV. We had voice and diction with Graham Bernard, and we used to go to Carnegie Hall Studios for dance movement for actors, where we learned how to do things like faint without killing yourself. We had fencing—which I hated because I couldn't do it—and makeup, contemporary plays, cold readings.

When I tell my students now that I spent six months doing nothing but cold readings in a class with Ezra Stone, they look at me funny. I went to school five days a week, eight hours a day. The Wing taught me how to work, how to relax, and how to be free and honest. I notice a lot of actors in America these days are very uptight when they get an opportunity because they don't have the training and the background.

Being the only Negro at the Wing (except for James Earl Jones, who was in my TV acting class for one semester) didn't bother me because people were always telling me how talented I was and I knew it. That didn't make me arrogant—it made me more determined to be a success. It freed me and opened me up to suggestions. I would listen, and I was like a sponge absorbing everything about my craft. That training made me able to work with anybody and everybody. When a director tells me, "No," I say, "Oh, okay." And I go home, do my homework and come back with something else.

My teachers at the Wing decided to take five students whom they thought especially promising and put us all together for our classes. I was one of those chosen, and the five of us had a wonderful advisor named Bill Hansen. We worked on everything. Frank Bera and I were sort of Bill's pets, and he coached us on the nunnery scene from *Hamlet*. Whenever the school had people coming around visiting and wanted to show off the students, they got me and Frank to do the nunnery scene.

The radio teacher, Arthur Hanna, was directing a couple of soaps, and he put me on one. Arthur had this part on the "The Right to Happiness," and it wasn't a black part necessarily, because I think she was a secretary. One night after class, Arthur told me "I want you to be on the show tomorrow." Oh my God, I just couldn't believe it.

Still, my parents were a little disappointed, and not only because they wanted me to go to Howard. At that time there were no black role models for acting.

I knew I wanted to be an actress because I lived in the movies. Bette Davis and Irene Dunn were my favorites. I adored Irene Dunn because she could sing and act and everything. Later I discovered Anna Magnani and wanted to be like her.

I didn't want to do the stereotyped roles my parents were afraid I would fall into. As I've grown older and had more appreciation for women like Hattie McDaniel, Louise Beavers and Ethel Waters, I have realized that they were fine actresses who never had the opportunities to realize their full potentials.

A great hero to us was Paul Robeson. The first time I saw him in person was also the first time I saw Lloyd Richards as an actor, playing an old slave. Frank Silvera was starring in the title role of an Off-Broadway play called *Nat Turner*.

On the night I attended, Paul Robeson was in the audience and I almost had a heart attack. At the intermission, nobody moved. And that was during the time when everybody smoked. Everybody was waiting to see what Paul Robeson was going to do. Since he didn't go out to smoke, nobody else got up, either.

They didn't bother him for autographs or anything. They just sat there waiting for the second act to start.

When I finished my training at the Wing, I started pounding those pavements like everyone else trying to get work. I worked as a sales clerk and part-time barmaid, did dozens of showcases for no pay, and participated in demonstrations demanding more and equal opportunities for performers of minority races.

My next professional job, after the radio soap, was on a Sunday morning religious show called "Lamp unto My Feet." That was in the days of live TV. I dropped off my pictures and resumes at the networks like everyone else, and when a story came up about a young Negro couple they went through their file and called me in to audition. I went crazy when I got it.

That was the first time my mother ever saw me do anything. She watched the TV show and told all the neighbors.

I did background work and under-fives on all the TV shows—whatever I could. I belonged to AFTRA and SAG, and I didn't think I was ever going to get an Equity show.

Finally I got *Take a Giant Step*, when one of my Wing teachers directed it. It went Off Broadway and ran over a year. I think we made five dollars a week during rehearsals and forty dollars a week during the run. Jean Dalrymple saw me in it and that led to my Broadway debut as Dolly May in *The Wisteria Trees* at City Center.

When I was younger I met people like Rosetta LeNoire, who was very nice to me and sort of took me under her wing. She and her husband were always inviting me to their house for dinner. I was personally very fortunate, considering the limitations for black actors. And of course the Negro Ensemble Company was just the icing on the cake.

I realized very early in my career that a black woman who was a size eight—at the time—with a cafe-au-lait complexion and who couldn't sing or dance, was never going to be a star. So, being a practical person I decided I just wanted to work at what I loved to do, and thanks to the NEC I realized that dream.

There was a much smaller group of black actors in those days, before *Raisin in the Sun* and the NEC. We all knew each other and were constantly talking about the need for a theatre of our own where we could develop black actors, playwrights, directors, stage managers, administrators, crews.

Lea Scott, Frances Foster and Sullivan Walker in Nevis Mountain Dew
(Negro Ensemble Company)

Douglas Turner Ward hadn't wanted to be an actor—he took acting classes with Lloyd Richards because he thought it would make him a better playwright. Doug was very disciplined on the national tour of *Raisin* and saved his money. He came back to New York and took time off to write *Day of Absence* and *Happy Ending*. Then he raised enough money to get them on at the St. Marks Playhouse, and we were a huge hit.

The New York Times asked Doug to write an article for the Sunday section, and he wrote about the need for an autonomous black theatre. The head of the Ford Foundation read it and called him to make a proposal. With the help of Robert Hooks and Gerald Krone, our company manager, he did, and this trio became the organizers of the NEC. The Ford Foundation gave them a grant to start the NEC in the summer of 1967.

We had contracts for fifty-two weeks, and you can't imagine what that was like. Among the original company members were Rosalind Cash, Arthur French, Moses Gunn, Denise Nichols, Esther Rolle and Hattie Winston. Paul Mann and Michael Schultz were our acting coaches, Louis Johnson our dance instructor and Kristin Linklater our speech and voice instructor. Lloyd Richards conducted the advanced acting workshops.

Douglas Turner Ward's feeling was that the actors were from different backgrounds and training, and needed to develop a common vocabulary to work together. The company had a three-month orientation period, from which evolved a true ensemble mind-set.

We were pulling together for something we believed in. There was a lot of gossip among black actors about the NEC; not vicious, but more of an excuse to explain why they were not selected. Once an actress was telling Esther Rolle, who is dark-skinned, that Doug only invited light-skinned women to work with the NEC.

Doug also took a lot of flak from the black community the first year for doing some plays by whites. Peter Weiss's *Song of the Lusitanian Bogey* had previously been performed in Sweden by whites; after seeing *Happy Ending* and *Day of Absence*, Weiss had gotten in contact with Doug and told him the play was about colonialization and was written to be acted by blacks. The NEC also took an Australian play, *Summer of the Seventeenth Doll*, and set it in Louisiana for a black cast, and we did Wole Soyinka's *Kongi's Harvest*, a play by a black but not an American.

Song of the Lusitanian Bogey was our first production and its success was mind-boggling. We thought doing the play would be a good experience, but we had no idea of the attention and recognition we would receive. We soon began to get offers literally from all over the world. Our first tour was to the 1968 World Theatre Festival in London—we were the first United States representative invited in the thirty years of that festival. In 1972 we represented the U.S. in the cultural activities at the Munich Olympics. In 1977 we went to

Australia and participated in a festival of colored people from all over the world. Gradually the NEC became known everywhere.

Hundreds of plays by black authors poured in. Some of them had been written years and years before and put away because no one was interested in doing them. It took time to sort those out and to develop new playwrights.

We had a studio theatre upstairs that had about eighty-five seats. We could direct if we wanted to try, so I did Samm-Art Williams' first play. He was just a kid, and it wasn't very good, but he had talent—and the experience he got as an actor and playwright helped him get to *Home*.

Deepening a character emotionally instead of enlarging it was one manifestation of our work process. As an example, I was asked to play Wilhemina Brown, the eighty-three-year-old drunken woman in *The River Niger*. That was the beginning of my playing older roles. People sometimes meet me now and say, "Oh, you're not nearly as old as I thought you were." I guess that's better than the other way around.

I had my doubts about the part, but I took it. The real challenge, in terms of deepening the character, came with finding the reason why she drank.

When the curtain came up, I was running around the house looking for a bottle, and finally found some bourbon, and the scene got lots of laughs. The audience laughed at this drunken old woman for two acts, and then in the third act—remember the days when plays had three acts?—I had a monologue about how my husband had been lynched. The text didn't say this, but I tried to convey that I drank because I'd never gotten over grieving for my husband. When our first audience laughed at my monologue, I got angry with myself.

I don't get angry at audiences—I feel if they laugh when they shouldn't *I'm* doing something wrong—and as a way of showing that this woman was more than a funny drunk, I worked on her grief. If the audience started to snicker, I thought, "No, no you don't." It wasn't a matter of pausing to make them listen—though I did some of that— it was reaching down as far as I could into that well of loneliness and grief and making it the first time those feelings had ever been expressed.

Sometimes I'd cry, sometimes not. Paul Mann always said you should try not to cry rather than try to cry—or to laugh. I haven't worried about it. If a play says I'm supposed to laugh and I can't come up with a big laugh, I'll giggle, or smirk—just do the best I can. So whatever I do is not a lie and it's spontaneous in the moment.

It seems unnatural for me to talk about NEC in terms of "And then I did . . ." because we were an ensemble. Even when we were not in a production, we said, "*We're* doing thus-and-so," "*We* got great reviews," "*Our* next play will be. . . ." We discovered early on that the more we worked together, the more we stood out as individuals. This was our salvation, the technique that made NEC productions so good, so honest, so exciting. Everyone was free to make helpful suggestions to one another. No stars—the play was the star, and our job was to serve it.

It's no difference to me whether I'm doing *Sty of the Blind Pig* at the Alley Theatre, James Baldwin at Center Stage, *Fences* at Seattle Rep or Charles Fuller here in New York. I serve the play, and I work the same no matter where I am.

Mule Bone, which was directed by Michael Schultz, is a perfect example of this approach. The authors—Zora Neale Hurston and Langston Hughes—the language—the people of Eatonville, Florida —are the stars.

As black people we have to be very conscious of being true to our culture. We express ourselves best in terms of emotion. White critics sometimes miss what that means.

At the NEC we did Philip Hayes Dean's *Sty of the Blind Pig*. I played a frustrated young woman who loved a man but never consummated that love. He dies in a plane crash, and there is a highly charged scene in which I start reading the obituary of this young man in my church and go off into a wild dybbuk-like kind of behavior, screaming and yelling and crying and writhing on the floor. We got great reviews for the play, but the *Village Voice* critic said he was appalled that they allowed me to overact so in the funeral scene.

Now black people who came to the play sometimes had to be taken out of the auditorium because it reminded them of a funeral they had been to and brought back the whole emotional experience for them. Black people *do* try to climb into the grave, *do* try to pull the body out of the casket.

I hated going to funerals when I was younger—they were a horrible experience—and I don't go to funerals today. When we read that review about how the funeral was overacted, we laughed, because we understood that the critic didn't know. He had never been to a black funeral.

What people need to do when they see something on the stage that is from black culture is understand that we are not exaggerating. We are presenting it to you as it is, just as they do in the Yiddish theatre and the Irish theatre and the Latino theatre. What you see is their knowledge and their experience and the background of their culture. But for some reason, when we as African-Americans do something, white critics tell us what's right and wrong about our culture. They don't realize it, but that's what they're doing. It annoys us that they trivialize it, because they have not experienced it.

We can go wrong. When we did Soyinka's *Kongi's Harvest* at the NEC, we didn't understand the play, so we misinterpreted it. Africans and African-Americans have different cultures. But the critics loved *Kongi*, because there were drummers and singing and half-naked girls and African dance. The fact that we weren't really getting to the essence of the play didn't phase them, 'cause they didn't know either.

I think what is needed more than anything now is for some black people with money to start producing our own plays and films so that we can do what we want and do things as we know they should be done. Really, it's as simple as that. We need the money—we need the resources—to be able to revive plays like *Mule Bone* and let people know about Zora and Langston and other neglected old black writers as well as new ones. I was in a Langston Hughes play when I was about eighteen years old, and here it's forty years later before I'm in another.

Theatre for me is a religious experience, and for over twenty-five years my main house of worship has been the Negro Ensemble Company. The NEC has been through some changes over the years, but it has always been a beacon for black artists and craftspeople. In the beginning it was a beacon in the wilderness, and thousands of black performers who would mostly have played servants and other stereotypes—if they worked at all—have had a chance to grow because of the NEC and other companies that have developed. Black authors couldn't hope to write a *River Niger*, much less *A Soldier's Play* or *Fences* or *The Piano Lesson*, and get New York productions and win Pulitzers and Tonys, until the NEC created an artistic home for them, and then Lloyd Richards went to the O'Neill Center.

If I appear to be overly protective towards the NEC, it's because I am spiritually and emotionally devoted to its doctrine.

I'm interested in nontraditional casting because I would get to do parts that I would like to do, but I'm also interested in terms of bringing forth the cultures of various people. If I were to play Linda in *Death of a Salesman*, I wouldn't try to play a white lady—I would be a black lady in those circumstances. I don't think of nontraditional casting as black and Asian and Hispanic actors trying to be white. But I don't think we need to do *Salesman* with a black cast—I'd much rather do a play by Charles Fuller or August Wilson or Steve Carter.

I was invited to speak at the first National Symposium of the Non-Traditional Casting Project, which took place in New York in 1988. I told two stories that I felt illustrated nontraditional casting. One was about doing a commercial on location in Pennsylvania, and not discovering until the third day of the shoot that the fine actor playing my husband was legally blind. The second story was about playing in *The Gin Game* at the Victory Theatre in Dayton, Ohio. The director, Ed Stern, had wanted me to play the role so much that he was willing to bring the other actor, the stage manager, the assistant stage manager and himself to rehearse *Gin Game* during the day while I was playing in *Amen Corner* at night at Baltimore's Center Stage. Emery Battis, the actor I was playing opposite, was white. When we opened the show in Dayton, not one reviewer mentioned that I was black.

I was always very proud of being black. When the CBS soap "The Guiding Light" called me four years ago to play Vera, Alexandra Spaulding's housekeeper, I had no qualms. I told them I would be happy to do it, but Vera would be a woman with integrity, pride, intelligence and a sense of humor. And I don't spell sense of humor "buffoon." Vera is Alexandra's friend as well as her housekeeper, as all "white" housekeepers in soaps are. I am proud that both white and black people stop me in the street and say, "I love the way you play Vera."

I see every experience as an opportunity to learn. In thirty-nine years of working professionally, whether it's on or Off Broadway, regional theatre, films or TV, it's all not-for-profit.

Every job I've ever had, the first thing I'm told is, "You know this is low budget." I think this happens to most black actors. It's all not-for-profit to us. Therefore each assignment is approached with the same integrity and discipline: learn your lines; know your blocking; hit your marks; be on time; don't change your costume or makeup without permission; give your all every performance or on each take; don't do anything you wouldn't want your family—your grandchildren—to see.

Theresa Merritt, who was the original Ma Rainey in August Wilson's play, *Ma Rainey's Black Bottom*, is also in *Mule Bone*. She and I talk sometimes about the difference in the young people nowadays. They think everything is due them. We had to work so hard for everything we got. We're glad to see them with more opportunities, but I think it would be healthier for them if they had to pay a little more dues.

Most young people in this industry have gone to college. They have the academic background and they think, "I should be given this and I should be given that." It's difficult sometimes not to say, "Hold it. You get what you earn." Hopefully they'll learn.

I always try to help the talented. I was teaching at Herbert Bergoff Studios until I started to rehearse this play, and when the show closes, I'll probably go back to HB. I do a scene-study class, with emphasis on the use of the tools: imagination, observation, discipline.

I'm a discipline nut. I enjoy teaching because I find it keeps me sharpened. I was reluctant to start, and Joe Walker, who wrote *The River Niger*, kept after me to do it. That's how I came to be artist-in-residence at City College of New York.

I didn't think I had the skills to teach, but as the students would ask me a question and I would answer, I'd think, "Gee, I didn't know I knew that!" I'd been doing it, but I didn't know I had the ability to articulate it.

When I realized I could and was being helpful, and the young people seemed to like me, it was a good feeling. The first time I saw my name on somebody's resume as a teacher, it was a *very* good feeling.

Sometimes students say, "Oh, Miss Foster, I was going to do a scene from *Sty of the Blind Pig* or *The River Niger*, and when I got the script, your name was there!" They're afraid to do the scene for me because I was the first to play the role. I don't know how many roles I have created since I've been with the NEC. Every new play that I did, I was the first to do that role. What more could an actress ask?

I wanted to be the best actress I could be, and I decided when I was very young that I didn't care about being a star. I think that was very good for me and kept me healthy. I just wanted to work and to be good.

This afternoon I was out in the audience at intermission, collecting money for Broadway Cares, and a lady said, "I've been watching you since 1967, Miss Foster. You are wonderful." This is a nice lady, an aged black lady who loves to go to the theatre, and that takes care of my ego, 'cause she was sincere.

It makes me very happy. It makes me very proud. That's all I need.

Twelfth Night *(American Repertory Theatre)*

*D*orcas in The Winter's Tale *isn't much of a role, but when Cherry Jones played her in the BAM Theater Company's 1980 production, she was clearly Somebody. Pretty in an apple-cheeked, fresh-scrubbed way, gawky like a colt, the recent Carnegie Mellon graduate had an offbeat presence. In the twelve seasons since that New York debut, Cherry Jones has found an artistic home at the American Repertory Theatre in Cambridge, Massachusetts. There and at such varied locales as the Oregon Comtemporary Theatre, Portland Stage Company, Arena Stage and Goodman Theatre, she has acted leading roles from Shakespeare and Calderon to Brecht, Shaw and Coward. For her third Broadway role, as Liz in* Our Country's Good, *she received a 1991 Tony nomination. The following season she won an Obie for her performance of Anna in the Circle Rep production of* The Baltimore Waltz *and Chicago's Joseph Jefferson Award as the title character in the Goodman Theatre production of* The Good Person of Setzuan.

When I first came to New York, there were several actresses who seemed to be in everything: Meryl Streep, Joan MacIntosh, Mary McDonnell, Alma Cuervo, Christine Estabrook, Mary Beth Hurt,

Laurie Kennedy. I remember looking up to them as my professional big sisters, and as role models in terms of the work they chose to do.

I've been thinking about my greatest influences lately because Colleen Dewhurst just died, and she is at the top of the list. I saw her in *A Moon for the Misbegotten* when I was sixteen. I was sitting right at the railing of the theatre balcony, and as soon as she walked out onstage I grasped that railing and didn't let go for the entire performance. I was already five feet eight inches tall, and to see a great big powerful woman onstage was so important for me at that age! And to know never to hold back on that power and to be proud of it. One of my daydreams was to play Colleen Dewhurst's daughter . . .

I had a great fantasy life growing up in Paris, Tennessee. I lived in these woods right across the street from my home. My friends would come out for lunch and supper, but I had to be pulled out by my hair because I would go in there and create all these different worlds. I was someone different every day.

The most precious gift of my childhood was a beautiful little wooden sword that the grandfather of playmates handcrafted for me when I was seven. I had it for about twenty minutes. My mother took it away and hid it because she was terrified that someone was going to have an eye put out. I mourned for that sword the rest of my childhood. I would dream about it. It was my Excalibur.

And when I went home for Christmas last year, the sword was leaning against the hearth—Mother had found it. It was exactly as I'd remembered—an elegant little stick of wood and silver with a graceful hilt. I brought it home to New York, hung it up on my wall, and the next day I got a phone call from the American Repertory Theatre in Cambridge saying that I was being named in a lawsuit (along with the theatre, Andrei Serban and Robert Brustein) because of a freakish accident that had happened with a sword when we were doing *Twelfth Night*.

I played Viola in Andrei's production, and we all thought my duel with Sir Andrew Aguecheek was such an innocent, safe little fight that our even bothering to rehearse it before each show was a joke. Robert Stanton and I would put our swords together above our heads and do this little dance around and bring the crossed swords down to waist level, and I would break to run away. Well, during one of the first performances, I pulled away and started my run across the stage, and to my horror realized that my sword was no longer in my hand. The hilt had caught on the lining of Robert's gauntlet, catapulted onto the floor of the stage, and gone point first right into the front row.

I ran down to the lip of the stage and here was this dear man sitting there looking up at me, and I said, "Sir, are you all right?" He answered, "I'm fine," and just as he said that I realized that about two inches below his right eye was a puncture wound—almost like a small-caliber gunshot wound—and a slight laceration going up his cheekbone. And I said, "No sir, you're not all right. You've been injured and you'd better go take care of that right now." He looked up at me like I was a Looney Tune coming right off the screen and said, "After the play." I said, "No sir, you'd better go right now." He was in shock; he didn't realize how badly he was injured. He left, I started to shake, and Jeremy Geidt, who was playing Sir Toby Belch, picked up his sword and attacked me, which was the next thing in the sequence of events. The poor audience then had to sit through two or three more serious sword fights.

We heard the man was all right, and I kept wanting to contact him but was advised not to by the folks in the theatre because there might be a suit. Nearly three years later, I found out I was being sued. The man finally settled out of court for a very small amount and four season passes to the theatre.

My mother's mother, Thelma Cherry—I called her Fa-Fan—wanted nothing more than for me to be an actress. I was put into a creative dramatics class when I was six or seven. We did a lot of turning into birds and into shoelaces and into the wind. I think the most important thing that happened in those classes was that someone told me, "You are good at this."

It was about the only thing I *was* good at. I had a lot of really smart playmates, and I was a below-average student. I just didn't get it. I was very slow, and things I didn't know and should have known scared me. They still do to a certain degree.

I had a dear drama teacher named Ruby Krider, who got a strong

national forensics league going in my home town. My senior year, I
won second in the nation in original oratory. I got through high school
going to these speech competitions and doing well; my teachers always
cut me a little slack because they realized I did have a talent.

My junior year, through Miss Ruby, I got to go to the High School
Institute of Speech and Drama at Northwestern. That was the first
time I met people from other parts of the country who were as
interested in theatre as I was. I asked one of the coaches about drama
schools and she mentioned Carnegie Mellon. I sent them my college
entrance test scores, which were lousy, and they wrote back congrat-
ulating me on them! I thought, "This is the place for me."

Carnegie Mellon was going through a big transition period when I
was there. We had a different head of the department every year, and
of course each new head would bring in new acting teachers who told
you to forget everything you'd ever learned, that they had the one true
way. I watched some of my classmates believe that, which troubled
me, because I think one should be an agnostic with acting teachers as
well as with God. The manipulation with acting teachers is tremendous, and a number of kids from my class actually had nervous
breakdowns. What I learned from having so many acting teachers at
Carnegie was how to work with every style of director that can come
down the pike.

When I graduated and came to New York in 1978, I was twenty-one,
5'8", heavy, with a little-girl face, and no one knew what in the world
to do with me. I figured my career would begin at thirty-five, and I was
going to have to find some way to support myself until then. Fortunately it wasn't that long, because I got fired from waitress jobs—I
was too slow. I couldn't be a receptionist because I would panic with all
those foreign-sounding names—where I grew up everyone was
Brown, Smith or Jones. I did hold onto a job behind a counter in a
trendy Upper West Side health food store. I would go for my auditions
from there.

I auditioned for Emily Mann at the Brooklyn Academy of Music for
a little ingenue role. I knew I was wrong for it, but Emily saw
something in me she liked and gave me the job. I became part of the
BAM Theatre Company, which was the greatest gift in the world to a

twenty-two-year-old who was sort of a misfit in New York City but very committed to a real theatrical career.

The opening show of the season was David Jones' production of *The Winter's Tale*, in which I played Dorcas. Then came the ingenue role: I played the daughter of Laurie Kennedy and Gerry Bamman in Rachel Crothers' *He and She*, and I felt so inadequate! I had no experience playing a sixteen-year-old girl. I wasn't interested in sixteen-year-old girls. I loved Laurie and Gerry, but I did not have a lot of fun doing my part.

I was not asked back for the second season of BAM, and I was upset about that. They made so much of how we were all company members and would be back next season, and then I got the letter saying they just didn't need me. I was crushed. I went home to Tennessee, and got a call to come back and audition for Rosalind in *As You Like It* at ART. This crazy Rumanian, Andrei Belgrader, had seen me in *He and She* and thought I might be a good choice. I couldn't believe it.

Bob Brustein had just brought all the kids who were in the show with me up from Yale—ART was going into its second season in Cambridge. I was surrounded by all these dang MFA students, so I'd scope out the ones I thought were the most maternal or paternal and go and ask them how to beat out a line or what something meant, 'cause I was really out of my league. I think what got me through it was my sincerity and energy. It also helped that the production was a pop-up fairy tale. I went right from Rosalind to Helena in Alvin Epstein's production of *A Midsummer Night's Dream*. Alvin had cellos under my speeches, which was kind of frightening, but I survived.

When I was back in New York, I heard that ART was going to Europe the following summer. I called up Bob Brustein, who was always very kind to me, and asked if my name could be thrown in the pot for next season, and he immediately asked me to be part of the entire season and go to Europe with them. So I became a full-fledged company member.

We did *Sganarelle* and toured it all over New England to get our muscles exercised for touring in Europe for three months. And we did *Ghosts* and *Journey of the Fifth Horse* by Ronald Ribman and Wedekind's *Lulu*. I wasn't in Lee Breuer's original production of *Lulu*, but when we went to Europe I was thrown in as a backup singer in one of the lesbian-countess groups, and was Lulu's understudy. I took over the role when we were in Yugoslavia, and I got the huge bouquet of roses and the television and film crews trying to beat down my door to interview me. If you only get to play Lulu once, Yugoslavia is definitely the place to do it.

Bob Brustein and I have a sort of father-daughter relationship. Many of my friends at ART still think of Bob as their Dean, even after fifteen years. That makes it hard to go into the office and talk about next season's roles, because you still feel like a kid around him. I don't feel like that. I really feel more like a daughter. Bob and I have disagreements like family members do, and at the same time we're fiercely protective of one another.

Ghosts is the only time I've ever worked with Bob as a director, and I remember we sat up in his office for two or three weeks, analyzing every line, every word, every verb. Kathleen Widdoes was playing Mrs. Alving, and we were surrounded by all these men with pipes, sitting around and puffing and going on and on about Ibsen. Kathleen and I would roll our eyes at each other—we wanted to scream and say, "Let's just go downstairs and *do* it." At one point, in this crowded little room where you could hardly even get up and go out the door without having to step over three people, Bob looked at me and said, "It says here, darling, that Regina is to walk boldly out of the room. Let's see what that would look like." And I said, "Well, Bob, don't you think we ought to wait till there's actually some room downstairs where I can stride boldly, 'cause I'm not going to be able to do much in these two feet up here."

Since 1980, the only years that I was not involved in ART were '84, '86 and '87. Its location is just one of the great things about it. The first thing I did when I got Rosalind was take my entire life savings, which was eight hundred dollars, and buy a moped. I could moped in twenty minutes to Walden Pond after rehearsals and take a sunset skinny-dip. And the ocean and the mountains are so close. Cambridge itself is not as totally WASPy as people sometimes think. In the eleven years I've been there, I've noticed greater diversity around the Square.

What I love most about ART is my family that I have there. I love standing onstage next to Jeremy Geidt and Tommy Derrah, whom I've been acting with since I was twenty-three. We've all grown up together. I've watched Jeremy go from an out-of-breath, overweight, heavy-smoking and drinking mess into a beautifully disciplined tee-totaller and nonsmoker whose acting has just grown and grown. Jeremy and Jan Geidt are my surrogate parents.

Tommy Derrah has always been a great inspiration. He's one of the most marvelously physical actors I have ever known, yet he's absolute magic for me at his stillest. As Feste in *Twelfth Night*, he was so still at times it just took your breath away. His Feste was tired and bitter but still needing to make a buck, and it just broke your heart.

It's great, too, when you've spent so much time at a place and worked with so many people who've been jobbed in. I go to auditions in New York and I know practically every third person in the room because I've worked with them or with their best friends. Doing four or five productions a year, which is the greatest luxury in the world, you really build up a wealth of relationships in the business.

I have found that if I'm at ART for two years, I need to be in New York for a while. If I'd worked there exclusively for the last decade and then come back to New York, I'd almost have to start all over again. This way people in New York know who I am.

My first Broadway show was *Stepping Out* in 1986. It was a British play about a group of adults taking a tap class. I got no rhythm, and I'm still amazed that Tommy Tune cast me. Tommy and Marge Champion taught us how to tap dance, and we had so much fun, even though we weren't a hit.

In my second Broadway show, I played Lady Macduff in the Glenda Jackson-Christopher Plummer *Macbeth*. I'd always adored Glenda Jackson, so I was in pig heaven. I had no pride. Every night after we were both dead, like a little tiresome puppy I would end up in Glenda's dressing room and we would sip a warm Guinness stout between us, and wait for curtain calls and talk.

Growing up in regional theatre where you know what you're doing, who the director's going to be, how much money and how much time you have, I sometimes can't believe that adults run Broadway. It seems like a bunch of kids who don't have a clue about what they're doing.

The *Macbeth* started off with Ken Frankel directing, but the producers were immediately dissatisfied with Ken and moved on to Robin Phillips. Poor Robin only had about two-and-a-half weeks to get the show up on its feet, and I don't understand why you would give someone two or three weeks to put *Macbeth* up and then send it out on the road.

Then we were reviewed in Toronto, and of course all the critics knew every Robin Phillips production from his years at the Stratford Festival, so we were nothing new to them. In fact, he was using some of his old tricks because he had no *time* to do a new production. We got creamed in Toronto and Robin sort of faded out of the picture and then Zoe Caldwell came in. She thought that Robin had busied up the play and set out to strip it down to the bone, which made Glenda very unhappy because Robin had done some wonderful things that really breathed life into the production and made it interesting. That was my second Broadway flop.

I was really crushed when *Our Country's Good* didn't make it last spring. I mean, we got good reviews and the tickets were twenty-four dollars and it still closed. I guess the budget limit is four hundred thousand dollars for Broadway Alliance productions, and you just can't get a show up and keep it running and advertise it, especially when there are no stars, with that kind of money. There's nothing to bring in the typical theatregoer who doesn't know about a wonderful new playwright named Timberlake Wertenbaker. I think the Broadway Alliance is shooting itself in the foot by not allowing for enough advertising money.

The longest any of my Broadway shows has lasted is two months. It's just a killer playing to dwindling houses, especially if your heart's really in it. *Stepping Out* was the worst because it was the first. We played *Macbeth* in a three-thousand-seat house in Pittsburgh and sold out every night, and then pulled into New York City and weren't even full during previews, when they paper like mad. I guess the word was out that it wasn't a very good production, but I would've thought people would come just to hear Glenda and Christopher recite *Macbeth*. But no.

During *Our Country's Good*, we used to peek through the big fire curtain and someone would say, "The balcony looks a little better than it did last night." Someone else would say, "There wasn't *anyone* in the balcony last night." And then the first someone would say, "Oh I know, there are *three* people tonight." You feel angry knowing what's going on on Broadway and what's not, and you're in a decent show, with cheap tickets, and you're dying.

Broadway has turned into Las Vegas. The hotels that have been put up look like Vegas hotels, so they need Vegas entertainment. People from my home town come to New York to go to the theatre and I ask, "What are you going to see?" and of course, to my horror, it's always *Phantom*, *Les Miz* and *Miss Saigon*.

I would go to the end of the world to work with Andrei Serban. He's a reason I've spent so much time at ART. I worship the guy. He can be the most impossible man on earth, and at the same time the most infectious. He just gets you in his spell, and I've never worked with a director who creates a world like Andrei does. And he's so theatrical. There are so few directors who know how to be theatrical and not just get lost in theatricality. Andrei has sometimes been accused of that, but his heart is always in the text and he never does things just for effect. He wants to keep surprising the audience, but there's a reason for everything he does.

I started with him in *Sganarelle*, the Molière short plays that we took to Europe. We went everywhere—Avignon; Edinburgh; a little tiny festival in Italy; Israel; Yugoslavia; Holland—ah, it was incredible. Then we marched straight into his production of *The Three Sisters*.

I don't know how I'll ever do another *Three Sisters*. It's one of those experiences I want to keep pristine and pure in my memory. Andrei made us fall in love with the air we were breathing in this Chekhov play.

He took us on a field trip to see an incredible film called *Unfinished Piece for Player Piano*. It's sort of a version of *Wild Honey* and *Platanov*, and he wanted us to see it because of the atmosphere. And he sat and read to us from the letters of Chekhov, day after day, until we were all completely in love with Chekhov's world and with the huge emotions of the Russians.

*Cherry Jones, Tom
Hewitt and Derek
Smith (foreground) in*
Life is a Dream
*(American Repertory
Theatre)*

American actors tend to take things so literally and seriously. Andrei
wanted us to understand that playing Chekhov even close to one level
is so wrong—that his characters are up and down and taking you by
surprise every minute with their emotions. It's an Eastern European
thing that you cannot believe until you've seen it, which is why he took
us to the film. There's a character in the film who's so distraught that
he tries to commit suicide, but two hours later he's laughing and
dancing in the fields at dawn with everyone else. Also, most English
translations are as heavy as the Victorian furniture that usually fills
productions. We used a Jean-Claude van Itallie adaptation which was
really wonderful.

I was in love with the whole experience—with Andrei and everyone
in it, and with my role, Irina. She was my first truly strong connection
to a character, outside of scene work. During rehearsals, when I came
to Irina's big speech in which she says "I can't think anymore, I can't

work, I can't remember the Italian for *ceiling*," I would just break
down with the frustration of this young girl who was seeing life as it
was going to be. Then when we got into previews, I could no longer
cry. I think it was because I felt so personally connected to that young
girl that I had mourned along with her and had shed tears until there
were no more left. So I changed the feeling behind the speech from
frustration and hurt to anger. When I said, "I can't work," I was saying,
"I can't act anymore." The tears would be angry tears, which I think
worked for Irina. Maybe it's not classically right, but it made her a
much stronger, more interesting young woman.

Sometimes when Vershinin was going on and on about what the
world will be like four or five hundred years from now, I would look
out into the audience and think that fifty or sixty years from now,
maybe no one in this theatre would be left. We were going through
this world together, and that's what makes the community of theatre
and the ritual of it so exciting. We are on this planet for such a brief
time, and this was who we're on it with. I would watch, in my mind's
eye, as pockets of the audience just faded away, until scattered across
the house were maybe fifteen or twenty people, and then it would get
down to nine and then to four, until there would be one lonely person
left sitting in that audience—the last witness of that evening and of
that community. It certainly put me in a Chekhovian mood, and made
me feel privileged to be there with that body of folks.

The whole experience of *Three Sisters* was like that. Anyone who
talks about that production talks about the same glowing memories.
The director Carey Perloff told me that she came up to visit some
friends and caught a matinee, and between the matinee and evening
show called her friends and said, "I'm sorry, I've got to stay and see it
again," because she was so moved by it.

This is just funny, but I remember Andrei coming up to me and asking,
"Cherry, Cherry, are you losing weight?" I said, "I think I've lost a
couple of pounds." He said, "No, no, no, no, no. You must keep those
cheeks. You're so Russian. You're like a little cherub, you must keep
those cheeks." So I ate ferociously, trying to stay plump and Russian
and full.

Andrei has always been on me about what happens to my work

when I get in front of an audience. I'm almost painfully open in the rehearsal room, but when we start previews there's something in me that closes down, as though the audience is an intruder at a private event. I become a little more presentational. Andrei accuses me of wanting to please them. I think it's more holding back from the audience because I love the rehearsal process so much that I have not been doing the work for *them*. I've been doing it for the love of it and for the camaraderie, and I feel like, "Who invited these people in here? This is *our* game." I do think that counting off the audience in *Three Sisters* was part of my attempt to love them.

In *Twelfth Night*, when we were first working on "Make me a willow cabin at your gate," Andrei kept telling me, "Just say it. Don't act it, just say it." And when I was really able to do that—and it wasn't every time by a long shot—there was a spirituality that came through it. That sounds corny, but I was doing less than I've ever done in a role and it moved me—it moved everyone in the room. But when I got into previews, I started to act it, because I froze up and couldn't be that open with a body of people I didn't know. I couldn't trust that just saying it would mean as much to them as it had to us in the rehearsal room. So I started to jazz it up a little bit and pump it out there, as the "Shake-spearean Actress." That's one thing I really thank Andrei for getting after me about, because it can absolutely kill a character or performance.

So many directors are looking for what they want out of you. Andrei, when he's given enough time, does a lot of improvisation. He'll do things that allow you to bring your strongest suits out. He knows people are best when they're free. He enables you to feel so good about yourself, physically and emotionally and intellectually, and then he'll pick the plums of your personality and your strengths as an actor. That's what he will start to infuse into the production, with every character in the play. He makes you feel that it's a true collaboration.

When we were working on the first scene between Viola and Olivia in *Twelfth Night*—when Viola first comes to bring the suit from the Duke—Andrei had me play her like a cocky little ruffian. I thought, "That'll be fun to play—oh, I like this!" Just as I got really comfortable feeling the cock of the walk, he said, "Now, Cherry, you must play her as if she were Christ." That wasn't half as much fun as the ruffian had been. At one rehearsal, when Maria made fun of me, I started to lash out with the lines and Andrei said, "Uh, uh, uh, uh, uh, what did Christ do? He turned the other cheek." So I turned the other cheek and swallowed my pride. Then he had me do the scene again and play the angry Christ, the Christ who ran the moneychangers out of the temple. We ended up interweaving these versions of the character so that there was really a person in there, one who was always able to take you by surprise.

Andrei didn't come in on the first day of rehearsal and say, "I want you to fall as madly in love with Olivia as you do with the Duke." Instead, he blocked such a gentle, beautiful sensuality into the first scene with Olivia that I started to wonder what was going on. By the time we got to the second major scene between them, when Viola starts to leave having said, "I'm not in love with you," and Olivia calls her back and she comes, I remember Andrei asking, "Why does she go back?" I said, "She goes back because she wants to go back, she doesn't want to leave." He said, "Right. Now you're getting it." And I said, "You mean . . . ?" He said, "Ha! Now you see?"

I never felt that I was having to manipulate the text to Andrei's will. In the production, it was a wonderful moment when he had me racing up this flight of stairs—very steep, no railings. It was sunset, overlooking the Mediterranean, and going into dusk during the course of the scene. It was just gorgeous. When Olivia, my beautiful dear friend Diane Lane, would call me, I remember leaping from about the sixth stair all the way down and then running to her.

Andrei's take on *Twelfth Night* is that, as often happens in life, no one really ends up with the mate they should have ended up with. It's the way things worked out, and the way society is. I know that often *Twelfth Night* is done in a dark, somber way. This production was not. It was unpredictable and very colorful. At the end of the play, Andrei's image for "The rain it raineth every day" was almost like *The Umbrellas of Cherbourg*. There was a tableau of umbrellas against this beautiful cyc, as the fog and the mist rolled in, and you saw people going off into this misty existence together, bound in by fog.

Andrei did want me to be in love with the Duke, which I think is always the difficult thing for the Violas, because Orsino is so impossible. I mean, that's the problem for all of Shakespeare's breeches-heroines—their mates are so hapless and hopeless. Orlando in *As You Like It*, Bassanio in *The Merchant of Venice*, Posthumus in *Cymbeline* . . . they're all kind of losers.

In the "Patience on a monument" scene, the Duke is saying that a woman's love can't compare with a man's, and Viola is desperately trying to make him understand that he's wrong. For the "Patience" speech, Andrei had me move to the center of the front lip of the stage and literally do an angel on a monument, "Smiling at grief." Orsino was at my knees, holding onto me, and the monument dissolved into an embrace of Orsino, and then he broke off to send me back to Olivia with a long kiss that sent me reeling. Viola is at her most vulnerable at that moment. She's right on the brink of losing it.

I got to play my first lesbian in *Cloud Nine* at Arena Stage. The few times I've played a character of my own sexual persuasion have been fun. But I also love playing heterosexuals. I love and adore men and find them very attractive—I've just never fallen in love with one because I am gay.

I can't think of a time professionally when it seemed threatening to be out in the open about it. My life's mate, Mary O'Connor, is such a part of my every minute, we are so happy together, that it's always very easy in conversation for me to drop in something about my sweetheart, Mary. I always try to let people know, almost on the first day of rehearsal, so there's never a moment three weeks later when they're suddenly surprised or taken aback. And because it's the wonderful theatre world, people are always so loving and immediately embracing of Mary because she's such a terrific person. In fact, sometimes I feel like old friends from productions call me to find out how Mary is.

I've always known I was gay, and from my earliest memories of movies, when characters talked about the theatre, there were jokes about homosexuals, so it was the one profession in the world where I knew there were gay people. It was a haven in my mind's eye, even as a little girl.

When I was growing up in a small town in Tennessee, most of the blacks I knew worked for whites, and in the dignified society of the rural South, whites were, without even knowing it, constantly condescending to blacks. At a very early age, I think I felt kind of black, because I knew that I, too, was going to grow up to be in a minority.

I knew that those "poof" jokes in the movies were unkind and showed a lack of tolerance, but I was not yet an adult homosexual, and so black jokes hurt a lot more, because I *knew* blacks. I was brought up by a black woman named Odessa, who taught me things and gave me things I can never repay. I could never, ever dream of condescending to a black person, because the most intelligent, worldly, fun, savvy person I knew was Odessa.

One of the most stinging moments of my childhood was the day Martin Luther King was killed. My parents were not racist but my grandparents were, because they were of that world and of that generation. We had a cousin of Odessa's working in our home, and I was sitting at the table when the news came through that King had been shot, and I remember my grandmother saying to Vernel, Odessa's cousin, "Well, I really think it's for the best. He was starting to really stir up trouble and people were getting so angry, and maybe it's a blessing in disguise. Don't you think so Vernel?" I remember Vernel, I'm sure fighting back the tears and the anger and just probably wanting to strangle my grandmother, saying, "Yes, ma'am." I raced out of the room sobbing, feeling that awful guilt of being white amongst whites who think they're better, and wanting your skin to change color, just so you're not one of them anymore.

Here I go back to *Twelfth Night* again, because in Andrei's production Sir Toby was played in such a dark way that there were times when Viola really was in great peril, because of intolerance, and I think that who I am and what I am and where I grew up helped me a great deal. I knew the frustration, I knew the anger, I knew the fear of a world that is intolerant and continues to want to hurt people for differences. At the end of the play—when all in the world Viola wants to do is run away with Olivia—because of society, she can't. She has to make a critical decision, and puts out her hand and goes with the Duke. That was very charged for me.

We went from *Twelfth Night* to *Major Barbara*, and I had a very difficult time. I used to say, "Why doesn't Shaw give me some words that would help me understand who this little preacher is?" Barbara has a lot of lines, but in an odd sort of way she is sketched in. Also I despised her at first because I saw her as a pampered young woman who was power hungry, and found that she could have power in the Salvation Army.

We were doing *Twelfth Night* while rehearsing Shaw, so I was tired, and I had the flu practically the entire second half of the season. I couldn't get well because I had no time to rest. And there's no way you can make *Major Barbara* theatrical, like you can make a Shakespeare or a Gozzi theatrical. Andrei always chooses texts that allow him to be theatrical, and clearly that's where my taste lies. Michael Engler, who directed *Major Barbara*, is much more of a traditionalist, and your feet are planted in the earth when you're doing Shaw. You don't have the wide wings of Shakespeare anymore. So I was feeling brought down to earth in a big way.

I finally realized that Barbara is sincere in wanting to help people. But like many who want to help people on a grand scale, she has equally that need for power. Also she has about three nervous break-downs, because emotionally she's turning on a dime throughout the entire play. She puts her whole being into the Salvation Army and then realizes that it's as corrupt as everything else in the world, and she's brought down and crushed.

The final breakdown is that amazing speech she has at the end of the play, which I think is almost sheer madness. I delivered it more like Mussolini than Wendy Hiller, because once again Barbara has found that high horse she could climb back up on. Michael Engler was the one who encouraged me to take the speech beyond the normal playing level of that scene. He really pleased me with that direction.

I did fall in love with Barbara, because she is just so much bigger than life, and once I forgave her for not being a perfect human being, I learned how to love her flaws. Also it's exciting to play a girl moving into womanhood. I think Cusins should not quite know what he's gotten himself into with Barbara. By the end she is like someone so close to madness that they terrify you. I'm sure many Shavian scholars would argue that point with me, but then I challenge them to act Barbara, because she's a bitch to play. She really is.

. . .

Though I don't want to direct, I can get kind of bossy sometimes. I'll watch a director, even Mr. Serban—especially Mr. Serban—in his tech weeks, when he goes completely berserk. He'll have all of his toys there, and he's like an indulgent child. He'll start to muck around and destroy the fragility or the beauty of a moment he's created. There's a little perverse devil inside of him. I'll be sitting behind him and I'll yell, "How could you destroy that moment for your own childish need to tweak the audience's nose?" And he'll say, "Really? Really? You think it was better the other way?" And I'll say, "Yes, it was better. Put it back!"

My last two seasons at ART, I watched myself grow, for the first time maybe ever, role to role. I'm not intellectual or analytical, and usually I don't notice things even if I trip over them, but the roles were so phenomenal that I was able to mark the growth. Inside of twelve months I went from Rosaura in Calderon's *Life Is a Dream* to Viola to Major Barbara to Grusha in Brecht's *Caucasian Chalk Circle*. I was ill, I was exhausted, I think I was delirious through half of it, but my concentration and my focus were absolute. I came to understand that the lot of the heroine is a very lonely one.

Everything in a play where there is a hero or heroine is set up to be an obstacle for that character. You go from one obstacle to the next, keeping your mind on where you're going, even if you don't know exactly where that is. You cannot allow yourself the luxury of extra business onstage. You have got to be clean and precise. Something happens with your heart rate and your adrenalin as a heroine, because it's you against the world. When your character is allowed to make those brief, real, human connections with other characters in the play, where they feel safe enough to do that—for Viola it's with Feste—those scenes are magical because the audience gets to see you let your guard down.

There has to be a stillness in your soul. That is what Andrei meant about just saying, "Make me a willow cabin," and being so concentrated within the character that the words can fly purely out of an instrument that is grounded and still and simple.

I wish every actor in the world got to play the great parts at some point in their careers. I don't think most do because society is so concerned about beauty or stereotypes of the leading man or the leading lady.

There's nothing like acting when you and a few other characters carry a play on your shoulders. It's the easiest acting there is. The smaller roles are harder because you have to do so much more work.

If you're onstage ninety percent of the time, you never leave that fantasy world. You're not going off into the greenroom and getting a Coke and having to figure out how to ground yourself and go back out there. You're moving through this incredible fantasy with almost no break, and when the breaks come—certainly in Andrei's productions, because they're so incredibly physical—they are like breaks for an athlete. Every night I played Viola I would come off drenched—my clothes would be soaking wet, and I'm not a sweater. I'd come off and I'd drink two bottles of water, suck on a peppermint and run back on. The breaks are about getting back out there with enough liquids to get you through the rest of the evening.

I don't know that I'll get to play that many more heroines in productions and with directors that are the be-all and the end-all. I know in my heart—I knew it at the time—that that year would always be—oh, I'm getting choked up—*will* always be a gift from the theatre and from those directors and everyone I worked with. Every waking moment was about going out there to do those women who were so exceptional. I felt like a little piggy actress playing all of those roles. I felt that they should have been shared, but I wasn't going to say no. In the end I knew that I had to leave ART for a while, because anything after that would be such a letdown.

I injured my knee in a rehearsal for *Caucasian Chalk Circle*, which almost made it easier. My knee popped completely out of joint and the ligament was severed, so I had to have it rebuilt. It's healing, but just last week I was asked to read for *Saint Joan* and I had to say no because the one thing I simply cannot do yet is kneel. I'm hoping I will have another shot at her because I really would love to do it.

When we're not working, that's the work, and when we are working, that's the vacation, in a way. I always find I feel so alive and sparkling and articulate when I'm working, and when I'm not working I move into this sort of dull gray cloud. I feel that my senses are somewhat dulled because I'm not being challenged creatively. It's a perfectly normal reaction, I guess, but I usually feel that I should be doing more. One thing I do is a lot of cleaning.

I also take part in a program called the Village Visiting Neighbors, which is about the only thing I've done for anybody else since I've been in New York. I think most actors have a desire to do something for others, but our schedules are so hectic and unpredictable. Village Visiting Neighbors is sort of like computer dating—they hook you up with an elderly person they think will suit you, and I've done that, when I've been in town, for about five years. My elderly friend is named Elizabeth, and she's eighty-nine now. She used to live near me, but now she is in a nursing home way out in Brooklyn, in a scary neighborhood, so I don't get out there as often as I should because it's a whole-day affair. I'll make plans to see her and then an audition will come through, so I never let her know when I'm coming because I'm always afraid I'll disappoint her.

While I'm in New York I'd like to do a couple of film roles. I've done about seven tiny parts before, but I would like to really get my foot in the door. At the age of thirty-four, I want another ace to play when the theatre roles thin out. I will always be happy to play anything and everything, so I'm not already mourning the young women who will be behind me; I just want to know that there'll be something ahead of me that can keep me employed as an actress. Jane Alexander has been able to do film work while maintaining her life in the theatre.

ART is my home. They took a raw kid from Tennessee and made a huge investment in me. They made a big leap of faith that I would be worth their while in the end, and they've showered me with love and support. Many of my dearest friends have come from those experiences. The happiest times of my life have been in my little one-room apartment in Cambridge, shuttling back and forth between that theatre and home, going from rehearsal to choking down some supper and jumping into that evening's performance. I hope to expire on that stage at the age of ninety-six.

Peer Gynt *(Hartford Stage Company)*

*M*y criticism teacher, Harold Clurman, urged his students to save
superlatives for the rare occasions when nothing else would do—
prescient advice for a phenomenon like Mark Lamos's staging and
Richard Thomas's portrayal of the title role in the 1989 Hartford Stage
Peer Gynt. When Thomas played the first scene at the top of his energy,
like a comet blazing across the sky, I remember thinking, "This is
incredible! But he can't keep it up; he'll be dead in two hours." Six hours
later he ended the play still blazing. Known throughout the world as
John-Boy on the television series "The Waltons" (for which he received
an Emmy Award in 1973), Thomas has pursued parallel careers in front
of the camera and on stage for most of his life. He is also a teacher,
director and poet (three books published since 1974, and winner of a
Friends of Robert Frost Award). Though he directed many episodes of
"The Waltons," he was in pre-production conferences for his first staging
of a play—The Red Badge of Courage at the Kennedy Center's children's theatre—when he gave me two interviews in January of 1993.
Meeting Richard Thomas, I understood what Hartford Stage public
relations director Howard Sherman meant when he told me: "It is only
when you spend some time with Richard that you realize what a brilliant
acting job John-Boy Walton was. So much of America believes that

Richard is John-Boy—a quiet, introspective, slightly removed character
—and he's not that at all. He's such a bundle of energy, and so much
more."

The greatest and worst night of my life was the first preview of *Hamlet* at Hartford Stage. You think you can't get through it. It's just too big. Eventually you resign yourself to the fact that your Hamlet is never going to be perfect—Wednesday night this speech'll be great, Thursday night that speech'll be great . . . if you're lucky. But when you first play it, the curtain's going up and you have to be Hamlet until they carry you off. There ain't nobody going to say, "We have to stop now because this poor fellow really needs a break and it's okay, Richard, you don't have to do all of it."

When I came offstage after the performance, my initial reaction was, "I did it! I got through it! I played Hamlet!" Then you realize, almost in the same moment, that it's not enough to get through it. You have to play it well. And you have to do it again tomorrow.

That first preview was really awful, and all Mark Lamos could say when he came backstage was, "What happened baby, what happened?" It was so sad. I think Mark was having serious doubts and fears. I can easily portray an essentially noble character, and I love poetry—I've been reading and writing poetry since I was a kid. I was always playing *into* the nobility, *into* the poetry. I think Mark just hated that I had not yet learned to play *against* those qualities.

I don't think about my life biographically, so it's hard for me to mark way stations, but the first time I got onstage is probably the most important. I was six years old and singing "You Gotta Have Heart" in a summer stock production of *Damn Yankees*. Then I replaced the boy who played John Roosevelt in *Sunrise at Campobello* on Broadway. That was important, because I wasn't working with my family, I was on my own.

My mom and dad were principal dancers in Alicia Alonso's company in Cuba for several years, then they toured with the New York City Ballet, and then they opened a ballet school in Manhattan. My early years were spent backstage at the ballet and the school, and working in New York theatre and live television.

I remember the first time I really said to myself, "I'm an actor. This is what I do." I was eight years old and in the middle of a performance as John Henry in *The Member of the Wedding* at Equity Library Theatre. I could feel the lights. I could sense the audience out there and the stage space around me. . . .

Playing Geraldine Page's son in the Actors Studio Broadway production of *Strange Interlude*, when I was around eleven, was an incomparable experience. I was kind of the Studio's mascot. Jane Fonda took me to watch classes all the time, and when they needed a kid in a scene or in a playwrights or directors unit project, they'd ask me. The Studio was my first real contact with a group of actors together for a particular purpose. There was a certain style, a company atmosphere that I knew from growing up in the ballet—very different from the free-agent status of most actors in American theatre.

I wasn't a Studio disciple, but I was raised to consider myself an heir to Stanislavski. My first copy of *An Actor Prepares* was given to me when I was ten. And I read it! That sense of heritage was heightened by working at the Studio, though I wasn't privy to all the subtleties of the Method. As a kid, the idea of acting is native to you—it's all one and hasn't split off into different technical aspects. What came across most was how passionate everybody felt about what they were doing.

In *Strange Interlude*, I had the opportunity to work with extraordinary actors: Geraldine Page, Ben Gazzara, Pat Hingle, Jane Fonda and Franchot Tone, and with Jose Quintero as director. Gerry Page treated me like her son. She took me to lunch, she helped me order, she took care of me. Now *that* was very much in keeping with the Method. I was made a member of the family. With those actors and Jose, I was plunged beyond professionalism into a realm of emotional commitment that was very, very powerful.

When you're raised in the ballet you learn about what makes a dancer: dedication, self-sacrifice, technique, professionalism, subsuming one's individuality in the rehearsal process with the choreographer. What you don't necessarily see or learn is the emotional contact that's made between performer and role: the alchemy that takes place between the steps and the artist who brings them to life. The actor's technique is so much more elusive; and—when it's reduced to its elements: movement, voice and intellect—so incomplete. The work I experienced with the Actors Studio was filled with a passion that is the heart of the acting process at its most revelatory, exciting and, I think, American.

Strange Interlude was done on a turntable. I was in the seventh act, and when the sixth was on, I was alone on the other side of the drop that separated the sets. I listened to Gerry play that sixth act every performance, and you could set your watch on the inflections and music of her voice. You didn't know exactly what was going to happen—there was always the possibility of something new—but I was aware of how consistent Gerry was and yet how fresh every time.

She could also break down the formality. When somebody in an early performance yelled, "We can't hear you," she stopped and said, "Okay, let's go back. What didn't you hear?" But that was probably the first time I became aware of a rigorous sense of marking places in the text and in performance: the great parallel techniques of consistency and freshness.

I had worked with a lot of wonderful people in New York and done five Broadway shows by the time I finished high school. I was in my third year at Columbia University—in the oriental studies department, because of my interest in Chinese poetry—when I left to do my first movie. "The Waltons" came along, and I was gone from the theatre from 1968 until 1974, when I played the Dauphin in *Saint Joan* at the Ahmanson Theatre. I left as a sixteen-year-old juvenile and came back above the title—as a star—in a classic play. There is an enormous lacuna there.

I had started in front of the cameras at almost the same time as my stage debut, and my technique in film had developed continuously from little boy actor on, but my technique for the theatre had this great gaping hole. The minute I hit rehearsal, I realized how much catching up I had to do. I was with actors who had played Shaw: Ken Ruta, Keene Curtis, Joe Maher, Tom Lacy, Jimmy Naughton . . . an exemplary theatre cast. I considered myself a theatre actor whose career had just gone down a different path for a while, but in terms of understanding how to act Shaw, I was a sad and sorry case of inexperience.

I find Shaw very hard to work with. His prose is jagged. It doesn't come trippingly off the tongue, nor does it lend itself to a naturalistic process of connection between text and inner life. To be "on the line" is really important. That doesn't mean you're not thinking and feeling on the line, it just means that relishing the argument rather than resisting it is at the heart of playing Shaw.

When I did *Saint Joan*, I knew that I could never again let a significant amount of time pass between theatre productions. It was difficult, because you can't be a star and say, "I'm going back and play a bit part in Ibsen." I knew I was going to be moving in a stellar position while I was learning what I needed to catch up with my technique in the theatre.

I've since worked onstage almost every year, sometimes several times in a season. I've alternated Sergius and Bluntschli with Johnny Rubinstein in *Arms and the Man* at the Pasadena Playhouse, and done Dick Dudgeon in *The Devil's Disciple* at Williamstown, where I've played three seasons. I was Billy in the Los Angeles production of *Streamers* and Ken Harrison in a national tour of *Whose Life Is It, Anyway?* I didn't always feel I was as good as I wanted to be, but you can't stay offstage because you're not ready. You have to get onstage and *get* ready.

I never had any vocal training. I know I have a peculiar voice, but it's very distinctive. Strangers hear me talking and turn around and go, "Is that you?" I do all these books on tape, but because my voice is not deep and is more in the larynx than in the head or chest, it doesn't have a lot of timbre. On top of that, I have a fifty percent hearing loss. . . .

Around 1981, a friend who has a lot of hearing problems told me, "You have symptoms of hearing loss." I'd have the stereo on and my wife or son would turn it down. I wouldn't hear the phone or the doorbell. We had triplet daughters in '81, and I would sleep through their crying at night. When my wife realized what my problem was, she'd just wake me up—thank God, because you need as much help as you can get with three, and I was happy to do it. I just didn't hear them! My friend said, "You've got a hearing problem," and took me to her doctor.

I have a condition called cochlear otosclerosis, in which the inner ear slowly loses its sensitivity to sound, especially in the higher pitches—

like a baby's cry. It tends to happen to men in their mid-thirties. My condition has been arrested, but the hearing loss can't be reversed, so the doctor suggested that I wear hearing aids in both my ears. They make a tremendous difference. Before I knew I had this problem, a couple of weeks into any production I would begin to feel vocal strain. I don't believe that any actor who's onstage is not aware of the pitch and timbre of the voice as it reverberates from the back of the house. If you're not feeling where you are vocally in the space, it affects your vocal production. After I put in the hearing aids, I never had another sore throat.

I got the hearing aids around the time when I first went to Williamstown, where I worked with the vocal coach, Liz Smith. I thought, "You've got a hearing problem. You've tended to get this tired throat. Let's get all the information you can. Let's do the exercises. Let's do the work." If I have any vocal quality at all it's because I felt it was an area where I wasn't any good, so I made it my business to spend every day working with Liz.

I think sometimes we try to excel in areas where our limits are. I grew up on the Upper West Side of Manhattan and was always being chased. I was never a fast kid, but I ended up being the fastest in my school, because I knew I had to move or get beaten up.

I think the first thing to become comfortable with as an actor is language. My first language was Spanish. We lived in Cuba when I was a baby and spoke Spanish at home. Then, as a boy growing up in an ethnically diverse neighborhood of Manhattan, I spoke Spanish a great deal. My wife Alma is a first generation Mexican-American, so our children are a real Anglo/Mexican mix. There have always been two languages spoken in the home, though our kids don't use Spanish as much as I wish they would.

I think hearing different languages very young opened my ear to an amazing number of accents, not only different foreign languages but the different kinds of English. For the Kennedy Center's American College Theatre Festival program, I've taught at colleges and universities for several years, and I always tell my students, "Learn language. The languages of the sixteenth century, the seventeenth century, the eighteenth century . . . these are your legacy."

Nikos Psacharopoulos at Williamstown was very good at talking about the different language styles of playwrights such as Chekhov, Shaw and Williams. The only way to get what you need as an actor is to do it and do it and do it: do the plays; do more of them; do different playwrights; get the sound of those playwrights into your body. My mother and father worked with Jerry Robbins, Anthony Tudor and George Balanchine, and each choreographer had a unique way of working with the body. The same is true with playwrights. When we, as American actors, approach all playwrights as if they were the same, using an inner technique that we've learned for some naturalistic school, we cheat ourselves of the opportunity to place our tools in context. There is a joy and a relish in bringing your gifts to bear in different dramaturgical environments.

I came back to Broadway in 1981, replacing Chris Reeve as Kenneth Talley, Jr. in *The Fifth of July*. Circle Rep had a play it wanted to keep going and needed a star who might bring in audiences. I don't know if Lanford Wilson and Marshall Mason were "Waltons" fans; I don't know if they'd ever seen me. They couldn't have thought I was a stinker, because it's a play you can't do if you're a bad actor—it's a fabulous, fabulous part. I love Lanford Wilson's plays and his dramatic sensibility.

The Fifth of July is kind of an American *Cherry Orchard* in which the cherry orchard doesn't get sold. Kenny Tally is a veteran who lost both of his legs in Vietnam (he wears artificial ones in the play). Prior to the war, he wanted nothing more than to be an English teacher, but now he feels like a victim and is giving up his teaching career and selling the family home to travel with his male lover and find out what he wants to do. The story is about how he learns to accept the loss of his legs, live within the family and go on with his life and his work.

I read the play and thought, "This is fantastic." I went to see it and felt, "I *have* to do this part." I knew Kenny was a character I *needed* to act, and I knew exactly how I wanted to play him. I also felt I knew what the play needed in terms of balance.

Lanford always writes an entertaining character who is dominant but who is *not* where the emotional axis of the play turns. In *Burn This*, he features Pale, but the play is about Anna's decision. In *Fifth of July*,

Richard Thomas in
Danton's Death
(Alley Theatre)

there's Gwen, a childhood friend of Kenny's who's a copper heiress—
she fancies herself a rock singer and wants to buy the Talley home to
turn it into a recording studio. . . . Lanford always gives a great part to
somebody who does not have to do the emotional work of the play.

With Swoosie Kurtz's performance as Gwen being so colorful and
fabulous—as the role demanded—I felt the play needed to be brought
into balance so that—on the other side of Gwen—you had Kenny
Talley being the person you needed desperately to care about. Kenny is
a wickedly funny person, with a brand of gay humor that can be
outrageous and cutting; there are jokes which need to be delivered
with a certain music and pace I'd heard growing up. Kenny needed to
be much funnier in the beginning in order to be much more poignant
later on.

I knew Lanford had an attitude about a television star coming in. The first thing he said when we met was, "What do you know about gay people?" And I thought, "Well, wait and see." I was raised around gay people. My "uncles" in the ballet and theatre were gay. They were a major part of my life as a child and were almost invariably people I really enjoyed—they were funny and warm and emotional and affectionate. I felt very connected to their world. It's a sensibility I absorbed, a color on my palette.

I didn't make a choice about how I was going to portray Kenny as a gay person. I just played the character as I heard him inside my head. I didn't say, "Well, Chris is playing it rather straight, I'm going to be different." It was purely instinct.

Marshall Mason was already doing another show, so I had only one or two rehearsals with him and then the stage manager, Freddy Reinglas, worked with me. I saw the show every night. I learned so much about the role from watching Chris Reeve. I saw him do beautiful performances. I worked like an understudy, because Marshall's direction was so brilliant and the actors were so in love with each other on the stage that what I needed most to do was fit into the ensemble. I had one dress rehearsal with the cast, and went on that night. Lanford came backstage and said, "Boy, did we get lucky!"

The day the reviews came out was one of the happiest in my life. That was a major moment, because the critics could have killed me—I could have had my birthright snatched away. If they'd called me a stinker, I might have had to spend another ten years earning legitimacy in the New York theatre. An actor shouldn't have to get validation from that source, but critical acceptance is a very important factor, especially from people like Frank Rich of the *New York Times*.

It certainly influences an audience. I think the people who were there my first night knew something exciting was happening; but after audiences had been told by reviewers *how* exciting it was, they came and laughed at all the jokes and it was great.

People basically still need to be told what to think and feel about things. The same thing just happened in Robert Wilson's production of *Danton's Death* at the Alley Theatre in Houston. Our first audiences came, looked and went, "Oh my God, what's this?" Then all those fabulous reviews came out and they knew the show was great and came to enjoy it.

I was asked to join Circle Rep after *The Fifth of July*. I've done a couple of readings for them and played Treplev in *The Seagull*. Everybody who's a member of Circle Rep has a kind of love/hate relationship there—I think the politics involved in running *any* company eventually get to the actors and piss 'em off. But I think it's a great organization or I wouldn't have been a member since 1981.

After *The Seagull* I got a call saying Peter Sellars was interested in having me do the title role in *The Count of Monte Cristo* for the American National Theatre at the Kennedy Center in Washington, D.C. It turned out that Dunya Ramicova, a costume designer I had worked with at Williamstown, had told Peter he should work with me.

Peter and I had a fantastic talk on the phone about the play, and he called back and said, "I want you to do it." I had never met him, and I never read for him. I think he had never seen me onstage—he'd probably never even seen me on television. Peter makes decisions his own way. I went to Washington, he brought me into rehearsal, and it was one of the greatest experiences I ever had.

Working with Peter was my first contact with a directorial style that I could identify as being related to the choreographic work I had seen my parents do. In rehearsals for *Monte Cristo*, I saw that it wasn't going to be a naturalistic production—we were going to be given very specific physical movements which would be used in relation to an overall vision. And I knew that I could accomplish those things without sacrificing my own inner nature as an actor. In doing Balanchine's steps, Allegra Kent did not give up her persona and her greatness as an artist . . . so I knew that I could take very rigorous and formal physical work and get a lot of life into it.

I don't know how much Peter got from *me*, except he could put anything on me and I would try to make it work. I learned to work with directors by watching my parents work with choreographers: you get the steps and you try them; if the steps don't work, you change them. Try it first and ask questions later. Model it for the director. Let him look at it. If it doesn't feel right in you or on you, say why. He'll probably know before you do, because he's looking at it.

In *Monte Cristo*, I had a sense of being larger than life, playing beyond naturalism and yet having everything fully felt. I felt transformed in that role. I started with my own persona—fair-haired, eager, callow, filled with energy and youthfulness. It was a beginning in which everyone could accept me as an idealistic young sailor with a girlfriend, and then I went totally off into outer space when the character is sent to prison and returns to confront his enemies as the mysterious Count.

I had enormous help. At one point during rehearsals I said, "Peter, how am I going to do this? I can't age enough for the character." He said, "Oh, I ought to apologize. I should have told you that you're gonna be in all this makeup. There's gonna be wigs . . . you're gonna be red in this act and blue here . . . nobody's even going to know who you are!" I thought, "Thank God. The production will be doing some of the work for me." I had a sense of carrying the play in a leading role, but also of having my performance totally supported by an overall theatrical vision. I loved it. It's the same feeling I had when I worked with Mark Lamos, when I worked with Robert Wilson, and funnily enough when I worked for Jerry Zaks in *The Front Page* at Lincoln Center . . .

Although Jerry is quintessentially a Broadway director, he's no more realistic or naturalistic in his way than Peter. The world of a Jerry Zaks production is not about "Let's live in the moment." It's very artificial. He uses who you are, but he puts it exactly where he wants it, moment by moment . . . and he wants it to be right there every night. Jerry's work is highly formal, but being part of a vision which does not depend entirely upon you—which you merely need to inhabit—can be very liberating.

Dunya Ramicova also put me together with Mark Lamos. She designed *Citizen Tom Paine*, which we did for the Philadelphia Theatre Company and at the Kennedy Center. While we were on the train to Philadelphia one day, she said, "You must work with Mark Lamos. He's a person whose sensibility you will love and he will love yours. He does the most beautiful Shakespeare productions."

Mark called a few weeks later and said, "Dunya thinks we should get together. She tells me you want to do Shakespeare." I said, "I want very much to do Shakespeare, but I don't want to learn by doing itty-bitty parts, because I don't have the time to give to that process. I'm going to have to jump in with both feet somewhere, over my head." After a brief discussion about playing the Duke in *Measure for Measure*, Mark asked, "Well, how about Hamlet?"

I had played only two Shakespeare roles before—the princes in *Richard III* (one at Stratford when I was thirteen, and the other for Joe Papp when I was fifteen). Who is the greater fool: the man who agrees to do Hamlet even though he's not prepared, or the man who turns it down because he's not prepared? You're damned if you do and if you don't. Being the greedy actor I was, I just jumped in.

I instinctively felt Hamlet, while the most famous of Shakespeare's parts, is not necessarily the most impossible for a young actor who already has a certain amount of experience in the theatre. Mark said to me, "You will find, Richard, that it will wrap itself around you. You will be able to be Hamlet according to whoever you are at this time of your life." That turned out to be true. Hamlet is an actor-friendly part.

Mark and I were soulmates from the first. I know he has his reservations about my work, but he also believes in me. I think Mark's a wonderful soul and a wonderful, wonderful person of the theatre. He loves and knows music, dance and opera, and he's not interested in things just being naturalistic.

One of the things I love about Mark's productions is that the play does not have to conform to a chronological reality. *Hamlet* was in no period at all. The royal family had a kind of dowdy, European-royalty look—sensible shoes; very good fabrics, but not very interesting cuts. Gertrude was in Jackie Kennedy hats, Polonius wore a cutaway, and the father's ghost was late-nineteenth-century Germanic. Characters used walkie-talkies and microphones. I killed Polonius with a .38 pistol.

On John Conklin's set, the play took place in an eighteenth-century theatre, very probably a court theatre in a palace, which was either being torn down or restored. There was scaffolding and a fabulous chandelier wrapped in plastic that was either being taken out or protected during renovation. There was a sense of the court, a sense of an older period, and a sense of the new. You couldn't tell if Elsinore was crumbling or being rebuilt.

Mark talked at one point about having it all take place in a bunker, or having it in the desert. He throws ideas around like that, but he doesn't make the period of the production control the play. He creates a world for the production. That helped me enormously as Hamlet, because I felt free from the constraints of acting in an Elizabethan or Shakespearean style. I felt I could use my own body language as a twentieth-century American.

I always got nervous for the first soliloquy. I found myself wanting to say to the other actors, "Don't leave me." It's at that point you become aware that the fourth wall is broken—that you're an actor doing a part that's been done a million times, that this is a famous bit, and that the audience knows the words as well as you do. (You never have to worry about going up in *Hamlet*, because there's always someone in the audience who can give you the line. I could hear them speak "To be or not to be" along with me. It was like a musical—you know, they go to see *Hello, Dolly!* and they hum the song? Well, they hummed *Hamlet!*)

I always loved "Oh what a rogue and peasant slave am I." I'm not sure I did it very well, but one of the reasons I like it is that the soliloquy is so active. "To be or not to be" I feel I missed sometimes. Then it was like the guy who wants so badly to take a picture of the Pope that he never gets to *see* the Pope. He knows he took the picture, but he missed the experience.

Hamlet turned out to be a great success critically and at the box office. Mark and I said, "We've done *Hamlet*, what else is there?" One night outside the theatre, he said, "You make your list. I'll make mine." And *Peer Gynt* was on both our lists.

I'd always wanted to play Peer, and I think it was a great show from the very beginning. Mark's imagination is wide open—he invented from day to day. The unbelievable scene of the storm at sea was done with a big black plastic sheet, like trash bags. Mark said, "Hey, somebody go back there and grab it. Let's see if you can make a wave. Oh, this is great!" We played, and it just evolved into the storm. Peer is infantile, and Mark said, "If you're gonna act like a big baby, we're gonna put you in a cradle," and John Conklin designed a fabulous set with a toy motif. It had things like miniature houses, Arabs riding around on hobbyhorses, and a tiny luxury liner that sailed, exploded and sank.

The rehearsal period was unbelievably exhausting, physically, but I think I may be one of the few actors who has the kind of energy to sustain it. I just have barrels. It's a gift. It has a bad side, because it plays into overworking and overselling and a kind of show-and-tell acting, and sometimes I can let energy substitute for choices. But I have the energy and Mark knew he had an actor who could get through it.

The only time it ever got rough was when we were doing the last act and I was being the old man but *not* being an old man, because Peer is infantile right to the end—he learns great lessons with each part of his life and promptly forgets them. We went round and round about whether to age him, and in the scene of his mother's funeral I didn't know whether to be an old man, whether to use an old voice . . . I didn't know what the hell to do. Mark was trying to give me physical solutions and I wasn't ready to adopt them because I didn't know where I was coming from. I got freaked and said, "Mark, I can't. I just don't know how to do this for you." We never had an argument or fight, but he became impatient with me. It was as if he said, "Just do it," and I thought, "If I don't know what I'm doing, I *can't* do it."

Mark came to me at the end of the day and said, "You know, what I realized is, if you lose courage here, we're all dead. If you lose that sense of 'I can do it,' we're all gonna go with you." He was right. It's like being a tightrope walker. You can't look down or you'll fall. What I did not feel in a position to say was, "Well, if you don't want me to look down, give me something to do that's going to keep me looking up." But he said, "Don't lose heart. You got it. It's gonna be good. Don't let fear conquer you." The minute he said that I understood, and the problem just went away.

I loved the six-hour marathons when we did both parts of the play in one day, with a dinner break. I loved all the performances. I didn't get all of the character I wanted to, but I knew there were moments that would make the rest work. I had to get the laugh at the end of Peer's first speech, when he's spinning the tale about catching the deer, after "and then I came home." I knew if I could go through that long, long, long, long speech, say that line and let the audience know it could laugh two minutes into the play, I was halfway home. And I knew that at the top of the second half, if I could find in myself and embody Peer's mean, selfish, middle-aged, "Fuck you, I'm a slave trader and I love it" unchained greed, they would buy the second half. Those were things that needed to be accomplished. But basically it was just fun.

My daughters were eight years old at the time, and they came to see the show. I didn't know where they were seated—I couldn't see them until we got to the troll scene, where I had to drink this great goblet of troll-piss. I looked up and there were my girls—two of them in the front row and the third just behind—looking right at me. As I lifted up this thing to drink, I could see all three of them go "Ewwwwwww," and make all these horrible faces. It was wonderful.

My children may have been some inspiration for Peer, but I think it was my own infantilism and my narcissism as an actor that I really used. I mean, let's face it: all of the totally self-centered needs of the actor are perfect for playing Peer Gynt. The ego is unmatched. I'm very much in touch with the part of me that is just like a big baby: "All I want is what I want. I'm gonna eat, I'm gonna spit on you, I'm gonna shit on you, I'm gonna scream." I felt incredibly powerful.

It's common knowledge that for years a lot of people thought I was gay. That may be related to John-Boy Walton being a male character who was sensitive. I'm not gay, but that doesn't preclude having a sense of closeness to people struggling and needing to be recognized as full members of society, and admiring the fact that they seem to have dealt with AIDS better than any other segment of the population.

I haven't done enough about AIDS. I haven't been on any big panels; I haven't given large segments of my fortune; I haven't made any inroads in Congress, in Washington. I *have* performed Lanford Wilson's one-man AIDS play, *A Poster of the Cosmos*, in some benefit situations, but I think my contribution has been paltry. If I've achieved anything, it's in being unafraid to portray gay people and lifestyles openly.

People come to see me in plays because they like me. A lot of people probably *dis*like me intensely as an actor, and you can't help that. You can't please *some* of the people *any* of the time. But there is generally a sense that people like and feel comfortable with me. They would come to see *The Fifth of July* and I could feel, five minutes into the play—when they realized Kenny was gay—a kind of gasp. I thought, "Maybe I'm flattering myself, but if anybody can get 'em over to this side of the fence, I can, because they trust me, they have a feeling of empathy with me." And sure enough, by the end of the play, audiences which had started out uncomfortable with the situation were wanting Kenny and his lover to stay together, accepting them as part of the family.

Terrence McNally's *Andre's Mother*, which I did as a film with Sada Thompson, is a gorgeous piece of writing about a mother meeting the lover of her son who has died of AIDS. I adored the part. Terrence wants it all from you. If you do a Terrence McNally play, you're gonna get emotionally naked, you can't escape that. *Andre's Mother* was like that. *The Lisbon Traviata* was like that—I played Stephen, the gay man who kills the lover who's leaving him, in the San Francisco/Los Angeles production of that one.

If you play Stephen, there is no nightmare you can keep from going through—it's emotionally the most grueling material I know, much more than Hamlet. And it happened at a time in my life when I was in great personal pain. I felt I was able to bring a part of myself to the stage that I had never been able to before—not in Stephen's sexuality, but in things about music, about opera, about getting through a midlife crisis. Stephen is a tragic character. There were times when I thought, "Damn you, Terrence, damn you, give me some shelter, give me something to hide behind—send me to England, for God's sake. At least Shakespeare sends Hamlet to England for a while. Give me a break!" But there was no break. Terrence is not afraid of grand passion. He knows that we carry great big emotions within us, emotions that can move the earth. . . .

I don't know if anybody else feels this way, but I think we all have a wall around us, a sort of unseen barrier that can't be broken through. Actors talk about losing themselves, but I think good acting is making yourself fully present. I mean, yourself in the role, which is probably the most difficult thing to do but what makes it come alive in the theatre. You can put on all the noses you want, you can empathize all you want, you can turn yourself inside out, but unless you yourself are fully present, it will be a diminished experience for you and the audience. Still, there's this barrier sometimes that you feel you can't break through. *Lisbon Traviata* made me break it, which was both horrifying and very cleansing.

This year I had vowed that I would not work in the theatre because I had to make more money, for personal reasons. Then the Alley Theatre called my agent and asked if I would consider playing Danton in Robert Wilson's production of *Danton's Death*. Now if anyone was missing on my résumé, from the short list of directors I most want to work with, it was ole Bob. I told my agent, "Of all the people in the world I wish *hadn't* asked me this year! How can I not do it? I have to do it . . . I can't do it . . . I have to . . . I can't." A week went by and I thought, "Wait a minute. This is probably the greatest gift you could have right now. Forget about your miserable personal life, forget about making money, go do something for *you*. What you love more than anything is to get on the stage with a director who's gonna push you off the cliff and go off with you." So I said, "Okay, I'm coming," and it was an incredibly satisfying experience.

Bob has what he calls the visual book, which is set before the dialogue is rehearsed. What he does is plan every movement and give each a number, and you learn the numbers before you start to work on the text. He'll say, "Okay, Richard, put your right hand on top of your head and turn upstage. . . ." You do the moves and the numbers—"One, two, three, four. . . ." When you start on the text, you get in your first position and as you read the dialogue, he calls the numbers and you make the corresponding moves. It's the strangest experience you've ever had, because you're trying to remember numbers and moves which may or may not have anything to do with the text. Sometimes it's amazing how the two *do* come together. That's the alchemy the actor creates.

There's a moment in the play where Danton is addressing the Convention: he knows that he has to get the people on his side or Robespierre will continue the Reign of Terror and he'll be one of its victims. Bob gave me a series of very specific gestures, and underneath them created this incredible crescendo of the crowd. Through the sound system, which was all around the theatre, it got louder and louder and louder. As I heard the sound rising, the sense of controlling the crowd, of swaying it to my side, came through the gesture of bringing my arm forward, and the feeling of bringing the crowd to me and keeping it where I needed came from moving the arm to my chest.

As I began to do the gestures in rehearsal, I started to alter them slightly to bring them in line with what I was playing. I became a collaborator in the process, because as it came in contact with my living of the text, a gesture was naturally modified. Even though the formal gesture and the text were not necessarily conceived to refer to one another, through the alchemy of performance the actors brought them together.

I loved the process. The challenge was how heightened and how artificial you could get, because you still had to be a human being. Bob is not interested in automatons. He says that form is "boring boring boring boring. It's the performer who brings it to life. You make it yours." And he means it. He loves the form—it's a formal theatre— but it's brought to life by the flame in the artist.

On some level you are using your own psyche, bringing feeling into a formalized structure. The biggest problem in working for Bob is trying to figure out what he wants. You ask yourself, "Is my vocal delivery flat enough, is it too flat, is this too emotional for Bob, is this too cold, is it phony, is it real?" The danger is that when you spend all your time wondering what the director is thinking, you take yourself out of the center of your process and place the director there. If that happens, you can no longer bring yourself completely to your work.

Once you can get Bob out of your inner rehearsal process and take the chance of bringing yourself into his work, the magic begins. If he doesn't like something he tells you: "That's too precious, Richard . . . that's great right there . . . that's hard enough . . . bigger here. . . ." He's not interested in your subtext, he's not interested in your inner life, he doesn't care how you get what you need (you could be thinking about a shopping list), but he wants you vigilant, listening, looking.

Bob wants you to lay down the tools and the banner of naturalism. He says naturalism is a lie. I differ with him in that I think naturalism as a style has as much legitimacy as formalism. We had a birth of naturalism to cleanse and purify the melodramatic histrionics of the late nineteenth century. Formalism is an antidote to the mire of behavioral naturalism we subsequently found ourselves in. There's a reason for changes of style, and each is legitimate. Actors can have great fun with formalism. I wish more actors recognized its value.

My problem as an actor has always been that I work too hard. I use more energy than I need, I'm more ready than I need to be, I make more decisions than I need to make before I need to make them. It's one reason that I actually have more trouble in film than on the stage, because being in the space of a theatre allows for higher energy.

I've never regarded the theatre as a place to stretch, as if it were some kind of gym where you go to exercise and then you do the real work someplace else. Nor have I regarded it as a duty, like a maiden aunt you have to visit every six months or she might not leave you in her will. That's baloney. I *gotta* be on a stage. I will *never* get enough of it. It gives me intense pleasure. If it didn't, I'd probably be doing something else, because it certainly doesn't give me a lot of money.

There is virtually no financial incentive to work in the theatre. Actors who work there twice as much earn half as much as in the other media. I'm very lucky. I am able to work in the theatre because I have another career that supports me and my large family. I wish more actors had such options. Actors are driven out of the theatre because there is so much more comfort, so much more security, so much more recognition in film and television. But I'll tell you this: when all the electronic media are buried in the dust, theatre will rise up out of it.

Stage Appearances

(*Note:* Television, film and directorial credits—often extensive—have been excluded here due to space limitations. Theatres cited frequently are abbreviated as below.)

Abbreviations:

ACT/S, A Contemporary Theatre (Seattle)
ACT/SF, American Conservatory Theatre (San Francisco)
ANT, American National Theatre
APA, Association of Producing Artists
APT, American Place Theatre
ART, American Repertory Theatre
ASF, American Shakespeare Festival
ATC, Arizona Theatre Company
ATL, Actors Theatre of Louisville
B, Broadway
BAM, Brooklyn Academy of Music
BTF, Berkshire Theatre Festival
Circle, Circle Repertory Company
CITS/OB, Circle in the Square, Off Broadway
CITS/B, Circle in the Square, Broadway
CP, Charles Playhouse
CPH, Cleveland Play House
CS, Center Stage
CSF, Champlain Shakespeare Festival
ELT, Equity Library Theatre
GJRC, Great Jones Repertory Company
GLTF, Great Lakes Theater Festival
LCT/B, Lincoln Center Theater on Broadway

LCT/N, Lincoln Center Theater at the Mitzi Newhouse
LCT/VB, Lincoln Center Theater at the Vivian Beaumont
MRT, Milwaukee Repertory Theater
MTC, Manhattan Theatre Club
MTF, Mark Taper Forum
NEC, Negro Ensemble Company
NATE, Native American Theatre Ensemble
NYSF, New York Shakespeare Festival at Delacorte Theater in Central Park
NYSF/LC, New York Shakespeare Festival at Lincoln Center
OB, Off Broadway
PH, Playwrights Horizons
Public, New York Shakespeare Festival at the Public Theater
ST, The Shakespeare Theatre
SCR, South Coast Repertory
SRT, Seattle Repertory Theatre
TAG, Tacoma Actors Guild
TRC, Trinity Repertory Company
WTC, Whole Theatre Company
WTF, Williamstown Theatre Festival

+ Transfer to other venue, tour, etc.
* Obie Award
• Drama Desk Award
† Theatre World Award
‡ Tony Award
(Other awards listed individually)

FRANCES CONROY

Education/Training: Neighborhood
  Playhouse; Dickinson College;
  Drama Division of the Juilliard
  School.
Professional stage debut: ensemble, *Measure for Measure* (NYSF, 1976).
1977–78: Prudence Duvernoy, *Camino Real;* Cordelia, *King Lear;* Kattrin, *Mother Courage* (Acting Company).
1978–79: Diana, *All's Well that Ends Well* (NYSF); *Antigone;* Lady Capulet, *Romeo and Juliet;* Pearl, *Broadway;* Charlotte Bronte/Amy Lowell/Sappho/Mary Shelly/Dorothea Brooke/Virginia Woolf, *The Other Half* (Acting Company).
1979–80: Isabella, *Measure for Measure* (Yale); Jo, *The Lady from Dubuque* (B); Desdemona, *Othello* (NYSF).
1980–81: Woman in Skirt, *Girls, Girls, Girls* (Public); Sally, *Sally and Marsha* (Yale); Christine, *The Sorrows of Stephen* (Public).
1981–82: Julia, *Zastrozzi* (Public); Zena Frome, *Ethan Frome* (Long Wharf); Miranda, *The Tempest;* Donna Elvira, *Don Juan* (Guthrie).
1982–83: Megs Church, *Painting Churches* (Second Stage).
1983–84: Sonya, *Uncle Vanya* (La MaMa); Kevin, *To Gillian on Her 37th Birthday* (CITS/OB); Rosalind, *As You Like It* (Arena).
1984–85: Elmire, *Tartuffe* (Yale); Louisa May Alcott, *Romance Language* (PH); Kate, *The Taming of the Shrew* (ASF).
1985–86: Elizabeth, *Richard III* (Old Globe); Mrs. San Francisco, *Mrs. California;* Louisa May Alcott, *Romance Language* (MTF).
1987–88: Samantha, *Zero Positive* (Public);

Ann Whitefield, *Man and Superman* (Roundabout).
1988–89: Mrs. Gibbs, *Our Town* (LCT/B).
1989–90: Marion French, *The Secret Rapture* • (Public+); Frankie Lewis, *Some Americans Abroad* (LCT/N+).
1990–91: Anna Petrovna, *Ivanov* (Yale); Agnes Eggling, *A Bright Room Called Day* (Public); Hesione Hushabye, *Heartbreak House* (SCR).
1991–92: Catherine Forrest, *Two Shakespearean Actors* (LCT/B); Sally Truman, *Lips Together, Teeth Apart* (MTC/OB).
1992–93: Patricia Hamilton, *The Last Yankee* (MTC).

CLAYTON CORZATTE

Education: University of Alabama
  (Alumnus in the Arts Award, 1993).
Professional stage debut: Lachlan, *The Hasty Heart* (Barter).
1951: Carlton Fitzgerald, *Light Up the Sky;* Bassanio, *Merchant of Venice* (Barter).
1952–53: ensemble, *Thunderland* (outdoor drama); Haemon, *Antigone;* Apollodorus, *Caesar and Cleopatra;* Lysander, *A Midsummer Night's Dream;* Ensign Pulver, *Mister Roberts* (CPH).
1953–54: Richard, *The Lady's Not for Burning;* Michael, *The Male Animal;* Young Covey, *The Plough and the Stars;* Antony/Cassius, *Julius Caesar* (CPH); Servant, *She Stoops to Conquer;* Lysander, *A Midsummer Night's Dream;* Ferdinand, *The Tempest;* ensemble, *The Crucible* and *A View from the Bridge* (Group 20).
1954–55: Edgar, *Venus Observed;* Judas, *Family Portrait;* leading male, *The*

Girl on the Via Flamina; LeBeau, *As You Like It* (CPH); Paris, *Romeo and Juliet;* Brother Martin, *Saint Joan;* Richard, *The Lady's Not for Burning;* Messenger, *Electra;* Mortimer, *Henry IV, Part 1;* Warwick, *Henry IV, Part 2* (Group 20); Vernon, *Henry IV, Part 1* (Brattle+).

1955–56: Laertes, *Hamlet;* Eben, *Desire under the Elms;* Bud, *Best Foot Forward;* ensemble, *The Ponder Heart;* Don John, *Much Ado about Nothing* (CPH); Billie, *Abe Lincoln in Illinois;* Hodge, *Shoemaker's Holiday;* Mr. Tattle, *Love for Love;* Romanville, *Ring Round the Moon;* Student, *Faust, Part 1;* Lentulus, *Androcles and the Lion* (Group 20).

1956–57: Sakini, *Teahouse of the August Moon;* Mathematician, *Tiger at the Gates;* Danny, *Night Must Fall;* Sergeant, *Time Limit* (CPH); Oberon, *A Midsummer Night's Dream;* Decius, *Julius Caesar;* Surrey, *Henry VIII* (Shakespeare Under the Stars).

1957–58: Romeo, *Romeo and Juliet;* Bing, *Brother Rat;* Johnny, *Juno and the Paycock;* Sean, *Pictures in the Hallway;* Secretary, *Mademoiselle Colombe;* Reporter, *The Doctor's Dilemma* (Arena); Dick Dudgeon, *The Devil's Disciple;* Ariel, *The Tempest;* Jack Chesney, *Charley's Aunt;* Sean, *Pictures in the Hallway;* ensemble, *Ah, Wilderness!* (Toledo).

1958–59: Richard, *The Lady's Not for Burning* (ELT); Mercutio, *Romeo and Juliet;* Longaville, *Love's Labour's Lost;* Vernon, *Henry IV, Part 1* (Old Globe).

1959–60: Reporter, *The Gang's All Here* (B), Cranley, then Stephen, *Portrait of the Artist as a Young Man* (OB).

1960–61: Sebastian, *Twelfth Night;* Ariel, *The Tempest;* Eros, *Antony and Cleopatra* (ASF); Puck, *A Midsummer Night's Dream;* Cleomenes, *The Winter's Tale* (ASF tour); Hugo/ Frederick, *Ring Round the Moon* (Vassar College).

1961–62: Feste, *Twelfth Night;* Gratiano, *The Merchant of Venice;* Clarence, *Richard III* (Old Globe); Charles Surface, *The School for Scandal;*

Constantine, *The Seagull*;* Puck, *A Midsummer Night's Dream;* Mr. Stevens, then Zack, *The Tavern;* Osvald, *Ghosts;* Bassanio, *The Merchant of Venice;* Claudio, *Measure for Measure* (APA).

1962–63: Cranley, *Portrait of the Artist as a Young Man;* Con Boyle, *Juno and the Paycock;* Father Arnall, *The Barroom Monks* (OB); Osric/ Reynaldo, *Hamlet;* Cleante, *The Miser;* Kulygin, *Three Sisters* (Guthrie).

1963–69: Leslie, *The Hostage;* Leandre, *Scapin;* Blind Soldier, *Penny for a Song;* The Actor, *The Lower Depths;* Hector, *Man and Superman;* Laudisi, *Right You Are;* Gregers, *The Wild Duck;* Narrator, *War and Peace;* Juvenille/Angel, *Judith;* Firs, *The Cherry Orchard;* Young Walt, *We Comrades Three;* Charles Surface, *The School for Scandal;* Guard, *Exit the King;* Aubrey Piper, *The Show-Off;* Tony, *You Can't Take It with You* (APA+); *The Show-Off* (National Tour).

1969–70: Duke, *Measure for Measure* (Goodman); Mosca, *Volpone;* Brian, *Joe Egg;* Sparkish, *The Country Wife;* Playwright, *Once in a Lifetime;* Father, *The Initiation;* Teller, *In the Matter of J. Robert Oppenheimer* (SRT).

1970–71: Him, *A Village Wooing;* Chandebise/Poche, *A Flea in Her Ear;* Valere, *The Miser;* Richard, *Hay Fever;* Northumberland, *Richard II* (SRT).

1971–72: Vagabond, *The Tavern* (MRT); Contestant, *Adaptation* (SRT).

1972–73: Banquo, *Macbeth;* Adam, *The Diaries of Adam and Eve* (SRT); Chief Justice, *A Conflict of Interest;* Brian, *Joe Egg* (ACT/S).

1973–74: ensemble, *Jacques Brel;* Tom Daley, *That Championship Season;* ensemble, *Life, Love and Other Laughing Matters* (SRT); Old Man, *The Chairs* (ACT/S).

1974–75: Polonius, *Hamlet;* Doctor, *The Waltz of the Toreadors* (SRT); ensemble, *The Hollow Crown;* George, *Of Mice and Men* (ACT/S).

1975–76: *Caesar and Cleopatra* (CPH); Lyman, *Bus Stop* (Intiman).

1976–77: Jack Tanner, *Man and Superman* (CPH).

1977–78: Hogan, *A Moon for the Misbegotten;* Chebutykin, *Three Sisters;* Manders, *Ghosts* (Intiman); Moricet, *13 Rue de L'Amour* (SRT); Henry Carr, *Travesties;* Touchstone, *As You Like It* (ACT/S).

1978–79: Herdal, *The Master Builder* (SRT); Her Father, *Fantasticks* (ACT/S).

1979–80: Aslaksan, *An Enemy of the People;* Gremio, *The Taming of the Shrew;* Actor, *The American Clock* (SRT); Major Pollack/Mr. Malcolm, *Separate Tables* (Grays Harbor College).

1980–81: Gibson, *Artichoke* (ACT/S); Edgar, *The Dance of Death* (SRT); Uncle Freddy, *Bent* (Empty Space); Edgar, *Play Strindberg* (Oregon Contemporary).

1981–82: Ernest, *Bedroom Farce;* Duke, *Two Gentlemen of Verona* (SRT); *Billy Bishop Goes to War* (ATL).

1982–83: Friar Laurence, *Romeo and Juliet;* Mr. Pincus, *The Front Page* (SRT); *Billy Bishop Goes to War* (TAG).

1983–84: Rev. Dickey, *The Ballad of Soapy Smith;* Tom Olley, *Make and Break;* Adam, *As You Like It* (SRT); Niles Harris, *Angels Fall* (ACT/S).

1984–85: Dr. Blinder and others, *Execution of Justice* (Empty Space); Nat, *I'm Not Rappaport* (SRT); Quartermaine, *Quartermaine's Terms;* Stanley Berent, *End of the World with Symposium to Follow;* Dr. Hornby, *A Kind of Alaska;* Dispatcher, *Victoria Station* (ACT/S).

1985–86: Praed, *Mrs. Warren's Profession;* Drummle, *The Second Mrs. Tanqueray;* Yens, *Vikings;* Dwornitchek, *The Play's the Thing* (Intiman); Gardner Church, *Painting Churches* (Portland Repertory); Herbert, *The Return of Herbert Bracewell* (TAG); Grandpa, *You Can't Take It with You* (Theatre Project).

1986–87: Leo, *Danger: Memory* (SRT); Dr. Rank, *A Doll House* (Intiman); Fezziwig, *A Christmas Carol* (ACT/S).

1988–89: Duke of York, *Richard II* (ST); Ivar, *Oh Pioneers* (SRT); Bob Jackson, *Pack of Lies* (Portland Repertory); Polonius in *Hamlet* and *Rosencrantz and Guildenstern Are Dead;* Father/Captain/Doctor, *Frankenstein* (Intiman).

1990–91: Earl of Shrewsbury, *Mary Stuart* (ST); Sir Anthony Absolute, *The Rivals;* Uncle, *Aristocrats* (Intiman); Bradley, *The Cocktail Hour;* Pashka, *Egorushka* (Empty Space); Jorgensen, *Other People's Money* (ATC); Grandpa, *You Can't Take It with You* (Seattle Group).

1991–92: Dillwyn Knox, *Breaking the Code* (Alice B.); Ernest, *Rumors* (TAG); Malabranca, *Sunsets and Glories;* Fezziwig, *A Christmas Carol* (ACT/S); ensemble, *Catherine;* Messenger, *Antigone* (Intiman).

OLYMPIA DUKAKIS

Education/Training: Boston University.
Professional stage debut: Mrs. Cleveden-Brooks, *Outward Bound* (theatre and date unavailable).

1960: Madalena, *The Breaking Wall;* The Caretaker, *The New Tenant* (OB).

1961–62: Sabina Stefano, *The Opening of a Window* (OB); Emilia, *Othello;* Louise Harrington, *Five Finger Exercise;* Helen Hobart, *Once in a Lifetime;* Mrs. Botticelli, *J.B.;* Evdokia Romanoff, *Romanoff and Juliet;* Anna Berniers, *Toys in the Attic* (WTF).

1962: Widow Leocadia Begbic, *A Man's a Man** (OB); Mary Tyrone, *A Long Day's Journey into Night* (McCarter).

1963: Henriette, *Crime and Crime* (OB); Mary Tyrone, *Long Day's Journey into Night;* Charlotta, *The Cherry Orchard;* Amalie Freud, *A Far Country;*

Maxine, *Night of the Iguana;* ensemble, *Birthday Party for Shakespeare;* Mommy, *American Dream* (WTF).

1964: Anne Dowling, *Abraham Cochrane* (B); Chrysothemis, *Electra* (NYSF); Step-Daughter, *Six Characters in Search of an Author* (CP).

1965: Serafina, *The Rose Tattoo* (Studio Arena).

1966–67: Irma, *The Balcony;* Gertrude, *Hamlet; Mother Courage* (CP).

1967: Tamora, *Titus Andronicus* (NYSF); Mrs. Benthal-Green/Mother/Stepney Green/Debden, *Father Uxbridge Wants to Marry* (APT).

1968: Helena, *The Memorandum* (Public); Clytemnestra, *Iphigenia at Aulis;* Sophie, *White Liars;* Gypsy, *Camino Real;* Pauline, *The Seagull* (WTF).

1969: Ingrid/Greenclad Lady/Anitra, *Peer Gynt* (NYSF); Ranevskaya, *The Cherry Orchard* (WTF).

1970: Olga, *Three Sisters* (WTF).

1973: Goya, *Baba Goya* (APT; OB as *Norish the Beast*); Shen Te, *The Good Person of Setzuan* (WTF).

1974: Ilse, *Who's Who in Hell* (B); Pauline, *The Seagull* (WTF).

1975: Tatiana, *Enemies* (WTF).

1976: Olga, *Three Sisters;* Lady, *Orpheus Descending* (WTF).

1976–77: *Mother Ryan* (New Dramatists); Serafina, *The Rose Tattoo* (WTC).

1977–78: Ella, *Curse of the Starving Class* (Public); *Mother Courage;* Nurse Ratched, *One Flew Over the Cuckoo's Nest* (WTC).

1978-79: Hecuba, *The Trojan Women;* Martha, *Who's Afraid of Virginia Woolf?* (WTC).

1979–80: [?], *A Cat in the Ghetto;* Vladimir, *Waiting for Godot* (WTC).

1981: Ranevskaya, *The Cherry Orchard* (WTC).

1982: Filumena, *Snow Orchid* (Circle).

1982–83: Sara Melody, *A Touch of the Poet* (WTC).

1984: Madame Arcati, *Blithe Spirit* (WTC); Aase, *Peer Gynt* (WTF).

1985: Soot Hudlocke, *The Marriage of Bette and Boo** (Public); Mrs. Alving, *Ghosts* (WTC).

1986: Sophie Greenglass, *Social Security* (B); Arkadina, *The Seagull* (WTC).

1987–88: Serafina, *The Rose Tattoo* (WTC).

1988–89: Ereshkigal, *The Goddess Project;* Winnie, *Happy Days* (WTC); *Mother Courage* (WTF).

1991–92: Amanda, *The Glass Menagerie* (TRC); *Mother Courage* (GLTF).

FRANCES FOSTER

Education/Training: American Theatre Wing.

Professional stage debut: Dolly May, *The Wisteria Trees* (B, 1955).

1956: Violet, *Take a Giant Step* (OB).

1958: Tituba, *The Crucible* (OB).

1959–61: Ruth, *A Raisin in the Sun* (B+).

1962–63: Mrs. Ash, *The Last Minstrel* (OB).

1963–64: Sarah Washington, *Nobody Loves an Albatross* (B).

1965: Vi, *Happy Ending;* Supervisor and Aide, *Day of Absence* (OB).

1968: Olive Leech, *Summer of the Seventeenth Doll;* Ogbo Aweri, *Kongi's Harvest* (NEC).

1968–69: Lady, *God Is a (Guess What?);* Maydelle, *String;* Madeleine, *Malcochon* (NEC).

1969–70: First Village Woman, *Man Better Man;* Luann Johnson, *Brotherhood;* Second Operator, *Day of Absence;* ensemble, *Akokawe* (NEC).

1970–71: Mrs. Vanderkellan, *Behold! Cometh the Vanderkellans* (OB); Mrs. Mi Tzu, *The Good Person of Setzuan* (LCT/VB); Rosalee Pritchett (NEC).

1971–72: Alberta Warren, *The Sty of the Blind Pig;* Mrs. Drayton, *A Ballad Behind the Bridge* (NEC).

1972–73: Wilma, *Love Gotta Come by Saturday Night;* Wilhelmina Brown, *The River Niger* (NEC+).

1974–75: Gremmar, *The First Breeze of Summer* (NEC+).

1976: Mama, *Livin' Fat* (NEC).

1976–77: Lena, *Boesman and Lena* (MTC); Alberta Warren, *The Sty of the Blind Pig* (Alley).

1977–78: Aunt Duke/Potion Lady, *Mahalia* (New Federal); Maumau, *Daughters of the Mock* (NEC).

1978–79: Everelda Griffin, *Nevis Mountain Dew* (NEC, Arena).

1979–80: Mrs. Potts, *Big City Blues* (NEC).

1980–81: Ash, *Zooman and the Sign* (NEC); Emma, *A Full-Length Portrait of America* (ATL).

1981–82: Ash, *Zooman and the Sign* (NEC); Sister Margaret, *Amen Corner* (CS); Fonsia Dorsey, *The Gin Game* (Victory).

1982–83: ensemble, *Do Lord Remember Me* (APT); Berenice, *The Member of the Wedding* (BTF).

1983–84: ensemble, *Do Lord Remember Me* (New Federal).

1984–85: *Henrietta* (NEC). Obie Award for Sustained Excellence of Performance.

1985–86: Cassie, *House of Shadows* (NEC); Rose, *Fences* (SRT).

1986–87: Tituba, *Crucible* (Arena).

1989–90: Betty, *Matinee* (OB); Viola, *Ground People* (APT).

1990–91: Sister Lewis, *Mule Bone* (LCT/B).

1980–81: ensemble, *The Haggadah* (Public).

1981–82: Lullabye, *Lullabye and Goodnight* (Public).

1982–83: Solvieg, *Peer Gynt* (Guthrie); ensemble, *Broadway Babylon—the Musical that Never Was* (OB).

1983–84: Abby, *Hello I'm Not in Right Now* (White Barn).

1984: *Fela* (Tapia Theatre, Puerto Rico); *Peter Pan* (Centro de Bellas Artes, Puerto Rico).

1985: Lady Mortimer, *Henry IV, Part 1* (ANT); Marianne, *Tartuffe*; Annette, *The Game of Love* (GLTF).

1986: Helena, *A Midsummer Night's Dream* (WTC); Regina, *Ghosts* (GLTF); Julia, *Lucky Lucy and the Fortune Man* (Writers').

1986–87: Maria, *Neapolitan Ghosts* (Yale); Jennie, *Portrait of Jennie* (BTF).

1987–88: Aldonza, *Man of La Mancha* (Denver Center, George Street); Lucy, *Dracula, a Musical Nightmare* (Stage West); Bride, *Blood Wedding* (GLTF).

1988–89: Viola, *Twelfth Night* (Capital).

1989–90: Emilia Pavese, *Tamara* (OB); Varya, *The Cherry Orchard* (Capital).

1991–92: Maria Valdez, *Nick and Nora* (B); Sarah Brown, *Guys and Dolls* (B).

JOSIE DE GUZMAN

Education/Training: Boston Conservatory of Music.

Professional stage debut: ensemble, *Nightclub Cantata* (CP, Arena; 1977–78).

1978–79: Lidia, *Runaways* (Public+); Gia Campbell, *Carmelina* (B).

1979–80: Maria, *West Side Story* (B+).

ANTHONY HEALD

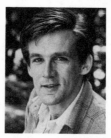

Education/Training: Michigan State University.

Professional stage debut: Nicky Holroyd, *Bell, Book and Candle* (Houghton Lake Playhouse, 1963).

1963: Dr. Locke, *Not in the Book*; Bibi, *The Happy Time*; Leblache, *A Shot in the Dark*; Policeman, *King of Hearts* (Houghton Lake).

1964: Mr. Esmond, Sr., *Gentlemen Prefer Blonds;* Don Blades, *The Best Man;* Burt, *Riverwind;* Man, *Sunday in New York* (Enchanted Hills).

1965: Dr. Baugh, *Cat on a Hot Tin Roof;* Munro Murgatroyd, *Dirty Work at the Crossroads;* Paul Cunningham, *The Typists;* Young Man, *Hello, Out There;* Peter, *A Taste of Honey* (Indianhead).

1966: Harry Berlin, *Luv;* Peter, *The Zoo Story;* Cocky, *The Roar of the Greasepaint, The Smell of the Crowd;* Old Actor, *The Fantasticks* (Indianhead).

1967: Pierre, *The Madwoman of Chaillot;* Leander, *Scapin;* Balthasar, *Romeo and Juliet;* Sylvio, *Servant of Two Masters;* Bardolph, *Henry IV, Part 1* (Asolo).

1968: Nickles, *J.B.;* Cliff, *Look Back in Anger;* Lysander, *A Midsummer Night's Dream;* Koby, *The Visit;* Haemon, *Antigone;* Mick, *The Caretaker* (Asolo); Constantine, *The Seagull;* Jack Hunter, *The Rose Tattoo* (Hartford).

1969: Gump, *The Waltz Invention;* Joey, *The Homecoming;* Franz/The Chief Clerk, *The Trial;* Clarence, Jr., *Life with Father* (Hartford); Lysander, *A Midsummer Night's Dream;* Peter, *The Kitchen;* Joey Percival, *Misalliance* (MRT).

1970: Prince Rudolph, *The Prince of Peasantmania* (MRT).

1971: Donald, *The Boys in the Band* (Hartford).

1974: Cockney Boyfriend, *There's a Girl in My Soup;* Lou, *The Gingerbread Lady;* Artie, *The House of Blue Leaves;* Frank, *Mrs. Warren's Profession;* Mortimer, *Arsenic and Old Lace;* Perchick, *Fiddler on the Roof;* Joe, *The Time of Your Life;* Paul, *Barefoot in the Park;* Annas, *Jesus Christ, Superstar* (BoarsHead).

1975: Antonio/Stephano, *The Tempest;* Charles, *Blithe Spirit;* Macbeth; Billy Bibbitt, *One Flew Over the Cuckoo's Nest;* Paul, *6 Rms Riv Vue* (BoarsHead); Charles, *Blithe Spirit* (Stage Door).

1976: Servant, *The Amorous Flea;* Carlos, *Savages;* Johnny Tarleton, *Misalliance;*

Felix, *The Owl and the Pussycat;* James, *That Championship Season;* Paravicini, *The Mousetrap;* Sky Masterson, *Guys and Dolls;* Milt Manville, *Luv* (BoarsHead).

1977: Richard, *The Lion in Winter;* Marcus Lycus, *A Funny Thing Happened on the Way to the Forum;* Brick, *Cat on a Hot Tin Roof;* Young Marlowe, *She Stoops to Conquer;* Minister, *Habeas Corpus;* E.K. Hornbeck, *Inherit the Wind;* Tony, *Dial "M" for Murder* (BoarsHead); Edmond, *Long Day's Journey into Night;* Richard, *Ah, Wilderness!* (MRT).

1978: Esker Mike, *Esker Mike and His Wife Agiluk;* Dr. Rank, *A Doll House* (Workshops, NYC).

1979: Andrea, *Galileo;* Ambrose Kemper, *The Matchmaker;* Serge, *Bonjour, La, Bonjour* (Hartford); Orpheus, *The Electra Myth* (ELT).

1980: ensemble, *The America Project* (ATL); ensemble, *Fables for Friends* (PH); Tom, *The Glass Menagerie* (Lion).

1981: Jones/Maples, *Inadmissable Evidence,* Gunner, *Misalliance†* (Roundabout).

1982: Aston, *The Caretaker;* Henry Grenfel, *The Fox* (Roundabout); Wayne Foster, *The Wake of Jamey Foster* (B).

1982–83: Derek, *Quartermaine's Terms** (Long Wharf+).

1983: Donald, *The Philanthropist* (MTC).

1984: Fluellen, *Henry V** (NYSF, also St. Clair Bayfield Award); Charlie, *The Foreigner** (OB).

1985: *Digby** (MTC); Figaro, *The Marriage of Figaro* (CITS/B).

1986: Bill, *Principia Scriptoriae* (MTC).

1987–89: Lord Evelyn, *Anything Goes* (LCT/VB).

1989: Stephen, *Lisbon Traviata* (MTC+); Robert, *Betrayal* (BTF).

1990: Elliot, *Elliot Loves* (Goodman, OB).

1991: Higgins, *Pygmalion* (Roundabout); John Haddock, *Lips Together, Teeth Apart* (MTC+).

1992: Hough, *A Small Family Business* (MTC on B).

RICHARD JENKINS

Education/Training: Illinois Wesleyan.
Professional stage debut: Family member,
  Son of Man and the Family (Trinity
  Repertory Company, 1970).
[All work at TRC except as noted]
1970–71: Curtis, *The Taming of the Shrew;*
  Steward, *Love for Love;* First Const-
  able, *The Threepenny Opera;* Man,
  You Can't Take It with You.
1971–72: Diomedes, *Troilus and Cressida;*
  Alain, *The School for Wives.*
1972–73: Butler, *Lady's Audley's Secret;*
  Alain, *The School for Wives;* Salinas/
  Headsman, *Royal Hunt of the Sun;*
  Warder/Pawtucket/Toastmaster/
  Young Fisherman, *Feasting with
  Panthers.*
1973–74: McPherson/Newsman/An Ele-
  gant Fireman, *Aimee;* Sheriff, *Brother
  to Dragons.*
1974–75: Constable Brown, *Well Hung;*
  Jumper, *Jumpers;* Landolph, *The Em-
  peror Henry;* John Bland, *Seven Keys
  to Baldpate.*
1975–76: German Worker, *Cathedral of
  Ice;* Duke of Milan, *Two Gentlemen
  of Verona;* Lord/Huddy/Captain/
  Soldier, *Bastard Son.*
1976–77: Victor Chandebise, *A Flea in Her
  Ear;* George, *Of Mice and Men;* Bing
  Ringling, *Rich and Famous.*
1977–78: *Ethan Frome;* Teach, *American
  Buffalo;* Raul, *Seduced;* Moon, *The
  Real Inspector Hound;* Richard Pawl-
  ing, *The Shock of Recognition.*
1978–79: Tom, *Father's Day;* Moe Axelrod,
  Awake and Sing; Biff, *Death of a
  Salesman.*
1979–80: Paul Verral, *Born Yesterday;*
  Semyon Semyonovich, *The Suicide;*
  Vladimir, *Waiting for Godot.*
1980–81: Jerry, *Betrayal;* Charlie Martin,

On Golden Pond; Hickey, *The Iceman
  Cometh;* Philip Hill, *Whose Life Is It,
  Anyway?;* Frederic/Policeman, *The
  Elephant Man;* Bruno, *The Magnifi-
  cent Cuckold* (Yale).
1981–82: Bob Cratchit, *A Christmas Carol;*
  Poche, *A Flea in Her Ear;* Pavel
  Ivanovich, *Dead Souls;* Austin, *True
  West;* O'Neill Conference.
1982–83: Stephano, *The Tempest;* Jack Ab-
  bott, *In the Belly of the Beast* (Yale);
  Torvald, *A Doll House* (Long Wharf);
  Johnny Case, *Holiday.*
1983–84: Eddie, *Fool for Love* (TRC,
  Dallas Theatre Center).

CHERRY JONES

Education/Training: Carnegie-Mellon.
Professional stage debut: Eva, *Absurd Per-
  son Singular* (Carnegie-Mellon
  Theatre Company, 1978).
1980: Dorcas, *The Winter's Tale;* Millicent,
  He and She (BAM); Rosalind, *As You
  Like It;* Helena, *A Midsummer
  Night's Dream* (ART).
1981–82: Celia, *Sganarelle;* Elizaveta,
  The Journey of the Fifth Horse;
  Regina, *Ghosts; Lulu* (ART);
  Julia, *Fallen Angels* (Oregon
  Contemporary).
1982–83: Irina, *Three Sisters;* Courtesan,
  The Boys from Syracuse; Helen, *Baby
  with the Bathwater;* Lady Teazle, *The
  School for Scandal* (ART).
1983–84: Liz, *The Philanthropist* (MTC);
  Sally Bowles, *I Am a Camera* (Ameri-
  can Jewish); Maud/Linn, *Cloud Nine*
  (Arena); Elizabeth, *Cheapside* (White
  Barn).
1984–85: Kitty, *The Ballad of Soapy Smith*
  (Public); Princess of France, *Love's
  Labour's Lost;* Jodie, *Gillette;* Sara,

Claptrap (ART); Varya, *The Cherry Orchard* (John Drew).

1985–86: Cecily, *The Importance of Being Earnest* (OB).

1986–87: Lynn, *Stepping Out* (B); Sara, *Claptrap* (MTC).

1987–88: Lady MacDuff, *Macbeth* (B); Dorine, *Tartuffe* (Portland Stage); Fran, *Big Time* (ART+).

1989–89: Cherestani, *The Serpent Woman;* Sofya, *Platonov;* Merry Chase, *Mastergate;* Elise, *The Miser;* Rosaura, *Life Is a Dream* (ART).

1989–90: Viola, *Twelfth Night;* Major Barbara; Sylvia, *The Lost Boys;* Grusha, *Caucasian Chalk Circle;* Angela, *King Stag* (ART).

1990–91: Regan, *King Lear* (ART); Hoskins/Brotherton, *Light Shining in Buckinghamshire* (New York Theatre Workshop); Liz, *Our Country's Good* (B).

1991–92: Anna, *The Baltimore Waltz** (Circle); *The Good Person of Setzuan* (Goodman); Constance Ledbelly, *Goodnight Desdemona (Good Morning Juliet)* (CSC).

1993: Josie Hogan, *A Moon for the Misbegotten* (CS).

JAMES EARL JONES

Education/Training: University of Michigan, American Theatre Wing.

Professional stage debut: Johnson in *Personal Appearance* (Manistee Summer Theatre, 1953).

1953: (as Jim Jones) small roles in seven plays, including Officer Brophy in *Arsenic and Old Lace* (Manistee).

1955: (as Todd Jones) small roles in nine plays, plus Antonio in *Twelfth Night* (Manistee).

1956: (as Todd Jones) *Othello;* Conjure Man in *Dark of the Moon;* roles in six other plays (Manistee).

1957: (as James Earl Jones) Sergeant Blunt, *Wedding in Japan* (OB); roles in five plays (Manistee).

1958: Edward, *Sunrise at Campobello* (B).

1960: Harrison Thurston, *The Cool World* (B); Abhorson, *Measure for Measure;* Williams, *Henry V* (NYSF).

1961–62: Deodatus Village, *The Blacks* (OB); Cinna, *Infidel Caesar* (B); Roger Clark, *Clandestine on the Morning Line* (OB); ensemble, *The Apple* (Living Theatre); Ephraim, *Moon on a Rainbow Shawl†*; Lord Marshall/Gardner's assistant, *Richard II;* Oberon, *A Midsummer Night's Dream* (NYSF). Obie Award for *Clandestine, Apple* and *Moon.*

1962–63: Mario Saccone, *P.S. 193;* George Gulp, *The Love Nest* (OB); Caliban, *The Tempest;* Prince of Morocco, *The Merchant of Venice* (NYSF).

1963–64: *Mister Johnson* (ELT); Rudge, *Next Time I'll Sing to You* (Phoenix); Zachariah, *The Blood Knot* (OB); Camillo, *The Winter's Tale* (NYSF).

1964–65: Ekart, *Baal** (OB); *Othello •* (NYSF+).

1965–66: Philippeau, *Danton's Death* (LCT/VB); Arnie/Bo, *Bohikee Creek* (OB); Junius Brutus, *Coriolanus;* Ajax, *Troilus and Cressida* (NYSF).

1966–67: *Macbeth* (NYSF Mobile Theater); ensemble, *A Hand Is on the Gate* (OB).

1967–68: Lennie, *Of Mice and Men* (Purdue University); Jack Jefferson, *The Great White Hope* (Arena).

1968–69: Jack Jefferson, *The Great White Hope •* ‡ (B).

1970–71: Boesman, *Boesman and Lena* (CITS/OB); Tshembe Matoseh, *Les Blancs* (B); *Othello* (MTF).

1972–73: Claudius, *Hamlet* (NYSF); Lopakhin, *The Cherry Orchard* (Public).

1973–74: Hickey, *The Iceman Cometh* (CITS/B); *King Lear* (NYSF).

1974–75: Lennie, *Of Mice and Men* (B).

1977–78: *Paul Robeson* (B).

1979–80: Steve Daniels, *A Lesson from Aloes* (B); *Timon of Athens* (Yale).

1980–81: Steve Daniels, *A Lesson from Aloes* (B); Judge Brack, *Hedda Gabler* (Yale).
1981–82: *Othello* (ASF+).
1982–83: Julius Nkumbi, *The Day of the Picnic* (Yale); Sam, *"Master Harold" . . . and the boys* (National Tour).
1985–86: Troy Maxson, *Fences* (Yale, Goodman).
1986–87: Troy Maxson, *Fences* • ‡ (B+).

RANDALL DUK KIM

Education/Training: University of Hawaii.
Professional stage debut: Tribe Member, *Hair* (Las Vegas, 1969).
1971: Monsewer, *The Hostage* (Hunter College); Cassius, *Julius Caesar;* Gremio, *The Taming of the Shrew* (CSF); Shlink, *In the Jungle of Cities* (Public).
1972: Tam Lum, *Chickencoop Chinaman* (APT); *Titus Andronicus;* Touchstone, *As You Like It;* Dr. Caius, *The Merry Wives of Windsor* (CSF); Prince Myshkin, *Subject to Fits* (ST); Pantalone, *Servant of Two Masters* (ELT).
1973: Friedrich Engels, *The Karl Marx Story* (APT); *Richard III;* Puck, *A Midsummer Night's Dream;* Capulet, *Romeo and Juliet* (CSF); Criminal, *Baba Goya* (APT, OB as *Nourish the Beast*).
1974: Fred Eng, *Year of the Dragon* (APT); Trinculo, *The Tempest* (NYSF/LC, St. Clair Bayfield Award); *Pericles* (NYSF).
1974–75: *Richard III;* Tranio, *The Taming of the Shrew;* Mr. Callahan, *Streetscene;* Criminal, *The Threepenny Opera* (ACT/SF).

1975: Puck, *A Midsummer Night's Dream;* Pedro, *Don Juan* (Yale).
1976: *Richard II* (OB); *Hamlet* (Honolulu); Prospero, *The Tempest* (Indiana); Howard, *Wildflowers* (Circle).
1977: *Walt* (American Players Theatre/D.C.).
1978: Nanno, *Night of the Iguana* (CS).
1978–79: *Hamlet;* Bishop Nikolas, *The Pretenders;* Menasha, *Teibele and Her Demon;* Zhevakin, *The Marriage* (Guthrie)
[All following at American Players Theatre except as noted]
1980: *Titus Andronicus;* Puck, *A Midsummer Night's Dream.*
1981: *King John;* Egeon, *The Comedy of Errors.*
1982: Launce, *Two Gentlemen of Verona;* Petruchio, *The Taming of the Shrew;* Chorus/Friar Laurence, *Romeo and Juliet.*
1983: Dr. Pinch, *The Comedy of Errors;* Tamburlaine the Great, Part 1; Sir Nathaniel, *Love's Labour's Lost;* Peter Quince, *A Midsummer Night's Dream;* Romeo, *Romeo and Juliet;* Gremio, *The Taming of the Shrew.*
1984: Capulet, *Romeo and Juliet;* Sir John Falstaff, *The Merry Wives of Windsor.*
1985: Brutus, *Julius Caesar;* Shylock, *The Merchant of Venice;* Chubukov, *The Marriage Proposal.*
1986: *Hamlet;* Dr. Caius, *The Merry Wives of Windsor;* Svetlovidov, *Swan Song.*
1987: Malvolio, *Twelfth Night; Ivanov.*
1988–89: Prospero, *The Tempest* (ATC); Storyteller, *The Legend of Oedipus* (WTF); Chu-Yin, *Marco Millions;* Herbert Soppitt, *When We Are Married* (ACT/SF).
1989: *King Lear;* Starveling, *A Midsummer Night's Dream; Oedipus Rex.*
1990: Prospero, *The Tempest;* Stockman, *An Enemy of the People.*
1991: Arnolphe, *The School for Wives* (ATC, Zony Best Actor Award); Stockman, *An Enemy of the People;* Orgon, *Tartuffe.*

JANE LIND

JOAN MACINTOSH

Education/Training: New York University School of the Arts.

Professional stage debut: Eulahlah, *Body Indian* (NATE/La MaMa, 1972).

1972–73: Eulahlah, *Body Indian;* Wolf, *NA HAAZ ZAN;* Coyote Trails, *Sapsucker;* Nun/Princess Pocahontas, *Foghorn* (NATE/La MaMa+).

1975: Hecuba *(The Trojan Women),* Chorus *(Electra, Medea): Fragments of A Trilogy* (GJRC/La MaMa+).

1976: Water Seller, *Good Person of Setzuan* (GJRC/La MaMa).

1977–78: Kirizuzu, *Night Club* (La MaMa); Yellow Woman, *Black Elk Speaks* (ST).

1979: Bright Eyes, *Footprints in Blood* (American Indian Center of Omaha).

1980–81: Yellow Woman, *Black Elk Speaks* (OB).

1981–82: Balladeer, *"49"* (American Indian Community House Theatre).

1982–83: Katherine, *The Taming of the Shrew;* Woman, *Two for the Road* (Alaska Rep tour); Mother, *The Little Black Fish* (Theatre for the New City).

1983–84: Eileen Joe, *The Ecstasy of Rita Joe* (OB).

1987: Hecuba/Chorus, *Fragments of a Trilogy; Summer Face Woman* (La MaMa).

1988–89: Hera, *Another Phaedra via Hercules* (La MaMa); *Angalak* (Open Eye).

1989–90: Raven-Monkey, *The Book and the Stranger* (La MaMa); Katherine Rose, *The Independence of Eddie Rose* (Ensemble Studio).

Education/Training: Beaver College, New York University School of the Arts.

Professional stage debut: Agave, *Dionysus in '69** (Performance Group).

1967–78: (with the Performance Group in New York and on tour); Dark Power, *Makbeth;* Clementine, *Commune*;* Becky Lou, *The Tooth of Crime;* Mother Courage, *Mother Courage and Her Children;* Marilyn Monroe, *The Marilyn Project;* Jocasta, *Oedipus;* ensemble, *Sakonnet Point;* Jean Harlow, *The Beard.*

1977–78: Joan Dark, *St. Joan of the Stockyards* (Encompass).

1978–79: Sister/Creatures, *Alice in Concert;* rock ensemble, *Dispatches;* Jane, the Bag Lady, *Runaways* (Public).

1979–80: Nell, *Endgame* (MTC); Alice, *Plenty* (Arena); Ellis, *Killings on the Last Line* (APT).

1980–81: Frau Rasch, *Request Concert •* (Women's Interart).

1981–82: Suzanne, *Three Acts of Recognition* (NYSF/LC).

1982–83: Stella, *Screenplay* (Arena); Judy, *Sore Throats* (Repertory Theatre of St. Louis).

1983–84: *Hedda Gabler;* Masha, *Three Sisters* (Guthrie).

1984–85: Sally Talley, *Talley's Folly* (Yale).

1985–86: Irma, *The Balcony* (ART).

1986–87: Joan, *Cleveland* (BACA); Jana, *Whispers* (Open Space); Cass, *Consequence* (Women's Project); Elizabeth I, *Almost by Chance a Women: Elizabeth* (Yale).

1987–88: Mama, *A Shayna Maidel* (OB); Portia, *Julius Caesar* (Public).

1988–89: Inanna, *The Goddess Project*

(WTC); ensemble, *Our Town*
(LCT/B); Queen, *Cymbeline* (Public).
1989–90: ensemble, *Orpheus Descending*
(B); Goneril, *King Lear* (WTC).
1990–91: Gotchling, *A Bright Room Called
Day* (Public); Anna, *Night Sky*
(Women's Project).
1992–93: Polina, *The Seagull* (National Actors Theatre).

JOHN MAHONEY

Education/Training: Quincy College, West-
ern Illinois University.
Professional stage debut: Mr. Wallace, *The
Water Engine* (St. Nicholas Theatre,
1977).
1977: Doctor/Surgeon/Guru, *Ashes* (St.
Nicholas).
1978: Canon Mick O'Byrne, *Philadelphia,
Here I Come* (Steppenwolf).
1979: Dad, *Funeral March for a One-Man
Band;* Mr. Dussel, *The Diary of Anne
Frank* (St. Nicholas); Clancy/Dr.
Barnes, *Waiting for Lefty;* Birdboot,
The Real Inspector Hound
(Steppenwolf).
1980: Charlie, *Death of a Salesman;* Paul,
Absent Friends; Harry, *The Collection*
(Steppenwolf); John, *Balm in Gilead*
(Steppenwolf+); Vernouillet, *Celimare;*
Chudu, *The Prince, the Dwarf, and
the Blacksmith's Daughter* (St. Nich-
olas); Older Jackie, *First Confession*
(City Lit).
1981: multiple roles, *Savages;* Spooner, *No
Man's Land;* Major Petkoff, *Arms and
the Man;* Candy, *Of Mice and Men;*
Wyatt Earp, *The Great American
Desert* (Steppenwolf).
1982: Captain Locke, *The House;* Law-
rence, *Loose Ends;* Simon. *A Prayer
for My Daughter;* George

Stott, . . . *And a Nightingale Sang*
(Steppenwolf); Basil, *The Coarse Act-
ing Show* (Cross Currents Cabaret).
1983: Stuart, *Beyond Therapy* (Pheasant
Run); Roland, *Taking Steps* (Body
Politic); Gibbs, *The Hothouse,* Mr.
Webb, *Our Town* (Steppenwolf).
1984: Birger, *Ballerina;* Dr. Prentice, *What
the Butler Saw;* Walter, *The Price*
(Northlight); Robert, *Stagestruck*
(Steppenwolf); Oronte, *The Mis-
anthrope* (Court).
1985: Harold, *Orphans†* (Steppenwolf+);
Grandpa, *You Can't Take It with You*
(Steppenwolf).
1986: Artie Shaughnessy, *The House of
Blue Leaves‡* (LCT/N+, also Clarence
Derwent Award).
1987: Harry Brock, *Born Yesterday*
(Steppenwolf).
1989: Quentin, *After the Fall* (National
Jewish).
1990: *Uncle Vanya* (Goodman); Peter Rav-
enswaal, *Wrong Turn at Lungfish*
(Steppenwolf).
1991: John Cleary, *The Subject Was Roses*
(Roundabout).
1992: Marty Frankel, *The Song of Jacob
Zulu* (Steppenwolf).

PAUL MCCRANE

Professional stage debut: Adolf-Friedrich in
The Physicists (McCarter Theatre,
1976–77).
1977–78: Johann Franz, *The Berserkers*
(New Dramatists); Bert, *Landscape of
the Body* (Academy Festival, Public).
1978–79: Eddie, *Runaways* (NYSF on B);
ensemble, *Dispatches* (Public).
1979–80: Jeff, *Split* (Second Stage).
1980–81: Christopher, *Sally's Gone, She
Left Her Name* (CS); Ronnie

Shaughnessy, *The House of Blue Leaves* (BTF).

1981–82: Carlo, *Crossing Niagara* (MTC); Aloysius "Wishy" Burke, *The Curse of an Aching Heart* (B); Rovo, *Hunting Scenes from Lower Bavaria* (MTC).

1982–83: Ricky, *Hooters* (Hudson Guild); O'Neill Conference.

1983–84: Chick/Kit/Vinnie/Bernard/Clay/Andy, *Fables for Friends* (PH); Leslie, *The Hostage* (Long Wharf); Orlando, *As You Like It* (La Jolla).

1985–86: Don Parritt, *The Iceman Cometh* (B).

1986–87: Edmond, *Long Day's Journey into Night* (Portland Stage).

1987–88: Timmerman/Bartender, *Right Behind the Flag* (PH); Norman, *Moonchildren* (Second Stage); O'Neill Conference.

1989–90: Flowers, *Briarpatch* (Ensemble Studio); Rick, *Six Degrees of Separation* (LCT/N); O'Neill Conference.

1990–91: Larry, *The Country Girl* (Roundabout); Rick, *Six Degrees of Separation* (LCT/VB).

1991–92: Andrei, *Three Sisters* (McCarter); O'Neill Conference.

ISABELL MONK

Education/Training: Towson State University, Yale School of Drama.

Professional stage debut: Columbine, *Flavio Betrayed* (The Comedia Company, 1975).

1978–79: ensemble, *As You Like It* (Yale).

1979–80: Timandra, *Timon of Athens;* Ghost/ensemble, *Ubu Rex* (Yale).

1980–81: Miss Lady, Lady Day, *The Resurrection of Lady Lester* (Yale).

1981–82: ensemble, *The Tempest* (NYSF);

Momma/Daughter, *Slow Drag Momma* (ATL); Louise Mae, *Rupert's Birthday;* Rodeo/French Fries, *Talking With* (ATL tour).

1982–83: Nancy Mannigoe, *Requiem for a Nun* (Guthrie).

1983–88: Antigone/Evangelist, *The Gospel at Colonus* (BAM+).

1984–85: Narrator, *Sister Susie Cinema* (tour); Dorine, *Tartuffe;* Maria, *Twelfth Night* (Guthrie).

1985–86: Gwenn Craig/V.P., Harvey Milk Democratic Club, *Execution of Justice* (B); Madeleine Caderousse/La Charconte/Officer Dyrne, *The Count of Monte Cristo* (ANT).

1986–87: Audrey West, *End of the World with Symposium to Follow;* Nurse/Actress, *The Day Room;* ensemble, *The Good Person of Setzuan* (ART).

1987–88: chorus, *Elektra* (CSC); Gloucester, *King Lear* (George Street).

1988–89: Mary, *Ladies* (Music-Theatre); Spirit-Woman, *The Warrior Ant* (BAM).

1989–90: Gloucester, *Lear** (Mabou Mines); Kadijz, *The Screens;* Baroness/eleven other roles, *Candide;* Maryina, *Uncle Vanya;* Cariola, *The Duchess of Malfi* (Guthrie).

1990–91: Mistress Quickly, *Henry IV, Parts 1 & 2* and *Henry V;* Fortune Teller, *The Skin of Our Teeth;* chorus, *Medea* (Guthrie).

1991–92: Linda, *Death of a Salesman;* ensemble, *Fantasio;* Simone Evrard, *Marat/Sade* (Guthrie).

1992: Clytemnestra, *Iphigenia in Aulis/Agamemnon/Electra;* Paulina, *The Winter's Tale* (Guthrie).

JOE MORTON

Education/Training: Hofstra University.
Professional stage debut: Jesse, *A Month of Sundays* (OB, 1968).
1969: Mark, *Salvation* (OB).
1970: tribe member, *Hair* (B).
1971: Willy Thomas, *Prettybelle* (tour); Charlie, *Charlie Was Here and Now He's Gone* (OB).
1972–73: Samuel Adams, *Two If By Sea* (CITS/OB); Arlecchino/Lead Singer, *Tricks* (B); Valentine, *Two Gentlemen of Verona* (B); Walter Lee, *Raisin* (Arena).
1973–75: *Raisin*† (B).
1976–77: Shoulders, *G.R. Point* (Phoenix); Styles/Buntu, *Sizwe Bansi Is Dead* (Pittsburgh Public).
1977–78: Aaron, *Titus Andronicus;* George, *Daddies;* Molinaro, *The Bridgehead;* Shooter, *Third and Oak;* Styles/Buntu, *Sizwe Bansi is Dead* (ATL).
1979–80: Caliban, *The Tempest* (ASF); Autolycus, *The Winter's Tale;* Lucius, *Johnny on a Spot* (BAM); Caliban, *The Tempest* (Shakespeare & Company).
1980–81: Lysander, *A Midsummer Night's Dream;* *Oedipus Rex;* Kite, *The Recruiting Officer;* navel officer, *The Wild Duck* (BAM).
1981–82: Eastern Habim, *Oh, Brother!* (B); Historical Event, *How I Got That Story* (GeVa); Valentine, *Two Gentlemen of Verona* (Pennsylvania Stage).
1982–83: Sam Dodd, *Rhinestone* (Richard Allen Center).
1983–84: Peter, *Souvenirs* (OB).
1984–85: Tom Brody, *Private Territory;* Oliver Manzi, *Advice to the Players* (ATL).
1985–86: Cutting Ball, *Cheapside* (Round-

about); Ty Fletcher, *Tamer of Horses* (Crossroads).
1986–87: Ty Fletcher, *Tamer of Horses* (Los Angeles Theatre Center); Barney Walker, *Honkey Tonk Nights* (B); Mama Zaza, *Almost by Chance a Woman: Elizabeth* (Yale).
1987–88: Orestes, *Elektra* (CSC); Oedipus, *The Legend of Oedipus* (WTF).

HOWIE SEAGO

Education/Training: California State University, Northridge.
Founder-director Happy Handfuls (deaf children's theatre troupe, Los Angeles, 1973–76).
Founder-actor-director Deaf Moose Theatre (1992–).
Professional stage debut: *Gilgamesh* (National Theatre of the Deaf, 1980).
1980–82: *Gilgamesh;* Achilles, *The Iliad, Play by Play;* Narrator, *Ghost of Chastity Past* (National Theatre of the Deaf).
1982–83: Beast, *Beauty and the Beast* (Honolulu); Orin, *Children of a Lesser God* (Hawaii Performing Arts Company).
1984–85: Orin, *Children of a Lesser God* (Asolo).
1985–87: Fadinard, *Italian Straw Hat;* Mortimer, *Arsenic and Old Lace* (National Technical Institute for the Deaf).
1986–87: *Ajax* (ANT+, Helen Hayes Award, Dramalogue Award).
1987: Caliban, *The Tempest* (La Jolla); Howie, *Prison-Made Tuxedos* (Music-Theatre).
1988: Enkidu, *The Forest* (BAM+).
1990: Lou, *Seeing Place* (San Diego).

1991: Tom, *Nancy and Plum* (Seattle Children's).

FREDA FOH SHEN

Education/Training: American Conservatory Theatre.
Professional stage debut: Shogun's wife, *Pacific Overtures* (B, 1976).
1976: Leilani, *One, Two Cups* (OB).
1977: Court dancer, *The Bourgeois Gentleman* (ACT–SF).
1977–78: Royal dancer and wife, *The King and I* (B).
1978–79: Servant, *My Fair Lady;* Isabelle, *Ring Round the Moon* (Santa Rosa).
1980–81: Tuptim, *The King and I* (Alliance); Selina, *Loose Ends* (Alaska).
1981–82: Chi Chi/Date/Mariko, *Yellow Is My Favorite Color* (Pan Asian); Isabel D'Orsay, *Gun for the Roses* (ATL); Nerissa, *The Merchant of Venice* (Syracuse).
1982–83: Nancy Wing, *Yellow Fever* (Pan Asian); Lady Nijo/Mrs. Kidd, *Top Girls* (Public).
1983–84: Nancy Wing, *Yellow Fever* (Pan Asian); Tashiro, *The Longest Walk* (APT).
1984–85: Pearl Concubine, *Empress of China* (Cincinnati).
1985–86: Joanna Lu, *Execution of Justice* (B); Rosa, *The Ups and Downs of Theophilus Maitland* (Dallas); Fujin Macbeth, *Shogun Macbeth;* Hero, *Much Ado about Nothing* (Shakespeare Festival of Dallas).
1986–87: Fujin Macbeth, *Shogun Macbeth* (Pan Asian+); Miranda, *The Tempest* (Theatre for a New Audience); Queen Isabelle, *Richard II* (NYSF).
1988–89: Princess Kukachin, *Marco Millions* (ACT/SF).

1989–90: Carmen, *The Balcony* (Hudson Guild).
1990–91: Leeann, *A Piece of My Heart* (Philadelphia Festival); Gyoko, *Shogun: the Musical* (B); Elizabeth, *Necessities* (Old Globe).
1991–92: Sun Hong-Tien, *A Small Delegation* (Philadelphia Festival); O'Neill Conference.

JOSEF SOMMER

Education/Training: Carnegie Institute of Technology.
Professional stage debut: Bodo, *Watch on the Rhine* (Carolina Playmakers, 1943).
1943–46: Dinosaur, *The Skin of Our Teeth;* Newsboy, *Our Town; Master Pierre Pathelin* (Playmakers).
1951: ensemble, *Unto These Hills* (Kentucky outdoor drama).
1954–56: Aguecheek, *Twelfth Night;* Charles, *Blithe Spirit;* Howard, *Picnic;* Thomas Mendip, *The Lady's Not for Burning* and roles in 15 other plays (Gateway).
1957: ensemble, *Wilderness Road* (Kentucky Summer).
1962: Ross, *Richard II;* Vernon, *Henry IV, Part 1* (ASF).
1963: Captain, *King Lear;* Music Master, *Caesar and Cleopatra;* Balthazar, *The Comedy of Errors;* Montjoy/Cambridge, *Henry V* (ASF).
1964: Rivers, *Richard III;* Antonio, *Much Ado about Nothing;* Player King/First Player, *Hamlet* (ASF).
1965: Cominius, *Coriolanus;* Albany, *King Lear;* Capulet, *Romeo and Juliet* (ASF).
1966: Malvolio, *Twelfth Night; Henry IV, Part 2; Julius Caesar;* Fourth Tempter, *Murder in the Cathedral* (ASF).

1967: *The Father* (SRT); Malvolio, *Twelfth Night;* Dumain, *All's Well that Ends Well* (Old Globe).

1968: John of Gaunt, *Richard II;* Don Armado, *Love's Labour's Lost;* The Captain, *Androcles and the Lion* (ASF).

1969: *Tartuffe; Henry IV, Part 1;* Serjeant Musgrave, *Serjeant Musgrave's Dance;* Paul Sycamore, *You Can't Take It with You;* Ezra Mannon, *Mourning Becomes Electra;* Bobby, *The Visit;* Eddie Carbone, *A View from the Bridge; [?] Look Back in Anger;* George, *Who's Afraid of Virginia Woolf* (SRT).

1970: King of France, *All's Well that Ends Well;* Ghost/First Player, *Hamlet* (ASF); Brabantio, *Othello* (ASF+).

1970–71: *The Latent Homosexual;* Hovstad, *An Enemy of the People;* Ted Bacon, *The Selling of the President;* Society Gentleman, *The Time of Your Life* (ACT/SF).

1971: Defense, *The Trial of the Catonsville Nine* (B); Artie, *The House of Blue Leaves* (SRT); Dr. Karl Yaegar, *Children! Children!* (B).

1972–73: Skrobotov, *Enemies;* Antonio, *The Merchant of Venice* (LCT/VB); Cassius, *Julius Caesar* (ASF).

1973–74: Schmidt, *Full Circle* (B).

1974–75: Arnold J. Pilger, *Who's Who in Hell* (B); William, *The Dog Ran Away* (Ensemble Studio); Salisbury, *Richard III* (Long Wharf).

1975–76: Thomas Jefferson, *The Estate* (Hartford); Camillo, *The Winter's Tale* (McCarter).

1976–77: Interviewer, later Brian, *The Shadow Box* (B); Camillo, *The Winter's Tale* (ASF).

1976–79: Brian, *The Shadow Box;* Inquisitor, *Saint Joan;* Arnold, *Alphabetical Order;* Yahov Shalimov, *Summerfold* (Long Wharf).

1977: Max, *The Archbishop's Ceiling* (Kennedy Center); Francis, *Spokesong* (Long Wharf).

1978: Arnolphe, *The School for Wives* (WTF).

1978–79: Francis, *Spokesong* (CITS/B); Alan, *Drinks Before Dinner* (Public).

1979–80: Cliford A. Faddington, *The 1940's Radio Hour;* Dr. Michael Emerson, *Whose Life Is It, Anyway?* (B).

1980: George, *The Lady and the Clarinet* (MTF).

1981: Menelaus, *The Greeks* (WTF).

1982: Joshua Hickman, *Lydie Breeze** (APT).

1982–83: George, *The Lady and the Clarinet* (Long Wharf+); Martin Engel, *Black Angel* (Circle); Mr. Holt, *Knife in the Heart* (WTF).

1984: Victor Marsden, *Love Letters on Blue Paper* (Hudson Guild); Troll King, *Peer Gynt* (WTF).

1985: Rev. Hugh Burton, *Bullie's House* (Long Wharf).

1986: Dr. Kopriva, *Largo Desolato* (Public).

1987: Andrey Botvinik, *A Walk in the Woods* (Yale).

1990: Andrew, *Love Letters* (Yale); Polonius, *Hamlet* (Public).

1991: Anton Schill, *The Visit* (Goodman).

1992: Chebutykin, *Three Sisters* (McCarter).

RICHARD THOMAS

Education/Training: Columbia University.

Professional stage debut: Singer, *Damn Yankees* (Sacandaga Garden Theatre, 1957).

1958: John Roosevelt, *Sunrise at Campobello* (B).

1959: John Henry, *The Member of the Wedding* (ELT).

1963: Young Gordon Evans, *Strange Interlude* (Actors Studio on B).

1964: Edward, Prince of Wales, *Richard III* (ASF).

1965–66: Eric, *The Playroom* (B); Richard, Duke of York, *Richard III* (NYSF).

1967–68: Roger, *Everything in the Garden* (B).

1974: Dauphin, *Saint Joan* (Ahmanson
Theatre, L.A.).

1976–77: *Merton of the Movies* (Ahmanson
Theatre, L.A.).

1977–78: Billy, *Streamers* (Westwood Playhouse, L.A.).

1980: Ken Harrison, *Whose Life Is It, Anyway?* (National Tour).

1981: Kenneth Talley, Jr. *The Fifth of July*
(Circle on B).

1984: Treplev, *The Seagull* (Circle); Dick
Dudgeon, *The Devil's Disciple;* The
Writer, *Vieux Carre;* Husband, *La
Ronde* (WTF).

1985: Edmund Dantes, *The Count of
Monte Cristo* (ANT); *Citizen Tom
Paine* (WTF).

1986: Hildy Johnson, *The Front Page*
(LCT/VB); alternated Sergius and
Bluntschli, *Arms and the Man* (Pas-
adena); Man, *Two Figures in Dense
Violet Light* (Kennedy Center); Rev.
Hooper, *Hawthorne Country;* Dr.
Makarov, *Barbarians* (WTF).

1987: *Citizen Tom Paine* (Philadelphia
Theatre, Kennedy Center).

1988: *Hamlet* (Hartford).

1989–90: *Peer Gynt* (Hartford), Andrew,
Love Letters (OB+), Adam, *Square
One* (Second Stage).

1991: Stephen, *The Lisbon Traviata*
(MTF+).

1992: Danton, *Danton's Death* (Alley).

JEFF WEISS

Professional stage debut: one-man show
(El Coyote Gallery, 1962 [?]).

1964: *Waiting Boy* and *Prevarications* (La
MaMa).

1966–67: *And That's How the Rent
Gets Paid* (La MaMa); *A Funny
Walk Home* (Caffe Cino); Tad,
Spofford (B). Obie Award for *Rent*
and *Walk.*

1969–70: Julius Esperanza, *Gloria and Esperanza; The International Wrestling
Match** (La MaMa).

1972: Nevius Voorhees, *Locomotive Munch*
(La MaMa).

1973: *And That's How the Rent Gets Paid,
Part Two; Pushover: An Oldfashioned
Homosexual Mystery Play* (La
MaMa).

1977: *Good Sex* (La MaMa).

1979–80: Dr. Faustus, *Dr. Faustus Lights
the Lights* (Judson Poets Theatre);
Lyle Woomelsdorf, *Dark Twist* (La
MaMa); *And That's How the Rent
Gets Paid, Part Three** (Performing
Garage).

1981: *Convergent Lives* (Limbo Lounge).

1983: *And That's How the Rent Gets Paid,
Part Four: the Confessions of Conrad
Gehrhardt* (Performing Garage).

1985–86: Ghost/Player King/Osric, *Hamlet*
(Public); Theseus, *A Midsummer
Night's Dream* (PepsiCo).

1986–87: Bensinger, *The Front Page*
(LCT/VB).

1987–88: Porter/Siward/Witch, *Macbeth*
(B+); Menenius, *Coriolanus*
(McCarter).

1988–89: Simon Stimson, *Our Town*
(LCT/B).

1989–90: Representative Sellers/Wylie
Slaughter, *Mastergate* (B).

1990–91: Scrooge, *A Christmas Carol* (Mc-
Carter); Bobo, *Casanova* (Public).

1991–92: *Hot Keys** (Naked Angels);
Shakespeare/Claudius/Polonius, *The
Fifteen Minute Hamlet;* Magnus, *The
Real Inspector Hound*
(Roundabout).

Jeff Weiss also appeared at The Good
Medicine & Company in *Two Dykes;
Coming Attractions; Last Gasps; Kill
the Children; The Rise of Louis Bi-
mbo; Teddy and the Social Worker;
Gangster Review; A Pig Fart; The
Corpse that Walks Like a Mother;
Horsemeat* and *Uxmal.*

Theatres Cited

(Founding and, where applicable, closing dates are indicated, except where I could not locate the records. Theatres with missing dates are marked by an *)

NEW YORK CITY

The Acting Company 1972–
American Jewish Theatre 1974–
American Negro Theatre 1940–1953
American Place Theatre 1964–
American Theatre Exchange at the Joyce Theatre 1985–1991
Association of Producing Artists 1960–1970 (APA-Phoenix 1964–69)
BACA Downtown Theatre (Brooklyn Arts and Culture Association) 1978–91, 1993–
Brooklyn Academy of Music (BAM) 1861–
  BAM Theatre Company 1976–78
  BAM Theater Company 1979–81
  Next Wave Festival 1983–
Caffe Cino 1958–67
Chelsea Theater Center 1965–86
Circle in the Square 1951–
Cricle Repertory Company 1969–
CSC (Classic Stage Company) 1967–
The Cubiculo (NYC base of the National Shakespeare Company) 1968–
Encompass Theatre 1975–
Ensemble Studio Theatre (EST) 1971–
Equity Library Theatre (ELT) 1943–1989
Hudson Guild Theatre 1896–1990
Judson Poets Theatre 1961–1981
La MaMa ETC 1962–
Lincoln Center Theater 1964–
Lion Theatre Company 1974–1990
Living Theatre 1951–
Mabou Mines 1970–
Manhattan Project 1970–1975
Manhattan Theatre Club 1970–
Naked Angels 1986–
Native American Theatre Ensemble 1972–
New Dramatists 1949–
Negro Ensemble Company 1967–
New Federal Theatre 1970–
New York Shakespeare Festival 1954–
New York Theatre Workshop 1979–
Ontological-Hysteric Theater 1968–
The Open Eye: New Stagings 1972–
*Open Space Theatre
Open Theatre 1963–1973
Pan Asian Repertory Theatre 1977–
The Performance Group 1967–1980
Phoenix Theatre 1953– (APA-Phoenix 1964–69)
Playwrights Horizons 1971–
Repertorio Español 1969–
Richard Allen Center 1969–

371

Ridiculous Theatrical Company 1967–
Roundabout Theatre Company 1965–
Second Stage Theatre 1979–
Shaliko Company 1972–
Theatre for a New Audience 1979–
Theatre for the New City 1970–
Women's Interart 1969–
The Women's Project 1978–
WPA Theatre 1977–
The Wooster Group 1967–
Writers' Theatre 1975– (moved to Chicago
    1992)

OUTSIDE OF NEW YORK CITY

Academy Festival Theatre (Lake Forest,
    IL) 1967–1979
A Contemporary Theatre (Seattle, WA)
    1965–
Actors Theatre of Louisville (KY) 1964–
Alaska Repertory Theatre 1976–1988
Alice B. Theatre (Seattle, WA) 1984–
Alley Theatre (Houston, TX) 1947–
Alliance Theatre Company (Atlanta, GA)
    1969–
American Conservatory Theatre (San
    Francisco, CA) 1965–
American National Theatre at the
    Kennedy Center (Washington, D.C.)
    1985–86
American Players Theatre (Spring Green,
    WI) 1979–
American Repertory Theatre (Cambridge,
    MA) 1979–
American Shakespeare Festival (Stratford,
    CT) 1955–1982
Arena Stage (Washington, D.C.) 1950–
Arizona Theatre Company (Tucson/
    Phoenix) 1966–
Asolo State Theater (Sarasota, FL) 1960–
Barter Theatre (Abingdon, VA) 1933–
BoarsHead: Michigan Public Theatre
    (Lansing) 1970–
Body Politic Theatre (Chicago, IL) 1966–
Brattle Theatre (Cambridge, MA) 1949–
    1954
Capital Repertory Company (Albany, NY)
    1980–
Center Stage (Baltimore, MD) 1963–
Champlain Shakespeare Festival
    (University of Vermont, Burlington,
    VT) 1959–88

Charles Playhouse (Boston, MA) 1958–
    1973
Cincinnati Playhouse in the Park (OH)
    1960–
City Lit Theater Company (Chigaco, IL)
    1979–
Court Theatre (Chicago, IL) 1955–
Cleveland Play House (OH) 1915–
Crossroads Theatre Company (New
    Brunswick, NJ) 1978–
Dallas Theatre Center (TX) 1959–
Deaf Moose Theatre (Seattle, WA) 1992–
Denver Center Theatre Company (CO)
    1980–
Empire State Institute for the Performing
    Arts (Albany, NY) 1976–
Ensemble of Theatrical Artists (Honolulu,
    HI) 1967–69
Empty Space Theater (Seattle, WA) 1971–
George Street Playhouse (New Brunswick,
    NJ) 1974–
GeVa Theatre (Rochester, NY) 1972–
Goodman Theatre (Chicago, IL) 1925–
Goodspeed Opera House (East Haddam,
    CT) 1963–
Great Lakes Theater Festival (Cleveland,
    OH) 1962–
Group 20 (Avon Old Farms, CT and
    Wellesley, MA) 1953–1960
Guthrie Theater (Minneapolis, MN) 1963–
Hartford Stage Company (CT) 1964–
Hartman Theatre Company (Stamford,
    CT) 1975–1987
*Hawaii Public Theater (Honolulu, HI)
    1976–
Honolulu Theatre for Youth (HI) 1955–
Indiana Repertory Theatre (Indianapolis,
    IN) 1971–
Intiman Theatre Company (Seattle, WA)
    1972–
La Jolla Playhouse (CA) 1947–
Long Wharf Theatre (New Haven, CT)
    1965–
Los Angeles Theatre Center (CA) 1985–92
Mark Taper Forum (Center Theatre
    Group, Los Angeles, CA) 1967–
McCarter Theatre Center for the
    Performing Arts (Princeton, NJ)
    1960–
Milwaukee Repertory Theater 1954–
Music-Theatre Performing Group/Lenox
    Arts Center (MA) 1971–
National Jewish Theater (Chicago, IL)
    1986–

National Theatre of the Deaf (Waterford, then Chester, CT) 1967–

New Jersey Shakespeare Festival (Madison) 1963–

New Mexico Repertory Theatre (Albuquerque) 1983–

Northlight Theatre (Evanston, IL) 1974–

Old Globe Theatre (San Diego, CA) 1937–

O'Neill Theater Center/National Playwrights Conference (Waterford, CT) 1964–

Oregon Contemporary Theatre (Lewis and Clark College/Portland) 1981–1983

Oregon Shakespeare Festival (Ashland) 1935–

Organic Theater Company (Chicago, IL) 1969–

Pasadena Playhouse (CA) 1918–1969; 1986–

Pennsylvania Stage Company (Allentown) 1977–

PepsiCo Summerfare (Purchase, NY) 1980–1989

Pheasant Run (Chicago, IL) 1963–

Philadelphia Drama Guild (PA) 1956–

Philadelphia Festival Theatre for New Plays (PA) 1981–

Philadelphia Theatre Company (PA) 1974–

Pittsburgh Public Theater (PA) 1975–

PlayMakers Repertory Company (Chapel Hill, NC, formerly Carolina Playmakers) 1918–

Portland Repertory Theater (OR, formerly Willamette Rep) 1980–

Portland Stage Company (ME) 1974–

Repertory Theatre of St. Louis (MO, formerly Loretto-Hilton Repertory Theatre) 1966–

Seattle Group Theatre 1978–

Seattle Repertory Theatre (WA) 1963–

Shakespeare Festival of Dallas (TX) 1972–

Shakespeare Theatre (Washington, D.C., formerly Shakespeare Theatre at the Folger) 1970–

Shakespeare under the Stars (Antioch College; Yellow Springs, OH) 1952–56; 1960–67

South Coast Repertory (Costa Mesa, CA) 1964–

StageWest (Springfield, Mass) 1967–

St. Nicholas Theater Company (Chicago, IL) 1974–81

Studio Arena Theatre (Buffalo, NY) 1965–

Syracuse Stage (NY) 1974–

Tacoma Actors Guild (WA) 1978–

Theatre '47 (Dallas, TX) 1947–1959

Theatre Project Company (St. Louis, MO) 1975–

Toledo Festival of Comedy (OH) 1958

Trinity Repertory Company (Providence, RI) 1964–

Victory Theatre (Dayton, OH) 1974– (Founded as Turner Opera House, 1866; renamed Victoria Theatre, 1989)

Whole Theatre Company (Montclair, NJ) 1973–89

Williamstown Theatre Festival (MA) 1954–

Wisdom Bridge Theatre (Chicago, IL) 1974–

Yale Repertory Theatre (New Haven, CT) 1966–

SUMMER STOCK THEATRES

Buzzard's Bay Theatre (MA) 1957

*Edgartown Summer Theatre (MA)

Enchanted Hills Playhouse (Syracuse, IN) 1961–

Gateway Playhouse (Bellport, NY) 1952–

Houghton Lake Playhouse (MI) 1963–1968

*Indianhead Mountain Playhouse (Wakefield, MI)

John Drew Theatre (East Hampton, NY) 1931–

*Kentucky Summer Theatre

Manistee Summer Theatre (MI) 1951–1963

*Sacandaga Garden Theatre (NY)

Santa Rosa Summer Repertory Theatre (CA) 1972–

*Stage Door Summer Theatre (Port Huron, MI)

White Barn Theatre (Westport, CT) 1947–